Longman Guide to
Shakespeare's Characters

★

KENNETH McLEISH

Longman Guide to
Shakespeare's Characters

A Who's Who of Shakespeare

★

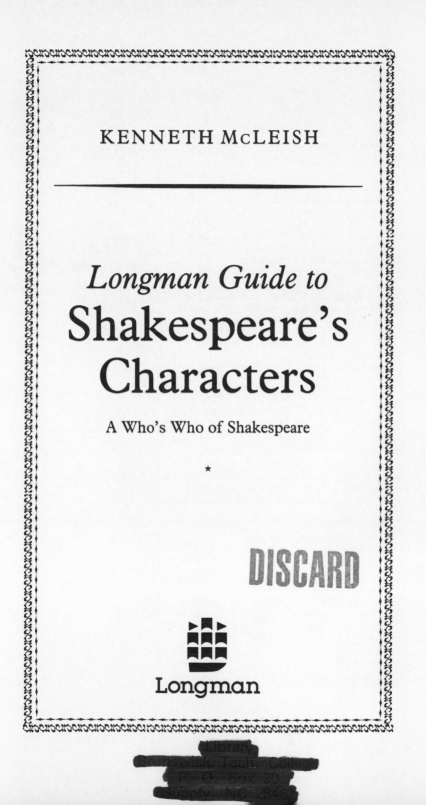

Longman

Longman Group Limited,
Longman House, Burnt Mill, Harlow,
Essex CM20 2JE, England
and Associated Companies throughout the world.

First published 1985

British Library Cataloguing in Publication Data

McLeish, Kenneth
   Longman guide to Shakespeare's characters
   1. Shakespeare, William—Characters—
   Dictionaries
   I. Title
   822.3'3   PR2989

   ISBN 0-582-89253-8

Computer typeset in 9/11pt Linotron Plantin
by Computerset (MFK) Ltd., Ely, Cambridgeshire.

Printed in Great Britain
by Hazell Watson & Viney Ltd.,
Aylesbury

Introduction

MEETING SHAKESPEARE'S CHARACTERS is like strolling through a small but populous town, being introduced to every single inhabitant: over a thousand people from countesses to constables, gallants to gamekeepers, friars to whores – even the condemned man in the prison-cell and the village witch – get to shake our hands. The amazing thing about these people is that although they are all the product of one man's imagination, they are no more clones than are the people of a real-life town: except in the matter of amorous young aristocrats and the attendant lords and ladies they grow up to become, Shakespeare seldom repeats a character-type.

For scholars, characterisation is one of Shakespeare's main structural devices: what his people are determines, and is determined by, the unfolding meaning of the action. For actors and directors, character-individuality is often the peg on which to hang a whole interpretation, a means of turning the play from words on a page to a living, blood-pulsing simulacrum of human life. But for both groups, as for ordinary spectators and readers, the very proliferation of Shakespeare's characters is one of the greatest glories of his work, second only perhaps to poetry. It is because we recognise common humanity in his people, and because we identify with it, that his plays still live – and it is this aspect of his art, above all others, which this book celebrates.

In this who's who of Shakespeare, all his characters are listed alphabetically. There is also a summary of each of the thirty-eight plays – also listed with the same alphabetical sequence.

Nick McDowell and, as always, Valerie McLeish gave me much help and encouragement during the writing, and Anne Nash typed the manuscript's early draft; to all, and to Trevor R. Griffiths who read the text, my warmest thanks.

Kenneth McLeish

● *for Michael and Tricia Sargent* ●

About the author

Kenneth McLeish studied at Worcester College, Oxford, where he obtained degrees in Classics and Music. Having been a schoolmaster, a professional musician, an actor, director and playwright (for theatre and television), he took up freelance writing and broadcasting in 1975. His voice is often to be heard on BBC Radios 3 and 4. He reviews regularly for *The Literary Review, Country Life* and *The Listener*, and has written more than forty books including *The Penguin Companion to the Arts in the Twentieth Century, The First Oxford Companion to Music, The Theatre of Aristophanes* and *Children of the Gods*.

Aaron (*Titus Andronicus*)
With two exceptions, the main characters in *Titus Andronicus* are one-dimensional, and their dimension is villainy. They want power or they want revenge, and their method of getting them (sadistic murder) is as unemotional as the answer to a mathematical equation. The exceptions are LAVINIA (a sweet child 'curiously lopped', who spends much of the play handless, raped and tongueless) and Aaron the Moor. Aaron is as much a villain as anyone else – it is he who arranges the mutilation of Lavinia, and sets up a scheme to frame TITUS' sons for a murder of which they are innocent – but his crimes are committed with self-awareness and gusto, and so have a dimension beyond horror. (He is the only character in the play who ever laughs.)

The Greek word *eiron* means 'pretender', someone who plays a part (it is the origin of the English word 'irony'), and part-playing is the key to this Aaron's character. He plots and schemes, cheats and lies – and revels in every twist and turn of his own villainy. There is no real need, for example, to bury a bag of gold and a body in a pit, then tumble two young men into it so that they will be condemned of murder on circumstantial evidence – the whole thing could have been organised more economically – but the scheme's baroque extravagance, its 'staging', is what appeals to Aaron and is its justification: its outcome is secondary. We may find Aaron's actual deeds repellent, but his self-delight is infectious, and creates that complicity with a dramatic character which is essential to the enjoyment of any theatre-show.

In a later, more developed, play Shakespeare might have put our seedling sympathy for Aaron to dramatic use. Aaron loses everything: his mistress (TAMORA, wife of the Roman emperor) gives birth to a 'blackamoor baby', a 'coal-black calf', Aaron's child, and his fatherly affection for it brings about his capture, the revelation of his crimes, and his punishment. (He is buried up to the neck and left to starve; we never learn the baby's fate.) As with the character of TITUS in the play, Shakespeare might have used Aaron's sufferings to trigger remorse or anguish in him, some complexity of emotion to extend his character. As it is, once Aaron realises that he is trapped, and doomed, he reverts to his original ironical style, and in a spectacular confession (delivered from the top of a ladder) not only admits his misdeeds but glories in them. His confession is the most satisfying scene, dramatically, in the play, and has the most pompous, peacocking poetry (e.g. the catalogue of Aaron's life of villainy which begins 'Even now I curse the day – and yet, I think,/Few come within the compass of my curse –/Wherein I did not some notorious ill...'). But for all its magnificence, it remains melodrama, not tragedy: Aaron is Captain Hook, the villain we love to hate, and nothing more. (He is a character-clone of RICHARD in *Richard III*, written in the same year, and his scenes are the only ones in *Titus Andronicus* to match the sister-play. In fact, if it had not been for all those cardboard Romans, alternately slicing one another and speaking turgid thoughts in turgid verse, *Aaron the Blackamoor* might have been one of young Shakespeare's juiciest plays.)

Abbess *(The Comedy of Errors)*
Dignified, indeed headmistressy, she refuses to release ANTIPHOLUS I from sanctuary. ('Be patient, for I will not let him stir...'.) Soon afterwards, confronted with her long-lost twin sons and husband, she lets joy seep through her dignity, to brief but moving effect. ('Thirty-three years have I but gone in travail/Of you, my sons, and, till this present hour,/My heavy burden ne'er deliver'd./The Duke, my husband and my children both,/And you two calendars of their nativity,/Go to a gossip's feast, and joy with me:/After so long grief, such felicity!')

Abergavenny, Lord *(Henry VIII)*
With BUCKINGHAM and NORFOLK, he opens the play by voicing dislike of WOLSEY – and his feelings are justified, for he is arrested soon afterwards and taken to the Tower.

Abhorson *(Measure for Measure)*
Public executioner, proud of his 'mystery' and unwilling to teach it to POMPEY. A man of few words (in fact no more than a dozen lines), he is, like so many Shakespearean kings and courtiers, characterised more by his trade than by what he says.

Abraham *(Romeo and Juliet)*
Servant of the Montagues, whose appearance with a fellow-servant at the start of the play provokes a quarrel with SAMPSON and GREGORY. He speaks only a few, suitably uncompromising lines: 'Do you bite your thumb at us, sir?'; 'You lie'.

Achilles *(Troilus and Cressida)*
Greek lord, traditionally the noblest warrior of them all, though he spends much of the play like a child in a huff, putting on a 'savage strangeness' to his fellow-commanders and refusing to see them, then being hurt and angry when they, in turn, walk past his tent pretending not to recognise him. ('They passed me by/As misers do by beggars, neither gave to me/Good word nor look. What, are my deeds forgot?') His chosen companions are the wasp-tongued clown THERSITES and the youth PATROCLUS and he is surrounded by a band of devoted

Myrmidons and keeps aloof, it seems, from every other soldier in the Greek army. His aloofness is shattered only when HECTOR kills Patroclus, and his fury then is more like that of a vicious child than of the man of honour he thinks himself. ('Come here about me, you my Myrmidons./Mark what I say. Attend me where I wheel,/Strike not a stroke, but keep yourselves in breath,/And when I have the bloody Hector found/Empale him with your weapons round about...'.) One of the play's main themes is the way true dignity and true moral standing are replaced by conceit, and Achilles' self-regard is the most apparent, most arrogant and deadliest of all.

Adam (*As You Like It*)
Loyal old servant who takes ORLANDO's side against OLIVER, lends him his life-savings and follows him into exile. He is (so he tells us) over 80, and is prone to an old man's verbosity; but he is as impetuous as he is honest, and his simple-hearted goodness is matched by his humanity. Adam is a figure from melodrama, and a plot-contrivance (it is because Orlando has to find him food that he bursts in on and becomes a follower of the DUKE in the Forest of Arden; after Orlando joins the duke, Adam vanishes from the action); but his combination of physical frailty and mental sturdiness makes him an interesting character as well as a necessary one.

Adrian (*Coriolanus*)
Volscian messenger who meets the Roman spy NICANOR on the road and hears his news. His chief characteristic is the pleasure he gets from meeting a fellow-professional: the freemasonry of espionage, it seems, transcends even patriotism.

Adrian (*The Tempest*)
ALONSO's courtier.

Adriana (*The Comedy of Errors*)
It would have been sufficient for the play to leave Adriana characterless, just one more strand in the farcical complication of the plot. But Shakespeare has considered her predicament (married to, and in love with, a bossy bore), and the reactions and feelings he gives her add depth to the superficial misunderstandings which fuel the action. Adriana loves ANTIPHOLUS II and tries hard to be a good wife to him ('Thou art an elm, my husband, I a vine...'), and his inexplicable behaviour at first leads her to despairing reflection on the balance of their relationship. ('Hath homely age th'alluring beauty took/From my poor cheek? Then he hath wasted it./Are my discourses dull? Barren my wit?.../That's not my fault: he's master of my state.../Since my beauty cannot please his eye,/I'll weep away what's left, and weeping, die'.)

Then, when she finds out that Antipholus II is seeing a courtesan, and that he has (as she thinks) proposed a love-affair to her own sister LUCIANA, Adriana bursts out in fury against him – and tempers it with

3

love. ('He is deformed, crooked, old and sere,/Ill-fac'd, worse-bodied,
shapeless everywhere,/Vicious, ungentle, foolish, blunt, unkind,/
Stigmatical in making, worse in mind...', but 'My heart prays for him,
though my tongue do curse...') At the end of the play, as the tangle is
resolved, her lines do relapse into the conventional ('I see two
husbands, or mine eyes deceive me'), but we have seen enough of her
spirit in earlier scenes to wonder how their relationship will develop
once the play is over – not the commonest of questions one asks of
marriages in farce.

Aegeon *(The Comedy of Errors)*
Father of ANTIPHOLUS I and ANTIPHOLUS II, an aged, sad old man. At
the start of the play he explains, at great length, how his sons were
parted as babies in a shipwreck; at the end of the play he is reunited
with both of them and with his long-lost wife, the ABBESS. The DUKE
calls him 'hapless'; he describes himself as 'hopeless and helpless'; these
adjectives, plus a tendency to long-windedness, sum up his character.

Aemilius *(Titus Andronicus)*
SATURNINUS' courtier.

Aeneas *(Troilus and Cressida)*
Of the two main Trojan leaders in the war, HECTOR is headstrong and
passionate, Aeneas pragmatic and cool. His main function is
diplomatic, notably in the exchange of CRESSIDA for the prisoner
ANTENOR, and his speeches seldom rise above silky courtesy, even to
his most deadly enemies. ('Health to you, valiant sir,/During all
question of the gentle truce./But when I meet you arm'd, as black
defiance/As heart can think or courage execute.')

Agamemnon *(Troilus and Cressida)*
Greek commander-in-chief, a swaggering nonentity. The other Greek
leaders defer verbally to his absolute authority, and then do exactly as
they please. The play's main characters are the younger lords, chafing
at the futility of their existence; Agamemnon, the commander who
decides everything but does nothing, is one of the main authors of that
futility, as the house-of-cards ceremoniousness of his scenes tellingly, if
never explicitly, makes clear.

Agrippa *(Antony and Cleopatra)*
OCTAVIUS' friend, who proposes the marriage between ANTONY and
OCTAVIA, and later welcomes Octavia to Rome when Antony deserts
her. He is one of the senior members of Octavius' entourage; for all
that, he has few words in the play and shows little character.

Aguecheek, Sir Andrew *(Twelfth Night)*
There is a long tradition of playing Sir Andrew as a lanky, sad-faced
loon, a kind of Shakespearean Stan Laurel. He certainly has the brains
of a flea, and he is certainly melancholy – 'What is *pourquoi*? Do or not
do?', he says plaintively at one point. 'I would I had bestowed that time

in the tongues that I have in fencing, dancing and bear-baiting. O, had I but followed the arts!' – and he is prone to outbursts of manic activity (dancing, jumping with rage, duelling) which are a gift to a physical comedian. But the text consistently describes a different kind of person altogether, a peppery, dim-witted squire from the shires, more like Bob Acres in Sheridan's *The Rivals* than (say) SLENDER in *The Merry Wives of Windsor*. MARIA, always perceptive about other people, says of him, 'For all that he's a fool, he's a great quarreller, and, but that he hath the gift of a coward to allay the gust he has in quarrelling, 'tis thought among the prudent he would quickly have the gift of a grave', and we see his bellicosity and cowardice in action when he challenges VIOLA/ Cesario to a duel, only to be beaten by Viola's twin SEBASTIAN. The chief reason for casting him as lugubrious and thin is, perhaps, to match him with Sir Toby BELCH, to create a Laurel-and-Hardy-like double-act, and although this interpretation is as arbitrary as any imposed from outside the text, it is both marvellously playable and a considerable help in deepening Sir Toby's otherwise shallow character. Some of the dialogue between the two of them, indeed, could be transposed unaltered into a Laurel and Hardy script. (*Sir Andrew*: 'O, if I thought that, I'd beat him like a dog.' *Sir Toby*: 'What, for being a puritan? Thy exquisite reason, dear knight?' *Sir Andrew*: 'I have no exquisite reason for it, but I have reason good enough.')

Ajax *(Troilus and Cressida)*

Greek warlord. He is a dolt, with no redeeming qualities: THERSITES aptly calls him a 'mongrel, beef-witted lord'. We first see Thersites yapping insults at him, and Ajax responding with feet and fists; soon afterwards, grossly flattered by ULYSSES and the other Greek commanders into fighting HECTOR, he responds with the same instinctive preference for brawn, not brains. ('If I go to him, with my arméd fist/I'll push him o'er the face'; 'An a' be proud with me, I'll pheeze his pride...'.) He comes out to fight like a turkey-cock ('Thou, trumpet! There's my purse./Now, crack thy lungs and split thy brazen pipe.../Come, stretch thy chest and let thy eyes spurt blood:/Thou blow'st for Hector'), and this attitude persists throughout the duel. ('I am not warm yet; let us fight again.') Only when Hector breaks off the fight, on the grounds that Ajax is his cousin, does he step out of character, fawning instead of snarling ('I thank thee, Hector:/Thou art too gentle and too free a man...'), suggesting that his 'famous cousin' pay a VIP visit to 'the Grecian tents' and obsequiously introducing him to his superiors ('Great Agamemnon comes to meet us here'). Association with Hector also turns his head in another way: when we next see him in battle (preparing to challenge TROILUS) it is as one of the most honourable, straightforward and heroic of all the Greek lords, as if, alone of everyone in the play, he is fulfilled by fighting, ennobled by contact (however bloodthirsty) with noble men. (*Diomedes*: 'Troilus, I say!' *Ajax*: 'What wouldst thou?' *Diomedes*: 'I would correct him.'

Ajax: 'Were I the general, thou shouldst have my office/Ere that correction.../I'll fight with him alone.')

Alarbus *(Titus Andronicus)*
TAMORA's eldest son. He has the gory distinction of being the first person to be hacked to death in the play. He does not even have time to speak.

Albany, Duke of *(King Lear)*
We first see Albany bewildered by LEAR's fury at GONERIL ('My lord, I am guiltless, as I am ignorant,/Of what hath mov'd you...'), and then, when he hears the facts, filled with handwringing dismay ('How far your eyes may pierce I cannot tell:/Striving to better, oft we mar what's well'). His wife Goneril snappishly dismisses him as a 'milk-liver'd man', a fool 'more attack'd for want of wisdom/Than prais'd for harmful mildness'. But as the play proceeds he grows in authority, until discovery of EDMUND's and Goneril's love-affair leads him to arrest Edmund and set up the trial-by-combat which leads to Edmund's death. He ends the play as a statesman, handing over power to EDGAR and to KENT ('Our present business/Is general woe; friends of my soul, you twain/Rule in this realm and the gored state sustain'). The part is small and the lines are colourless, but the character's growth from ignorance to understanding lifts it above routine.

Alcibiades *(Timon of Athens)*
Athenian military commander, TIMON's only true friend. (The only reason he does not help Timon financially is that he is himself in exile at the time.) He is young and fiery – when Timon says jovially at the first banquet, 'You'd rather be at a breakfast of enemies than a dinner of friends', he answers, 'So they be bleeding-new, my lord, there's no meat like 'em' – and he is loyal to people rather than to conventions, pleading before the Senate for the life of a drunken comrade who killed a man, and closing the play by forgiving rather than destroying the Athenian people. He is the only 'noble' character in the play, the only man apart from FLAVIUS with generosity of spirit, and his lines when he is banished – save that the part is smaller and never tragic – echo not so much bitter Timon as CORIOLANUS in another era and another play. ('I have kept back their foes/While they have told their money and let out/Their coin upon large interest, I myself/Rich only in large hurts – all those for this...?')

Alençon, Duke of *(Henry VI Part One)*
Brave French lord, whose fighting-fitness is his only character.

Alexander *(Troilus and Cressida)*
CRESSIDA's servant, who describes to her the blow AJAX gave HECTOR on the battlefield, 'the shame whereof hath ever since kept Hector fasting and waking'.

Alexas *(Antony and Cleopatra)*
CLEOPATRA's major-domo, a man of considerable dignity (verging on pomposity) but no personality.

Alice *(Henry V)*
KATHARINE's maid who gives her English lessons ('De hand, de fingres, de nick, de bilbow'). She is deferential, but delightfully prone to giggles (e.g. at the idea that the English should use indecent words like 'foot' and 'count').

All's Well that Ends Well

Helena's father, a doctor, has left her magic healing potions in his will. She is in love with Bertram, Count of Rousillon, a snobbish youth in the service of the sick King of France, and, in return for healing the king, Helena asks him to order Bertram to marry her. Horrified at having so to demean himself, Bertram exiles himself to Italy immediately after the marriage, aided by the boastful, cowardly Parolles, his flatterer. He sends Helena a note saying that he will only accept her as his wife if she gets a ring from his finger and becomes pregnant with his child, adding the caustic PS that this, in his opinion, means 'never'. Nothing daunted, Helena sets off after him to Florence, disguised as a pilgrim. She lodges with a widow, whose daughter Diana is trying to seduce Bertram; she arranges to change places with Diana, sleeps with Bertram and gets the ring.

While this scheme is in progress, Parolles' fellow-officers Dumain and Dumain, irritated by his boasting, trick him into revealing his true, cowardly colours to Bertram. The scales fall from Bertram's eyes, but he has other matters on his mind: seduction of 'Diana' and return to France immediately afterwards (for he has heard that Helena is dead and there is therefore no impediment to going home). Back at the French court, Bertram is about to be betrothed to the daughter of the good old lord Lafeu when Diana appears, brandishing a ring – not Bertram's ring, but one the King of France earlier gave to Helena – and accusing Bertram of promising marriage and then betraying her. He angrily calls her a liar and a harlot, and she is about to be arrested when Helena comes in, pregnant and wearing Bertram's heirloom ring. The conditions of Bertram's silly letter have been exactly carried out, and he agrees, as cheerfully as possible under the circumstances, to spend the rest of his life with Helena.

Alonso *(The Tempest)*
King of Naples, who long ago took PROSPERO's dukedom from him and gave it to ANTONIO. He is misguided rather than black-hearted, and he is punished by being made to think that his son FERDINAND has drowned. ('He receives comfort like cold porridge,' SEBASTIAN callously remarks; Alonso himself says, 'I am attached with weariness,/To th' dulling of my spirits'.) When he hears from ARIEL that Ferdinand's 'death' is due to his own wickedness, he immediately becomes contrite,

and his change of heart paves the way for radiant joy when Ferdinand is found alive. ('Now all the blessings/Of a glad father compass thee about!')

Ambassador *(Hamlet)*
Arrives with FORTINBRAS at the end of the play, bringing news that ROSENCRANTZ and GUILDENSTERN are dead; says only five lines.

Ambassador *(Henry V)*
Head of the French delegation who sneeringly tells HENRY the DAUPHIN's message that 'There's nought in France/That can be with a nimble galliard won', and even more scornfully delivers his present, a barrel of tennis balls.

Amelia *(The Comedy of Errors): see* **Abbess**

Amiens *(As You Like It)*
Attendant lord in the Forest of Arden, notable chiefly because he sings. (His rendition of 'Under the Greenwood Tree' throws JAQUES into exquisite melancholy.) He may be one of the unnamed Lords dressed as foresters who are the DUKE's 'co-mates and brothers in exile' later in the play; in that case he speaks several speeches, and sings several more songs, including 'Blow, blow, thou winter wind'.

Andromache *(Troilus and Cressida)*
HECTOR's wife, who in a single emotional scene urges him to heed omens of disaster and not to fight ACHILLES. ('O be persuaded! Do not count it holy/To hurt by being just!') She fails, begs Hector's father PRIAM to forbid him outright to go, and is sent out of the room by Hector for her pains. ('Andromache, I am offended with you./Upon the love you bear me, get you in.')

Andronicus, Marcus *(Titus Andronicus): see* **Marcus Andronicus**

Andronicus, Titus *(Titus Andronicus): see* **Titus**

Angelo *(The Comedy of Errors)*
Goldsmith who delivers a chain to (the wrong) ANTIPHOLUS, and then has (the right) Antipholus arrested for refusing to pay for it. Hurt bewilderment is his main characteristic.

Angelo *(Measure for Measure)*
At base, Angelo is exactly the same kind of person as MALVOLIO in *Twelfth Night*: a dessicated puritan who is corrupted and destroyed by lust. Sir Toby, in *Twelfth Night*, says to Malvolio, 'Dost think, because thou art virtuous, there shall be no more cakes and ale?', and Malvolio, though he would dearly like to answer 'Yes', is in no position to command it. But Angelo has precisely that power, and has far more serious sins to cure than gluttony or drunkenness. None the less, we feel that his power of correction gives him no joy: he is more like an actuary, examining every particle of the law and making sure, in a

finicky, good-day's-work way, that it is carried out. 'We must not make a scarecrow of the law', he says, 'Setting it up to fear the birds of prey,/ And let it keep one shape, till custom make it/Their perch and not their terror.' This is the speech of a man concerned only for the law, heedless both of the human beings it exists to control and of their reasons for the things they do. For such a man, personal feelings are not so much irrelevant as dangerous, the cause of the very lapses he has been appointed to amend. Angelo absolutely rejects ISABELLA's and others' pleas to temper justice with mercy, and even allows himself a piece of grim sophistry at their expense: 'I show pity most of all when I show justice:/For then I pity those I do not know,/Which a dismiss'd offence would after gall,/And do him right that, answering one foul wrong,/ Lives not to act another.' It is the attitude of an Inquisitor: neither estimable nor evil, it applies the rules of scientific or mathematical logic to human lives in an attempt to rule the unruly and govern the ungovernable.

If that were all there was to Angelo, he would indeed be Malvolio's clone, and his downfall would be similarly farcical and unedifying: capering cross-gartered hurts nothing but pride, and involves no change of basic personality. But the trap that snares Angelo is far more complex than Malvolio's simple ambition: he is caught in the (again Christian) double-bind of knowing perfectly well what sin he is committing and being unable to prevent himself. He says, 'What is't I dream on?/O cunning enemy, that, to catch a saint,/With saints dost bait thy hook! Most dangerous/Is that temptation that doth goad us on/To sin in loving virtue...' – in short, the lust he sees in himself is not primarily physical (for Isabella's body) but metaphysical, a longing to rape the moral power in her which he sees as a distorted image of the virtue he has always aspired to in himself. His passion is pitiful, and all the more so because of his self-awareness and self-disgust.

After this revelation, Angelo's personality seems to become as uncomplicated as his actions, and it is utterly unlikeable. He behaves as if he is terrified out of his wits: physically terrified of what will happen to him if his behaviour is discovered, and even more morally terrified at his inability to climb out of the abyss he has found within himself. He responds with uncaring ferocity when Isabella threatens to unmask him. ('Who will believe thee...?/My unsoil'd name, th'austereness of my life,/My vouch against you, and my place i' the state,/Will so your accusation overweigh/That you shall stifle in your own report/And smell of calumny.') When the deed is done, as he thinks, and Isabella has given in to him, he still sends the PROVOST word that CLAUDIO must be executed – and there seems no reason for it but malignity. When he hears news of the DUKE's imminent return, he plants the idea in ESCALUS' mind that the Duke's actions 'show much like madness; pray heaven his wisdom be not tainted' – an insinuation whose only motive can be self-preservation; when the Duke does return and the accusations against Angelo begin, he counters them with a hard-faced intransigence which is subtler than guile itself, only to fall into abjectness ('O my dread lord...') when he discovers that the Duke, in disguise, has witnessed every one of his transgressions. In the end, like a Christian penitent, he begs for the 'grace' of 'immediate sentence and sequent death', as if it were a kind of absolution. That he is denied this, and is instead put through the cruel charade of forced marriage, confiscation of all his worldly possessions, a pretence that he is being led away to death, and, finally, arbitrary reprieve, is tragedy, not comedy. At the start of the play he had nothing, no human qualities whatsoever, and did not know it; at the end he is exactly the man he was before, and knows himself. In dramatic terms we might expect this, in some way or other, to be a progression from darkness to light, to be as illuminating and cathartic as (say) the progression to self-knowledge in *King Oedipus*. And it is not. We pity Oedipus, because his reversal is overwhelming and enormous; we pity Malvolio, though his reversal is trivial and ludicrous; we feel no pity at all for Angelo, and the reason lies either in the 'dark philosophy' some critics attribute to the play, or to the absence of true tragic dignity in Angelo's own character. Either we know too much about him in the first half of the play, or too little in the second; either way, he fails to change or to grow before our eyes, and that, except in melodrama or comedy (neither of which *Measure for Measure* wholeheartedly is) is less a tragic than a dramatic flaw.

Angus *(Macbeth)*
Scottish lord who deserts MACBETH before the final battle, on the grounds that 'Now he does feel/His secret murders sticking on his hands;/Now minutely revolts upbraid his faith-breach/... Now does he feel his title/Hang loose about him, like a giant's robe/Upon a dwarfish thief.'

Anne, Lady *(Richard III)*
Daughter-in-law of Henry VI, widow of his son EDWARD whom RICHARD killed (in *Henry VI Part Three*). She veers between hatred of Richard and fascination: wooed over her father-in-law's body at the start of the play, she at first shouts her rage ('Out of my sight! Thou dost infect mine eyes!'), but then, like a broken horse, submits in a couple of lines and agrees to marry him. Later, and not unexpectedly, she comes to wish that her crown 'were red-hot steel to sear me to the brains', and joins with Queen ELIZABETH and the Duchess of YORK in grief for the dead princes in the Tower. (Their antiphonal grieving-and-cursing sessions are among the most artificial, most spectacular, set-pieces in the play.) When Richard decides to marry Queen Elizabeth's daughter for dynastic reasons, he orders STANLEY to put it about that Anne is ill; soon afterwards she vanishes, to reappear as one of the GHOSTS which haunt Richard before Bosworth.

Antenor *(Troilus and Cressida)*
Trojan lord captured by the Greeks and later exchanged for CRESSIDA.

Anthony *(Romeo and Juliet)*
Servant of CAPULET, who speaks one less-then-immortal line ('Ay, boy, ready') in the scene of bustle preparatory to the Capulets' masked ball.

Antigonus *(The Winter's Tale)*
Good old lord who tries to argue LEONTES out of his jealous rage ('You are abused, and by some putter-on/That will be damn'd for't'), is given baby PERDITA to expose on the coast of Bohemia to live or die, and is soon afterwards pursued by a bear and eaten. Puzzled loyalty to Leontes and deference to his voluble wife PAULINA are his main character-traits.

Antiochus *(Pericles)*
Wicked king of Antioch. He sets all his DAUGHTER's suitors a riddle, killing any who fail to answer. The answer is the girl herself, and the riddle refers to her incest with Antiochus, so when PERICLES guesses the answer, Antiochus orders THALIARD to murder him. Antiochus is a cardboard villain, of no interest in himself. His death after being struck by lightning is announced in Act Two, and is the most intriguing thing about him. ('When he was seated in his chariot/Of an inestimable value, and his daughter with him,/A fire from heaven came and shrivell'd up/Their bodies, even to loathing...')

Antiochus' daughter *(Pericles)*
She speaks two lines, wishing PERICLES luck in guessing the riddle, the answer to which is that she is committing incest with her father. Later, we hear that she has been burned to death with her father, after being struck by lightning.

Antipholus I (Antipholus of Syracuse) *(The Comedy of Errors)*
A rich young merchant visiting Ephesus, he is troubled by the town's reputation as 'full of cozenage,/As, nimble jugglers that deceive the eye,/Dark-working sorcerers that change the mind,/Soul-killing witches that deform the body' – and his suspicions are confirmed by the way people keep giving him money, invitations and jewellery as if they've known him for years. Sometimes this delights him – 'I see a man here needs not live by shifts,/When in the streets he meets such golden gifts' – but generally it alarms him, and in the end he rails against ADRIANA (who thinks he is her husband ANTIPHOLUS II) so violently – 'Dissembling harlot.../...confederate with a damned pack...' – that she takes him for a lunatic and he is forced to seek sanctuary in an Abbey.

The other part of Antipholus' character, set against this bewilderment and alarm, is a cheerful, joky relationship with his servant DROMIO I. They are forever interrupting the action to exchange wisecracks, and in one scene, after Dromio escapes from the clutches of fat Nell the kitchen-maid, they have a splendid time comparing her body to a globe of the world and imagining, ridiculously or salaciously, where various countries might be situated.

In many ways, Antipholus I is the stock farce hero, more interesting as the butt of lunatic action than in himself. But he is not only bewildered and discomforted: he has a robust opportunism, a zest for taking things as they come (for example, making overtures to LUCIANA even though she clearly thinks he is her sister's husband), and that and his wit make him a far more rounded character than his morose brother Antipholus II. He is the hub of the action and the 'hero' of the play.

Antipholus II (Antipholus of Ephesus) *(The Comedy of Errors)*
A serious-minded young merchant, making his way in the world and very conscious of his social position, he is thrown totally off-balance when the pattern of mistaken identities begins. Unlike his brother ANTIPHOLUS I, however, he takes no pleasure in his bafflement: he becomes ever surlier, ever more convinced that other people are playing cruel practical jokes on him, and his responses (e.g. proposing to give to a courtesan the gold chain he ordered for his wife) are not so much spirited as spiteful. He is the stock farce bore, literal-minded and humourless, and the wilder the world grows the more pompous and long-winded he makes himself. It is hard, for example, not to imagine general yawns onstage as he embarks on his catalogue, to DUKE SOLINUS in the last act, of the events of his most uncomfortable day. ('My liege, I am adviséd what I say,/Neither disturbéd with th'effect of wine/Nor heady-rash, provok'd with raging ire,/Albeit my wrongs might make one wiser, mad...')

Antonio *(The Merchant of Venice)*
Antonio, the merchant of the title, is a mean-spirited, unsociable man. Surrounded by friends at the start of the play, he immediately announces his melancholy ('In sooth, I know not why I am so sad') which isolates him from their merriment; offered a truce as well as money by SHYLOCK ('I would be friends with you, and have your love') he is so disdainful that he refused at first even to speak to him – his speech accepting the bond is made to BASSANIO; when his argosies are thought lost and he is taken to court, he spurns all proffered help (e.g. Bassanio's offer to pay back the money) with a determination to suffer ('I do oppose/My patience to his fury') which is pig-headed and ungracious rather than noble or reasonable. He stirs race-hatred into the unlovely brew. Long before the trial-scene gives him justification to dislike Shylock, he sneers (to Bassanio) 'The devil can cite scripture for his purpose' and (to Shylock) 'If thou wilt lend this money, lend it not/As to thy friends.'

It could be argued that Antonio's willingness to accept the bond in the first place is a generous action, to help his friend Bassanio: he certainly surrounds it with the trappings of fulsome generosity. ('Go, presently inquire, and so will I,/Where money is, and I no question make,/To have it of my trust or for my sake'.) But he only borrows because he is certain that the bond will never be called in, that in less than two months, when his ships come home, he will have 'thrice three times' its value, and his behaviour when his hopes are dashed is more like that of a disappointed child than a grown man of any business acumen. His only disinterested action in the play comes right at the end, when he intercedes with PORTIA for Bassanio – 'I dare be bound again,/My soul upon the forfeit, that your lord/Will never more break faith advisedly' – and this small piece of generosity comes too late to counter the view that he, not Shylock, is the most amoral and least likeable man in Venice.

Antonio (*Much Ado about Nothing*)

LEONATO's brother, an old gentleman greedy to enjoy every moment of life. At the masked ball he flirts with HERO's maidservant URSULA, pretending to be someone else (but given away by his senile twitch: 'I know you by the waggling of your head'); he is brisk and jolly with Hero, just like everyone's idea of the applecheeked, favourite uncle. His best scene comes after Hero's disgrace, when he agrees to pretend to CLAUDIO that she is dead, and joins Leonato in splendid tirades of fake rage at Claudio. ('Come, follow me, boy, come, sir boy, come, follow me!/Sir boy, I'll whip you from your foining fence,/Nay, as a gentleman I will.') He speaks only 54 lines in the entire play, but they are crammed with personality, and make him a swaggering counterpart to Leonato.

Antonio (*The Tempest*)

PROSPERO's brother, who twelve years before the play began usurped his throne in Milan. We first see him in the opening storm scene, venting his rage on the BOATSWAIN ('Hang, cur, hang, you whoreson, insolent noisemaker'), and our sour view of him remains unchanged throughout the play. He jokes sarcastically with SEBASTIAN about GONZALO's loyalty to ALONSO (and his boring turns of speech); he plots with Sebastian to murder Alonso while he sleeps ('What a sleep were this/For your advancement'); he is restrained from villainy by Prospero's magic but unchanged by it. At the start of the play Prospero described him as 'The ivy which had hid my princely trunk/And suck'd my verdure out on't', and at the end, although he has returned Prospero's dukedom and been forgiven for his treachery, we are given no signs at all that he will amend his wicked ways: if peace and justice reign in Milan for evermore, it will be in spite of him.

Antonio (*Twelfth Night*)

Sea-captain friend of SEBASTIAN, who survives the shipwreck with him and offers to go with him into Illyria. He is later much confused when he finds VIOLA dressed as a boy and takes her for Sebastian, but before things get too complicated he is arrested and disappears from the play until the unravelling of the last act, when he is on hand to tell everyone who Sebastian really is.

Antonio (*The Two Gentlemen of Verona*)
PROTEUS' father, persuaded by PANTHINO to send his son to Milan to further his education. A characterless, middle-aged aristocrat.

Antony (Marcus Antonius) (*Julius Caesar; Antony and Cleopatra*)
In *Julius Caesar*, a play full of politicians and crammed with arguments about ends and means, Antony at first seems to stand alone: he symbolises action, military excellence and a loyalty to people and country which transcends (or never once involves) intellectual calculation. In real life, such heroic integrity might seem admirable but dull; in the play, it makes him a foil for other characters. In particular, his preference for action is the mirror-image of BRUTUS' love of thought, and his steadfastness contrasts with CASSIUS' pliability; of the other people in the play, only CAESAR and PORTIA can match him for singlemindedness.

As the action of the play unfolds, however, Shakespeare exploits what we think we know of Antony to marvellous effect. In the opening scenes, which are largely used to show Caesar's tyrannical disposition and the growing hysteria and conviction of the conspirators, Antony speaks less than half a dozen lines, and their tone is summed up by the punctilious (not to say obsequious) 'When Caesar says "Do this", it is performed'. He is one of a group of satellites, and our interest is in the sun they surround; we hardly notice him. Our shock is therefore all the greater – it is one of the play's main theatrical surprises – when after the assassination he suddenly makes ironical political advances to the conspirators, flings himself on Caesar's corpse in an outpouring of personal emotion paralleled by no other character (not even Brutus ever rises to such passion), and finally woos the mob in a scene of poetic rhetoric so persuasive (of the theatre audience as well as of the Roman CITIZENS he is addressing) that he virtually steals the play. Finally, in the negotiations with Brutus before Philippi (where he reverts to the character of simple, honest soldier), his unwavering pride in decisive action is matched against Brutus' equal pride in a viewpoint reached by intellectual self-persuasion. The passion we know is bottled up in both characters, though never shown here, adds to the tension which makes the scene.

In *Antony and Cleopatra*, Antony is the same mixture of bluntness and passion as in *Julius Caesar*, but whereas there the passion was under control, let out only occasionally and by design, here it rules unchecked. As he has grown older, Antony has surrendered to the pleasure-principle, to the force of the irrational (expressed not only in lust for CLEOPATRA, but in drink, in a love of pomp and flattery, and in apoplectic anger when his will is crossed): he has lost himself. While other Romans make war or politics, he makes love; he is a tragic hero whose downfall arises from his nature and is inevitable from the start of *Antony and Cleopatra*.

Constantly throughout the play, Antony reaches for the cloak of his former single-mindedness, and finds it rags. Cleopatra refers to this quality dismissively – 'A Roman thought hath struck him' – and his tragedy is that where the root of his being was once action, it is now, precisely, no more than thought. When Cleopatra sails away from the climactic sea-battle of the play, he wheels his ship and goes after her 'like a doting mallard': all is lost on a whim, as casually (to the outside observer) as if on the turn of a card or a throw of dice. He rounds furiously on Cleopatra afterwards – their quarrel is the reason she plans to feign death – but his anger is really rage against himself, and is another surrender to irrationality.

A key feature of *Antony and Cleopatra* is the way the play revolves not round a single character but round a couple. They are host and parasite, as symbiotic as the partners in a double-act, and we are left continuously in doubt who gains and who loses by the relationship. This ambivalence is given a particular, sexual edge. Cleopatra's skittishness, her playacting, is 'masculine' (by the terms of Shakespeare's day, if not of the liberated twentieth century): its purpose is to dominate. By contrast, Antony's hesitancy, his willingness to lapse into the role of 'strumpet's fool', is 'feminine', a fact which is condemned by his Roman compatriots. The contrast between Cleopatra's certainty of purpose (she knows just what her flirting is meant to achieve) and Antony's self-indulgent helplessness (if he is a fly in a spider's web, he loves it) is both psychologically fascinating and dramatically powerful. We are not intrigued by the lordly, grizzled Antony who confronts OCTAVIUS, but by the grotesque, amorous youth he makes himself for Cleopatra. He says, 'These strong Egyptian fetters I must break,/Or lose myself in dotage' – and because we know that he lacks the character-qualities to break the fetters, we feel a goosepimply, ironical satisfaction, a mixture of sympathy and 'I told you so', as we watch him struggle.

Antony and Cleopatra

The root of the tragedy is the pull between public duty and private pleasure. Antony is one of the three rulers of Rome (the others are Octavius Caesar and Lepidus), but is neglecting his military duties because he is passionately in love with Cleopatra, Queen of Egypt. She flirts with him like a naughty child; it's never clear whether her passion is for him or for splitting Roman power apart. Antony's obsession with Cleopatra leads him first to quarrel with Octavius and Lepidus and then to open war. Even then he might have won, if Cleopatra had not sailed away from the battle, and he had not turned his ship and followed her. His military career and self-esteem both in ruins, he attempts suicide, then succeeds, and Cleopatra, rather than be taken by the Romans and paraded through the streets of Rome, kills herself (by means of a snake hidden in a basket of figs) and lies beside her lover in death. This simple plot-line is merely the play's peg; the main interest lies in the complex characters of Cleopatra and Antony, and in the superb, ecstatic poetry which everyone (even common soldiers, even messengers) is given to speak.

Apemantus *(Timon of Athens)*

Apemantus belongs most nearly to the Cynic school of philosophy. Cynics believed that most of the values of human society, including friendship, generosity and the rule of law, were a sham, and they spent their lives denouncing them with a barking vehemence which earned them their name (the word cynic means 'dog-like'). Apemantus' repartee is as sharp as any Shakespearean clown's, but has no shred of humour in it: when someone says to him, for example, 'You're a dog', he replies, without a moment's pause for thought, 'Thy mother's of my generation: what's she, if I be a dog?' He refuses to eat with TIMON, on the grounds that 'if I should be bribed too, there would be none left to rail upon thee,' and is the only person in the first half of the play to perceive that 'a number of men eats Timon, and he sees 'em not'. Towards the end, he softens. He goes to Timon in exile, ostensibly because 'men report/Thou dost affect my manners' but actually to offer him help; but when he is spurned he reverts to his former character, and the scene dissolves into acid hatred. *(Timon:* 'I'll beat thee, but I should infect my hands.' *Apemantus:* 'I would my tongue could rot them off.' *Timon:* 'Away, thou issue of a mangy dog...' *Apemantus:* 'Would thou would burst.' *Timon:* 'Away, thou tedious rogue! I am sorry I shall lose a stone by thee.' *(Throws a stone at him) Apemantus:* 'Beast!' *Timon:* 'Slave!' *Apemantus:* 'Toad!')

Apothecary *(Romeo and Juliet)*

With great reluctance, he supplies ROMEO with poison. In most other dramatists' hands, he would be a tiny or silent cog in the plot; Shakespeare gives him a full scene with Romeo, highlighting his poverty and allowing Romeo a splendid outburst against hard cash. ('There is thy gold, worse poison to men's souls,/Doing more murder in this loathsome world/Than these poor compounds that thou may'st not sell...')

Apprentices *(Henry VI Part Two)*

Loutishly support PETER in his duel with HORNER.

Aragon, Prince of *(The Merchant of Venice)*

PORTIA's suitor, who chooses the silver casket. A Spanish grandee, he is all fire and flashing eyes, both before he chooses the wrong casket ('Fortune now/To my heart's hope!') and afterwards. ('What's here? The portrait of a blinking idiot!.../How much unlike my hope and my deservings!')

Archidamus *(The Winter's Tale)*
Exaggeratedly polite courtier, whose language is an Everest of elegant
self-deprecation: his country is so inferior to his hosts', he claims, that
if they ever visit it his people 'will give you sleepy drinks, that your
senses, unintelligent of our insufficience, may, though they cannot
praise us, as little accuse us'.

Arcite *(The Two Noble Kinsmen)*
The more dashing and less interesting of the two young men in the
play, Arcite lives his life like the hero of a swashbuckling adventure
film, in a whirl of disguises, duels, affairs of honour and vows of
undying loyalty. He seems constantly to be watching himself in the
mirror of his own admiration, and his end is suitably ironical: thrown
from his horse in a victory-gallop, he gives the girl he loves to the
cousin who has been his beloved rival, and breathes his last at the very
moment of reconciliation. Such a character belongs more to the age of
chivalry, in which the story of *The Two Noble Kinsmen* originated, than
to the world of Renaissance sensibility, and though Shakespeare has
been at some pains to turn PALAMON into a Romantic, psychologically
interesting hero, he has left Arcite more or less alone, as two-
dimensional as a knight in a gorgeous medieval tapestry.

Ariel *(The Tempest)*
'Airy spirit' freed by PROSPERO from an imprisonment imposed on him
by the witch Sycorax, and bound to Prospero thereafter in a kind of
grudging servitude. Ariel is the chief agent of Prospero's magic,
perplexing the villains, delighting MIRANDA and FERDINAND, and
leading CALIBAN, STEPHANO and TRINCULO a muddy dance through
middens and horseponds. For all his insubstantial nature, he is subject
to human emotions: 'How now? Moody?' Prospero asks him at one
point, and later he teaches Prospero himself a lesson in compassion.
(*Ariel*: 'Your charm so strongly works 'em/That if you now behold them
your affections/Would become tender.' *Prospero*: 'Dost thou think so,
spirit?' *Ariel*: 'Mine would, sir, an I were human'.) His chief emotions,
yearning for freedom and innocent delight in his butterfly life – he is no
malevolent sprite, like the PUCK of *A Midsummer Night's Dream* – are
expressed in one of his many songs in the play: 'Where the bee sucks,
there suck I,/In a cowslip's bell I lie;/There I couch when owls do
cry./On the bat's back I do fly/After summer merrily./Merrily, merrily
shall I live now,/Under the blossom that hangs on the bough.' Ariel
spends much of the play dressed as a sea nymph, and indeed the role is
often played by a woman.

Armado *(Love's Labour's Lost)*
Armado is one of a gallery of characters so similar (PISTOL in *Henry IV
Part Two* and *Henry V*, CAIUS in *The Merry Wives of Windsor*,
AGUECHEEK in *Twelfth Night*, STEPHANO in *The Tempest*) that we may
wonder if they were not all written for the same actor. If so, he was a

rare comedian, with a range of funny voices, a gift for rolling mock-rhetoric and a tatterdemalion magnificence which filled the stage.

Armado is a Spanish grandee, a puffed-up fool. HOLOFERNES addresses him as 'Most military sir'; others call him a plume of feathers and a weathercock. He is ludicrously equipped with a minute, cheeky page-boy, MOTH, who outsmarts him in every sentence – and his self-importance is so invincible that even when he notices, he never once believes his ears. Unlike most of Shakespeare's foreigners, however, he has a Falstaffian familiarity with the English language, a rhetorical panache which is the farce-equivalent of BEROWNE's high poetry. (He says to COSTARD, for example, 'By my sweet soul, I mean setting thee at liberty, enfreedoming thy person; thou wert immured, restrained, captivated, bound'.)

Love's Labour's Lost is one of the most schematically organised of Shakespeare's plays, and one of its most pleasing linkages, cutting across the main groups of lords, ladies and low-life characters, is that between Armado and Berowne. They are opposite aspects of the same character – folly and melancholy, fantasy and seriousness, capering and pondering – and the crossing of their destinies (in Costard's mixing-up of their love-letters) is a hinge of the action, driving Berowne to reveal even more seriousness (the depth of his love) and Armado even more foolishness (the depth of his self-regard). Appropriately, as the play moves from giddiness to seriousness, Armado's importance wanes; but in the first half he is a main contributor to the sunlight-dazzle of words and actions, the mayfly who leads the dance.

Artemidorus *(Julius Caesar)*

Greek prophet who tries to give CAESAR a letter warning him of the conspiracy. He is grandly brushed aside with the words 'What touches us ourself shall be last serv'd'.

Artesius *(The Two Noble Kinsmen)*

Appears 'with attendants' in the dumb-show which starts the play (a wedding-procession and dance). There is no indication of who he is, what he does or what his character is like.

Arthur, Duke of Bretagne *(King John)*

JOHN's nephew and the rival to his throne. A saintly child, whose little-lord-Fauntleroy charm ('Alas, what need you to be so boisterous-rough?/I will not struggle, I will stand stone-still') disables HUBERT from blinding and killing him. Shortly afterwards, in a turn of events characteristic of this play of the absurd, he jumps from the castle battlements crying 'Good ground, be pitiful and hurt me not', and kills himself.

Arviragus *(Cymbeline)*

Younger of CYMBELINE's sons brought up in Wales (where he goes under the name Cadwall). He is a youth of about 17, and like his brother GUIDERIUS is chiefly characterised by a kind of unaffected, healthy-young-animal charm: lines like *Guiderius*: 'I am throughly weary.' *Arviragus*: 'I am weak with toil, yet strong in appetite' are typical.

As You Like It

Orlando, younger son of Sir Roland de Boys, has been kept in rural serfdom by his wicked brother Oliver, and when he demands his patrimony Oliver plots with the wrestler Charles to disable him. But Orlando defeats Charles, and escapes his brother's vengeance by going to the Forest of Arden with his loyal old servant Adam. Also in the forest are Rosalind (whose father, the old Duke, has been banished by *his* wicked brother, Duke Frederick, and whom Orlando has met at the wrestling match), Celia and Touchstone, the court jester. Rosalind is by now disguised as a boy (Ganymede), and when she finds that Orlando is in love with her, she encourages him to practise his courting on her, safe (so she thinks) in her disguise.

The other occupants of the forest include the old Duke (Rosalind's father) and his court, among them the melancholy lord Jaques, and a collection of shepherds and other rustics including Silvius (who loves Phebe) and Phebe (who loves 'Ganymede'). The Forest of Arden gradually works its enchantment on all these people, and by the end of the play the wicked Oliver and Duke Frederick have changed their ways to good, Orlando and the old Duke are restored to their lands and properties, and every pair of lovers (Rosalind and Orlando, Celia and Oliver, Phebe and Silvius, Touchstone and the lumpish Audrey) are united in happiness. Only Jaques, that amateur of human despondency, is left – and he goes into a monastery to see what he can learn from 'these convertites'.

Attendant *(The Winter's Tale)*

Reports, with breathless anguish, the death of the child MAMILLIUS.

Audrey *(As You Like It)*

TOUCHSTONE's beloved, she is a goatherd, and apparently (to judge by what he says to her) is ungainly and ugly. She is a butt for his humour and says little, but the part offers splendid opportunities for a physical comedienne.

Aufidius, Tullus *(Coriolanus)*

Volscian war-leader, CORIOLANUS's rival and enemy. At the start of the play, indeed, he seems to be Coriolanus' clone, a fearless fighter of genius who despises the common people, and when the two men meet on the battlefield they talk with the banter of people who have been each other's familiars for years. (*Coriolanus*: 'I'll fight with none but thee; for I do hate thee/Worse than a promise-breaker.' *Aufidius*: 'We hate alike:/Not Afric owns a serpent I abhor/More than thy fame I envy. Fix thy foot.'

Despite Coriolanus' and Aufidius' apparent relaxation with one another, there have already been plain hints of what is to come, that their relationship is not the hearty, Queensberry-rules affair it seems: LARTIUS, for example, has already reported Aufidius as saying 'that of all things upon the earth he hated/Your person most; that he would pawn his fortunes/To hopeless restitution, so he might/Be call'd your vanquisher'. In the light of this, his friendly welcome after Coriolanus banishes himself from Rome can been seen for the slyness it really is, and he becomes a plotter as black-hearted and dissembling as any IAGO. Lines like 'When, Caius, Rome is thine/Thou'rt poorest of all; then shortly art thou mine' cast a deep shadow over his apparently pure-hearted nobility at the beginning of the play. Like Iago, he gives only perfunctory reasons for his vendetta – 'I rais'd him, and I pawn'd/Mine honour for his truth!...' – but his need to destroy Coriolanus, which leads him to encourage the assassins in the final scene, must be deeper-rooted than irritation at being out-heroed or ill-thanked for generosity. Aufidius can be played simply, as a two-timing, melodramatic villain (the lines are fustian enough), or subtly, as a flawed reflection of Coriolanus' flawed magnificence, his Lucifer; either way, the relationship between them is more crucial to the meaning of the play even than Coriolanus' relationship with his mother or with the Roman CITIZENS and the tribunes who speak for them.

Aumerle, Duke of (*Richard II*)

Aumerle begins as one of RICHARD's most fawning courtiers ('How brooks your grace the air,/After your late tossing on the breaking seas?'), but in the Parliament-scene in Act IV, when BAGOT and others challenge him before BOLINGBROKE, he suddenly begins to twist and rage, switching on a hot-headed, furious rhetoric of which he has previously shown no hint. The explanation comes in the same scene, when an anonymous lord calls him 'forsworn Aumerle'. He is a shifty courtier, a place-seeker and a flatterer, honey-sweet when things are going his way, viper-quick when cornered. Quickness becomes his main characteristic in the rest of the play (the conspiracy scenes which dominate Act V): discovered by his own father YORK to be plotting against Bolingbroke (and therefore to have lied in the Parliament scene), he gallops to London to beg forgiveness before York can accuse him. He is a lordly equivalent of BUSHY, BAGOT, GREEN and those other 'caterpillars of the commonwealth' who nibble Richard's state, and his false loyalty is strongly contrasted with his father's honesty. He appears as Duke of York in *Henry V*, but the only two lines he speaks ('My lord, most humbly on my knee I beg/The leading of the vaward') give no clue at all to his character, devious or otherwise.

Austria, Archduke of (*King John*)

Ally of PHILIP of France against the English. Although his bluster overawes JOHN, he is mocked and tormented like a bullied child by the BASTARD, and can think of no way to deal with it; in the end he meets the Bastard in battle and has his head cut off.

Autolycus *(The Winter's Tale)*
In Greek myth Autolycus was a grand trickster, a king descended from
Hermes, god of crooks, himself. In *The Winter's Tale* he is a petty thief
and conman, preying on the gullible rustics of Bohemia. His stock-
in-trade is disguise: he pretends to be a muggers' victim, rolling on the
ground in fake agony until the CLOWN bends over him and he can pick
his pocket; he goes to the sheep-shearing festival disguised as a pedlar
and sells his entire stock of worthless trinkets; when he is forced to
change clothes with Prince FLORIZEL he immediately begins to play the
aristocrat as if to the manor born. His main victims are the SHEPHERD
and the Clown, and the three of them have scenes of integrated,
'professional' fooling which set them somewhat apart from the other
characters in the play.

Autolycus is charming and personable, able to sing well (e.g. in the
catch he performs with MOPSA and DORCAS) and treated with affection
rather than scorn even by those he cheats. The source of his charm rests
in his delight in his own roguery, the feeling that he does what he does
for fun as much as for profit. His professional skill, and his rollicking
use of language, are seen at peak when he talks to the Shepherd and the
Clown, disguised, and, pretending that he has no idea who they are,
calls the father 'an old sheep-whistling rogue, a ram-tender' and says of
the son that he will be 'flay'd alive, then 'nointed over with honey, set
on the head of a wasps' nest, then stand till he be three-quarters and a
dram dead, then recovered again with *aqua-vitae* or some other hot
infusion, then, raw as he is, and in the hottest day prognostication
proclaims, shall he be set against a brick wall, the sun looking with a
southward eye upon him, where he is to behold him with flies blown to
death'.

Auvergne, Countess of *(Henry VI Part One)*
In one of the most intriguing episodes of the play, she plans to capture
TALBOT and win fame 'as Scythian Tomyris by Cyrus' death'; but
though this ambition proves her to be well-read, her cunning is no
match for Talbot's, and she ends up inviting him to dinner instead of
killing him.

Bagot, Sir William (*Richard II*)
The highest-ranking of RICHARD's three 'creatures', and the chief
'caterpillar of the commonwealth', Bagot actually says or does very little
in the play to justify his loathly reputation. His moment of glory comes
at the start of the Act IV Parliament-scene, when he accuses AUMERLE
of plotting against BOLINGBROKE, and so sets the nobles at one
another's throats.

Balthasar (*Romeo and Juliet*)
ROMEO's servant, who takes him the (mistaken) news that JULIET is
dead and accompanies him to the tomb. He speaks quite a number of
lines; concern for his master is his chief character-trait.

Balthazar (*The Comedy of Errors*)
Friend of ANTIPHOLUS II who is invited for dinner and persuades him
not to break the door down when he is locked out but to eat at an inn
instead.

Balthazar (*The Merchant of Venice*)
PORTIA's servant, sent to Padua to fetch lawyer's clothes.

Balthazar (*Much Ado about Nothing*)
Attendant on DON PEDRO who looks after the music and sings the song
'Sigh no more, ladies'. Like most of Shakespeare's musicians he is
given a few lines to speak, a character-cameo: in his case, he makes
somewhat inept attempts at Benedickian wit.

Bandits (*Timon of Athens*)
There are three of them. They come across TIMON digging for gold, and
he shares it among them on the grounds that their trade is one of the
most honest in the world. They are so impressed by him that they vow
to give up their thievery, at least 'as soon as there is peace in Athens'.

Banquo (*Macbeth*)
MACBETH's fellow-general, who visits the WITCHES with him and
understands how their prophecy awakes ambition in him. After
DUNCAN's murder he is suspicious of Macbeth ('Thou hast it now:
King, Cawdor, Glamis, all/As the weird women promis'd, and I fear/
Thou play'dst most foully for it . . .'), but before he can say or do
anything he is murdered in his turn, and his only subsequent

appearance is as a ghost, shaking gory locks and making faces which only Macbeth can see.

Baptista *(The Taming of the Shrew)*
KATHARINA's and BIANCA's father, the standard silly old fool of farce. He constantly, warily, puts his head into the lion's jaws of his daughter's temper ('Why, how now, daughter Katharine? In your dumps?'), and regrets it.

Bardolph *(Henry IV Parts One and Two; Henry V; The Merry Wives of Windsor)*
One of FALSTAFF's drinking-companions, notable less for character than for his warty, carbuncular face and large red nose (which is compared to a brazier, a lantern, a warming-pan). Takes bribes to free two of the scarecrow army in *Henry IV Part Two*; forces a truce in the quarrel between NYM and PISTOL in *Henry V*; goes to fight at Agincourt, but steals from a church and ends on the gallows. The part offers plenty of opportunities for rant and swagger, but little else; Bardolph is constantly the second fiddle to others.

Bardolph, Lord *(Henry IV Part Two)*
One of the minor rebel leaders, with SCROOP, against King Henry; he has no special characteristics, and vanishes from the action about halfway through the play.

Barnardine *(Measure for Measure)*
Drunken reprobate in the same prison as CLAUDIO. Despite the PROVOST's apt description of him – 'A man that apprehends death no more dreadfully but as a drunken sleep, reckless and fearless of what's past, present or to come; insensible of mortality and desperately mortal' – he vigorously refuses to be executed (so that his head can be disguised as Claudio's and sent to ANGELO) on the grounds that he's not ready ('They shall beat out my brains with billets, I will not consent to die this day'). In the end he is pardoned by the DUKE.

Bassanio *(The Merchant of Venice)*
Generosity is the hallmark of Bassanio's character. His friends have only to say, as GRATIANO does, 'I have a suit to you', and he immediately answers 'You have obtained it'. He is short of money to woo PORTIA simply because he has lavished it: 'I have disabled mine estate/By something showing a more swelling port/Than my faint means would grant continuance'. He is horrified by the terms of SHYLOCK's bond, and offers to give up his suit to Portia rather than see ANTONIO accept them. When the 'lawyer' (Portia in disguise) asks for Portia's keepsake-ring in lieu of a fee, he indignantly refuses, and then gives it away because Antonio begs him to do so. He is an unequivocally honest man, so straightforward that he appears something of a fool. But it is straightforwardness which wins him a shoal of friends in Venice and a rich heiress for a wife – he chooses Portia's lead casket, instead of gold

or silver, because 'the world is still deceived with ornament' – and he gives the impression by the end of the play that he is well on the way to humanising Antonio and showing Portia what true love is.

Bassanius *(Titus Andronicus)*
SATURNINUS' brother and rival, in love with LAVINIA. He finds out about TAMORA's love-affair with AARON, and dies for it. He has no time to show much character, but what there is is a more strong-willed version of his brother's black-hearted selfishness.

Basset *(Henry VI Part One)*
Follower of SOMERSET and member of the red-rose faction. He quarrels with VERNON and takes him before HENRY for judgement – as a result of which Henry tries to unite YORK and Somerset with him against a more pressing enemy, the French.

Bastard (Philip Faulconbridge; Sir Richard Lionheart) *(King John)*
Of Shakespeare's early plays, only *Richard III* rivals *King John* for quality of verse, variety of plot and black-farce irony, and the Bastard in this play outmatches even RICHARD as a dramatic character. If the neglect of the whole play is remarkable, the overlooking of this part by leading actors, directors and managements is inexplicable: it ranks with EDMUND, IAGO or MACBETH themselves.

We first see the Bastard claiming the Faulconbridge lands and titles from his wimpish brother Robert, only to be told that he is the illegitimate son of Richard Cœur-de-Lion; he is immediately given a knighthood and a new identity (Sir Richard Lionheart) and is promoted to be the confidant of King JOHN himself. This abrupt and amazing turn of events exactly suits his mood, for he is cynical, humorous and amoral, a gambler with fate who has nothing to lose. (As he puts it himself, in one of the fine soliloquies which stud the play, 'Mad world! Mad kings! Mad composition!/Gain be my lord, for I will worship thee!') At first, as well as John's right-hand man, he makes himself a kind of lordly jester, pricking the pomposity of PHILIP of France, Cardinal PANDULPH and above all the Archduke of AUSTRIA (whom he torments by capping everything he says with the daft phrase 'And hang a calf-skin on these recreant limbs'). He is capering, reckless and rude, and brings colour to the living-dead world of John and his courtiers; no wonder he wins the support of the formidable Queen ELINOR, his grandmother who is the first to acknowledge his true father's character in him. ('The very spirit of Plantagenet!/I am thy grandam, Richard: call me so').

As the play continues, Plantagenet qualities increasingly take over the Bastard's character, and he sheds the cap and bells he has chosen for himself (though he still goes, with relish, on a money-raising tour of Northern monasteries, and gleefully brings back not only bulging coin-sacks but the lunatic prophet PETER of Pomfret). He dazzlingly fights England's enemies (bringing in Austria's head to prove it), practises statecraft with HUBERT, SALISBURY and PEMBROKE after the death of ARTHUR, and by the play's final act has been transformed into a heroic and charismatic leader. ('O inglorious league!/Shall we, upon the footing of our land,/Send fair-play orders and make compromise,/ Insinuation, parley and base truce/To arms invasive? Shall a beardless boy,/A cocker'd silken wanton, brave our fields/And flash his spirit in a warlike soil,/Mocking the air with colours idly spread,/And find no check...?'). He squares up to the Dauphin LEWIS, no longer with the careless mockery of the earlier quarrel-scenes but with a ringing patriotism worthy of HENRY V himself: 'Now hear our English king:/ For thus his royalty doth speak in me.../This apish and unmannerly approach,/This harness'd mark and unadvised revel,/This unhair'd sauciness and boyish troops,/The king doth smile at, and is well prepared/To whip this dwarfish war, these pigmy arms,/From out the circle of his territories.' His epitaph for John ('Art thou gone? I do but stay behind/To do the office for thee of revenge,/And then my soul shall wait on thee in Heaven/As it on earth hath been thy servant still...') is one of the most dignified and heartfelt utterances in the play, beggaring cynicism.

This line of development could be continued to the end of the play, converting what began as heartless farce to (equally heartless) patriotic masque. But to do this would bleach away the Bastard's wit and his lateral stance to life, and leave him a clothes-horse for pageantry like all the other lords, merely more self-aware and sharper-tongued. An alternative – fitting the irony of John's unexpected death from poison on the very brink of triumph – is to let the Bastard keep his cynicism, let it run arm-in-arm with his nobility, and leave him to kneel to the slender majesty of Prince HENRY ('I do bequeath my faithful services/ And true subjection everlastingly') and to carry the play to its end ('Come the three corners of the world in arms,/And we shall shock them...') not with the hollow jingoism on the surface of the words but on a characteristically equivocal, sardonic and sarcastic note.

Bastard of Orleans *(Henry VI Part One)*
His name is the most interesting thing about him, and it goes unexplained. He introduces LA PUCELLE to CHARLES as 'the holy maid... ordained to raise this tedious siege'; thereafter he leads the French army with ALENÇON, REIGNIER and the others, bravely, loyally and colourlessly.

Bates, John *(Henry V)*
One of the common soldiers who talk to the disguised King HENRY on the eve of Agincourt. Although he wishes he were somewhere else (e.g. buried up to the neck in 'Thames water'), he announces his intention of fighting bravely for his country.

Bavian *(The Two Noble Kinsmen)*
The 'driveler' or 'baboon' in a morris-dance, he takes part in the dance

the COUNTRYMEN are preparing for Duke THESEUS. He says only two
words, 'Yes, sir', the standard Shakespearean allocation for a non-actor
in a musical or dancing scene.

Bawd *(Pericles)*
Brothel-keeper's wife, furious with MARINA for destroying trade. ('Fie,
fie upon her! She's able to freeze the god Priapus, and undo a whole
generation.') She sees LYSIMACHUS as the saviour of her whole
enterprise, and urges Marina, 'without any more virginal fencing' to
'use him kindly'; when Marina refuses, she briskly orders BOULT to
'crack the glass of her virginity, and make the rest malleable'.

Beadle *(Henry VI Part Two)*
Thrashes SIMPCOX at St Albans.

Beatrice *(Much Ado about Nothing)*
LEONATO's witty niece, the best friend of his daughter HERO. She is
utterly set against marriage, and mocks would-be suitors so mercilessly
that few pay court to her. Her bubbly, carefree attitude is summed up,
with somewhat rueful admiration, by Leonato: 'There's little of the
melancholy element in her... She is never sad but when she sleeps –
and not even sad then, for I have heard my daughter say she hath often
dream'd of unhappiness and wak'd herself with laughing.' For all that,
there is something alienating about Beatrice's wit. She is never serious,
and her dazzle of words is like a shield against true communication,
true dialogue. (For example, she smothers Leonato's well-meant
remark, 'Well, niece, I hope to see you one day fitted with a husband'
with the lengthy, funny and unanswerable reply, 'Not till God make
men of some other metal than earth. Would it not grieve a woman to be
over-master'd with a piece of valiant dust? To make an account of her
life to a clod of wayward marl? No, uncle, I'll none: Adam's sons are
my brethren, and truly, I hold it a sin to match in my kindred.')

If Beatrice's wit makes her admired, it also makes her lonely: though
everyone but she can see it, her sharpness about BENEDICK ('He wears
his faith but as the fashion of his hat: it ever changes with the next
block') disguises longing for him, and the match between them is as
inevitable as it seems unlikely. Hence her total change of manner after
the trick played on her in the orchard (where Hero and URSULA let her
overhear them saying how passionately Benedick is in love with her).
She never speaks another unserious word. She declares that she will
'tame her wild heart' to Benedick's 'loving hand'; but before their love
can be properly declared, Hero's wedding is broken off, and she is so
full of concern for her friend and of rage at the way she has been
wronged that she urges Benedick to fight a duel with CLAUDIO.
(*Beatrice*: 'O God that I were a man! I would eat his heart in the
market-place.' *Benedick*: 'Hear me, Beatrice — ' *Beatrice*: 'Talk with a
man at a window? A proper saying!' *Benedick*: 'Nay, but, Beatrice — '
Beatrice: 'Sweet Hero, she is wrong'd, she is slander'd, she is undone.'

Benedick: 'Beat — ' *Beatrice*: 'Princes and counties! Surely a princely testimony, a goodly count, Count Confect...'.)

This development – she and Benedick, from being the most artificial people in the play, are turned by love into the most human and sympathetic – colours our enjoyment of their final scene together, when they spar with words as they have always done but it is now clear that they are irrevocably, deeply in love and that they both know it, and Benedick demonstrates that the ideal way to deal with 'Lady Tongue' is not with words, but with action. (*Benedick*: 'Come, I will have thee. But by this light, I take thee for pity.' *Beatrice*: 'I would not deny you. But by this good day, I yield upon great persuasion, and partly to save your life, for I was told you were in a consumption.' *Benedick*: 'Peace. I will stop your mouth'. (*Kisses her*).)

Beaufort (*Henry VI Part Two*): *see* **Winchester**

Bedford: *see* **Prince John**

Belarius (*Cymbeline*)
Loyal lord banished by CYMBELINE twenty years before the play begins, and now living in the Welsh woods under the name of Morgan. He is grizzled, brave and honest, a worthy foster-father to GUIDERIUS and ARVIRAGUS, a doughty fighter against the Romans, and a man so free from mean-spiritedness that he bows the knee to Cymbeline, restores his sons to him and offers him loyalty without a word more about his own ill-treatment than that he is 'indeed, a banish'd man;/I know not how a traitor'.

Belch, Sir Toby (*Twelfth Night*)
OLIVIA's uncle, a bluff, self-indulgent man who soaks himself in all life's sensual delights. He is his niece's house-guest, a permanent hanger-on who carouses with the servants, mocks the steward and brings in undesirables of all kinds (including Sir Andrew AGUECHEEK, the most unlikely person in the world to be Olivia's suitor, at least until MALVOLIO volunteers.) He is bluster and roister incarnate, a plum-pudding of a man, and he has no moral scruples whatsoever: he milks Sir Andrew of his cash (so far, 'some two thousand strong, or so'), and proposes, for general entertainment, that the 'mad' Malvolio be locked in a dark room and cruelly tormented. At the end of the play, beaten by SEBASTIAN, he staggers out with Sir Andrew speaking words of what sound like remorse ('Will you help? An asshead and a coxcomb and a knave, a thin-faced knave, a gull...'), and some performers read the bitterness of these lines back into his earlier appearances, making him not merely a cheerful drunk but a hollow man, terrified by his own emptiness, joking and carousing to keep reality at bay. We are told at the end that MARIA has married him.

Benedick (*Much Ado about Nothing*)
The growth in Benedick's character corresponds with the development

of the play. The arch of the part (and of the play) is a simple movement
from lightheartedness to sadness and back again, and it is set against a
progression from artificiality (games-playing) to seriousness (true
feelings) in a way which satisfies the intellect as well as the emotions.
Making one character exemplify the play's development in this way is
an Aristotelian idea, much used in Greek tragedy. It appears
occasionally in Shakespeare's histories (*Richard II*, *Henry V*) or
tragedies (*Macbeth*, *Lear*), but in none of his comedies but this one –
and the result is to make Benedick one of the most substantial of all
Shakespeare's comic lords.

At the start of the play, like BEATRICE, Benedick seems little but an
opinionated, razor-tongued wit, incapable or disdainful of seriousness.
When, for example, CLAUDIO asks him to describe HERO, he ripostes
with the merry but intensely irritating (to an eager lover) 'Do you
question me as an honest man should do, for my simple true
judgement, or would you have me speak after my custom, as being a
profess'd tyrant to their sex?', and continues avoiding the issue, with
shallow brilliance, to the end of the scene. At the masked ball, when he
is scornfully described (by Beatrice) as 'the Prince's jester' whose only
gift is 'devising impossible slanders' and who will eat no supper if his
jokes are not appreciated, he sulks. ('O she misused me past the
endurance of a block . . . !') This part of the play is all masquerade and
merriment, and as soon as the masks are removed the merriment begins
to die – and the same is true of Benedick. Long before he discovers that
Beatrice is in love with him, he is plunged into melancholy, and the
cause is love. He tells us, in the long soliloquy at the start of the
orchard- scene, that he will never fall in love lest love 'may transform
me into an oyster', but there is a distinct feeling that he is protesting
too much, and as soon as he overhears the news of Beatrice's affection,
he is hooked. ('I will be terribly in love with her. I may chance have
some odd quirks and remnants of wit broken on me, because I have
rail'd so long against marriage, but doth not the appetite alter? A man
loves the meat in his youth that he cannot endure in his age . . .')

At this point, just as Benedick is preparing to pay court to Beatrice,
the mood of the play turns to darkness. DON JOHN's plot against Hero
takes its course, and the action is concerned not with lighthearted
masquerades but with the black charade of BORACHIO and MARGARET
and with its consequences. Benedick, like Beatrice, slips into the
background. We know that they are in love, and we know that they are
sad, but there is no opportunity for them to discover one another's true
feelings, and the suspense in their relationship continues throughout
the marriage-scene and its outcome, when they are the only two people
onstage to show true concern for Hero or zeal to find out what the real
truth is. In this scene, Beatrice is furiously angry ('Kill Claudio!');
Benedick's part is subtler, and he shows as much eagerness to make
friends with her as indignation on Hero's behalf.

As soon as Borachio is arrested and confesses, the mood of the play reverts to happiness – except for Benedick and Beatrice, whose relationship is stuck where it was before. The last scenes are devoted to showing how they discover the truth about Borachio, and how they realise and admit the truth about their own relationship. In these scenes Benedick is just as sharp-witted as before (he tries to write Beatrice a love-song, but can't find the rhymes: 'I was not born under a riming planet, nor I cannot woo in festival terms'), but his arrows are directed at himself rather than at Beatrice or his companions, and instead of frivolity, passion underlies the jokes. (*Beatrice*: 'Will you go to hear this news, signior?' *Benedick*: 'I will live in thy heart, die in thy lap and be buried in thine eyes, and moreover I will go with thee to thine uncle's.') Finally, in the closing scene of the play, he abandons wit altogether, 'stops her mouth' with a kiss and orders the pipers to strike up the wedding-dance. It is the happy ending everyone has been longing for since the play began, and the anguish Beatrice and Benedick have been through to reach it (much of it self-induced) makes it all the more satisfying to see. If there is catharsis in comedy, if it purges the spectators' emotions as tragedy does, this is how the trick is done.

Benvolio (*Romeo and Juliet*)
ROMEO's cousin and closest friend, after MERCUTIO. He shares in the fantastical word-play characteristic of the young men, and is as willing as anyone else to duel with the Capulets. But he is altogether soberer than either Mercutio or Romeo: we first see him trying to prevent the servant's brawl, and then as a trusted confidant of old MONTAGUE. He is prone to melancholy: 'An hour before the worshipped sun/Peered through the golden window of the east,' he finely says, 'A troubled mind drave me to walk abroad...'; he is reminiscent less of an Elizabethan Englishman than of one of those grave young nobles on the fringes of Italian Renaissance paintings.

Berkeley (*Richard III*)
Silent attendant on Lady ANNE.

Berkeley, Lord (*Richard II*)
Messenger from YORK to BOLINGBROKE, swept from the limelight as soon as York himself appears.

Bernardo (*Hamlet*)
Officer of the watch at Elsinore. With MARCELLUS, he urges HORATIO to talk to the GHOST.

Berowne (*Love's Labour's Lost*)
Love's Labour's Lost is structured rather like a piece of music. Instead of following the fate of individual characters it uses groups (the lords, the ladies, the low-life characters), and the action deploys them like musical themes, developing character against character within each group and contrasting group with group. It is only in Act Five that all three groups come together, performing charades for one another and

exchanging identities in a flurry of cross-purposes, similar – as the critic Michael Stapleton has pointed out – to the ensemble which rounds off a Mozart opera.

Two characters, ARMADO and Berowne, stand out from this group-structure and highlight it. Both are 'loners' in the society around them – Armado because of his nationality, Berowne by temperament. Of the two, Berowne is the subtler dramatic creation. In the opening scenes he is very lightly characterised – one lord among several, a little more saturnine and sulkier than the others – but as the play develops he moves more and more apart, becoming a commentator on the action as well as a participant in it. He is the first lord to abandon the foolish vow of the opening, declaring, in a soliloquy of soaring eloquence and passion, that he has become the 'field-corporal' of 'this wimpled, whining, purblind, wayward boy,/This signior-junior, giant-dwarf, Dan Cupid'; in the eavesdropping scene he rounds on the other lords and delivers a second enormous, deeply felt and overwhelming soliloquy on love (a spoken aria) which sweeps away their pretence and (ironically) paves the way for the masks, tricks and deceits which crown Act Five.

Like BENEDICK's in *Much Ado about Nothing*, Berowne's conversion from frivolity to seriousness makes him more than a two-dimensional character. Keeping his passion in balance is tricky, and Shakespeare makes it no easier by cramming the actor's speeches with sonnets, rhyming couplets and multi-lined conceits. If the play falls flat, it can be because the actor playing Berowne fails to rise to these challenges; if it succeeds, if it achieves the perfection of chamber music, the credit should equally be his.

Berri, Duke of *(Henry V)*
French lord; silent.

Bertram *(All's Well that Ends Well)*
Count of Rousillon, the man chosen by HELENA as her future husband. He is young and sulky: told to marry Helena, he submits with remarkably ill grace ('I cannot love her, nor will strive to do't'); forbidden to go to fight in Italy, he swears, stamps his foot and finally goes anyway; faced in the trial-scene with DIANA claiming that he has ruined her, he pouts and prevaricates like a cornered schoolboy. ('She's impudent, my lord,/And was a common gamester to the camp'.) Rather than tell Helena to her face that he will not treat her as a wife, he scuttles out of the country and leaves her an insulting note; given the chance of humiliating his confidant PAROLLES, he jumps at it; before his overbearing mother and his lord the KING OF FRANCE, by contrast, he grovels. Shakespeare gives him no redeeming qualities whatever, and even his recantation at the very end ('If she, my liege, can make me know this clearly,/I'll love her dearly, ever, ever dearly') is so perfunctory and so hasty that we may wonder if Shakespeare wrote the lines at all, or lost patience with Bertram and sorted him out without plausibility or human feeling for his own creation. Just as Parolles is a

faint shadow of FALSTAFF, so Bertram is a third- or fourth-hand copy of the equally wilful but ultimately winsome young men of *As You Like It, Much Ado About Nothing* and *Love's Labour's Lost,* and his very colourlessness makes it hard to understand why Helena is so intent on marrying him.

Bevis, George *(Henry VI Part Two)*
Follower of CADE, on the grounds that 'virtue is not regarded in handicrafts-men'. Unlike his more bloodthirsty colleagues he is quiet and honest, and soon fades into the background of the action.

Bianca *(Othello)*
CASSIO's mistress. IAGO and EMILIA vigorously put it about that she is a harlot, but she denies it with equal vigour ('I am no strumpet, but of life as honest/As you that thus abuse me'). So far as her appearances in the play are concerned, she seems a normal girl, besotted with Cassio and furious when she thinks that the handkerchief he has given her to unpick belongs to another woman. She falls on his neck, sobbing, when she finds him wounded, and everyone embarrassedly hustles her off the stage. A small part, but spirited.

Bianca *(The Taming of the Shrew)*
Apparently a demure young miss, in whose mouth not the smallest butter-pat would melt, Bianca spends much of her time responding to wooers. With GREMIO and HORTENSIO, the fools, she is as bland as a doll, but with LUCENTIO she shows a coy slyness, a willingness to flirt, which is both pert and charming. (She construes Virgil with him: '*Hac ibat Simois* – I know you not – *hic est Sigeia tellus* – I trust you not – *Hic steterat Priami* – take heed he hear us not – *regia* – presume not – *celsa senis* – despair not'.) At the end, after slipping away under her father's nose to marry Lucentio in secret, she becomes (in terms of the play, at least) a wife so wilful and headstrong that she has to be taught a lesson in obedience by her once shrewish sister KATHARINA. Her flashes of independent-mindedness are brief (and the part itself is small), but they make her far more interesting to play than the porcelain innocent she at first appears to be.

Bigot, Robert, Earl of Norfolk *(King John)*
Attendant lord.

Biondello *(The Taming of the Shrew)*
LUCENTIO's second servant after TRANIO, he bustles about arranging the deception of BAPTISTA, pretending that Tranio is Lucentio and that Lucentio is a Latin teacher, finding a passer-by to play the part of Tranio's/Lucentio's father, and bringing word to Lucentio and BIANCA that they should slip out and be married. Beyond glee at the tricks he plays, he has no particular character.

Blanch *(King John)*
JOHN's niece, princess of Castile who is married off to LEWIS of France

in a doomed attempt to head off war between France and England. She
is a political pawn rather than a person, and though she speaks prettily
and dutifully ('My uncle's will in this respect is mine') there is little
about her to excite our interest or move our pity.

Bl(o)unt, Sir James *(Richard III)*
Follower of RICHMOND. One line.

Blunt, Sir John *(Henry IV Part Two)*
Son of the BLUNT of *Henry IV Part One*, grandfather of the BLUNT of
Richard III, Sir John in this play is merely a retainer of Prince JOHN.
He takes COLEVILE to execution; he does not speak.

Blunt, Sir Walter *(Henry IV Part One)*
One of the king's courtiers. The part is tiny (about two dozen lines in
all), but offers the actor a good death scene (when he persuades
DOUGLAS that he is the king, fights him in single combat and loses).
The BLUNT of *Part Two* is his son; the BLUNT of *Richard III* is his
great-grandson.

Boatswain *(The Tempest)*
Preoccupied with saving his ship from wreck in the storm, he is sharp
with ANTONIO, SEBASTIAN and the other lords who force their way up
on deck to give advice.

Boleyn, Anne *(Henry VIII): see* **Bullen**

Bolingbroke, Henry; becomes **Henry IV** *(Richard II; Henry IV Parts
One and Two)*
One of the most fascinating conventions of this century's *Richard II*
performances has been for two leading actors to alternate the parts of
RICHARD and Bolingbroke in the same production. The pleasure for the
audience is in seeing how each actor's personal and physical presence
affects the meaning of the production; for the actors, the challenge is
playing two utterly different but interdependent and mirror-image
parts. Richard's character is fixed from the start, undeviating, and is
gradually revealed as the play proceeds; the actor's chief tasks are to
keep the essence of the part intact without giving too much of it away,
and to balance the pettiness and shallowness of the man himself with
the soaring rhetoric of the lines he speaks. Bolingbroke's character, by
contrast, develops, and the actor's chief task is to show the moral
progression in him from simplicity to complexity, as he responds to the
changing situation. The part of Richard is all poetic show, a display of
vocal and physical pyrotechnics; the part of Bolingbroke is inward-
turned and veiled, strength of character colouring drab, conventional-
seeming lines.

At the start of *Richard II*, convention rules. Bolingbroke is hardly
differentiated from the other squabbling lords, and his adherence to an
absurd chivalric code ('Pale trembling coward, there I throw my gage';
'Further I say, and further will maintain/Upon his bad life to make all

this good,/That he did plot...') is as pompous and unthinking as
theirs. Even when Richard arbitrarily breaks off the duel between him
and MOWBRAY, and banishes them for no apparent reason but his own
royal whim, Bolingbroke bites the bullet and bends the knee as a loyal
subject should: like Richard himself, he believes unquestioningly in the
divinity of kings and in the need to obey them however capricious or
cruel the things they do. It is only after the death of his father GAUNT
and Richard's confiscation of the money and titles that should rightfully
be his that he returns from exile, and even then he claims to be more
concerned with restitution than with usurping the throne. But as
Richard's behaviour grows more and more extravagant ('What must the
king do now? Must he submit?/The king shall do it. Must he be
deposed?/The king shall be contented...'), Bolingbroke gradually
assumes regal authority and dignity. He becomes a hard, fair arbiter (in
the scene where the nobles challenge and counter-challenge one
another, or in the quarrel between AUMERLE and his father YORK), and
the more florid and unbalanced Richard's utterances become, the more
Bolingbroke's speeches are clipped and curt. ('Carlisle, this is your
doom:/Choose out some secret place, some reverend room,/More than
thou hast, and with it joy thy life...'.) Where Richard has been
concerned with the pomp and show of power, Bolingbroke is concerned
with its duties and responsibilities – a sharp moral point. Then, in the
very last moments of the play, he is confronted with news that EXTON
has killed Richard, and at once his moral certainty collapses and he
begins to brood on his own moral state rather than that of the country
('I'll make a voyage to the Holy Land/To wash this blood off from my
guilty hand'). In short, as soon as he becomes king he falls prey to
exactly the same fault as Richard, neurotic self-absorption.

Having established this mode, Shakespeare kept it intact for Henry's
character in *Henry IV*. The theme of moral growth continues, but is
transferred to the character of Prince Hal; the character of Henry
advances no further than it was at the end of *Richard II*. He is soul-
sick, eaten by guilt for Richard's death, by despair because he is too ill
to undertake a redeeming pilgrimage, by anguish at the civil wars which
rack the country, and above all by uncomprehending misery at his son's
apparent unsuitability to succeed to the throne. It is as if kingship is a
contagious and debilitating disease, and he is no more able to cope with
it than Richard was. From the no-nonsense commander of *Richard II*,
Henry becomes a sorrowful, insecure brooder, prone to maundering
soliloquies and enormous speeches of disappointment and disapproval.
(To Hal: 'I know not whether God will have it so/For some displeasing
service I have done.../But thou dost in thy passages of life/Make me
believe that thou art only mark'd/ For the hot vengeance and the rod of
Heaven/To punish my mistreadings...'.) But though this makes the
part hard to play – it is never easy portraying a miserable bore without
being miserable or boring – it is vital not to infuse it with sparks of the
Bolingbroke of old. The whole point of *Henry IV* is that Hal is learning

and growing in statesmanly qualities before our eyes, and part of that process involves taking over the moral qualities of regality from his father. At the end of *Part Two* Hal literally takes the crown, and when Henry discovers this he is finally released from the burden which has oppressed him since Richard's death: historically unlikely, perhaps, but a satisfyingly happy ending for such a pathetic, and sympathetic, dramatic character.

Bolingbroke, Roger *(Henry VI Part Two)*

Necromancer who conjures up the fake SPIRIT which traps ELEANOR Duchess of Gloucester. Of all the frauds, he has the best line in professional patter. ('Deep night, dark night, the silent of the night,/ The time of night when Troy was set on fire,/The time when screech-owls cry, and ban-dogs howl,/And spirits walk, and ghosts break up their graves...')

Bona, Lady *(Henry VI Part Three)*

French princess (sister-in-law of King LEWIS) intended to be married to EDWARD until he unexpectedly marries Lady GREY instead.

Borachio *(Much Ado about Nothing)*

DON JOHN's rascally henchman. He agrees, for 1000 ducats, to destroy HERO's reputation by flirting with her maid MARGARET (in Hero's clothes); later, when he is arrested and questioned by DOGBERRY, he is as tight-mouthed and truculent as any investigating officer could wish. But finally, when he thinks that Hero has died of shame, he repents, confesses and apologises to LEONATO, after which he is taken away by Dogberry and vanishes from the play. His change of heart is the most interesting thing about him, and its elevated, dignified language is in marked contrast to the run-of-the-mill villainy of his earlier scenes. ('Sweet prince, let me go no further to mine answer: do you hear me, and let this count kill me. I have deceived even your very eyes: what your wisdoms could not discover, these shallow fools have brought to light...')

Bottom, Nick *(A Midsummer Night's Dream)*

Athenian weaver, who takes the part of Pyramus in QUINCE's production. He is a one-man compendium of ham acting. At the casting-meeting he offers to play every single part, and is only satisfied with Pyramus (the lead) when he has worked out 'What beard were best to play it in'. At rehearsal he delivers the sound of his lines without the sense (*Bottom*: 'Thisbe, the flowers of odious savours sweet ...' *Quince*: 'Odours, odours'), and he crowns the actual performance with one of the most elaborate death-scenes ever staged. '(*Stabs himself*) Thus die I, thus, thus, thus./Now I am dead./Now I am fled./My soul is in the sky./Tongue, lose thy light,/Moon, take thy flight./Now die, die, die, die, die. (*Dies*)'.

In ordinary life, Bottom affects the same kind of orotund, stagy utterance, filling the air with verbiage and marvellously garbling the

English language in the process. When he hears that there is to be a lion in the play he strikes an attitude and exclaims 'God shield us! A lion among ladies is a most dreadful thing, for there is not a more fearful wildfowl than your lion living'. When he is introduced to the FAIRIES, he puts on an extravagant courtesy, quite oblivious of the fact that he is wearing an ass's head. And finally, when he comes out of his fairy trance, he reflects on the experience in a soliloquy whose words have almost entirely shed their everyday meanings and become wonderful. ('I have had a dream, past the wit of man to say what dream it was... The eye of man hath not heard, the ear of man hath not seen, man's hand is not able to taste, his tongue to conceive nor his heart to report what my dream was. I will get Peter Quince to write a ballet of this dream: it shall be called Bottom's Dream because it hath no bottom, and I will sing it at the latter end of a play before the Duke ...')

Bottom's other main characteristic, good-heartedness, allies him to the burghers of *The Merry Wives of Windsor* or to the FISHERMEN in *Pericles*. He loves the world and everyone in it, and his geniality is nowhere better seen than when he thinks himself king of the fairies, and allots tasks to his subjects with a bonhomie which irradiates the role: of all the parts he takes in the play, this is the one that fits him best. (*Bottom*: 'Give me your nief, good Mounseer Mustardseed. Pray you, leave your courtesy, good Mounseer.' *Mustardseed*: 'What's your will?' *Bottom*: 'Nothing, good Mounseer, but to help Cavalery Peaseblossom to scratch. I must to the barbers, Mounseer, for methinks I am marvellous hairy about the face, and I am such a tender ass, if my hair do but tickle me, I must scratch.' *Titania*: 'What, wilt hear some music, my sweet love?' *Bottom*: 'I have a reasonable good ear in music. Let's have the tongs and bones.')

Boult *(Pericles)*

Servant of the brothel who buys MARINA from the PIRATES and then, when she begins 'freezing' the customers, is ordered to 'crack the glass of her virginity' and teach her both humility and the tricks of her trade. Until now, he has seemed no more than an unintelligent ruffian; but she sweet-talks him, too, and persuades him to slip her out of the brothel into an honest house. (He remains credulous, even so: '... since my master and mistress have bought you, there's no going without their consent: therefore I will make them acquainted with your purpose, and I doubt not but I shall find them tractable enough...'.)

Bourbon, John, Duke of *(Henry V)*

The uncle of King CHARLES OF FRANCE (and therefore treated by Shakespeare as an elder statesman), he makes one brave and mettlesome speech during the battle of Agincourt ('... he that will not follow Bourbon now,/ Let him go hence, and with his cap in hand,/ Like a base pandar, hold the chamber door...'); the next we hear of him is in the list of honourable Frenchmen killed in the fighting. The BOURBON in *Henry VI Part Three* is his bastard son.

Bourbon, Lewis (*Henry VI Part Three*)
Lord Admiral of France, the bastard son of the BOURBON in *Henry V*.
He appears in one scene only, with his master LEWIS, and does not
speak.

Bourbon, Louis (Admiral of France) (*Henry VI Part Three*)
Attendant on King LOUIS; he does not speak.

Boy (*Much Ado about Nothing*)
BENEDICK's servant. Asked to fetch a book, he cheekily says that
Benedick has it already. But he speaks only six words, and has no time
for character.

Boy (*Measure for Measure*)
Sings 'Take, O take those lips away' to MARIANA at the moated grange.

Boyet, Lord (*Love's Labour's Lost*)
Companion and protector of the PRINCESS and her ladies, he is as silver-
tongued and artificial as the conceited French courtiers in *Henry V*; but
where the conceit there is presented ironically, as a kind of tragic flaw,
here it is nothing but soap-bubble exuberance. BEROWNE says of him
'this fellow pecks up wit as pigeons peas,/And utters it again when God
doth please;.../This gallant pins the wenches on his sleeve;/Had he
been Adam, he had tempted Eve.../The stairs, as he treads on them,
kiss his feet' – and the description exactly fits Boyet's character. There
is some hint that he is older than the ladies, a middle-aged gallant
(MARIA, for example, calls him 'Cupid's grandfather'); if this is so, his
young man's coquetry mismatches his years as strikingly as MOTH's
knowing chatter outsoars his youth.

Brabantio (*Othello*)
DESDEMONA's father, an elderly and 'reverend signior'. He is distraught
at the news that OTHELLO has stolen his daughter, and reviles him in
the most overt lines of racist abuse in the play. He arraigns Othello
before the Duke of VENICE ('She is abus'd, stol'n from me and
corrupted/By spells and medicines bought of mountebanks'), only to
withdraw, heartbroken, when Desdemona herself announces that she
has married Othello for love, and now owes him the duty she formerly
gave her father. Brabantio's part is small, and the speed with which he
moves from rage to despair is both pitiable in itself and a foreshadowing
of the change which is to happen to Othello as the play develops.
Forthrightness is his main characteristic, but his rudeness is masked by
the sumptuous language in which he expresses it: even in the abyss of
misery, his phrases can make us warm to him. ('Come hither, Moor:/I
here do give thee with all my heart/Which, but thou hast already, with
all my heart/I would keep from thee. For your sake, jewel,/I am glad at
soul I have no other child:/For thy escape would teach me tyranny,/To
hang clogs on them...')

Brakenbury, Sir Robert *(Richard III)*
Lieutenant of the Tower of London, blockishly loyal to whichever
member of the York family is on or nearest to the throne. He arrests
CLARENCE on EDWARD's instructions, and tells RICHARD that 'His
majesty hath straitly given in charge/That no man shall have private
conference,/Of what degree soever, with your brother' (to which
Richard silkily replies, 'Brakenbury,/You may partake of everything we
say'). He is determinedly unaware of Clarence's future, even when he
hands him over to the MURDERERS ('I will not reason what is meant
hereby,/Because I will be guiltless from the meaning'). Later, on
Richard's orders, he bars Queen ELIZABETH, the Duchess of YORK and
ANNE from visiting the Princes in the Tower, and in his zealous
confusion makes a revealing slip of the tongue. (*Brakenbury*: 'I may not
suffer you to visit them:/The King hath strictly charged the contrary.'
Elizabeth: 'The King? Who's that?' *Brakenbury*: 'I mean the Lord
Protector...') Though his loyalty is doltish rather than reasoned (he is
another of the rabbits snake-Richard mesmerises), he is not an
unworthy man, and is honourably mentioned after the battle of
Bosworth as one of those who died fighting bravely.

Brandon *(Henry VIII)*
Arrests BUCKINGHAM and ABERGAVENNY for treason.

Bretagne, Duke of *(Henry V)*
French lord, notable chiefly for his scornful temper and vivid turn of
phrase.('Normans, but bastard Normans,/Norman bastards. *Mort de ma
vie*! If they march along/Unfought withal, but I will sell my
dukedom/To buy a slobbery and a dirty farm/In that nook-shotten isle
of Albion...')

Brother *(The Two Noble Kinsmen)*
JAILER'S son, a child who humours his mad sister, the Jailer's
DAUGHTER, in a scene as tear-jerking as any in Victorian melodrama.

Brutus, Junius *(Coriolanus)*
One of the two 'bald tribunes' who inflame the Roman mob against
CORIOLANUS. Unlike the fire-brand SICINIUS, he is quiet-spoken and
sly, so that even his most honest-seeming arguments (e.g. when he
urges that Coriolanus 'hath serv'd well for Rome') sound double-edged.
He signals his insincerity as clearly as Dickens' Uriah Heep – 'Now we
have shown our power,/Let us seem humbler after it was done/Than
when it was a-doing...' – and also makes his political motives perfectly
clear: if Coriolanus ever becomes consul, he says, 'our office may... go
sleep'. His slipperiness is matched by cowardice: he shelters behind
Sicinius, always being the second to speak, and when Coriolanus pre-
empts argument by action, encamping outside Rome with the Volscian
army, he is reduced to impotent snivelling ('Would half my wealth/
Would buy this for a lie!'), has to beg the hated MENENIUS to 'make
trial what your love can do/For Rome', and immediately afterwards

vanishes from the play.

Brutus, Marcus (*Julius Caesar*)
Julius Caesar's chief 'characters' are groups – cabals, conspiracies, mobs, friendships – and its action constantly shows them forming, dissolving and reforming in response to the actions and attitudes of the people who compose them. For this purpose, Shakespeare had no need to create fully fleshed characters: since what matters is not who the people are but the qualities they stand for, stock figures – a ruthless dictator, a loyal friend, an ambitious politician, a spirited wife and so on – were quite enough. The exception is Brutus. Without him, *Julius Caesar* would be as schematic as an essay, as calculated as the politics it demonstrates. But his involvement, and the warmth with which his character is drawn, irradiate the action: *Julius Caesar* is 'his' tragedy just as much as *Hamlet* is HAMLET's.

Shakespeare's Brutus is fascinatingly different from the person in the ancient sources. To writers on Roman history (such as Plutarch) he was a stern moralist, descendant of that Brutus who banished the tyrannical Tarquin the Proud, son-in-law of Cato (the most upright man in the Republic) and a follower of the philosophy of Stoicism (which advocates an ascetic, self-denying life and declares involvement in public affairs a moral duty). Shakespeare retains all these 'Roman' ideas, but he blurs them – and in the process deepens Brutus' character – by giving him Renaissance sensibilities and a view of life which embraces such contemporary sixteenth-century ideas as More's utopianism and Montaigne's humanism. Brutus is a scholar, with a taper ever burning in his room, a book in his pocket and an absent-minded air. He is a kind-hearted human being first and a 'political animal' second: his concern for the boy LUCIUS shows this, as do his love for PORTIA – very un-Roman, and in marked contrast to CAESAR's attitude to CALPHURNIA – and his behaviour immediately after the assassination, when his first thought is not for power, but to reassure the trembling Senators that there will be no more deaths. He is prone to soliloquies (a favourite Shakespearean device for showing people trapped by their own sensibilities) and to outbursts of honesty (e.g. refusing to give people power merely because they can grease his palm) which infuriate the more practical CASSIUS. He is a rational being, and proud of it – and the result is that when irrational things happen (Portia's suicide, utterly unexpected; the appearance of Caesar's ghost, utterly against the laws of nature) his trust in his own 'reason' (the word is barbed) falters and his personal tragedy begins.

Because Brutus' character arouses our sympathy, it weights the entire moral argument of the play, showing us that political events do not move by their own cold logic, but at every stage incorporate human choices, human passions, human anguish and human mistakes. None the less, his moral rightness is tragically flawed by the very humanity which gives rise to it: it is precisely his injection of moral considerations into the political process which causes the collapse of the whole republican endeavour. He says, and knows in his mind, that 'There is a tide in the affairs of men' – but he is so used to thinking instead of doing that whenever the time for action comes, whenever the tide is on the flood, he misses it: his sensibility and his common sense never march in step.

Buckingham, Edward Stafford, Duke of (*Henry VIII*)
Son of the BUCKINGHAM of *Richard III*, grandson of the BUCKINGHAM of *Henry VI Part Two*. At the beginning of the play he mutters with ABERGAVENNY and NORFOLK against WOLSEY, calling him a 'butcher's cur', 'venom-mouthed', and complaining that 'no man's pie is freed/ From his ambitious finger'. Before the plot can proceed he is arrested for treason, accused before Henry and condemned to death. His scene as he is led to execution is as full of resigned dignity as his earlier scene was furious and vehement: only Wolsey, at the moment of *his* fall, has a soliloquy to equal Buckingham's. ('When I came hither, I was Lord High Constable/And Duke of Buckingham; now, poor Edward Bohun;/ Yet I am richer than my base accusers,/That never knew what truth meant...'.)

Buckingham, Edward Stafford, Duke of (*Richard III*)
Except for RODERIGO in *Othello*, Buckingham is the least intelligent person in all Shakespeare. The plays are full of naive youngsters, rustics, fops and fools, but all have a self-admiration and an irony he lacks. There is no tragedy in him, and no mystery: he consistently does the wrong thing because he is too slow-witted to work out consequences or alternatives, and Shakespeare denies him the pathos or innocence that might snare our sympathy.

Nothing could better suit the play. *Richard III* is about hypnotic malevolence, about a man who weaves word-webs for others and loves to watch them struggle – and unlike RICHARD's other victims, ANNE, CLARENCE or ELIZABETH (who have no idea what is happening until they are trapped beyond help), Buckingham knows perfectly well what Richard is like, and chooses to walk into his web because he thinks himself invincible. He would be the straight man in a double-act, except that straight men get their laughs by genuine complicity with their partners, by precise timing and by an obvious awareness that games are being played on them.

If Buckingham were grand enough to have a tragic flaw, it would be self-importance. He fawns on every king and prince who comes along (and no doubt imagines himself a devil of a politician for doing so). He toadies to Richard ('Think you, my lord, this little prancing York/Was not incensed by his subtle mother/To taunt and scorn you thus opprobriously...?'), and is so pleased with himself that he fails to notice Richard's abstracted reply ('No doubt, no doubt'). In the same way, his self-delight in the scene where he offers Richard the crown (the only scene where Richard actually needs him) is officious, ludicrous and marks him for an early fall. None the less, when that fall comes we feel no pity for him. He is asked to agree to the murder of the princes in the Tower, goes out to ponder his decision, and comes back to be told bluntly 'Well, let that rest'. He tries to remind Richard of his promise to make him Earl of Hereford, and Richard at first refuses to listen, then brushes him aside with 'I am not in the giving vein today'. In short, Buckingham thinks himself a suit of armour, and he is in fact shrugged off like an old coat – and we smile, never weep, to see it happen. Actors sometimes make his stupidity pathetic, and this undermines the play: Richard must be the only mysterious character, the one person whose personality puts him at risk, and Buckingham's blockheadedness is an essential part of creating that effect.

Buckingham, Humphrey Stafford, Duke of *(Henry VI Part Two)*
Father of the BUCKINGHAM of *Richard III*, this man is, with SOMERSET and SUFFOLK, one of the conspirators against GLOUCESTER. He arrests ELEANOR for witchcraft, and impatiently hurries Gloucester's own fall along ('He'll... hold us here all day./Lord Cardinal, he is your prisoner.') With Old CLIFFORD, he breaks up CADE's conspiracy by offering Cade's followers free pardons to desert him; he acts as intermediary between the king and rebellious YORK. He is decisive, energetic and effective, and his brisk brevity makes a welcome contrast with the protracted politicking, discussing and soliloquising of more senior lords.

Bullcalf, Peter *(Henry IV Part Two)*
A recruit to FALSTAFF's army, except that (like MOULDY) he bribes BARDOLPH to wipe him from the list.

Bullen, Anne *(Henry VIII)*
Though she is central to the plot, Anne appears only briefly in the play. We see her bantering with SANDS at a dinner-party, dancing with HENRY at the masked ball which follows it, and stiff-necked and formal at her coronation in Act Four. In between, in an eloquent scene, she confides to her attendant OLD LADY that she is reluctant to displace Queen KATHARINE or indeed to receive any honours from the king, and the Old Lady sharply advises her to seize with open hands whatever good luck fortune throws at her. She is demure, bashful and retiring ('I do not know/What kind of obedience I should tender.../Vouchsafe to speak my thanks and my obedience/As from a blushing handmaid, to his highness...'), and if what we know of her from history suggests that her feelings may be slightly less innocent than they seem, there is no hint of it in this play.

Burgundy, Duke of *(King Lear)*
An imperious youth, he listens uncomfortably to LEAR's dispossessing of CORDELIA (his intended bride), and then refuses to have anything more to do with her. (*Lear*: 'Will you, with these infirmities she owes,/Unfriended, new-adopted to our hate,/Dower'd with our curse and

stranger'd with our oath,/Take her or leave her?' *Burgundy*: 'Pardon me, royal sir./Election makes not up on such conditions.')

Burgundy, Philip, Duke of *(Henry V; Henry VI Part One)*
At the end of *Henry V*, Burgundy makes an impassioned plea for peace between England and France, asking 'what rub or impediment there is' that 'the naked, poor and mangled Peace,/Dear nurse of arts, plenties and joyful births,/Should not, in this best garden of the world,/Our fertile France, put up her lovely visage?' He urges HENRY's marriage with KATHARINE, and acts as Henry's intermediary with her. The part is small, but the character is lively and humorous. In *Henry VI Part One* he continues at first to favour the English, but is persuaded to back France against them by a rousing patriotic speech from LA PUCELLE. His character in this play is far less distinct: concern not to see his beloved France torn by war is once again his main motivation.

Bushy, Sir John *(Richard II)*
At first as unimportant-seeming as that other royal favourite, GREEN, Bushy reveals in his brief scene with the QUEEN a mellifluous courtier's turn of phrase. ('Each substance of a grief hath twenty shadows,/Which shows like grief itself but is not so;/For sorrow's eye, glaz'd with blinding tears,/Divides one thing entire to many objects...') To modern ears, there is something faintly camp about verbal conceits of this kind, especially in the mouths of minor characters; perhaps the same was true on Shakespeare's stage.

Butts, Sir William *(Henry VIII)*
HENRY's physician, who alerts him to the fact that CRANMER is being made to wait in a corridor, before the heresy-hearing, "'mongst pursuivants,/Pages and footboys'.

Cade, Jack *(Henry VI Part Two)*
Like most middle- and upper-class boys of his time, Shakespeare was
given an education modelled on that of ancient Rome. A large part of it
consisted of rhetorical training, putting speeches into the mouths of the
great men or women of history, justifying and explaining their actions.
(A Roman boy might assume the character of Hannibal; for an
Elizabethan, the subject might as easily be Cain, King Arthur or
Saladin.) When he began writing plays, Shakespeare carried this
rhetorical tradition into his dialogue: his 'noble' characters spend much
of their time explaining their political and other feelings in measured,
elegant verse which seldom seeks to differentiate one from another.

When it came to low-life characters, Shakespeare drew on a different
tradition: the comic interludes, mystery plays and rustic farce of
medieval fairs and churches. Here motivation mattered less than action
(and was very often explained in terms of character-stereotypes such as
the shrew, the cuckold, the renegade, the pietist and so on). The words
were plain and the action, however serious the subject-matter, was
often fast and slapstick. It is to this tradition that Cade and his
followers belong: indeed, *The Rebellion of Jack Cade* would make a
satisfying short interlude on its own, were it not (somewhat clumsily)
stitched into the main action of the play by the appearance of several
blank-verse-speaking 'noble' characters.

We are left in no doubt about Cade's character. He is a rogue, a liar,
a demagogue and a tyrant. He invents royal ancestry for himself, tosses
lordships to his followers like crumbs, and arbitrarily murders anyone
he dislikes (e.g. a CLERK whose only crime is the gentrified ability to
write his own name). Like many demagogues, he uses common speech
to give plausibility (but never clear explanation) to ideas about
government and human rights far outside the understanding of his
audience; like many revolutionary leaders, when he is challenged he
resorts to bluster and intimidation.

Implicit in all this is both a critique and a bland defence of upper-
class political morality. Cade's behaviour, like his 'court', is a replica of
the squabbling nobles in the main body of the play. Like Cade, they all
busily assert claims (real or invented) to birth nobler than the king's;
like him they have a neat line in rabble-rousing; like him, they scatter
honours and rewards like confetti; like him, they resort when cornered

to naked force. But the difference is as plain as the similarity. Because Cade and his followers are 'base', their claim to rule is bound from the start to fail; by contrast, since the aristocrats are 'noble', whichever of them wins the power-struggle is bound to grow into the dignity and moral stature of an office which is his by right of class.

As with the rhetorical speeches of the nobility, this outcome was probably one Shakespeare's own audience expected – and it allowed them to watch Cade's revolting followers with comfortable detachment, unworried even by Cade's unexpected moments of 'aristocratic' remorse (e.g. just after he sentences Lord SAY to death) or chivalric dignity (e.g. just before the fatal duel in IDEN's garden). The effect nowadays, when we are less at ease both with the tropes of oratory and the divine-right pretensions of the aristocracy, is often precisely the opposite: Cade and his 'rabblement', humorous, cheerful and farcical, can steal the play.

Caesar, Caius Julius (*Julius Caesar*)

Taking their cue, perhaps, from a single line in the play, 'Come on my right hand, for this ear is deaf', some acting companies give the part of Caesar to an elderly actor, whose silvery presence adds dignity to the part and provides, by the alchemy of casting alone, a nobility of character which weights our sympathy against the conspirators before a blow is struck. This is entirely false to Shakespeare. His Caesar is a tyrant, a man who (in CASSIUS' unminced words) bestrides the world 'like a colossus' while lesser beings 'Walk under his huge legs and peep about/ To find dishonourable graves'. And his tyranny is made worse because he chooses (like a silky Mafia boss, like the dictator of a modern banana republic) to dissemble it, to play the charade that he is an ordinary mortal like any other. He is plied with omens and portents of disaster if he goes to the Senate-house on the Ides of March, and decides, just because he feels like it, to ignore them; when he gives way to CALPHURNIA's pleading it is humouring her whims, not agreeing with her reasons – and he changes his mind equally arbitrarily as a result of DECIUS' flattery; he tells TREBONIUS that he has 'an hour's talk in store' for him, then patronisingly adds 'be near... that I may remember you'; in refusing to recall METELLUS' banished brother he contrives to compare himself to the North Star for constancy and to Olympus itself for firmness; in short, he is portrayed throughout as arrogant, insensitive, the very embodiment of irrational power and ripe for the assassins' knives.

The only real puzzle in the play, if Caesar is portrayed as starkly as the text demands, is why such a man should attract such loyalty, not only from ANTONY ('O pardon me, thou bleeding piece of earth!'), not only from the mob (whose love he buys) but from the far more complex, humane and morally judgmental BRUTUS. What are the qualities Brutus admires in Caesar – and how can they be brought out in performance without playing against the text? Perhaps this is the best reason for casting a distinguished elderly actor. Caesar's greatness now, in middle age, must be made to seem a matter of charisma rather than reality, a residue of what it was in youth, and, just as Brutus loved the man he used to be, so he is bound to hate the husk he has become. This interpretation adds to the sound political reasons for Caesar's death (which we, the audience, are constantly made to see), and to the self-serving ambition of the other conspirators (which Cassius embodies) the very human motives (in Brutus) of admiration disenchanted, of love betrayed – and it also throws the weight of the tragedy where it properly belongs, on Brutus.

Caesar, Caius Octavius (*Antony and Cleopatra*): *see* **Octavius**

Caithness (*Macbeth*)
Scottish lord who urges MENTEITH, LENNOX and ANGUS to desert MACBETH, and to offer as much blood in battle as is needed to 'dew the sovereign flower, and drown the weeds'.

Caius (*Titus Andronicus*): *see* **Gentlemen**

Caius, Doctor (*The Merry Wives of Windsor*)
Ebullient French physician, in love (or so he claims) with Anne PAGE, and convinced, in true farce fashion, that he is the only possible man for her. At one level he is a stock comic Frenchman, all bizarre oaths and inside-out syntax; he is also fierce as a terrier, forever barking at anyone he thinks has wronged him, and ready, if there is no one else to duel with, to challenge his own servant RUGBY to a sword-fight. Like all extravagant-foreigner parts in farce, this one has no other purpose than to amuse the audience, and the best way to play the lines is to go right over the top and have a wonderful time with them.

Calchas (*Troilus and Cressida*)
Trojan priest who deserts to the Greeks, and agrees to stay with them only if they bring his daughter CRESSIDA from Troy. A small part with little character.

Caliban (*The Tempest*)
PROSPERO's monstrous servant, a 'freckled whelp, hag-born, not honoured with/A human shape'. He is the beast in humanity made flesh, and spends the play resentfully muttering against Prospero ('This island's mine, by Sycorax my mother,/Which thou tak'st from me') or plotting his destruction with TRINCULO and STEPHANO. ('I'll yield him to thee asleep,/Where thou mayst knock a nail into his head'.) He is aware of beauty – 'The isle is full of noises' – and of the charms of the island (which he appreciates, indeed, more than Prospero does), but he lacks understanding and is therefore prey to his brutish senses, fawning on Stephano, for example, simply because he supplies the wine. At the end of the play, however, he reaches a sudden insight which puts him on a level with the humans – 'What a thrice double ass/Was I to take this drunkard for a god/And worship this dull fool': the island's magic wakens moral sensibility even in his stunted, misshapen soul.

Calphurnia (*Julius Caesar*)
CAESAR's wife. She appears always in her husband's shadow, and even her one big moment (the scene in which she tries to prevent him going to the Senate-house because of portentous nightmares) rests chiefly on a single speech ('... graves have yawned and yielded up their dead.../ And ghosts did shriek and squeal about the streets...'), and the interest is less in her panic than in Caesar's unfeeling egotism ('How foolish do your fears seem now, Calphurnia!/I am ashamed I did yield to them./Give me my robe, for I will go').

Cambridge, Richard, Earl of (*Henry V*)
Conspirator against HENRY, unmasked and arrested at Southampton before the fleet sails for France. An eager, fawning courtier ('Never was monarch better feared and loved/Than is your majesty...'), clearly signposted (by the CHORUS) as a hypocrite before he starts to speak.

Camillo (*The Winter's Tale*)
Loyal to principle rather than to people, he helps POLIXENES escape from Sicilia instead of poisoning him as his master LEONTES has ordered, and sixteen years later helps PERDITA and FLORIZEL elope from Bohemia after Polixenes (his new master) has forbidden their wedding. His clear view of what is right, regardless of other people's machinations, makes him a kind of fairy-godfather figure in the plot, and his character is an appropriate mixture of nobility and blandness. Leontes suggests that Camillo should marry PAULINA at the end of the play.

Campeius, Cardinal (*Henry VIII*)
The Pope's envoy, sent to help WOLSEY persuade KATHARINE to accept the annulment of her marriage and to warn Wolsey that there is gossip about him in the Vatican. Feline, silver-tongued and untrustworthy.

Canidius (*Antony and Cleopatra*)
ANTONY's officer, who complains after Actium that 'we are women's men', and is one of the first to desert Antony for OCTAVIUS, who promptly puts him in the front row to fight Antony.

Canterbury, Archbishop of (*Henry V*)
After the Prologue spoken by the CHORUS, there is a further expository scene, between the prelates of Canterbury and ELY. Its main purpose is to announce HENRY's change of character from headstrong youth to a king full of grace and regard. Canterbury then urges conquest of France, and gives as justification an enormously long (and tedious, as the politics are irrelevant) exposition of the ancient laws of succession. The lines are so many, and so dry, that simply speaking them gives Canterbury the character of a pedant; in modern performances they are usually drastically trimmed, and this barbering helps the character as well as the play.

Canterbury, Cardinal Bourchier, Archbishop of (*Richard III*)
Sent by BUCKINGHAM to fetch the boy Duke of YORK from sanctuary to the Tower. He is persuaded to let politics override religion, but the part is too small to allow this idea to be explored, and our attention, throughout his dialogue with Buckingham, is on Buckingham.

Caphis (*Timon of Athens*): *see* **Servants**

Captain (Roman) (*Cymbeline*)
Brings LUCIUS news from Rome that IACHIMO is coming with reinforcements.

Captain (*Hamlet*)
Norwegian officer who briefly explains to HAMLET the identity of the soldiers who are marching across the stage. (They are FORTINBRAS' army, on their way to Poland.) The role is tiny, and its main function is structural: to prepare the way for Hamlet's soliloquy, 'How all occasions do inform against me...'.

Captain (*Henry VI Part Two*)
Pirate with a bunch of prisoners for ransom (including SUFFOLK) and a lip-smacking turn of phrase (to Suffolk: 'Pole! Sir Pole! Lord!/Ay, kennel, puddle, sink, whose filth and dirt/Troubles the silver spring where England drinks!/Now I will dam up this thy yawning mouth/For swallowing the treasure of the realm;/Thy lips, that kiss'd the queen, shall sweep the ground...').

Captain (*Richard II*)
Appears with SALISBURY, and colourfully announces that because of supernatural portents ('The baytrees in our country all are wither'd,/ And meteors fight the fixed stars of heaven;/The pale-faced moon looks bloody on the earth...') the Welsh are deserting RICHARD's cause. He is sometimes claimed to be the same person as GLENDOWER in *Henry IV Part One*, on the grounds of linguistic similarity rather than historical likelihood.

Captain (*Titus Andronicus*)
At the start of the play, announces to the squabbling factions (of SATURNINUS and BASSIANUS) that TITUS is returning from the battlefield.

Captain (*Twelfth Night*)
Tells the newly-shipwrecked VIOLA that he last saw SEBASTIAN bound to a floating mast 'like Arion on the dolphin's back', and then helps her to disguise herself as a boy and seek employment at ORSINO's court.

Captains (British) (*Cymbeline*)
Arrest POSTHUMUS after the Roman defeat.

Capucius (Chapuys), French ambassador (*Henry VIII*)
Sent by HENRY to succour KATHARINE at the time of the divorce.

Capulet, Cousin (*Romeo and Juliet*)
Old friend and relative of CAPULET, who exchanges pleasantries with
him at the masked ball, rather after the manner of SHALLOW and
SILENCE in *Henry IV Part Two*.

Capulet, Lady (*Romeo and Juliet*)
JULIET's mother. She is far younger than her husband (indeed, she
seems to have married, and borne a child, at an age not much more
than Juliet's own), but she is characterised throughout as one of the
older generation who remain on the fringes of the action. Not only that,
but all the motherliness in the play is given to the NURSE (just as
fatherliness is given to Friar LAURENCE), and this makes Lady
Capulet's an even more wooden role. She is cool, wordly-wise and
imperious; her best moments are in the scene where CAPULET is trying
to persuade Juliet to marry PARIS, and there she plays a spirited peacemaker (saying, for example, to Capulet 'Fie, fie, what are you mad?';
'You are too hot'). But even there, in the end, she sides with her
husband and rounds on Juliet with the abrupt exit-lines, 'Talk not to
me, for I'll not speak a word./Do as thou wilt, for I'll have done with
thee.'

Capulet, Old (*Romeo and Juliet*)
JULIET's father. He could be little more than a dodderer, a one-
dimensional head of family whose pride at the start of the play leads to
a fall at the end. But two things make him interesting. First, he is a
generation older than his wife, and she is none the less devoted to him
as a husband and not as a father-figure. Second, he has as fiery a temper
as anyone in the whole play: he rounds on TYBALT when he thinks he is
about to fight a duel at the masked ball, and later, when Juliet refuses
to marry PARIS, he turns on her too ('Hang thee, young baggage!
Disobedient wretch!.../Get thee to church on Thursday,/Or never after
look me in the face'). If the feud between Capulets and Montagues has
no cause, his vehement temper is one of the main reasons for its
continuing. In the final scene, however, where emotions other than
pride are to the fore, he is not spectacularly humbled by Juliet's death
(as we might expect from what we know of him), but falls back into
stage convention.

Cardinal (*Richard III*): *see* **Canterbury**

Carlisle, Bishop of (*Richard II*)
Carlisle is often doubled with MOWBRAY, and at first sight it is hard to
see what possible attraction even that line-up could have for a leading
actor. (To say that the costumes – of lord and prelate respectively – are
gorgeous and the lines pompous and ceremonial is, in this day of high
professional acting-standards, not enough.) Carlisle supports RICHARD,
and is vehemently against his abdication: indeed, his finest moment is
in the Parliament scene just before the abdication, when he urges the
lords not to attack their Christian, anointed king. ('The blood of

English shall manure the ground,/And future ages groan, from this foul act;/ Peace shall go sleep with Turks and infidels,/And in this seat of Peace tumultuous wars/Shall kin with kin and kind with kind confound...') It is a marvellous outpouring, and the play stops for it: in fact, the actor who plays Carlisle is like an opera-singer brought in as guest to sing one superb, show-stopping aria – and perhaps that is the part's appeal.

Carriers (*Henry IV Part One*)
There are two of them, and they have a two-page, joky scene the purpose of which is to lighten the mood from the rebels' politicking which precedes it.

Casca (*Julius Caesar*)
The first of the conspirators to be recruited, and the first to stab CAESAR ('Speak, hands, for me!'). He is a blunt, drily witty man ('The rabblement shouted... and threw up their sweaty nightcaps, and utter'd such a deal of stinking breath... that it had almost chok'd Caesar... For my own part, I durst not laugh for fear of opening my lips and receiving the bad air'), and CASSIUS makes use of his somewhat affected simplicity to trap him into the conspiracy; even so, Casca finds a thunderstorm and other natural portents more persuasive than argument. After the murder he disappears from the play.

Cassandra (*Troilus and Cressida*)
Trojan priestess, sister of HECTOR, PARIS and TROILUS. She makes a handful of dramatic entrances, bursting in 'raving, with her hair about her ears' to shriek prophecies of disaster which no one heeds. ('Cry, Trojans, cry! A Helen and a woe!/Cry, cry! Troy burns, or else let Helen go!') In myth, she refused to sleep with Apollo, and he cursed her with the gifts of always speaking the truth and never being believed; in Shakespeare she is a melodramatic gibberer, kin to the spirit-conjurers of *Henry VI Part Two*, the SOOTHSAYER in *Julius Caesar* or the WITCHES in *Macbeth*.

Cassio, Michael (*Othello*)
OTHELLO's lieutenant, suspected by him of adultery with DESDEMONA. Cassio is a serious counterpart to AGUECHEEK in *Twelfth Night*, a similar blend of the woebegone ('I have very poor and unhappy brains for drinking: I could well wish courtesy would invent some other form of entertainment') and the peppery ('A knave teach me my duty? But I'll beat the knave into a twiggen bottle!'), and equally gullible: he believes every one of IAGO's insinuations without a moment's thought. In fact lack of thought is the secret of his military success, and when introspection is forced on him (in the 'reputation' scene) his character disintegrates and he becomes exactly the 'honest fool' required for Iago's schemes.

If what happens to Cassio parallels Aguecheek's gulling by Sir Toby BELCH, it also strikingly echoes the progress of Othello himself in Iago's hands. Cassio and Othello are identical in the way bravery in war depends on an absolute concept of honour (both their own and other people's) and in the ease with which this strength can be turned into a crippling flaw. The difference between them is one of dramatic stature. Cassio's personality-collapse is only momentarily devastating, leading to injury rather than death, and at the end of the play his reputation is undamaged – in his own eyes, one suspects, as well as in those of his superiors who give him the governorship of Cyprus. Othello's unquestioning trust in his own honour, by contrast, is a tragic flaw which leads to delusion, disgrace and death. In such circumstances, it is hard to make Cassio anything more than a slight character, dignified less by what he says than by his unwitting part in events far more significant than his own disgrace. Othello's plight is tragic, and we care about it; Cassio's is pathetic, and in the end interests no one but himself.

Cassius, Caius (*Julius Caesar*)

Unlike BRUTUS (who believes that if only the right purposes in life could be chosen, the way to fulfil them would be simple and obvious), Cassius is interested in means, not ends. Like most politicians, he knows exactly what he wants (in his case, power), and spends his time devising strategies to get it, persuading other people to agree with him and modifying his methods to suit each new set of circumstances without once changing his ultimate goal. Often, indeed, the chase seems to intrigue him just as much as the kill: a good example is the way he scurries about setting up the conspiracy, taking a different approach to each new recruit. (With bookish Brutus he adopts the slow course of planting anonymous notes, day after day, so that Brutus will ponder on their exhortations to liberate Rome until he thinks he thought of it himself; with blunt CASCA he exploits the occasion of a storm to talk of the gods' displeasure and urge immediate action before worse portents follow.) These, and not the scenes of generalship after CAESAR's funeral, are the times when we see his character at its most interesting and most complete.

Another political characteristic in Cassius is that when he is faced by a stronger personality or a mind apparently deaf to his arguments, he gives way (or appears to give way) rather than risk head-on defeat. (In the quarrel-scene, for example, when Brutus refuses to yield over taking bribes, he quickly turns the talk to other things.) This pliability is his ruin. He gives way, against his better judgement, over letting ANTHONY address the mob, and the result is a reversal of reputation for the conspirators; he leaves the parleying before Philippi to Brutus and Anthony, and where he and OCTAVIUS (another consummate politician) might have worked out a compromise, the others' prideful intransigence results in battle, the defeat of the conspirators and Cassius' own suicide. His ruin is personal, but his pliability is shown to be typical of politics in general, and the character chosen for him is thus part of Shakespeare's commentary on public and private honour throughout the play.

Cassius' manipulation of people and events suits the Epicurean philosophy which he proclaims at one point in the play (a pragmatic determination to 'live for each moment' rather than according to some grand, over-riding principle of life, as Stoics like Brutus do: see page 38); but it sits very ill with the rashness and ambition of his nature. He tries to school impetuosity out of himself (rather as Brutus tries to galvanise himself from anguished indecision into action) and it is because he fails to do so, because he hot-headedly accepts every challenge (e.g. swimming the Tiber fully-clothed) and flares up at every slight (e.g. the accusation that he has 'itchy palms') that he is destroyed. Although he and Brutus are presented as fire and ice throughout the play, they really represent each other's alter ego and both are examples of a favourite Shakespearean character-type, the man or woman destroyed less by outside events than by inconsistencies of personality within.

Catesby, Sir William (*Richard III*)
With RATCLIFF, RICHARD's chief favourite, and the agent of his villainy, instrumental in organising the deaths of CLARENCE and of HASTINGS and in the finding of TYRREL to kill the princes in the Tower. He is honey-tongued, deferential and as trustworthy as quicksand.

Catling, Simon (*Romeo and Juliet*)
Leader of the three musicians who perform an interlude between Acts Four and Five of the play. As well as playing 'Heart's ease', they debate with the clown PETER what the meaning is of the phrase 'Music with her silver sound'; Carling's view is that it is because of music's sweetness.

Cato, Young (*Julius Caesar*)
Valiant youth who runs headlong into the enemy shouting, 'I am the son of Marcus Cato, ho! I am the son of Marcus Cato, ho!', and so reminds BRUTUS (his brother-in-law) that he, too, has martial dignity and pride.

Celia (*As You Like It*)
Daughter of Duke FREDERICK, who accompanies her friend ROSALIND into exile. She plays a supporting role to Rosalind throughout, helping her in her masquerade with ORLANDO (and getting quite cross when she is too sharp with him); she is so lightly characterised that it comes as something of a surprise when she falls in love with the reformed OLIVER, and decides to marry him.

Ceres (*The Tempest*)
Dignified corn-goddess, who sings in the masque to entertain MIRANDA and FERDINAND. In some productions the part is taken by one of ARIEL's 'airy spirits'.

Cerimon *(Pericles)*
Old lord who finds THAISSA's body and sets to work to test his
restorative skills. He explains, at some length, that "'tis known, I ever/
Have studied physic, through which secret art,/By turning o'er
authorities, I have – /Together with my practice – made familiar/To me
and to my aid the blest infusions/That dwell in vegetives, in metals,
stones…' – but his cures are as effective as his explanations are long-
winded, and Thaissa is brought back to life. Many years later he is the
'reverent appearer' who tells PERICLES everything before Diana's temple
at Ephesus, and gives him proof that Thaissa is his long-lost wife.

Chamberlain *(Henry IV Part One)*
A humorous rogue employed at the Boar's Head Tavern; gives
information about rich travellers to the robbers and pickpurses who
drink there.

Chapuys *(Henry VIII): see* **Capucius**

Charles *(As You Like It)*
Wrestler commissioned by OLIVER to disable ORLANDO. Despite his
professional self-regard ('I wrestle for my credit, and he that escapes me
without some broken limb shall acquit him well') he is thrown by
Orlando and carried unceremoniously from the play.

Charles, Dauphin of France (later King Charles VII) *(Henry VI Part
One)*
We see Charles not as a dignified king but as an impetuous young
warrior, proud as a falcon (*Bastard*: 'See, noble Charles, the beacon of
our friend:/The burning torch in yonder turret stands.' *Charles*: 'Now
shine it like a comet of revenge,/A prophet to the fall of all our foes!').
Apart from his avenging-angel presence on the battlefield, the main
interest in his character is his relationship with LA PUCELLE: as soon as
he meets her he challenges her to single combat, then makes a
passionate and equivocal declaration of friendship ('Whoe'er helps thee,
'tis thou that must help me:/Impatiently I burn with thy desire…/Let
me thy servant, and not sovereign be:/'Tis the French Dauphin sueth to
thee thus'); thereafter he and she are presented as close comrades, equal
in their lust for military glory and the honour of France. When La
Pucelle is captured and burnt, however, Charles never mentions her
again, concentrating on peace-terms in a wooden, characterless way
("Tis known already, that I am possess'd/With more than half the
Gallian territories,/And therein reverenc'd for their lawful king…').
We end less intrigued with him than we began: he steps for a lively
moment out of the historical tapestry, only to step right back in again.

Charles V, King of France *(Henry V)*
HENRY's chief adversary, treated by Shakespeare more as a figurehead
than a dramatic character: the best lines go to his son the DAUPHIN and
others. He is often given spurious character in performance by being

played as a slack-witted geriatric, but though he is thought in real life to have been mentally unstable, the text of the play itself gives this interpretation no support.

Charmian (*Antony and Cleopatra*)
CLEOPATRA's confidential maid, a cheerful, giggly girl whose ambition (or so she tells the SOOTHSAYER) is 'to be married to three kings in a forenoon, and widow them all'. Her best moment comes in the monument, when she bids a lovely goodbye to the dead Cleopatra ('Now boast thee, death, in thy possession lies/A lass unparallel'd. Downy windows, close...'), and then uses the same asp to kill herself.

Chatillon, Duke of (*King John*)
French ambassador, with the standard chameleon courtesy of diplomats: he is the colour of whatever news he brings.

Chiron and Demetrius (*Titus Andronicus*)
TAMORA's sons. They are a murderous double-act, always appearing together, interchangeable in character and lines. They kill BASSIANUS, rape LAVINIA, frame TITUS' sons QUINTUS and MARTIUS for murder, try to kill AARON's infant son, and are finally beheaded and baked in a pie. They are like comic-opera villains deprived even of the dignity of music, and it is hard nowadays to take them seriously – a pity, since the momentum of the plot depends on them.

Chorus (*Henry V*)
The Chorus introduces each of the play's five acts, and speaks an Epilogue in the form of a sonnet. Part of the purpose is to explain the action, and to make the usual (ironical?) grovelling advances to the audience – 'Piece out our imperfections with your thoughts'. But Shakespeare uses this Chorus, as he does no other, to give the play a narrative grandeur nearer to epic poetry than drama: lines like 'From camp to camp through the foul womb of night/The hum of either army stilly sounds,/That the fixed sentinels almost receive/The secret whispers of each other's watch./Fire answers fire...' are reminiscent of Homer's *Iliad* or Virgil's *Aeneid*, and their bardic, incantatory style impregnates the play. It would have been tempting to make the dramatic scenes an illustration of the Chorus' narrative, like glimpses through a window; Shakespeare does this with the scenes in the French camp (which as a result are as unreal as charades), but he gives the English scenes a bustling, raucous verisimilitude, a downbeat rhetoric which directly contrasts with the Chorus' artificiality, and the interplay between the styles gives the play its dramatic impetus. (It serves the same purpose as the alternation in *Henry IV* of 'low-' and 'high-life' scenes, and allows Shakespeare, in passing, to draw his 'low-life' characters into the main dramatic action, as if all Britain were uniting, under King HENRY, to beat the French.)

Chorus (*Romeo and Juliet*)
Introduces the play ('Two households, both alike in dignity...'), and speaks once during the action (at the break between Acts One and Two; breaks between the other acts may have been filled with music). The Chorus' tightly rhythmed, elegantly rhymed verse (a sonnet, each time) helps to set the tone of rhetorical, artificial poetry which pervades the play.

Cicero, Marcus Tullius (*Julius Caesar*)
No hint is given in the play of Cicero's real-life character, a distinguished barrister and politician, the finest orator of his times and a fanatical (if somewhat muddle-headed) conservative opposed to CAESAR because he seemed set to overthrow tradition. Instead, he is a minor figure, an absent-minded elder statesman scathingly dismissed by the practical CASCA. (*Cassius*: 'Did Cicero say anything?' *Casca*: 'Ay, he spoke Greek.' *Cassius*: 'To what effect?' *Casca*: 'Nay, an I tell you that, I'll never look you in the face again... Those who understood him smiled... and shook their heads; but for mine own part, it was Greek to me...')

Cinna (*Julius Caesar*)
One of the conspirators; characterless.

Cinna the Poet (*Julius Caesar*)
Unfortunate man torn to pieces by a mob who mistake him for CINNA the conspirator. Under the circumstances, panic is all the character he has time to show.

Citizen (*King John*)
Canny local politician who, rather than declare his city Angiers either British or French (and so risk extermination by the other side), urges the marriage of BLANCH and LEWIS, a union which, he says, 'shall do more than battery can/To our fast-closed gates: for, at this match,/The mouth of passage shall we fling wide ope/And give you entrance'. One of the most splendidly boring burghers even Shakespeare (who delighted in the breed) ever created.

Citizen (*Romeo and Juliet*)
In a brief moment of glory at the end of the duel scene, he performs a citizen's arrest on BENVOLIO; apart from SAMPSON, GREGORY and ABRAHAM, the servants, he is the only indication we are given that ordinary folk in the Verona streets are affected by the Capulet–Montague feuding – and his distaste for it is plain.

Citizens (*Coriolanus*)
Of all Shakespeare's serious plays, only *Henry V* gives such prominent parts to ordinary people; but whereas there they are individually named and characterised, in *Coriolanus* they are undifferentiated, a many-headed mutter of SERVING-MEN, officers of the Senate, soldiers on sentry-duty, messengers, conspirators and, most vociferous of all,

citizens of Rome, the 'voices' Coriolanus despises but cannot survive without. Eight separate citizens thrust themselves from the crowd to speak, but apart from the sardonic Third Citizen and the rabble-rousing First Citizen (the man MENENIUS categorises as 'the big toe of this assembly' because he is the most forward and least useful part of it), they are less like identifiable people than the chorus-leaders in Greek tragedy.

The exception is the scene preceding CORIOLANUS's begging their 'voices' for his consulship, where the Second and Third Citizens indulge in heavy-footed banter. (*Third Citizen*: '... if all our wits were to issue out of one skull, they would fly east, west, north, south, and their consent of one direct way should be at once to all the points o' the compass.' *Second Citizen*: 'Think you so? Which way do you judge my wit would fly?' *Third Citizen*: 'Nay, your wit will not so soon out as another man's will. 'Tis strongly wedged up in a blockhead, but if it were at liberty, 'twould, sure, southward.' *Second Citizen*: 'Why that way?' *Third Citizen*: 'To lose itself in a fog...') In his adaptation of the play, which was concerned above all with the awakening of ordinary people to revolutionary consciousness, Brecht made the citizens and other commoners the main focus of the action; in Shakespeare they are more like an ever-changing, dangerous background, and their wavering loyalty and headstrong selfishness match Coriolanus' own.

Citizens *(Julius Caesar)*
Their chief function is to be a many-headed, fickle multitude, and their moment of glory comes in the Forum-scene after CAESAR's murder, when they are convinced first by BRUTUS and then, to the contrary viewpoint, by ANTONY. Four of them speak individual lines, but apart from the Second Citizen (a cobbler and a joker) they show little character but rowdiness.

Citizens *(Richard III)*
In a brief interlude between the death of EDWARD IV and the arrival in London of his son (the elder of the two doomed princes soon to be sent to the Tower), three Citizens have an impassioned political conversation deploring the state of the country, expressing popular unhappiness with events, but hoping for better things. They are sure that there can be nothing but 'woe to the land that's governed by a child'. Since we already know of RICHARD's dark plans for the princes, the Citizens' presence serves chiefly to stretch our expectation, and they need little individuality.

Clarence, George, Duke of *(Henry VI Part Three; Richard III)*
Son of YORK, brother of EDWARD and RICHARD. Unlike all of them, he is mild-mannered, and earns the description 'false, fleeting, perjur'd Clarence' more by vacillation than by villainy: even when he joins in the stabbing of EDWARD Prince of Wales, it seems to be less from conviction or vindictiveness than to keep his brothers company. He

consistently plays Cinderella to their Ugly Sisters, is largely ignored by
Edward (to whom, being younger, he poses no threat), but is a pebble
on Richard's path to the throne, to be kicked mercilessly aside (by
treachery, arrest, and drowning in a butt of wine). His terror makes
him vacillate: he can never decide whose side to be on in the power
struggle, and consistently picks the loser's. His scene in *Richard III*
with BRAKENBURY and the MURDERERS before he is killed is full of
pathos, and the nightmare he recounts is scalp-tinglingly vivid ('Lord,
lord, methought, what pain it was to drown!/What dreadful noise of
waters in mine ears!...'); but it is, alas, the only memorable moment in
his entire Shakespearean career.

Clarence, Thomas, Duke of *(Henry IV Part Two; Henry V)*
Second son of HENRY IV, the epitome of a loving son and brother (to
Prince HAL). Speaks mostly to his dying father in *Henry IV Part Two*;
silent character in *Henry V*.

Claudio *(Measure for Measure)*
Claudio, ISABELLA's brother, is the kind of youth people sometimes
describe as 'a healthy young animal': one who gives way to his sensual
appetites with never a thought for the consequences. He is bewildered
rather than indignant when he is arrested for impregnating JULIET,
whom he regards as his wife. His horror at the thought of death is
purely physical ('Ay, but.../To lie in cold obstruction and to rot...'),
and he has as little understanding of ISABELLA's intellectual vocation for
chastity as she has for his physical impetuosity. He is human frailty
personified, and he is the only truly 'innocent' person in the play, that
is, undevious, untainted and harmless. At the end, he is able to
continue his existence on exactly the same terms as before, as if the
events of the plot had never happened, and the reason is that he has
understood, and been affected by, not a single one of the moral issues
which have so altered everyone around him.

Claudio *(Much Ado about Nothing)*
HERO's beloved, an ardent young Florentine. In his juvenile way he is
as hot-headed as her father LEONATO: certainly he is equally willing to
believe the accusation that she is unfaithful, and speaks equally coldly
of vengeance. ('If I see anything tonight why I should not marry her
tomorrow, in the congregation where I should wed her, will I shame
her'.) His despair when he thinks her dead, and his puppyish eagerness
to make amends by doing anything Leonato suggests (even marrying a
'niece' sight unseen) are equally immature, and he would be a shallow,
unlikeable character – as over-conventional and spineless as he is made
to seem in some interpretations – were it not for the youthful ardour
and cheerfulness he shows elsewhere (e.g. in tricking BENEDICK into
thinking that BEATRICE loves him). Fecklessness is a rare characteristic
in Shakespeare's young men, but feckless is what he is.

Claudius (*Julius Caesar*)
BRUTUS' servant; no character.

Claudius (King) (*Hamlet*)
A veneer of melodrama overlies everything Claudius says or does. Whether he is playing the roles of king or of guilt-racked villain, part of the effect of the part comes from the swaggering, rolling lines he has to speak. It is difficult to underplay words like "Tis sweet and commendable in your nature, Hamlet,/To give these mourning duties to your father' or 'O, my offence is rank: it smells to heaven', and they give the part an orotund shallowness which is shared only by the GHOST and the PLAYER KING, both of whom, in their different ways, come straight from the melodramatic tradition in Elizabethan theatre.

   In public, Claudius makes himself 'every inch a king' (to borrow LEAR's phrase about himself). He speaks formal, poised lines which sound almost like rehearsed lessons and surround what he says with an aura, as if it were presented to people in a frame rather than spoken. He certainly never intends such remarks to be discussed or challenged, to lead to dialogue. In formal scenes, this is fair enough: no one needs to argue with 'Welcome, dear Rosencrantz and Guildenstern!/Moreover that we much did long to see you,/The need we have to use you did provoke/Our hasty sending' or 'I have sent to seek him, and to find the body./How dangerous is it that this man goes loose!'. But he uses the same style in conversation with intimates – 'His liberty is full of threats to all,/To you yourself, to us, to everyone./Alas, how shall this bloody deed be answer'd?' or 'Let's further think of this,/With what convenience both of time and means/May fit us to our shape' – and more than anything else, its contrived, self-conscious air is what gives us the feeling that he is a villain, speaking to stage-manage other people's reactions rather than saying what is in his heart.

   In private, Claudius is racked with remorse for his brother's murder. He shows this only rarely, and when he does it is as if it has boiled up uncontrollably, been forced out against his will. Before the scene where he eavesdrops on HAMLET and OPHELIA (the 'Get-thee-to-a-nunnery' scene), Claudius blurts out to the audience, unheard by anyone onstage, 'The harlot's cheek, beautied with plastering art,/Is not more ugly to the thing that helps it/Than is my deed to my most painted word./O heavy burden!' After the play-scene has 'caught his conscience', when he kneels to pray (alone, as he thinks: but Hamlet is eavesdropping), he writhes with a blend of self-disgust and terror. ('O wretched state! O bosom black as death!/O limed soul that, struggling to be free,/Art more engag'd...'.) The histrionic manner in which this private anguish is expressed raises doubts about Claudius' sincerity even with himself. Is his remorse as much play-acting as his public pomp? Certainly when he speaks the first aside quoted above, he is just about to use Ophelia to trap Hamlet into revealing that he is not as mad as he seems; even as he kneels to pray he knows perfectly well (as we do) that he has just plotted with ROSENCRANTZ and GUILDENSTERN to arrange Hamlet's death in England. Two-way irony affects everything he does. When we see him riding high in public, we know that he knows his inner rottenness; when we see him breast-beating in private, we know that he has no intention of abandoning the sins for which he writhes. He is either a kind of manic depressive of malignity, alternately swaggering and cringing but always evil, or else he is a hollow man in the way of Pirandello's characters three centuries later, so drained of true humanity that the performance he gives in life, with painful effort, is the only thing he is.

Cleomenes and Dion (The Winter's Tale)
Sent by LEONTES to consult the Delphic Oracle, they bring back the answer that HERMIONE is innocent. They have a tiny scene together exclaiming at the wonders of Delphi (which, in true if-it's-Tuesday-this-must-be-Belgium tourist style, they think is called Delphos); apart from this, they appear in Act Five encouraging Leontes to marry again.

Cleon (Pericles)
Governor of Tarsus who welcomes PERICLES' help in the famine and later agrees to bring up his baby daughter MARINA. When his wife DIONYZA has Marina murdered, as he thinks, he weakly tries to remonstrate ('O lady!... O Leonine!') and even attacks her with senile rage ('Thou art like the harpy,/which, to betray, dost, with thine angel's face,/Seize with thine eagle's talons...'). She brushes him aside ('I know you'll do as I advise'), and we later hear that he has died. Too few lines to show much character; what there are make him appear somewhat feeble-minded.

Cleopatra (Antony and Cleopatra)
Many of Shakespeare's character-decisions about Cleopatra flow from a single technical consideration: the fact that the part was written for a boy actor, who had to play convincingly and without embarrassment someone who was both a 'lass unparalled' and the 'serpent of old Nile' whose wiles ensnared and destroyed the finest soldier in the world. Although such technical constraints can be exaggerated – the boy was clearly an impressive actor, able to carry off lines like 'I shall see some squeaking Cleopatra/Boy my greatness i' the posture of a whore' and even (of the asp) 'Dost though not see my baby at my breast,/That sucks the nurse asleep?', and it is likely that once Shakespeare began writing, he let the character follow its own dramatic course, independent of stage considerations – each of the character-qualities he gives Cleopatra, and particularly her replacement of sexual seduction by coquettishness, of passion by play-acting, are both technically easier to perform than the alternative and psychologically more complex. Even today, when Cleopatra is played by mature women able to add every nuance of seductiveness, sexual ambivalence is one of the qualities in the part which make it great.

In history, Cleopatra was 28 when she met ANTONY (who was 14 years her senior), and 39 when she died; in the play, although references to her age are not shunned (she has borne several children; years before she met Antony she was Julius CAESAR's lover and beguiler), she behaves with a bouncy innocence more suited to a teenage heroine than to a mature woman. It is as if she is discovering the headiness of flirting for the first time, instead of having used it for her own political purposes for years.

Although people in the play constantly describe Cleopatra's beauty as calm, radiant and still (it is compared, for example, to rays of light or star-shine) we never once see her actually in repose. She is volatile, a flirt, a fidget; she seems to live each moment on tiptoe, without calculation and without regret. Since Shakespeare's time, psychologists have identified this kind of emotional restlessness as typical of an obsessive character – and it sits so ill with Cleopatra's known guile (to which reference is also made throughout the play) that we must assume either that she is, so to speak, two different people, or that her butterfly flirting is itself a performance, a strategy whose effects are precise and planned. Since we never see her alone, but always in scenes with other people, there is no way (e.g. soliloquy) for us to know her private thoughts, and this puts her sincerity in question throughout the play. If she is performing for everyone else – for CHARMIAN, for IRAS, for the messenger, for OCTAVIUS Caesar, even for the eunuch MARDIAN – why should we assume that her passion for Antony is real, not feigned? This is a central issue, and decisions made about it affect not only the acting of the part but the overall interpretation of the play.

None the less, although Cleopatra's devious complexity makes her the play's most interesting character, *Antony and Cleopatra* has two people at its heart, not one: like *Macbeth*, it centres on the relationship between a couple, and their behaviour singly or with other people is coloured throughout by what we know of them together. For this aspect of the play (and particularly the sharing of 'masculine' and 'feminine' qualities between the two characters) see the article about Antony on pages 14–15.

Clerk (*The Merchant of Venice*)
Reads a letter to the court in Venice, introducing PORTIA as a young Roman lawyer and asking that 'his lack of years be no impediment to let him lack a reverend estimation'.

Clerk of Chatham (Emanuel) (*Henry VI Part Two*)
The first person killed by CADE and his followers, on the grounds that because he can read and write he must be an aristocrat.

Clifford, John (Young Clifford) (*Henry VI Parts Two and Three*)
Lord CLIFFORD's son. At the end of *Henry VI Part Two*, finding his father's body, he eloquently vows revenge on YORK who killed him and on the entire York dynasty. He is the chief fire-brand of HENRY in *Part*

Three ('Patience is for poltroons'), and the first man to stab York in the assassination-scene; he is fatally wounded in battle, and dies after a deathbed speech as moving as the vengeance speech which began his military career. ('Come, York and Richard, Warwick and the rest./I stabb'd your fathers' bosoms; split my breast. *(Dies)*')

Clifford, Thomas, Lord *(Henry VI Part Two)*
Grizzled old royalist who puts down CADE's rebellion and is vehement against YORK. ('This is my king, York: I do not mistake,/But thou mistak'st me much to think I do./To Bedlam with him! Is the man grown mad?') He fights bravely at St Albans, and York kills him in single combat.

Clitus *(Julius Caesar)*
BRUTUS' slave; asked to help his master commit suicide, he refuses.

Cloten *(Cymbeline)*
CYMBELINE's stepson, the man Cymbeline has in mind as husband for his daughter IMOGEN. As his name suggests, Cloten is a crass, unthinking fool, mocked by his own lords behind his back (*Cloten*: 'That she should love this fellow, and refuse me!' *Second Lord, aside*: 'If it be a sin to make true election, she is damned.'), easily persuaded to disguise himself as Imogen's husband, follow her into exile and rape her. He is loud, uncouth and rude, and when he quarrels with true nobility, in the form of the king's long-lost (and disguised) son GUIDERIUS, he both figuratively and literally loses his head. His epitaph is spoken by Guiderius, the man who foreshortened him, and every word is apt. ('This Cloten was a fool, an empty purse:/There was no money in't. Not Hercules/Could have knock'd out his brains, for he had none:/Yet I not doing this, the fool had borne/My head as I do his'.)

Clown *(All's Well that Ends Well): see* **Lavache**

Clown *(Antony and Cleopatra)*
Delivers a basket containing asps to CLEOPATRA in the monument. In a one-page scene, he has a single joke ('I wish you joy o' the worm'), and repeats it every time they try to hustle him offstage. Like the PORTER-scene in *Macbeth*, the Clown's scene dissipates tension before a climactic moment, Cleopatra's death.

Clown *(Othello)*
Mocks the MUSICIANS who try to cheer up CASSIO, and is then used as a go-between, taking Cassio's request to DESDEMONA to plead for him and bringing Desdemona's reply. Everyone he speaks to is distracted with other matters (Cassio's lost reputation, Desdemona's lost handkerchief), and has no time for his somewhat laboured jokes.

Clown *(Titus Andronicus)*
Takes SATURNINUS a basket of pigeons and a bundle of letters TITUS

has written to the gods demanding vengeance. The object is to persuade
Saturninus that Titus is (a) insane and (b) dangerous. The clown has a
few clownish lines (*Titus*: 'Didst thou not come from heaven?' *Clown*:
'From heaven? Alas, sir, I never came there: God forbid I should be so
bold to pass to heaven in my young days'), but he is onstage for less
than three pages, and is dragged out and hanged soon afterwards.

Clown (*The Winter's Tale*)
AUTOLYCUS is the main comic role, and the Clown (somewhat
implausibly cast as the SHEPHERD's lumpish son) is his straight man,
eternally gulled by Autolycus' confidence tricks and eagerly believing in
every one of his disguises. He has, even so, two good individual
moments, one in his first appearance, on the seashore from which
ANTIGONUS has just been chased by a bear (I'll go and see if the bear be
gone from the gentleman, and how much be eaten...'), and the second
at the sheep-shearing festival, where he leads the jollity ('I love a ballad
but e'en too well, if it be a doleful matter merrily set down or a very
pleasant thing indeed and sung lamentably') and pays rustic court to his
beloved MOPSA.

Clowns (*Hamlet*): *see* **Gravediggers**

Cobweb (*A Midsummer Night's Dream*): *see* **Fairies**

Coleville, Sir John (*Henry IV Part Two*)
A rebel, captured (and mocked) by FALSTAFF, who hands him over to
Prince JOHN for execution.

The Comedy of Errors
There is such hostility between the towns of Ephesus and Syracuse that
any Syracusan found in Ephesus, unable to bail himself out, is
executed. The aged Syracusan Aegeon is caught in this trap, and begins
the play by explaining that many years ago his twin baby sons and their
twin baby servants were parted in a shipwreck, and that he is combing
the world to find the 'lost' Antipholus (son) and Dromio (servant). He
is given twenty-four hours to raise bail or die.

Next we see a chain of mistaken identities, as Antipholus of Syracuse
(Antipholus I) and his servant Dromio of Syracuse (Dromio I) are
mistaken for their twins Antipholus of Ephesus (Antipholus II) and
Dromio of Ephesus (Dromio II), and vice versa. Antipholus I knows
Ephesus's reputation as a town of wizards, conjurers and apparitions,
and is bewildered but not surprised as he is hailed by strangers in the
street, given money and a gold chain, even taken to dinner by a lady
(Adriana) who claims to be his wife and with whose sister Luciana he
falls in love. For his part, Antipholus II is barred from his own house
on the grounds that he is inside already, eating dinner, and is denied
the chain he ordered from Angelo the goldsmith on the grounds that he
has it already. The two Dromios are regularly sent on errands, only to
return to the wrong master, who disclaims all knowledge and thrashes

them for cheek.

The complications are unravelled when Antipholus II is first arrested for debt and then tackled as a lunatic (by the quack-doctor Pinch) and Antipholus I seeks refuge in an Abbey just as Aegeon and the Duke of Ephesus also arrive there. Aegeon recognises his son Antipholus II; Antipholus I and II discover each other and Antipholus II is reunited with his wife Adriana; the Abbess recognises Aegeon as her long-lost husband, and is revealed as the young men's mother; Antipholus I pays Aegeon's bail and frees him from execution, then goes off to marry Luciana. The two Dromios, left alone onstage, grin at one another, squabble amiably about which of them is the older, and go out hand in hand.

Cominius *(Coriolanus)*

Roman consul. He leads the army against the Volscians at Corioli, and later awards CORIOLANUS his honorific surname and sponsors him for the consulship. He is presented throughout as 'the good Cominius', an elder statesman whose thoughts are always for the good of Rome rather than for any single individual: 'I do love/My country's good with a respect more tender,/ More holy and profound than mine own life...' None the less, his admiration for Coriolanus leads him to offer to accompany him into banishment ('I'll follow thee a month, devise with thee/Where thou shalt rest...'), and later, like MENENIUS, to go and plead with him outside the walls of Rome. On each occasion he is respectfully but uncompromisingly rejected. His name is derived from the Latin word *comis*, 'cultured', and a kind of distant gentlemanliness marks his character even on the battlefield, even in the midst of a violent political slanging-match.

Conrade *(Much Ado about Nothing)*

Servant of DON JOHN and henchman of BORACHIO. He has two colourless scenes – one asking Don John why he is so melancholy and the other going with Borachio to the assignation with MARGARET and being arrested for it – and one lively one in which, questioned by DOGBERRY, he first plays the injured, innocent toff and then spoils everything by calling Dogberry an ass. His vehemence here is his main character-trait, and it is unheralded by his blandness in the earlier scenes.

Constable of France (Charles Delabreth) *(Henry V)*

Although conscious that the English are not the easy pickings the DAUPHIN thinks, the Constable spends the night before Agincourt dicing for them, and exchanging jokes and proverbs with the Dauphin and ORLEANS. During the battle he makes a passionate speech of encouragement, as fine rhetoric as HENRY's 'Crispin's day' speech (but carefully written in artifical, flowery conceits in contrast to Henry's man-of-the-people lines); we see him only once thereafter, in the depression of defeat, and his name is later mentioned with honour in the roll of the slain.

Constance *(King John)*

Widow of JOHN's brother Geoffrey and mother of the child ARTHUR.
She fights on Arthur's behalf with a verbal fury which makes weapons
seem superfluous: her spitting rows with ELINOR, in particular ('Thou
monstrous injurer of heaven and earth!'), are a high point in the early
part of the play. After the dynastic marriage of BLANCH and LEWIS, and
the capture of Arthur, she is reduced to railing at PHILIP and at
PANDULPH ('He talks to me that never had a son'), and finally we hear
that she has 'in a frenzy died'. The part is in one mode only, hysterical
rage, but the lines are plentiful and marvellous.

Cordelia *(King Lear)*

When Nahum Tate refurbished *King Lear* in 1681, equipping it with
new motivation (a love-affair between EDGAR and Cordelia) and a happy
ending, he made substantial changes to the character of Cordelia, and in
so doing established an image of her which has persisted in productions
ever since, even those using Shakespeare's (utterly different) original
text. She is presented as a dewy-eyed girl, radiant and wronged, a living
doll for her father to throw down at the start and pick up at the end.
The line of the part runs from bashful obstinacy in the opening scene
('... my love's/More richer than my tongue...') to concern over
LEAR's madness, as the last act begins, expressed in verse of almost Pre-
Raphaelite sugariness ('O my dear father! Restoration hang/Thy
medicine on my lips, and let this kiss/Repair those violent harms that
my two sisters/Have in thy reverence made...').

In Shakespeare's unreconstructed play, the only person who thinks of
Cordelia in these sentimental terms is Lear himself. He wants her to be
a puppet, and his sorrow over her death at the end has exactly the same
cause as his fury at the beginning: distress that she behaves differently
from what he had in mind. (At the beginning, she refuses to speak the
loving words he wants to hear; at the end, she dies.) No one else but
FRANCE has any time for her. BURGUNDY was marrying her dowry, not
herself; KENT's quarrel with Lear is more about Lear's unjust
behaviour than Cordelia's deserving; GONERIL and REGAN brush her
haughtily aside. (*Regan*: 'Prescribe not us our duties.' *Goneril*: 'Let
your study/Be to content your lord...'.) After the opening scene she
vanishes from the action for over an hour, to reappear as commander of
the French forces, vigorous, decisive and full of concern for Lear.
(*Messenger*: 'News, madam:/The British powers are marching
hitherward.' *Cordelia*: 'Tis known before. Our preparation stands/In
expectation of them. O dear father,/It is thy business that I go
about...'.) In the scene of Lear's recovery from madness, she is as
formal and statesmanlike towards Kent as she is loving towards Lear;
later, captured by the English and about to be led away to prison, she
shows leathery maturity rather than maidenly alarm. ('We are not the
first/Who, with best meaning, have incurr'd the worst./For thee,

oppress'd king, am I cast down;/Myself could else out-drown false
Fortune's frown.')

Cordelia appears, and speaks, in only four scenes, and is onstage as a
corpse for the play's closing pages. The part is small, and at least as
much of it shows tough-mindedness and self-possession as doe-eyed
innocence. Playing her less like Lear's plaything than like his daughter,
just as much the inheritor of aspects of his character as are Regan or
Goneril, changes the impression we form of his love for her, and so
alters the balance of the play as we perceive it – and both the play and
its spectators gain from that.

Corin (As You Like It)

Shepherd, older colleague of SILVIUS. His best moment in the play is
his discussion with TOUCHSTONE of the merits of the shepherd's life,
which reveals him as a rustic philosopher. ('Sir, I am a true labourer: I
earn that I eat, get that I wear, owe no man hate, envy no man's
happiness, glad of other men's good...')

Coriolanus

Caius Marcius is an unbending, arrogant aristocrat, whose inflexibility
wins every bout on the battlefield and loses every peacetime argument.
In particular, he despises the common people and their tribunes
Sicinius and Brutus, adding personal loathing to the class-hatred shown
by his aristocratic friend Menenius. After a famous victory at Corioli
against the Volsci and their leader Aufidius (his clone for military
genius, though a more circumspect and humane politician), he is given
the honorific surname Coriolanus, and is promised the consulship at
Rome if he will humble himself to beg the citizens' support. He does
so, reluctantly and with ill-concealed disdain, but Sicinius and Brutus
poison the people's minds against him and he furiously exiles himself
from Rome, allies himself with Aufidius and leads the Volscian army
against his own people. The Volsci are camped outside the city, and
Coriolanus' friends and relatives go to beg him to spare it. The friends
fail, but Coriolanus' mother Volumnia succeeds by a combination of
heroic rhetoric and withering maternal rage. Coriolanus makes a treaty
and leads the Volscian army back to Antium, where Aufidius accuses
him of treachery and organises a conspiracy to assassinate him.

Coriolanus, Caius Marcius (Coriolanus)

In the Romantic era, Coriolanus was often played as a tragic colossus, a
hero whose nature was too big for his countrymen to understand and
too expensive for them to afford. More recently he has often been
played as an outsider, a man (like LEAR, HAMLET or PROSPERO) infected
by the existential sickness, the need to find some way of defining
himself, of coming to terms with his own reality. Both interpretations
can be supported from the text; but to follow either without the other is
to sap the play's vitality, to turn it into a somewhat uningratiating tract.
Shakespeare depicts Coriolanus chiefly as a man of action, a war-

leader whose reflexes and instincts carry everything before him on the battlefield, who can be shut in alone with a townful of enemies at Corioli and come out bleeding but triumphant. His John-Wayne heroism requires no rationale, and his 'problem' lies, quite simply, in the facts that there are not enough physical wars to fight and that his macho tactics are unsuited to the subtler arguments of peace. He is used to getting what he wants by opening his mouth and roaring, and when he is attacked he redoubles his fury, like a blinkered bull. The play begins by contrasting his glory on the battlefield with his ungoverned and useless rage against the CITIZENS because they lack the consistency which is the hub of his own being. ('What would you have, you curs/That like neither peace nor war?... He that trusts to you,/Where he should find you lions, finds you hares,/Where foxes, geese;/you are no surer, no,/Than is the coal of fire upon the ice,/Or hailstorm in the sun') Its pivot-scene is the enormous brawl in Act Three, where he begins by trying to sweep hostile opinion aside by yelling, and ends up physically attacking the aediles and being dragged to safety shouting, like a punch-drunk prize-fighter, 'On fair ground I could beat forty of them'.

One source of this sterile bravado (which is the result less of arrogance than of bewilderment) is his upbringing: Shakespeare is at pains to show that just as his mother VOLUMNIA is stunting the conscience of his son Young MARCIUS by approving no instincts in him but bloodthirstiness, so she channelled Coriolanus into the beliefs that nobility and inflexibility are the same thing and that war-wounds (which at one point she gloatingly, gruesomely itemises on his body) are a coin that buys all honour. While Coriolanus has her approval, he needs no conscience; so long as she smiles on him, he needs no flatterers. Their view of each other, summed up by her remark 'O, he is wounded; I thank the gods for it' and his 'You were used to load me/With precepts that would make invincible/The heart that conn'd them', is a flaw in both of them, and when Coriolanus realises, in the intercession scene, that he must yield as always to his mother's promptings however incompatible they are with his new-found conscience, his fall becomes pitiable rather than just pig-headed. ('O my mother, mother, O!/ You have won a happy victory to Rome;/But for your son, believe it, O believe it,/Most dangerously you have with him prevail'd,/If not most mortal to him'.)

The discovery of his own hollowness, that grandeur is not enough, is the key to Coriolanus' character. He begins by thinking that supreme achievement confers supreme moral authority – when BRUTUS asks, after Coriolanus has once more reviled the Citizens, 'Shall the people give/One that speaks thus, their voice?' he grandly answers, 'I'll give my reasons,/More worthier than their voices' – but as the play proceeds his self-esteem crumples to the point where, encamped outside Rome and begged by his friends not to destroy his own people, he refuses even to acknowledge who he is: 'Coriolanus/He would not answer to...'. This is not the abasement of an Aristotelian tragic hero, chastised for *hubris*; it is ordinary human despair. Coriolanus' discovery of a void in himself where humanity should be, and his struggle to cope with it and at the same time to deal with the politicking of those who still think him a colossus to topple just because he is too big for them, is the battle which makes the tragedy.

Cornelius *(Cymbeline)*
Honest doctor commissioned by the QUEEN to provide poison in a box (to kill IMOGEN, though the Queen tells him it is to use on animals and 'observe th'effects'). He suspects her motives and substitutes a sleeping-draught. Later, he brings news to CYMBELINE that the Queen has confessed and died. His part is small, but his character (clear-eyed integrity) is strong and his lines are among the meatiest in the play.

Cornelius *(Hamlet): see* Voltimand and Cornelius

Cornwall, Earl of *(King Lear)*
Cornwall's part is small, and in one mode only: cold-hearted cruelty. His highhandedness towards KENT (putting him in the stocks for quarrelling with OSWALD) is matched by his murderous rage against the SERVANT who tries to stop him blinding GLOUCESTER, and his lip-smacking relish in the details of the blinding itself ('Out, vile jelly!/ Where is thy lustre now?') is designed more to speed the scene along than to make us think about his character. As the moral ambiguity of the play increases, he vanishes (killed by his own Servant) – and so he must, for there is no place for him in a world of randomness, of the possibility of good, of choice.

Costard *(Love's Labour's Lost)*
Cheerful buffoon, ARMADO's rival for JAQUENETTA. At the start of the play he is arrested for sitting on a bench and talking to Jaquenetta, and is handed over to Armado's custody, only to be freed to deliver a letter to Jaquenetta. As HOLOFERNES and SIR NATHANIEL gradually take over the 'low-life' action of the play, Costard becomes less important, until in the pageant of the Nine Worthies he takes the part (if not the swaggering magnificence) of 'Pompey the Big' and is unexpectedly and engagingly afflicted by stage-fright. He has none of the melancholy usual in Shakespeare's clowns: he is irrepressible, down-to-earth and uncomplicatedly funny, one of the few people, in this play about pretension, with absolutely no conceit at all.

Countrymen *(The Two Noble Kinsmen)*
There are four of them, and they rehearse and perform a morris dance before Duke THESEUS. Unlike the 'rude mechanicals' of *A Midsummer Night's Dream* (who plan a similar entertainment) they are not slapstick clowns but serious-minded yeomen: perhaps the parts were written for dancers, not actors, and are suitably undemanding.

65

Court, Alexander *(Henry V)*
Common soldier, mess-mate of BATES and WILLIAMS, who meets the
disguised King HENRY on the eve of Agincourt. He speaks one line only
('Brother John Bates, is not that the morning which breaks yonder?'),
and it is hardly redolent with character.

Courtesan *(The Comedy of Errors)*
Dignified rather than loud, she claims the gold chain ANTIPHOLUS II has
promised her, and later accompanies his wife ADRIANA in search of
him, to have him treated for lunacy.

Coventry, Lord Mayor of *(Henry VI Part Three)*
Appears with WARWICK on his city walls, but does not speak.

Cranmer, Thomas, Archbishop of Canterbury *(Henry VIII)*
Whatever history's view of him, Cranmer is presented in this play as a
man so holy, honest and simple that we begin to wonder how far
Shakespeare's tongue was in his cheek. At one point HENRY asks him
the question burning on all our lips: 'Know you not/How your state
stands i' the world, with the whole world?/Your enemies are many, and
not small...', and he replies with either innocent sincerity or
serpentine guile, 'God and your majesty/Protect mine innocence, or I
fall into/The trap is laid for me!' Henry duly protects him against the
commission trying him for heresy (the same commission as keeps him
waiting in a corridor like a lackey); Cranmer then acts as godfather to
the infant Princess Elizabeth, and speaks a long prophetic eulogy ('This
royal infant.../Though in the cradle, yet now promises/Upon this land
a thousand, thousand blessings...') which rounds off the play as
resoundingly as a peal of bells.

Cressida *(Troilus and Cressida)*
ULYSSES, who has no interest in finding good qualities in people, brands
Cressida as a harlot the minute he sees her: 'Fie, fie upon her!/There's
language in her eye, her cheek, her lip;/Nay, her foot speaks, her
wanton spirits look out/At every joint and motive of her body.' He is,
however, alone in this opinion: the most the other Greek commanders
allow themselves is a chaste, ceremonious kiss of welcome, and in Troy,
though Cressida beds with TROILUS, it is with the same ardour (of love,
not lust) and constancy as JULIET shows to ROMEO in *Romeo and Juliet*.
Her fidelity is stressed throughout her time with Troilus – she says 'If I
be false, or swerve a hair from truth.../...when they've said "as
false/As air, as water, wind or sandy earth,/As fox to lamb or wolf to
heifer's calf,.../Yea," let them say, to stick the heart of falsehood,/"As
false as Cressid"' – and there is no irony in her character, no wanton
subtlety to prepare us for her rapid succumbing to DIOMEDES'
seduction later on. Indeed, she seems as surprised as we are to find
herself lecherous, and her scene with Diomedes is a mixture of shyness
and coyness to the very end. The outcome of her affair with Troilus is
bleak, in keeping with the tone of the play – not realising he can hear

her, she confides to the audience, 'Troilus, farewell! One eye yet looks on thee,/But with my heart the other eye doth see'. But although what she does is made to seem both shocking and portentous, she never sacrifices our sympathy: even when she conforms in every detail to Ulysses' description of her, she still seems more a pure soul tragically corrupted than a votary of Venus, corrupt from the very start.

Cromwell, Thomas *(Henry VIII)*
WOLSEY's servant, loyal, obsequious and unimportant until his master's death, Cromwell then rises to a position of sufficient eminence to be secretary of the commission trying CRANMER for heresy. He spars with GARDINER on Cranmer's behalf, and rounds on the whole committee as soon as he sees that Cranmer has HENRY's support. There is a hint of the toady in his lines, but he is never so described, and the part is too small to round out this (or any other) characterisation.

Cupid *(Timon of Athens)*
Announces the arrival of a group of dancers dressed as Amazons, who dance with the guests at TIMON's first banquet. No character, but a pretty turn of phrase. ('Hail to thee, worthy Timon, and to all/That of his bounties taste! The five best senses/Acknowledge thee their patron, and come freely/To gratulate thy plenteous bosom:/The ear, taste, touch, smell, pleas'd from thy table rise;/These only now come but to feast thine eyes.')

Curan *(King Lear)*
Courtier who tells EDMUND the 'whisper'd...ear-kissing' rumour that CORNWALL and ALBANY are at loggerheads.

Curio *(Twelfth Night)*
ORSINO's courtier.

Curtis *(The Taming of the Shrew)*
PETRUCHIO's chief servant in the country, who listens to GRUMIO's account of PETRUCHIO's and KATHARINA's accident-plagued journey home from the wedding.

Cymbeline *(Cymbeline)*
In real life Cymbeline (Cunobelin) was one of the last Celtic British kings to stand against the Romans, and the father of Caratacus whose heroism and defiant nobility won the admiration even of the enemy who paraded him through Rome in triumph. In Shakespeare's play – which has nothing to do with this real history – Cymbeline is a fool, an absolute ruler whose decisions are arbitrary, unquestioned and devastating to himself and those he loves. (We never see how his actions affect his country: court life, with its silly intrigues and sillier masquerades, is as isolated from ordinary daily life as if it were in a box.) Cymbeline marries a malevolent witch and favours her clottish son CLOTEN, blind to his lack of charm; when his daughter IMOGEN secretly marries the noble POSTHUMUS instead of Cloten, he banishes

Posthumus and gives the girl into her step-mother's house-arrest;
earlier he banished from court the most loyal of his counsellors,
BELARIUS (who then stole his infant sons to bring them up untainted by
the manners of their father's court). He crashes about his life like a
caged rhinoceros, and the play's happy outcome is brought about by
others and seems to impinge on him as little as anything else – even his
witch-wife's death rouses him to no more substantial epitaph than 'O,
she was naught'.

What on earth is Shakespeare showing us – for the play is named
after this royal dolt? Is Cymbeline a tragically bemused old man, a cut-
price LEAR? Or is he a simpleton, elevated to royalty by the accident of
blood alone? Either interpretation is uncomfortable, and many
productions (of the few there ever are) prefer to make him a
characterless, cardboard figurehead, the pole round which the merry-
go-round of the play revolves. But this involves underplaying the
restlessness and danger which also lie in his lines. Maybe he is best
played as the enigma he seems, a man who claims to be 'amaz'd with
matter' but none the less, for good or ill, gets exactly what he wants.

Cymbeline

Twenty years before the start of the action, Cymbeline unjustly
banished Lord Belarius, and Belarius stole Cymbeline's baby sons
Guiderius and Arviragus to bring up in Wales, far from the corruption
of the court. Cymbeline has a daughter, Imogen, a scheming second
wife and a cloddish stepson, Cloten. He plans to marry Imogen to
Cloten, and when she secretly marries the honest nobleman Posthumus
instead, he banishes Posthumus and claps Imogen under house arrest.
Posthumus goes to Italy, where he wagers with Iachimo, a bored,
corrupt aristocrat, that Imogen's purity cannot be assailed; Iachimo at
once hurries to Britain, hides in a trunk in Imogen's bedroom, steals a
bracelet from her while she sleeps and uses it to persuade Posthumus
that she has been false to him.

Bitterly furious, Posthumus sends a letter ordering his servant
Pisanio to kill Imogen, but Pisanio instead disguises her as a boy (called
Fidele) and helps her escape to Wales, where she meets up with
Guiderius and Arviragus. Cloten decides to follow her to Wales and
rape her, and to this end dresses up in Posthumus' clothes; in Wales he
quarrels with Guiderius who cuts off his head. When Imogen discovers
the headless corpse, she takes it for Posthumus and is heartbroken.
Meanwhile, Posthumus himself has come to Britain with a Roman
invading-force led by Caius Lucius; they land in Wales and the British
forces (led by Cymbeline) and Welsh guerrillas (led by Belarius) beat
them and force surrender.

The last forty minutes of the play are an unknotting of complications,
a flurry of recognitions and repentances and a tying of loose ends:
Cymbeline is reunited with his long-lost sons, Posthumus is reunited
with Imogen, alliance is made with Rome, and everyone (except Cloten,

headless, and the queen, dead of apoplectic insanity) lives happily ever afterwards.

Dardanius (*Julius Caesar*)
Slave of BRUTUS who declines to help his master kill himself.

Daughter (*The Two Noble Kinsmen*)
No character in the whole Shakespearean canon belongs more firmly to the world of Jacobean masque than this JAILER's daughter who goes mad for love. We are given no reason for either her love or her madness, and she drifts in and out of the action with nothing much more to do than give (admittedly excellent) imitations of OPHELIA in *Hamlet*. ('Give me your hand... I can tell your fortune./You are a fool. Tell ten. I have posed him. Buzz./Friend, you must eat no white bread...'.) The daughter's presence is crucial to the plot (she has to free PALAMON from jail), but there was no need for all the dramatic embroidery, and it has the appearance of having been written up for a particularly talented actor. In talented hands, still, it can steal the play, but such a success would be due to the performer's and not the creator's magic, rather as a minor character with two good arias can steal an opera.

Daughter of Clarence (Margaret) (*Richard III*)
Child who with her brother bewails the murder of their father CLARENCE, one contrasting voice (childish treble) in a consort of weeping (Duchess of YORK; Queen ELIZABETH; her brother; herself).

Dauphin (*Henry V*)
Louis (or Lewis), son of King CHARLES V, this Dauphin is a haughty, exquisite young gallant. He despises the English, and is particularly scornful of HENRY, to whom he sends insulting messages and a barrel of tennis balls. He spends the eve of Agincourt in an elegant, punning conversation with the CONSTABLE, ORLEANS and others, comparing horses and mistresses and dicing over who will take most English prisoners. Orleans sums up his temper with the words, 'He longs to eat the English'; we see him twice at Agincourt, once urging on the troops and once bemoaning defeat ('O perdurable shame, let's stab ourselves./Be these the wretches that we played at dice for?'); he does not appear again.

Davy *(Henry IV Part Two)*
Justice SHALLOW's servant.

Decius Brutus *(Julius Caesar)*
The conspirator whose wheedling ('... when I tell him he hates
flatterers,/He says he does – being then most flattered') tempts CAESAR
to the Senate-house in the face of every portent, warning and entreaty.
He speaks twice in the assassination scene, then vanishes from the play.

Deiphobus *(Troilus and Cressida)*
Trojan prince, brother of HECTOR, TROILUS and PARIS, minor
character.

Demetrius *(Antony and Cleopatra)*
At the beginning of the play discusses with PHILO, ANTONY's break
with OCTAVIUS.

Demetrius *(A Midsummer Night's Dream)*
Initially in love with HERMIA, he is irritated to the point of rudeness by
HELENA's spaniel affection ('Hence, get thee gone, and follow me no
more'), but, under the influence of magic he is soon down on his knees
begging her to listen to his love-poetry. ('O Helen, goddess, nymph,
perfect, divine!/To what, my love, shall I compare thine eyne?') He
chases LYSANDER (actually PUCK, disguised) through the wood till he
tumbles asleep for weariness, and finally awakes to find that Helena at
last loves him as much as he loves her. (His earlier love for Hermia has
vanished like mist in the sun.) Hot-headedness sums him up: as with
Lysander and Hermia, what happens to him is far more interesting than
the sort of character he is.

Demetrius *(Titus Andronicus): see* **Chiron and Demetrius**

Dennis *(As You Like It)*
OLIVER's servant; except to usher in CHARLES the wrestler, he hardly
speaks.

Denny, Sir Anthony *(Henry VIII)*
Minor courtier attendant on the king; he speaks three lines.

Derby, Lord *(Richard III)*: *see* **Stanley**

Dercetas *(Antony and Cleopatra)*
ANTONY's friend, who tells OCTAVIUS news of his death. ('This is his
sword:/I robb'd his wound of it. Behold it stain'd/With his most noble
blood'.)

Desdemona *(Othello)*
Like JULIET in *Romeo and Juliet*, Desdemona is a child suddenly thrust
into adulthood by marriage, and quite unable to cope with it. Her most
natural behaviour was before her wedding, when she responded to
Othello's traveller's tales with 'a world of sighs', and played the game of
concealing her love from her father with a true adolescent's disregard

for the emotional consequences. (As IAGO says to OTHELLO, 'She did deceive her father, marrying you,/And when she seem'd to shake and fear your looks,/She lov'd them most.' That BRABANTIO might be devastated by the whole proceeding never seems to have entered her head.) Once she is married and in Cyprus, she throws herself into the game of being Othello's wife, the lady governess, and loves every adult minute of it, promising to help CASSIO, for example, with the eager words 'If I do vow a friendship, I'll perform it/To the last article. My lord shall never rest:/I'll watch him tame, and talk him out of patience;/His bed shall seem a school, his board a shrift;/I'll intermingle everything he does/With Cassio's suit...'

If all had gone well, this wide-eyed excitement would have been charming, and Desdemona would gradually have grown into the adult role she played. But as soon as things begin to go wrong, she reverts to being a frightened child, begging Iago to intercede for her to Othello as if Othello's rage is no more than a playmate's tantrum ('If e'er my will did trespass against his love.../Or that I do not yet, and ever did,/... love him dearly,/Comfort forswear me!'), and facing death itself with the kind of desperate prattle which – showing no understanding of the real issues – a little girl might use to avoid being smacked. ('And yet I fear you, for you are fatal then/when your eyes roll so. Why I should fear I know not,/Since guiltiness I know not; but yet I feel fear.') Even her last words, in the final rallying-moment before death, are as irrelevant to the main issues, and as preposterous, as they are pathetic. (*Emilia*: 'O, who hath done/This deed?' *Desdemona*: 'Nobody. I myself. Farewell./Commend me to my kind lord. O, farewell.') To the end she treats life as something to be played at with utmost seriousness, not lived, and her ambition to be a grownup, to be accepted on the terms she creates for herself, is one of the main ingredients in her somewhat over-emphatic charm.

Diana (*All's Well that Ends Well*)
Daughter of the WIDOW of Florence. She is named after the virgin huntress, goddess of the moon, and shares Diana's attributes, gladly letting HELENA sleep with BERTRAM in her place, and zestfully joining in the hunt to bring Bertram down. In the trial-scene, the picture of wronged innocence, she is slandered and insulted by Bertram, and is only saved from arrest by the rabbit-out-of-the-hat arrival of Helena.

Dick (*Henry VI Part Two*)
A butcher, one of CADE's most bloodthirsty and loudmouthed followers. ('The first thing we do, let's kill all the lawyers...')

Diomedes (*Antony and Cleopatra*)
CLEOPATRA's attendant, who tells the dying ANTONY that Cleopatra has not, as he thought, been killed.

Diomedes (*Troilus and Cressida*)
Although in Homer's *Iliad* (on Chapman's translation of which this play

is based) Diomedes is a lord, a commander of equal rank with ULYSSES, ACHILLES and others, in Shakespeare he is a noble underling: AJAX, for example, orders him about as if he were a subaltern. He plays no great part in the action of the first half, though he has one or two pithy speeches (e.g. on HELEN, 'She's bitter to her country. Hear me, Paris./ For every false drop in her bawdy veins/A Grecian's life hath sunk; for every scruple/Of her contaminated carrion weight/A Trojan hath been slain'). When he goes to fetch CRESSIDA from Troy he is stiffly polite with both her and TROILUS, and speaks only two words ('Even she') in the scene where the Greek commanders kiss her in turn, welcoming her to the camp. The surprise is therefore all the greater when we next see him flirting with Cressida and deftly, wittily seducing Troilus' love-token (an embroidered sleeve) from her. (*Diomedes*: 'What did you swear you would bestow on me?' *Cressida*: 'I prithee, do not hold me to mine oath./Bid me do anything but that, sweet Greek.' *Diomedes*: 'Good night'... *Cressida*: 'Diomed — ' *Diomedes*: 'No, no, goodnight. I'll be your fool no more...' *Cressida*: 'Hark, one word in your ear...') After the seduction he slips out of the main action again, and we see him only once more, being challenged and chased on the battlefield by Troilus. The part is small, and Diomedes' low standing among the Greek lords is vital to Shakespeare's purpose – for if Cressida were really as unflawed and as innocent as Troilus thought her, how could she ever betray him for someone so insignificant?

Dion *(The Winter's Tale): see* **Cleomenes and Dion**

Dionzya *(Pericles)*
Wife of CLEON and fellow-governor of Tarsus. At first she is noble and regal, grateful to PERICLES for ending the famine, and glad to look after his baby daughter MARINA. But when Marina grows up and overshadows her own daughter Philoten, she turns into the archetypal wicked stepmother of pantomime, and orders LEONINE to murder Marina. In a later scene we see Dionyza robustly rejecting Cleon's guilt-feelings over this supposed crime; later still, we hear that she is dead.

Doctor (English) *(Macbeth)*
Announces to MALCOLM and MACDUFF, who are at the English court, that the saintly English king is about to come forth and touch sufferers from the 'king's evil', since 'at his touch,/Such sanctity hath heaven giv'n his hand,/They presently amend'.

Doctor (Scottish) *(Macbeth)*
Watches LADY MACBETH during the sleep-walking scene, and then says that he can do nothing for her, since 'More needs she the divine than the physician'. He subsequently discusses her illness with MACBETH.

Doctor *(King Lear)*
Servant of CORDELIA who organises LEAR's cure from insanity. Professional kindness is his main characteristic.

Doctor *(The Two Noble Kinsmen)*
Kindly but pedantic, he questions the JAILER at length about the
symptoms of his DAUGHTER's madness, and then proposes the scheme
to cure her by letting the WOOER disguise himself as PALAMON and
make love to her in a darkened room.

Dogberry *(Much Ado about Nothing)*
Constable in charge of the WATCHMEN. Like most farce-scripts, the
lines of his scenes give only a shadow of the complete performance,
with little indication of the physical knockabout and ensemble-timing
which any competent group of actors might bring to them. In speech
Dogberry is pompous, garrulous and self-important, larding his lines
with long words which usually mean the exact opposite of what he
intends (e.g. 'Our watch, sir, have indeed comprehended two
auspicious persons...'). This is funny enough, in an obvious way; but
what makes the part glorious is endearing personality, not satire.
Dogberry's gentle bumbling (e.g. in the scene where he instructs the
Watchmen in their duties, among which are 'to make no noise in the
streets, for, for the watch to babble and talk is most tolerable and not to
be endured') is in the same class as SHALLOW's in *Henry IV Part Two*,
and the warmth of its depiction allows him, as a character, to transcend
the farcical circumstances in which he operates.

Dolabella *(Antony and Cleopatra)*
OCTAVIUS' ally. Left to take CLEOPATRA to Syria after OCTAVIUS leaves,
he gives her a moment alone with her maids in the monument, and
returns to find her dead.

Don John *(Much Ado about Nothing)*
DON PEDRO's brother. Defeated by him in battle and then insultingly
pardoned, he broods on revenge – 'I had rather be a canker in a hedge
than a rose in his grace' – and in particular plots to cross CLAUDIO, the
'young start-up' who 'hath all the glory of my overthrow'. He spends
his time thereafter feeding Don Pedro and Claudio lies, and his
plausible, hail-brother-well-met manner in those scenes contrasts with
his beetlebrowed malignity with BORACHIO. He is a straightforward
melodramatic villain and disappears from the play, unmourned, as soon
as he is discredited.

Don Pedro *(Much Ado about Nothing)*
Prince of Aragon whose visit to LEONATO begins the play. He is, on the
surface, a dignified and lordly aristocrat: BEATRICE, punning on
'Seville', calls him 'civil as an orange', and his public manner bears the
description out. At the masked ball he pretends to be CLAUDIO and
pays court to HERO on his friend's behalf. He is one of the few people in
the play able to trade witticisms with BENEDICK on equal terms, but is
quite happy to take part in the trick against him, persuading him to
love Beatrice by letting him overhear news that Beatrice is in love with
him. When he is told of the possibility of Hero's unfaithfulness, he

turns against her as abruptly as he decided earlier to woo her for
Claudio, and when unfaithfulness is proved and the wedding is
cancelled he is concerned above all for his own reputation. ('I stand
dishonour'd, that have gone about/To link my dear friend with a
common stale'.) Shakespeare allows him to make no subsequent
amends or apologies: like Claudio, he is paid for his coldness by being
tricked, in turn, by Leonato (at the second marriage, to the 'niece' who
turns out to be Hero in a mask), and in the rejoicing which ends the
play he speaks only one non-committal line. He is a shallow character: a
weathercock blown by the winds of his own vanity, too insignificant
(for all his rank) to merit our sympathy or our dislike.

Donalbain (*Macbeth*)
Younger son of king DUNCAN. He escapes to Ireland soon after his
father's murder, and disappears from the play.

Dorcas (*The Winter's Tale*)
Singer (in a catch with MOPSA and AUTOLYCUS) who also has a few lines
as a cheerful country wench.

Dorset, Thomas Grey, Marquess of (*Richard III*)
Elder son of Queen ELIZABETH. He takes his mother's part in her
argument with MARGARET, saying things like 'Dispute not with her: she
is lunatic', and being put down (by Margaret) with remarks like 'Peace,
master marquis. You are malapert.' But apart from this youthful
impetuousness, and his concern for his mother's ill-treatment by
RICHARD, he is given little character. He is sent to join RICHMOND's
rebellion, and is one of his retinue at Bosworth.

Douglas, Archibald, Earl of (*Henry IV Part One*)
Fiery Scots nobleman, a rebel against King HENRY. Rants about on the
battlefield of Shrewsbury, killing anyone he takes for the king; duels
with FALSTAFF (who fakes death); is arrested after Shrewsbury, and is
set free because of his chivalry and valour.

Dromio I (Dromio of Syracuse) (*The Comedy of Errors*)
His master ANTIPHOLUS I describes this Dromio as 'a trusty villain...
that very oft/When I am dull with care and melancholy/Lightens my
humour with his merry jests' – and this sums him up exactly. He is as
full of verbal caperings as a court jester, and eagerly joins his master in
wit-contests (e.g. a discussion about whether hairy men are more
cheerful than bald men, despite the hairs which fall into their porridge,
or the geographical discussion of fat Nell's body, big enough to be a
globe of the whole round world). He shares with Shakespeare's more
substantial clowns a delight in language, a love of words for their own
sake which results in waterfalls of inconsequential verbiage. Even
beatings provoke word-showers, and not even reporting his master's
arrest restrains his tongue. ('A devil in an everlasting garment hath
him:/One whose hard heart is button'd up with steel,/A fiend, a fairy,

pitiless and rough...'.) Like his master, he refuses ever to take life seriously, and this ironical stance (added to the irony of being taken, almost every time he enters, for someone else) lights up the play whenever he appears.

Dromio II (Dromio of Ephesus) *(The Comedy of Errors)*
Like his twin DROMIO I, this Dromio is a joker who refuses to take anything seriously. When ANTIPHOLUS I asks, 'Where are those thousand marks you had of me?' (referring to a large sum of money just given to Dromio I to put in safe deposit), he gives the insouciant and infuriating answer, 'I have some marks of yours upon my pate,/Some of my mistress' marks upon my shoulder,/But not a thousand marks between you both'. Sent for a crow(-bar) to force entry into his master's own house he quips, 'A crow without feather, master, mean you so?/ For a fish without a fin, there's a fowl without a feather./If a crow can help us in, sirrah, we'll pluck a crow together.' His part is smaller than Dromio I's, and he is less fully characterised. But his few lines nevertheless give the actor magnificent comic scope, and in particular make him a foil for the morose self-absorption of his master ANTIPHOLUS II.

Duke *(The Merchant of Venice): see* **Venice, Duke of**

Duke *(Othello): see* **Venice, Duke of**

Duke (Senior) *(As You Like It)*
ROSALIND's father, exiled before the play begins by his brother FREDERICK. He lives in the Forest of Arden, making of it a kind of rural paradise. The Duke is a dramatic contrivance rather than a character. He is incapable of recognising his own daughter through the boy's disguise she wears, and receives word that his brother has repented and restored all his lands with about as much emotion as if he had dropped a stitch in knitting. None the less, the part is not unrewarding to play: the lines are full of measured, unflustered dignity, and the Duke is the still centre around which the fantastical events and characters of the play revolve.

Duke (Vincentio) *(Measure for Measure)*
In the long gallery of Shakespeare's absolute rulers, which stretches from RICHARD in *Richard III* to PROSPERO in *The Tempest*, the Duke is one of the most puzzling and opaque personalities of all. He proposes and disposes; he never allows any questioning of his decisions, however strange they seem; he never entertains the slightest doubt about himself. Some readers and spectators (those who see *Measure for Measure* as philosophical and serious) have been driven by his absence of morality – not so much amorality as the feeling that he is above ordinary morality altogether – into equating him with the Gods or with God, even though the only real attribute he shares with the Old Testament Jehovah is a reluctance to make personal appearances. ('I

love the people,/But do not like to stage me to their eyes....') His disguise is thus a cloak for something else, and part of the fun of seeing the play is deducing what that is. Other people, taking the play for comedy, think of the Duke as a kind of malign leprechaun, whose meddling in people's lives is more for his own entertainment than for their benefit or chastisement. In that case his disguise is undertaken chiefly for the fun of it, like the other deceptions and impersonations in the play.

The problem, if the play is taken to be about the conflict between objective and subjective morality, is that the Duke's behaviour hardly stands up to scrutiny. He is happy to prostitute an innocent woman (MARIANA) to save ISABELLA's honour, and to have an innocent man's (BARNARDINE's) head chopped off instead of CLAUDIO's; he leaves his state in ANGELO's hands as much to test Angelo as to reform laxity in others, despite the possibly dire consequences to his people; he plays cat-and-mouse with everyone he 'helps', telling Claudio to be 'absolute for death' although he knows he will not be killed, falsely letting Isabella believe that Claudio has been executed, leading LUCIO on in an ever more self-condemnatory charade, sending Angelo to 'the very block/Where Claudio stooped to death' although he knows perfectly well that he is about to reprieve him, and finally, most arbitrarily of all to modern eyes, announcing his intention of marrying Isabella without once consulting her or taking into account her feelings about virginity or her vocation to be a nun. Feline cheerfulness is his main characteristic, whether he is zestfully planning the detail of fooling Angelo with a severed head disguised as Claudio's ('O, death's a great disguiser, and you may add to it. Shave the head and tie the beard...'), or stringing all parties along in the trial-scene, letting Isabella believe that her accusations are falling on deaf ears, and at the same time sowing doubts in Angelo's mind even while reassuring him that he is safe. ('By mine honesty,/If she be mad – as I believe no other –/Her madness hath the oddest frame of sense,/Such a dependency of thing on thing,/As e'er I heard in madness....')

If the Duke were truly like Shakespeare's other absolute rulers, we might expect him to give some clue, in soliloquies, to his real thoughts and motives. In fact he speaks only one soliloquy in the whole play, and it is a piece of rhyming doggerel more like a wizard's spell than a serious dramatic speech. It begins promisingly, if we are looking for motivation – 'He who the sword of heav'n will bear/Should be as holy as severe,/Pattern in himself to know,/Grace to stand and virtue go...' – but as the speech develops, it becomes clear that he is actually talking about Angelo, proposing to punish him for lapsing from a true ruler's moral eminence. ('Twice treble shame on Angelo,/To weed my vice, and let his grow!') In the trial-scene, he claims that 'like doth quit like, and Measure still for Measure' – and so it does, for everyone else in the action but himself. Is it just our modern way to read this as hypocrisy or to see the Duke as the most morally vacuous (and therefore flawed) person in the play, and would Shakespeare's audiences, more used to 'the divine right that doth hedge a king', have felt the same way about him as a character, or cared? If *Measure for Measure* is played as a comedy, and the Duke is no more than a cheerful puppet-master pulling the strings of other people's destinies, his moral opaqueness hardly matters. But if the play is serious, a philosophical examination wedded to a lively plot, then his moral attitude, and our attitude to it, are things which need establishing from the start.

Duke of Ephesus (Solinus) *(The Comedy of Errors)*
Stern but compassionate, he allows the 'hapless' AEGEON a day to raise the bail which will prevent his execution, and in the last act, when every plot-tangle has been unravelled, he pardons him and gladly goes to the 'gossips' feast' the ABBESS calls to celebrate her reunion with her family.

Duke of Milan *(The Two Gentlemen of Verona)*
SYLVIA's father, who tricks VALENTINE into telling him of the proposed elopement and banishes him, then, when his daughter follows Valentine into exile, chases after her to forgive them both and bring about the happy ending of the play. He seems the standard heavy father of this kind of play, save once, when he sends PROTEUS to 'slander Valentine' to Sylvia. Does he know, all along, what will happen? Is his tongue, perhaps, firmly in his cheek throughout? (*Duke*: 'What might we do to make the girl forget/The love of Valentine, and love Sir Thurio?' *Proteus*: 'The best way is to slander Valentine...' *Duke*: 'Then you must undertake to slander him...')

Dull, Anthony *(Love's Labour's Lost)*
Cloddish constable, whose main role is to stand around looking vacant. At one point HOLOFERNES says to him, '*Via*, goodman Dull! Thou hast spoken no word all this while', and he springs to attention and replies, with characteristic brick-brained zeal, 'Nor understood none neither, sir'. The moon-faced loon is a stock farce character, and is all the funnier as one member of a double- or triple-act, as here, with Dull, SIR NATHANIEL and Holofernes.

Dumain, Captains (1 and 2) *(All's Well that Ends Well)*
Fellow-captains with PAROLLES in the army in Italy. Annoyed by his boasting, they pretend to be foreign soldiers, kidnap him, blindfold him and terrify him into revealing all his companions' war-dispositions to the 'enemy commander' (actually BERTRAM, whom Parolles can't see). Their bustle, and their made-up language ('Throca movousus, cargo, cargo, cargo'; 'Biblibindo chicurmurco'), give them what character they have. *See also* LORDS.

Dumaine, Lord *(Love's Labour's Lost)*
Attendant lord on FERDINAND, the most strikingly characterised after BEROWNE. He is just as self-consciously exquisite as the others – his

opening words in the play are 'My living lord, Dumaine is mortified:/ The grosser manner of these world's delights/He throws upon the gross world's baser slaves' – but he is also blunter and more acid-tongued. His love poem, for example, is not a sonnet crammed with verbal felicities, like LONGAVILLE's, but a piece of unblushing doggerel ('On a day – alack the day! –/Love, whose month is ever May,/Spied a blossom passing fair/ Playing on the wanton air...'), and his behaviour during the play of the Nine Worthies, where he takes the lead in baiting HOLOFERNES, make him seem a man interested chiefly in himself, indifferent to everyone else or their opinion. He could be played as arrogant or world-weary; he is seldom likeable. At the end of the play he is treated with well-deserved disdain by his beloved KATHARINE ('Come when the king doth to my lady come;/Then, if I have much love, I'll give you some'), and replies, with sardonic deference, 'I'll serve thee true and faithfully till then': of all the play's characters, they have changed least, and allow no warm sentiment to thaw their icy games. Disdain is Dumaine's stock-in-trade, and it is both fun to play and an excellent foil to the ecstatic gush of his companion Longaville.

Duncan (*Macbeth*)
King of Scotland. A dignified elder, stern but just. Before he has time to establish personal character, as opposed to the aura of kingship, he is murdered.

Edgar (*King Lear*)
At the beginning of the play Edgar is purehearted and remarkably credulous, as if he had reached adulthood without ever noticing that there are villains in the world. He is easy meat for EDMUND: told of GLOUCESTER's displeasure, he accepts it at once, agrees to go armed, agrees to a pretend fight, and so confirms every one of the suspicions Edmund has planted in Gloucester's mind.

At this point, when he decides to go into exile and to disguise himself as Poor Tom the lunatic, Edgar's character utterly changes. He sheds his former blandness like a coat, and becomes ironical, calculating and devious. He begins to 'perform' his life, and the swaggering success of the performance creates him as a personality. 'Poor Tom' has far better lines than Edgar ever had – 'wine I lov'd deeply, dice dearly, and in women out-paramour'd the Turk; false of heart, light of ear, bloody of

hand, hog in sloth, fox in stealth, wolf in greediness...' – and the
charade is so effective that even his own father fails to recognise him.
He wanders in a landscape of surreal horror ('through fire and through
flame, through ford and whirlpool, o'er bog and quagmire', with
'knives under his pillow, halters in his pew... ratsbane by his
porridge...'), and his madness is so convincing that we wonder quite
how much is performance and how much is real. ('The foul fiend
haunts poor Tom in the voice of a nightingale. Hopdance cries in
Tom's belly for two white herring...').

The blackness Edgar discovers in himself extends to his treatment of
his blinded father. The trick he plays on him (describing imaginary
cliffs at Dover, and letting Gloucester think he is able to leap over them
and commit suicide), despite its good intentions, is as heartless in
execution as any of Edmund's manipulation of other people, and when
he shows compassion ('O thou side-piercing sight!) it is for LEAR, not
for Gloucester at all.

Soon afterwards, having heard from the GENTLEMAN about
GONERIL's and Edmund's plot on Lear's life, he changes character once
more, and becomes a stock noble avenger, brisk, brave and loyal. His
disguises now are brief and purposeful. He pretends to be a peasant,
and kills OSWALD; he goes to ALBANY disguised as a blunt yeoman, and
gives him a letter exposing Edmund; when the HERALD announces that
Edmund will defend his honour in single combat, Edgar accepts the
challenge disguised as a man whose 'name is lost,/By treason's tooth
bare-gnawn and canker-bit' – and, as Gloucester failed to recognise him
before, so Edmund fails now to recognise either his manner or his
voice. Edgar kills his own brother – his rise means Edmund's fall as
inevitably as Edmund's rise meant his – and is at last revealed as far-
sighted and patriotic, the only man fit (in Albany's words) to 'rule in
this realm, and the gored state sustain'. After the infantile but deadly
antics of so many other people in the play, his maturity is convincing
and comforting – and so it should be, after the terrible rites of passage
we have watched him undergo.

Edmund (*King Lear*)

Edmund is central to the plot, and whenever the play's action flags he
whips it into life. His stratagems against EDGAR, GLOUCESTER, ALBANY
and REGAN are clear in intention and swift in execution; like Satan at
the start of *Paradise Lost*, he soars.

The fact is, however, that *King Lear* is not primarily a play of action.
Its concern is less with events than with their wider meaning, and this
continually thrusts Edmund, as plot-manipulator, into the background:
he sets up an action only to stand back while it and its consequences
unfold. He is a one-dimensional character, as uncomplicated as the
black-hatted villain of a cowboy film, and the lack of compromise or
scruple is more interesting than he is himself. Like RICHARD in *Richard
III*, he shares his intentions with the audience, but his soliloquies lack

Richard's saturnine irony and self-delight, and his effect on others (e.g. Gloucester or Edgar) is due less to his own mesmerism than to their goodheartedness or moral blindness; as soon as he tackles villains subtler than himself (GONERIL; Regan) he is doomed.

The shallowness of Edmund's character (as opposed to the schematic fascination of his actions) is shown by the flat effect of his recantation and death in the play's last act. Other characters shed their illusions (Gloucester) or delusions (LEAR) and so achieve moral growth; those who do not (CORNWALL, Regan, Goneril) come to spectacular bad ends. But Edmund is left lying wounded onstage through several minutes of explanation (the unravelling of the Edgar, Goneril and Kent plot-strands), and then announces baldly, 'I pant for life: some good I mean to do/Despite of mine own nature' and reveals that he has ordered CORDELIA's execution – after which he is carried offstage like an unwanted prop, and the last we hear of him is the OFFICER's announcement 'Edmund is dead, my lord'. His death is insignificant, in marked contrast to the 'lusty stealth' of his conceiving or the blatancy of his ambition ('I see the business:/Let me, if not by birth, have lands by wit').

Edward of York (Earl of March, later King Edward IV) *(Henry VI Part Three; Richard III)*

At first sight, Edward seems a character of little resonance, and his extraordinary career (alternating on the throne with HENRY like a man in a weatherhouse) belies the bland, conventional lines he speaks ('O Warwick, Warwick, that Plantagenet/Which held thee dearly as his soul's redemption/Is by the stern Lord Clifford done to death'). Whenever he is king, he is stuffily regal; whenever he is not, he is brisk and furious ('Tush, man, abodements must not now affright us'/By fair or foul means we must now enter in,/For hither will our friends repair to us').

This apparent simplicity of character, however, masks Edward's true deviousness. He is, after all, YORK's son and RICHARD's brother, and though he never tells us, as they do, in brooding soliloquies what evil he means to do, his actions are just as ruthless and just as arbitrary. He gives way to lust in the matter of marrying Lady GREY, and brushes aside talk of consequences with a brusque 'I am Edward,/Your king..., and must have my will'; he is the first to draw dagger and stab dead young EDWARD, Prince of Wales – a most unkingly act; when he is firmly on the throne and all his enemies are defeated, he bounces up and down like a child at a party, crowing 'Now what rests, but that we spend the time/With stately triumphs, mirthful comic shows,/Such as befit the pleasure of the court?/Sound drums and trumpets! Farewell sour annoy!/For here, I hope, begins our lasting joy.'

Although Edward is never a monster of evil to equal (say) Richard, his self-indulgent recklessness is presented throughout as an evil force (utterly unlike TALBOT's noble recklessness in *Henry VI Part One*); in the same way, though his irony is nowhere near as developed as Richard's, it is sufficiently clear to make us wonder if his blander remarks may not have a sinister double-edge – certainly anyone would be a fool who took at face value lines like those he speaks when WARWICK deposes him: 'What fates impose, that men must needs abide;/It boots not to resist both wind and tide'. We are also constantly reminded, at each moment of Edward's triumph, that Richard is brooding on treachery in the shadows ('I/Stay not for the love of Edward, but for the crown'), and the foreboding this sets up undermines Edward's pomp and makes his self-satisfaction seem blinkered, fragile and pathetic: he is like a lamb dancing to the abbatoir.

In *Richard III* Edward's character changes yet again: he is depicted as a sick, saintly man ('Happy, indeed, as we have spent the day./Brother, we have done deeds of charity...'), whose final words before he is helped to his deathbed are 'Ah, poor Clarence', and who arouses neither our interest nor our sympathy.

Edward, Prince of Wales (*Henry VI Part Three*)
Fiery young boy, forever showing the spirit his father HENRY lacks. ('Speak like a subject, proud ambitious York!.../Resign thy chair, and where I stand kneel thou!') He is hacked to death by all three York brothers (EDWARD, RICHARD, CLARENCE) in front of his mother MARGARET; her lament ('O Ned, sweet Ned, speak to thy mother, boy!.../Butchers and villains, bloody cannibals!/How sweet a plant have you untimely cropp'd!') is – even for her – one of the most passionate outbursts in the play.

Edward, Prince of Wales (and, briefly, Edward V) (*Richard III*)
The elder of the two Princes in the Tower, he is a spirited boy who, on arrival in London for his coronation, says sharply to his uncle RICHARD, 'I want more uncles here to welcome me', and who encourages his younger brother YORK to ask to ride on Richard's back. As the children are led to the Tower, he tells his brother not to be afraid of 'dead uncles' (i.e. CLARENCE's ghost), but to beware of living ones; later, he is one of the ghosts who taunt Richard before Bosworth. ('Let us... weigh thee down to ruin, shame and death./Thy nephews' souls bid thee despair and die!')

Egeus (*A Midsummer Night's Dream*)
HERMIA's father. Irate that she loves LYSANDER and not DEMETRIUS, he tries to get THESEUS to forbid the young people to meet. He is little more than the standard furious farce father, and he is not softened by events: Theseus has to order him to give way and permit Hermia's and Lysander's wedding.

Eglamour, Sir (*The Two Gentlemen of Verona*)
Trusty, crusty old knight who goes with SYLVIA, as her protector, to look for banished VALENTINE. He is all chivalry, but is useless in a

crisis, unable to prevent even the incompetent OUTLAWS from kidnapping her.

Elbow (*Measure for Measure*)
Dim-witted constable who spends his time in the play arresting Mistress OVERDONE and POMPEY every time they open a new bawdy-house. In speech he is a poor relation of DOGBERRY in *Much Ado about Nothing*, using pompous malapropisms which utterly confuse what he is trying to say. ('If it please your honour, I am the poor Duke's constable, and my name is Elbow. I do lean upon justice, sir, and do bring in here before your good honour two notorious benefactors.') But Dogberry is motivated by human kindness and zest for his job, whereas Elbow is fuelled by moral outrage: this makes him both a darker and a more unsympathetic character. His attempt to have FROTH imprisoned for doing some unspeakable (or at least unspoken) wrong to Elbow's pregnant wife in the bawdy-house (unless it was in the pub) is utterly frustrated by Pompey's refusal to take the matter seriously or to give clear evidence, and all he can do in the end is rage, pompously, self-importantly and pitifully but never engagingly. ('Thou seest, thou wicked varlet, now, what's come upon thee: thou'rt to continue now, thou varlet, thou'rt to continue....')

Eleanor, Duchess of Gloucester (*Henry VI Part Two*)
A haughty, unintelligent woman whose ambition for her husband drives her to traffic in witchcraft. She is arrested, boxed on the ears by Queen MARGARET, subjected to public penance and banished to the Isle of Man. Apart from her foolish pride ('Methought I sat in seat of majesty,/In the cathedral church of Westminster,/And in that chair where kings and queens are crown'd'), the most intriguing thing about her is the devotion she inspires in GLOUCESTER. Although her part in her scenes with him is to nag and fret, his response is invariably tender and affectionate, and his sad speech when he sees her in penitent's rags ('Ah, Nell... thou aimest all awry!...) sums up both his fatal love for her and the zealous incompetence which marks her character.

Elinor, Queen (*King John*)
Mother of JOHN, Richard the Lionheart and Geoffrey, grandmother of the BASTARD and of ARTHUR. She is a formidable, flint-faced Plantagenet who fights hard to inject character into John and to support his claim to the English throne (especially against CONSTANCE, with whom she has some lively verbal duels); she recognises the Bastard's true worth as soon as she sees him ('I like thee well: wilt thou forsake thy fortune... and follow me?/I am a soldier, and now bound to France'); she disappears from the action after John's first victory over the French.

Elizabeth, Queen (*Henry VI Part Three; Richard III*): *see* **Grey, Lady**

Ely, Bishop of (*Henry V*)
In the long account of HENRY's reformed nature given at the start of the

play by CANTERBURY, he needs someone to speak his lines to, and Ely serves that purpose. His one powerful linguistic flight ('The strawberry grows underneath the nettle,/And wholesome berries thrive and ripen best,/Neighboured by fruit of baser quality...') seems all the more striking because of the hollowness of his other lines.

Ely, Bishop of (John Morton) *(Richard III)*

One of RICHARD's less prominent courtiers, notable chiefly because he brings in a spectacularly unlikely stage-prop. ('Where is my lord the Duke of Gloucester?/I have sent for these strawberries'...)

Emilia *(Othello)*

IAGO's wife, a simple soul whose affection is reserved not for her husband but for her mistress DESDEMONA. As the action of the play progresses, this affection drives her to stand up to OTHELLO ('I durst, my lord, to wager she is honest/... if you think other,/Remove your thought: it doth abuse your bosom'), to a general disgust with men's treatment of women ('... have we not affections,/Desires for sport and frailty, as men have?/Then let them use us well...') and finally to hysterical fury when she discovers Iago's treachery and Othello's guilt ('Villainy, villainy, villainy!/I think upon't. I think, I smell't. O, villainy...'; 'O murderous coxcomb! What should such a fool/Do with so good a wife?') She is the most honest and unaffected person in the play, and often, as a result, seems isolated from the machinations of the other characters onstage; her death-scene, in contrast to the contrived pathos of Desdemona's, is dignified and moving, without a trace of the sentimentality she sometimes showed in life. ('What did thy song bode, lady?/Hark, canst thou hear me? I will play the swan,/And die in music. "Willow, willow, willow" – /Moor, she was chaste; she lov'd thee, cruel Moor,/So come my soul to bliss as I speak true./So, speaking as I think, I die. I die.')

Emilia *(The Two Noble Kinsmen)*

HIPPOLYTA's sister, beloved by both PALAMON and ARCITE. She is a follower of Diana, the chaste moon-goddess, and could be as chilly and emotionally bland as that suggests, the typical 'pure damsel' every knight in chivalric fairy-tale makes the goal of his earthly aspiration. But Shakespeare – the quality of Emilia's lines suggests that their author was Shakespeare rather than his collaborator Fletcher – has made her a warm, confused human being, a sister to such heroines as IMOGEN or MIRANDA, and her discovery of emotion in herself is one of the most moving events of the play. She would like to be as poised, detached and superior as her sister and brother-in-law, and her earlier scenes show her in just such a light, discussing flowers with her WOMAN and people's pedigrees with THESEUS and Hippolyta in exactly the same cool tones. But as the play develops she has to face the facts, first that she is beloved by two young men to whom she has given no encouragement, and second that she must choose one of them and by so doing condemn the other to death. In true medieval style, she is the excuse for other people's quest for honour, and in true Renaissance style, she hates it. ('I had rather see a wren hawk at a fly/Than this decision: every blow that falls/Threats a bare life, each stroke laments the place/Whereon it falls...') The only emotional discovery she fails to make in the play – and given the circumstances of the plot, it would be hard to imagine things otherwise – is true love. In a more complex drama, Shakespeare might have given her desperate love for Palamon, cheated and frustrated until the very last moment; as it is, he (or Fletcher) checks this impulse, and Emilia is handed from cousin to cousin without revealing any more personal feeling than routine admiration. ('Thou art a right good man,' she says to Arcite on his deathbed, 'and while I live/This day I give to tears'.) The weakness of this particular 'happy ending' destroys Emilia's character before it can fully develop – a major disappointment, since she is otherwise the most interesting and most sensitively drawn person in the play.

Emilia (*The Winter's Tale*): *see* **Ladies**

Enobarbus, Caius Domitius (*Antony and Cleopatra*)
ANTONY's friend and second-in-command. He is a long-serving soldier, a plain man dazzled by Antony's personality. At first he shares Antony's delight at the luxury of Egypt and the beauty of CLEOPATRA ('The barge she sat on, like a burnish'd throne...'), but as the love affair proceeds and saps Antony's vitality for war, he turns away from him and eventually deserts to OCTAVIUS. His head tells him he is right (he says of Antony 'Sir, sir, thou art so leaky/That we must leave thee to thy sinking...', and of Octavius ''Tis better playing with a lion's whelp/Than with an old one dying'); but his heart is broken, and when Antony sends all his treasure after him he is utterly mortified ('I am alone the villain of the earth,/And feel I am so most'), and dies of grief. The head-and-heart conflict in his character mirrors Antony's, and an identical vacillation between love and honour destroys him; the way in which his leathery cynicism keeps warming into emotion, and his no-nonsense prose is replaced each time by lines of melting poetry, makes his part, though small, affecting to watch and satisfying to play.

Eros (*Antony and Cleopatra*)
ANTONY's slave who commits suicide rather than obey Antony's order to murder him.

Erpingham, Sir Thomas (*Henry V*)
A good old knight, the salt of the earth, treated with respect by everyone including HENRY. He lends Henry his cloak for the king's anonymous visiting of the soldiers on the eve of Agincourt. Elderly dignity and unhesitating loyalty are his character traits.

Escalus (*Measure for Measure*)
Good old lord, assistant to ANGELO in the DUKE's absence. He is

morally more indulgent than Angelo, but weaker-willed, and his objections to Angelo's harshness seldom amount to more than indignant questions. He rages briefly against the disguised Duke ('Why, thou unreverend and unhallow'd friar,/Is't not enough that thou hast suborn'd these women/To accuse this worthy man...? We'll touse you/ Joint from joint...'), but as soon as the Duke reveals his true identity he relapses into subservience.

Escalus *(Romeo and Juliet)*
Prince of Verona, who tries vainly to arbitrate in the feud between Montagues and Capulets, but is left at the end of the play with nothing to do but wring his hands ('Never was story of more woe/Than this of Juliet and her Romeo'). He is dignified, forceful and imperious, but (as suits his somewhat godlike function in the action, banishing one here, fining another there, condemning a third to death), he shows little human warmth or subtlety of character.

Escanes *(Pericles)*
As HELICANUS is PERICLES' second-in-command, so Escanes is Helicanus'. He is pleasant and honest, and his contribution to the action is minimal.

Essex, Geoffrey FitzPeter, Earl of *(King John)*
Chief Justice of England, who asks JOHN, at the start of the play, to adjudicate between Robert FAULCONBRIDGE and the BASTARD. He says three lines.

Euphronius *(Antony and Cleopatra)*
ANTONY's schoolmaster, sent to ask OCTAVIUS to allow him (Antony) to live in Egypt, or failing that 'to let him breathe between the heavens and earth,/A private man in Athens'. His requests fall on deaf ears.

Evans, Sir Hugh *(The Merry Wives of Windsor)*
One of Queen Elizabeth's real-life courtiers (her sergeant-at-arms) was a Welshman called Lewis Lloyd, a classical scholar fond of larding his speech with Latin words and allusions, and with a fine, bardic way with the English language. While no Shakespeare character is wholly based on him, his manner of speech seems to have affected two creations in particular, the turkey-cock FLUELLEN of *Henry V* and the farcical parson-schoolmaster Evans of this play. Evans is a kindly man, full of affability towards the young (e.g. to the boy William PAGE), and hail-fellow-well-met with adults. Even when he is challenged to a duel by the ridiculous, fantastical CAIUS, his good humour is hardly dented. His equability is nicely balanced by his horrendous mutilation of the English language, of which, in FALSTAFF's phrase, he 'makes fritters'. Evans' scenes with Caius are particularly bloodthirsty butcherings of language, stage Welshness battling stage Frenchness, and spoken English losing every bout.

Exeter, Duke of *(Henry V; Henry VI Part One)*
The king's uncle in *Henry V*, he plays a characterless but important nobleman's part, arresting the conspirators CAMBRIDGE, SCROOP and GRAY and acting as messenger to the French court. He movingly describes YORK's and SUFFOLK's deaths at Agincourt. In *Henry VI Part One*, as an elder statesman (the king's great-uncle), he bemoans the effects on the country of the dissension between GLOUCESTER and WINCHESTER, and repeatedly refers to prophecies, remarks and gloomy asides made in his hearing by Richard II and Henry V. Apart from this doddery political pessimism, he makes little contribution to the action.

Exeter, Henry Holland, Duke of *(Henry VI Part Three)*
Lancastrian, active in support of Queen MARGARET and HENRY Prince of Wales. He speaks less than a dozen lines.

Exton, Sir Piers *(Richard II)*
Mistaking BOLINGBROKE's words 'Have I no friend will rid me of this living fear?' as an encouragement to murder RICHARD, Exton rushes to Pomfret Castle and does the deed. His mistake about a matter so crucial to Bolingbroke's peace of mind makes him momentarily interesting, and the murder is the liveliest piece of physical action in the play.

Fabian *(Twelfth Night)*
One of Olivia's upper servants, perhaps a chief groom or head footman, who spends his time carousing with Sir Toby BELCH, FESTE and the others, and plotting with MARIA against MALVOLIO. He is a jovial, whimsical presence in most of the comic scenes, but speaks only a handful of lines and has no real character.

Fairies *(A Midsummer Night's Dream)*
There is a whole troop of them, TITANIA's servants, and they sing, dance and make merry throughout the play. Four of them, Cobweb, Peaseblossom, Moth and Mustardseed, bow ceremoniously to BOTTOM after his transformation, and delight him with their courtesy. In Shakespeare's time – as in the magical opera Benjamin Britten made of the play – the parts of the fairies were probably played by small boys, with the mixture of innocence and devilment that implies: the group who entertain Bottom, for example, are knowing in a most unangelic way.

Falstaff (*Henry IV Parts One and Two; The Merry Wives of Windsor;*
death movingly described in *Henry V*)

When he wrote *Henry IV*, one of Shakespeare's aims was to show the
education of a prince, his growth from undisciplined youth to the
measured, self-controlled dignity he would need as king. (This idea
chimes with a favourite theme of Shakespeare's 'history' plays, the
problems of balancing individual freedom against the claims of ordered
society.) To symbolise the unruly, self-indulgent society HENRY grows
up in, Shakespeare gives him headquarters in a tavern and a band of
low-life friends (drunk, ham actor, thief) led by the immoral, enormous
knight Sir John Falstaff. Falstaff was modelled on a real person (just as
Henry was modelled on the real Henry V – and about as true to life),
but he is also a splendid reincarnation of the Bragging Soldier of Roman
comedy and the Lord of Misrule from the Christmas festivities of
Shakespeare's youth, with an equal zest for earthly pleasures and an
equal ability to turn every occasion to his own advantage. (At the battle
of Shrewsbury he tries to claim credit for killing HOTSPUR; he invents
an army to embezzle the money for clothing and feeding it; when he is
beaten up in a highway robbery that goes wrong, he tells the story
afterwards in such a way that three assailants gradually turn into
dozens, and even though he loses the fight he very nearly takes all the
credit.)

Unlike the Lord of Misrule or the Bragging Soldier, however,
Falstaff is more than a straightforward farce-character. They exist
simply to make us laugh, and their personalities have neither variety
nor depth. Falstaff, by contrast, is perfectly aware that life is a charade,
and his decision to live without morality, to enjoy every moment for
itself without fretting over causes or consequences, gives him a
viewpoint on human existence which we can share or reject but not
ignore (it is part of the play's point), and makes him seem as complex
and vulnerable a human being as any we see around us in real life. He
fascinates; despite his faults we warm to him – and the result is that the
shock at the end of *Henry IV* (when Henry, now grown into the full
dignity of kingship, brushes aside Falstaff's hopes of power and wealth
with a curt 'I know thee not, old man') is as much a hammer-blow to us
as it is to Falstaff.

Falstaff's superb speeches (including some of the most succulent lines
in Shakespeare, e.g. when asked if he wants his 'pottle of sack' with or
without eggs, 'Of itself. I'll no pullet-sperm in my brewage'), and his
extravagant, subtle personality, have made him a favourite role for
generations of performers, despite the kilos of padding required to
make him barrel-bellied. As well as in *Henry IV*, he appears in one
other Shakespeare play, the farce *The Merry Wives of Windsor*. This is
fast and funny, but the Falstaff in it *is* merely a farce-character (a fat
fool tricked by the women he thinks are in love with him), lacks all the
subtlety he has in *Henry IV*, and could ably be played by a comic rather
than a dramatic actor (Oliver Hardy would have been superb).

Nonetheless, *The Merry Wives of Windsor* is one of the best-constructed farces in the business, and if *Henry IV* didn't exist to show us Falstaff's true character, we'd think his part in it a masterpiece.

Fang *(Henry IV Part Two)*
One of the law-officers brought by Mistress Quickly to arrest FALSTAFF. He fails.

Fastolfe, Sir John *(Henry VI Part One)*
Cowardly knight who leaves TALBOT to his fate at the battle of Patay – and would indeed, he says, abandon 'all the Talbots in the world to save my life'. Later, at HENRY's coronation, he brings a letter from BURGUNDY and tries to ingratiate himself with the king, but is publicly disgraced by Talbot, who strips off his garter insignia. Said to be the origin of FALSTAFF, but of no other interest – and even investigating that is like looking at an acorn and imagining an oak.

Father that hath kill'd his son *(Henry VI Part Three)*
Counterpart to the SON THAT HATH KILL'D HIS FATHER, notable for the quality of the lines he speaks ('What stratagems! How fell, how butcherly,/Erroneous, mutinous and unnatural/This deadly quarrel daily doth beget').

Faulconbridge, Lady *(King John)*
Mother of Robert FAULCONBRIDGE and the BASTARD. She is dignified and self-possessed, even when admitting adultery ('King Richard Coeur-de-Lion was thy father:/By long and vehement suit I was seduced/To make room for him in my husband's bed'); but she is a plot-contrivance only, a cipher, and makes little impression on the play.

Faulconbridge, Philip *(King John): see* **Bastard**

Faulconbridge, Robert *(King John)*
The BASTARD's bewildered brother, who hales him before the king claiming that he is trying to steal his lands. For his pains he keeps the lands, but sees the Bastard knighted and made the king's trusted familiar. The Bastard characterises him as 'a half-fac'd groat', and there is nothing in his handful of lines to suggest otherwise.

Feeble, Francis *(Henry IV Part Two)*
A woman's tailor, Feeble is the only one of FALSTAFF's tatterdemalion army recruits to show any zeal to fight.

Fenton *(The Merry Wives of Windsor)*
Willowy young gentleman who steals Anne PAGE from under her parents' noses. He is the standard young lover of farce, a handsome nonentity, and he is best characterised in the HOST's enthusiastic (not to say over-the-top) description: 'He capers, he dances, he has eyes of youth, he writes verses, he speaks holiday, he smells April and May...'

Ferdinand *(The Tempest)*
ALONSO's son, who falls in love with MIRANDA. He is an upright,
honest youth, tainted by none of his father's viciousness, and has no
need of the moral healing of PROSPERO's magic island; accordingly,
Prospero tests and confirms his love for Miranda instead of perplexing
him.

Ferdinand, King of Navarre *(Love's Labour's Lost)*
There is little to distinguish Ferdinand from the other young men
whose decision to make Navarre 'the wonder of the world' by turning
their court into 'a little Academe' is as deliciously doomed to failure as
it is ambitious. He is a well-mannered, exquisitely dressed adolescent
prince, proud of his new adulthood and utterly unsure of himself. The
main sign we are given of his authority is in the deference shown him
by others. In the final scene, when the tables are turned and the
PRINCESS and her companions start calling the amatory tune, he retreats
into a courteous but tongue-tied regality.

Feste (Fool) *(Twelfth Night)*
Feste is a bored, sad man in a kind of dazed shock at the follies of the
human race. Like all Shakespeare's Fools, he is simultaneously
liberated and cursed by his reputation for never taking anything
seriously, since his apparent frivolity – MALVOLIO contemptuously
dismisses him and his companions as 'the lighter people' – masks
agonising sensitivity to the misery of life. In Feste's case the mask is,
literally, 'playing the fool', and some of his dialogue (e.g. his sc   ~s
with VIOLA dressed as a boy) consists of humourless puns and \   .n
jokes deliberately stripped of heart or point. He seems the standard
broken-hearted clown or exhausted comedian: the mouth endlessly
grins and jokes, as if it had a motor of its own, but the eyes are dead.
He prefers to stand aside from events, and when he is drawn into them
(by Malvolio's cruelty) he plays a callous and unrelenting part,
manipulating other people like a puppeteer.

   If that were all, Feste would be a repellent character and *Twelfth
Night* would be grim and dark. But the play was written for a festive
occasion, and Shakespeare's intention was not bilious farce but sad-
happy, autumnal comedy. He achieves this atmosphere miraculously,
and in passing deepens Feste's character, by letting us see and share his
heartbreak at the world. Three times, Feste interrupts the play's action
to sing songs, and though 'O Mistress Mine,' 'Come Away Death' and
'When That I Was and a Little Tiny Boy' (the closing moments of the
show) have nothing to do with the plot, they are crucial to establishing
atmosphere. To change the mood of a play so simply is a feat of
dramatic writing – and to bring it off in performance needs acting skill
of the same order, and makes Feste one of the most challenging, though
briefest, of Shakespeare's major roles.

First Lord (*The Winter's Tale*)
Courtier who tries doggedly but unsuccessfully to head off LEONTES'
rage against POLIXENES and HERMIONE. In a later, characterless
appearance, he brings news of Polixenes' return to Sicilia, sixteen years
on, to look for FLORIZEL.

First Officer (*Othello*)
Leader of the Watch, who comes with BRABANTIO to arrest OTHELLO.

First Player (*Hamlet*)
Good-naturedly, the First Player lets HAMLET quote one of his own best
speeches at him, agrees to add a dumb-show and a new speech to the
play he is about to perform, and listens patiently to directions on how
to perform it. ('Speak the speech, I pray you...') We see his
barnstorming style at full tilt in the earlier scene, when he describes
Priam fighting hopelessly for Troy – 'Anon he finds him,/Striking too
short at Greeks' – and he tones it down only marginally for his
appearance in Hamlet's play. ('Full thirty times hath Phoebus' cart
gone round/Neptune's salt wash and Tellus' orbéd ground....') In
short, if he and his company take innocent pleasure in sending up their
employers ('Follow that lord, and look you mock him not', Hamlet
sternly advises them, as if they are naughty children), Shakespeare
takes just as much pleasure in sending them up for us. There is
powerful tension between the in-jokes about acting and the horror of
what is being enacted, and the First Player's hamminess also throws
light on the sort of performances (of madness; of remorse; of honesty)
Hamlet, CLAUDIUS and GERTRUDE are giving in the 'real life' outside
the Players' play.

First Player (*The Taming of the Shrew*)
In the Induction, he brings his troupe to the LORD's house and agrees
to perform for SLY.

Fishermen (*Pericles*)
There are three of them, the Master and his men Pilch and
Patchbreech. They work at Pentapolis, and rescue first PERICLES and
then his rusty armour from the sea. They have one scene, a mixture of
clownish comedy and homespun wisdom. (*Third Fisherman*: 'Master, I
marvel how the fishes live in the sea.' *First Fisherman*: 'Why, as men do
a-land: the great ones eat up the little ones.')

Fitzwater, Lord (*Richard II*)
Fitzwater squares up to AUMERLE and SURREY in the Parliament scene,
like a puppy snapping at lions. This is his moment; his only other
appearance in the play (telling BOLINGBROKE of victory over the rebels
at Oxford) is negligible.

Flaminius *(Timon of Athens): see* **Servants**

Flavius *(Julius Caesar)*
One of the tribunes of the people who appear at the opening of the play, trying to quieten the rebellious CITIZENS, and who are later 'put to silence' for removing scarves from CAESAR's statues. Apart from briskness, he has no character.

Flavius *(Timon of Athens)*
TIMON's steward. He is distressed by his master's career towards ruin – 'I bleed inwardly for my lord' – but is unable to get his attention for long enough to stop it. After Timon's exile, he goes to visit him – 'O you gods,/Is yond despis'd and ruinous man my lord?' – and is given the gold Timon has dug up, on the bleak condition that he hate and despise the human race. Later, he brings the SENATORS to try to persuade Timon back to Athens. For all that his part is small, his loyalty and sincerity light up the play.

Fleance *(Macbeth)*
BANQUO's son, a child. In both of his appearances he carries a torch to light his father's way, the first time on the battlements, the second time in the palace park, where they meet the MURDERERS. He says only one line.

Florizel *(The Winter's Tale)*
Handsome young prince who falls in love with PERDITA and elopes with her after his father POLIXENES forbids the match. He is like the principal boy in pantomime, and the chief feature of his role is the ringing, heroic rhetoric he has to speak. (Proposing to Perdita before his disguised father, for example, he says, 'O hear me breathe my life/Before this ancient sir, who, it should seem,/Hath sometime lov'd! I take thy hand, this hand,/As soft as dove's down and as white as it,/Or Ethiopian's tooth, or the fann'd snow/That's bolted by the northern blasts twice over.')

Fluellen *(Henry V)*
Swaggering turkey-cock Welshman, whose prickly pride in his nationality is matched only by his fantastical gobbling of the English language. ('I'll assure you, 'a uttered as prave worts at the pridge as you shall see in a summer's day. But it is very well; what he has spoke to me, that is well I warrant you, when time is serve...') His sound and fury could be there merely for laughs (e.g. when he quarrels with MACMORRIS, or forces PISTOL to eat his leek); but he is treated with cordial respect by HENRY, shows bravery in the fighting, and fleshes his windy rhetoric with genuine humanity and dignity (e.g. at the end of the scene with WILLIAMS, when he offers him a shilling and counters Williams' indignant refusal with 'It is with a good will; I can tell you, it will serve you to mend your shoes. Come, wherefore should you be so pashful? Your shoes is not so good. 'Tis a good shilling I warrant you,

or I will change it.').

Flute, Francis *(A Midsummer Night's Dream)*

Athenian bellows-mender. He is cast to play the heroine Thisbe in QUINCE's play, and finds it an embarrassing and awkward task. This is because he is a self-conscious youth – 'Nay, faith, let me not play a woman' he says; 'I have a beard coming' – but his gawkiness greatly enhances both his portrayal of hapless Thisbe and his (few) lines in the rehearsal-scenes.

Fool *(King Lear)*

Shakespeare wrote this part for Robert Armin, who had previously created the roles of FESTE in *Twelfth Night* and TOUCHSTONE in *As You Like It*. At the time of *King Lear* Armin was in his mid-thirties, presumably at the peak of his powers and as well-known to admirers of Shakespeare's acting-company as a famous comedian is to his audience today. This fame significantly affects the playing-style of comic parts (far more than actors' fame affects tragic parts, where the performers' personalities disappear into the roles they play), and a playwright can use the audience's expectation, confirming it or confounding it by giving the actor lines 'against type'. But whichever line Shakespeare took, the part of the Fool in his theatre had a resonance for the audience it is hard to recapture today, unless we imagine what one of this century's more distinctive comic actors (Zero Mostel? Jack Lemmon? Stan Laurel?) might have brought to it.

This ambiguity in performance is matched by scholarly confusion over what exactly the Fool is in the play to do. He is present only in the first half of the play (until LEAR is rescued and returned to sanity); after he disappears he is never again mentioned, unless Lear's remark 'And my poor fool is hang'd. No, no, no life!/Why should a dog, a horse, a rat have life,/And thou no breath at all?...' refers to him and not to CORDELIA, over whose body it is spoken. This disappearance has led to scholarly theory that he is some kind of *alter ego* for Lear, a walking conscience, and that when Lear regains his sanity he has no more need of him. Certainly the Fool constantly harps on Lear's foolish behaviour towards his daughters (*Fool*: 'Canst tell how an oyster makes his shell?' *Lear*: 'No'. *Fool*: 'Nor I neither. But I can tell why a snail has a house.' *Lear*: 'Why?' *Fool*: 'Why, to put his head in, not to give it away to his daughters and leave his horns without a case...'); equally, he tries his best to persuade Lear to shelter from the storm. But as soon as he fails, he reverts to a black, affectionless humour which has less to do with conscience than with the apocalyptic, Bosch-like desolation also tenanted by 'Poor Tom'. (*Lear*: 'O me, my heart, my rising heart, but down!' *Fool*: 'Cry to it, nuncle, as the cockney did to the eels when she put 'em 'i the paste alive. She knapp'd them 'o the coxcombs with a stick and cried, "Down, wantons, down!" 'Twas her brother that, in pure kindness to his horse, butter'd his hay.')

The closeness of the Fool's relationship to Lear bars him from intimacy with others. He spars with KENT, and his 'mad' scenes with the disguised EDGAR are more like contests of extravagant images than true dialogue. Lear's daughters and their husbands ignore his existence or treat him as a kind of human pet: when Cordelia leaves for France, they tell us, he 'pines away', more like a poodle than a man. He is bold in speech, but timid in action: when he goes into the hut to escape the storm, and finds 'Poor Tom' there, he runs out shouting for help and clutches Kent's hand like a terrified child. In short, the traditional view of him (summed up in the GENTLEMAN's words to Kent, that he 'labours to outjest' Lear's 'heart-struck injuries') is only partly true. He is a forerunner of Samuel Beckett's wasted derelicts, whose only buttress against the apocalypse is their cap and bells, and who know, even as they joke, that jokes are no help at all.

Fool (*Timon of Athens*)
Briefly talks with the SERVANTS who have come to claim payment from TIMON. He is APEMANTUS' friend, but shows none of his churlish character. He speaks only two dozen lines, and they are stuffed with the standard puns and quibbles of Shakespearean jesters. ('I think no usurer but has a fool to his servant: my mistress is one and I am a fool. When men come to borrow of your master, they approach sadly and go away merry, but they enter my mistress' house merrily and go away sadly. The reason o' this ...?')

Ford, Alice (*The Merry Wives of Windsor*)
Of the two 'merry wives' she is the one taking most risks by her pretended flirting with FALSTAFF. Her husband is a neurotically jealous man, forever arriving to search the house for lovers, and she is the one making all the assignations with Falstaff. She also dreams up ways for him to get out of the house unseen – in a laundry-basket; disguised as an old woman. Though her scenes with Falstaff are farcical, she is also out to teach her husband a lesson about marital trust, and this moral edge adds sharpness and humanity to the part.

Ford, Frank (*The Merry Wives of Windsor*)
Well-to-do citizen of Windsor, whose wife is one of the women courted by FALSTAFF. Because of the antics of others (Falstaff and his company; CAIUS; EVANS), less attention is often paid to the part of Ford than it deserves. He is a superb comic creation, a man racked by suspicion and jealousy, as humourless as MALVOLIO and as conceited as BOTTOM. The tricks played on Falstaff are also tricks played on him – he fails to notice Falstaff in the laundry-basket; he does not recognise him in his disguise as the old woman of Brainford – and the joke about his own disguise as 'Master Brook' is that it is no disguise at all, merely another declaration of the same suspicious character. He would be a one-dimensional (and slightly pathetic) character, were it not for his sudden *bonhomie* in the second half of the play, when relief that his wife is honest unlocks in him all the good-humoured humanity he has

suppressed till now, and he has a movingly serious speech of reconciliation ('Pardon me, wife. Henceforth do what thou wilt;/I rather will suspect the sun with cold/Than thee with wantonness...'), joins in the final tricking of Falstaff, makes cheerful jokes with Evans and Caius, and even finds a piece of ironical, platitudinous advice for his friend PAGE to comfort him for his daughter's elopement with FENTON: 'Stand not amazed. Here is no remedy./In love the heavens themselves do guide the state./Money sways lands, but wives are sold by Fate').

Forester *(Love's Labour's Lost)*
In a tiny scene during the deer-hunt, he speaks half a dozen lines, and his purpose is as a foil to the PRINCESS's wit. She deliberately misunderstands his advice as to where she can 'make the fairest shoot' as a slur on her beauty, then gives him money, 'fair payment for foul words'. He responds with the dignity of a retainer who knows his place but never sacrifices his self-respect.

Fortinbras *(Hamlet)*
Prince of Norway who is seen leading an army in the middle of the play and who returns at the very end to bring order and dignity to the affairs of Denmark. He is a figurehead, and the formality of his lines, essential for the drama, denies him character.

France, King of *(King Lear)*
When LEAR dispossesses CORDELIA at the start of the play, her two suitors are the King of France and the Duke of BURGUNDY. Burgundy haughtily refuses to marry her without her lands, but France ardently and generously accepts her. ('Fairest Cordelia, thou art most rich, being poor,/Most choice, forsaken, and most lov'd, despis'd;/Thee and thy virtues I here seize upon.')

Francis *(Henry IV Part One)*
Overworked waiter whose out-of-breath 'Anon, anon, sir', as he dashes from customer to customer, is a source of great hilarity to Prince HAL and POINS. The scene is slapstick fun for the actor playing Francis, and is also important for establishing Hal's ruthlessness.

Francis, Friar *(Much Ado about Nothing)*
Priest who officiates at HERO's and CLAUDIO's wedding. When it is broken off and Hero faints, he suggests the stratagem that she should be claimed to be dead, to bring about remorse in Claudio. His part in the plot is similar to Friar LAURENCE's in *Romeo and Juliet*, but he says far less, and there is no hint of moral censure in the words Shakespeare gives him.

Francisca *(Measure for Measure)*
Nun who lets LUCIO in to see ISABELLA.

Francisco (*Hamlet*)
Soldier guarding the battlements at Elsinore. He is jumpy and terrified because of the GHOST.

Francisco (*The Tempest*)
ALONSO's courtier, who tries to comfort him by telling him how FERDINAND swam bravely from the shipwreck, and therefore may not be drowned.

Frederick, Duke (*As You Like It*)
Wicked usurper, who takes his brother's lands and drives him into exile. He is a clone of OLIVER, and his part changes as abruptly from bad (at the start of the play, when he banishes ROSALIND) to good (when he meets a holy hermit, sees the error of his ways, makes restitution and retires to a monastery – all without once stepping onstage). He is a one-dimensional character, and his nastiness is best played with melodramatic directness, as a foil to the humanity of everyone else.

French Gentleman (*Cymbeline*)
Friend of PHILARIO, whose politeness to POSTHUMUS (apologising for quarrelling with him on an earlier occasion, 'when each of us fell in praise of our country mistresses') encourages Posthumus to claim that IMOGEN 'holds her virtue still', and IACHIMO to wager that she doesn't and that he can prove it. The Frenchman is essential to the plot, but he says little and his only character is that of cheerful conversationalist.

Friar Peter (*Measure for Measure*)
Brings ISABELLA and MARIANA where they can petition the DUKE on his return from Vienna.

Friar Thomas (*Measure for Measure*)
Assists the DUKE in his disguise.

Friends (*The Two Noble Kinsmen*)
There are two of them. The first brings the JAILER news that he is not to be punished for failing to prevent PALAMON's escape; the second breaks to him the sad news that his DAUGHTER is mad.

Froth (*Measure for Measure*)
Foolish burgher arrested with POMPEY for doing something nameless to ELBOW's pregnant wife. As Pompey tells the tale, all Froth was actually doing was cracking prune-stones in 'a lower chair in the Bunch of Grapes', and Froth's own slow-witted contributions to the evidence ('No indeed'; 'All-hallond Eve') suggest that cracking prune-stones may have been the major intellectual achievement of his life.

Gadshill *(Henry IV Part One)*
Highwayman associate of FALSTAFF; not to be confused with the *place* Gadshill, where the robbery takes place.

Gallus, Caius Cornelius *(Antony and Cleopatra)*
OCTAVIUS' officer, commander of the soldiers sent to arrest CLEOPATRA in the monument.

Gaoler *(Henry VI Part One)*
Keeper of the dying MORTIMER in the Tower of London.

Gaoler *(The Winter's Tale)*
Somewhat unwillingly admits PAULINA to see HERMIONE in prison, and (even less willingly) allows her to smuggle baby PERDITA out.

Gaolers *(Cymbeline)*
Manacling POSTHUMUS after he is captured in battle, and preparing him for hanging next morning, the First Gaoler has half a dozen speeches of lugubrious gallows humour ('The comfort is, you shall be called to no more payments, face no more tavern-bills...'); his assistant appears onstage for the time it takes to say four words, and that's all.

Gardeners *(Richard II)*
In one of the most famous 'common-people' scenes in Shakespeare, two gardeners compare the state of the country to that of an unpruned, weed-choked garden 'swarming with caterpillars'; the chief gardener then has the task of announcing to the QUEEN (who has been eavesdropping) that her husband RICHARD is BOLINGBROKE's prisoner. Like the PORTER scene in *Macbeth* or the GRAVEDIGGER scene in *Hamlet*, this one offers the chance for a show-stealing, two-page cameo appearance; the lines are not only intriguing in themselves, but are crucial to the plot, and the whole scene is a model of playwriting expertise.

Gardiner, Stephen, Bishop of Winchester *(Henry VIII)*
Leader of CRANMER's and CROMWELL's enemies, who speaks of Cranmer with furious disgust as 'a most arch heretic, a pestilence/That doth infect the land', and whose rage with Cromwell boils over, at the heresy trial, into a shouting-match. (*Gardiner*: 'Ye are not sound'. *Cromwell*: 'Not sound?' *Gardiner*: 'Not sound, I say.' *Cromwell*: 'Would

you were half so honest...' *Gardiner*: 'I shall remember this bold
language.' *Cromwell*: 'Do./Remember your bold life, too.') As soon as
HENRY intervenes, however, Gardiner sets aside his rage and grovels.
('Dread sovereign, how much are we bound to heaven/In daily thanks,
that gave us such a prince...', and later, *Henry*: 'Embrace and love this
man.' *Gardiner*: 'With a true heart/And brother love I do it.') His
change of heart is as perfunctory as it is amazing: there is nothing to
prepare us for it in what we earlier see or know of him.

Gargrave, Sir Thomas *(Henry VI Part One)*
Companion of SALISBURY and GLANSDALE, shot dead by the MASTER-
GUNNER OF ORLEANS.

Gaunt, John of, Duke of Lancaster *(Richard II)*
In real life Gaunt appears to have been irascible, arrogant and devious.
In *Richard II* (either for propaganda purposes – Gaunt was the ultimate
ancestor of the Tudor court – or because this was what he found in his
sources) Shakespeare presents him as an elder statesman, a founding
father, the epitome of honour and pure-hearted patriotism. In the first
scene of the play he urges obedience (to father, king and chivalric code)
on his son BOLINGBROKE; in the second scene he tries to persuade his
sister that vengeance should be left not in human hands but God's; in
the third scene, after Bolingbroke's banishment, he again urges
acceptance and bids him a brusque goodbye; a few scenes later he is
shown on his death-bed, and delivers what has since become the
anthem of every knee-jerk British patriot ('This royal throne of kings,
this sceptr'd isle.../This blessed plot...'), but is in fact a denunciation
of the way England's honour has vanished (or been bought, sold and
plundered) under RICHARD. The mangling of history for dramatic
purposes is as blatant as in *Richard III* – and as there, it is so superbly
done that Shakespeare's invented character has all but obliterated
reality.

General *(Henry VI Part One)*
Proud leader of the French defenders at Bordeaux. His one speech is a
ringing denunciation of TALBOT from the battlements. ('Thou ominous
and fearful owl of death,/Our nation's terror and their bloody scourge,/
The period of thy tyranny approacheth:/On us thou cannot enter but by
death...')

Gentle Astringer *(All's Well that Ends Well)*
An astringer is a keeper of goshawks, a person of considerable position
and dignity – and, in this case, a confidant of the sport-loving KING OF
FRANCE. He carries from HELENA to the king a petition against
BERTRAM supposedly written by DIANA.

Gentleman *(Hamlet)*
Announces LAERTES' furious return from France, hot to find the
murderer of his father. One lively speech.

Gentleman *(The Two Noble Kinsmen)*
Comes to fetch EMILIA to court to watch PALAMON and ARCITE duel for
her hand. Later, takes her news of Arcite's victory.

Gentlemen *(All's Well that Ends Well)*
The two Gentlemen tell the COUNTESS about BERTRAM's departure for
Italy, and deliver to HELENA his insulting message that there is nothing
for him in France 'until he have no wife' there. Extreme courtesy marks
their lines, and is their character.

Gentlemen *(Cymbeline)*
In the play's opening scene, the First Gentleman explains the story so
far to the Second Gentleman, enlightening him (and us) at some length
about CYMBELINE's banishment of BELARIUS twenty years before, and
the subsequent stealing of his two infant sons. The Gentlemen are here
to give information, and need no character; but at least during their
scene it is absolutely clear what is going on – the last time, cynics might
add, that could be claimed in this most labyrinthine play.

Gentlemen *(Henry VI Part Two)*
Captives of the pirates alongside SUFFOLK, the two of them bargain
cravenly about ransom and promise 'to write home for it straight'.

Gentlemen *(Henry VIII)*
In their first scene, the First Gentleman describes to the Second
Gentleman every detail of BUCKINGHAM's treason-trial, and they reflect
gloomily together on the contrast between the unpopular, triumphant
WOLSEY and the popular, doomed Buckingham. In their second scene
they watch, and commentate on, Anne BULLEN's coronation procession,
and the Third Gentleman conveniently arrives to describe events inside
the cathedral, out of our sight. In both scenes the Gentlemen are a
brisk, jolly and excited chorus: for all their forebodings about Wolsey,
they think that HENRY is the best of all possible kings and that his
England is the ideal place to live. A fourth, characterless Gentleman,
not part of this group, has a walk-on part to announce to Queen
KATHARINE the arrival of Wolsey and CAMPEIUS.

Gentlemen *(King Lear)*
One gentleman tells KENT that LEAR is wandering in the storm with
only the FOOL for company, and later seeks out Lear, has him taken
gently to CORDELIA, supervises his return to sanity, and keeps Kent
informed about the progress of EDMUND's and GONERIL's rebellion.
The other gentleman appears briefly in the final scene, holding the
bloody knife ('Tis hot, it smokes!') with which Goneril has killed
herself.

Gentlemen *(Measure for Measure)*
'Fantasticks' who exchange airy witticisms with LUCIO about moral
corruption and the law. They are shallow, loud and vain, and think
themselves devastatingly witty – an impression Shakespeare shatters

with every line he gives them. (*First Gentleman*: 'There's not a soldier of us all, that in the thanksgiving before meat do relish the petition that prays for peace.' *Second Gentleman*: 'I never heard any soldier dislike it.' *Lucio*: 'I believe thee, for I think thou never went where grace was said.')

Gentlemen (*Othello*)

There are four of them, companions in Cyprus of MONTANO, and their chief function is to announce the destruction of the Turkish fleet. ('News, lads! Our wars are done./The desperate tempest hath so banged the Turks,/That their designment halts: a noble ship of Venice/Hath seen a grievous wrack and sufferance/On most part of their fleet.')

Gentlemen (*Titus Andronicus*)

Their names are Publius, Sempronius, Caius and Valentine. Publius is MARCUS's son, the others are kinsmen of an unspecified sort. The first three join the shooting-party organised by Marcus, with whom they commiserate on TITUS' mental state; later, Publius, Caius and Valentine arrest DEMETRIUS and CHIRON.

Gentlemen (*The Winter's Tale*)

The three Gentlemen tell each other news of AUTOLYCUS' arrival in Sicilia with the bundle of PERDITA's baby-clothes, of the opening of the bundle and discovery of Perdita's real identity, and of the reconciliation of Perdita and LEONTES, Leontes and POLIXENES, Polixenes and FLORIZEL. Though they have plenty to say, their purpose is mainly structural – to prepare us for the suspense of the statue-awakening scene – and they have little character. The First Gentleman also appears elsewhere in the play, but simply as an announcer of comings and goings at court.

Gentlemen of Mytilene (*Pericles*)

There are a dozen gentlemen, lords and other minor characters in *Pericles*, and none has much character. The two gentlemen of Mytilene however, leap to life. They burst out of the brothel, amazed to 'have divinity preach'd there' by MARINA, and are so converted by her purity that they vow never to go back to bawdy-houses but to keep 'out of the road of rutting forever'. They have ten lines between them, and are two of the liveliest characters in the play.

Gentlewoman (*Macbeth*)

Calls the DOCTOR to witness LADY MACBETH's sleep-walking. Anxious and uncomprehending throughout her one brief scene.

George (*Henry VI Part Three*): *see* Clarence

Gertrude (Queen) (*Hamlet*)

Gertrude is a weak-willed, foolish woman hiding behind a façade of strength. She affects a distant, frosty hauteur, both in public (e.g. with ROSENCRANTZ and GUILDENSTERN) and in private (e.g. with HAMLET), and she would rather believe that Hamlet is mad than that he knows the truth. Even when Hamlet persuades her (in the closet-scene) that he is not insane, that he really saw the GHOST and really wants revenge, she agrees to cheat CLAUDIUS (by pretending that nothing has changed) rather than face him openly; OPHELIA's suicide unlocks pity in her rather than determination to set things right. She is a passive person, always the support and never the lead, and this continues right into the duel-scene, where she prefers to be a spectator rather than to influence events. Appropriately for such a useless, empty person, her death comes by a senseless accident (drinking the poison meant for Hamlet), accompanied by a line of feather-brained bravado: 'The Queen carouses to thy fortune, Hamlet'. In the context of the scene, surrounded by so many more significant events, her death has the uningratiating quality of seeming ludicrous rather than essential, and distracts us where it could have made us weep.

Ghost (*Hamlet*)

For the performer, this is one of the most rewarding cameo roles in Shakespeare. (There is a story that Shakespeare wrote it for himself.) In its first act appearances, the Ghost beckons and gibbers, and has a long scene with HAMLET telling him of its murder. ('Thus was I, sleeping, by a brother's hand/Of life, of crown, of queen, at once dispatch'd,/Cut off even in the blossoms of my sin...') In the Act Three scene between Hamlet and GERTRUDE, it reappears to Hamlet, 'to whet thy almost blunted purpose'. The part is small, and the Ghost's movements are the standard glidings, head-wagglings, beckonings and hand-wringings of melodrama, but the poetry of the lines is exceptional, and makes it one of the most dignified and moving spectres in drama.

Ghosts (*Cymbeline*)

After POSTHUMUS is captured by the British, and as he lies in jail awaiting execution, the ghosts of his father Sicilius, his mother and his two brothers appear to him, circling round and calling on JUPITER (in ringingly rhymed verse) to come down, confirm that Posthumus is innocent and 'take off his miseries'. Jupiter does exactly what they ask, and next morning Posthumus is reprieved on the very steps of the gallows. The ghosts are singers rather than actors, and without music their lines are as insubstantial as they are themselves.

Ghosts (*Richard III*)

On the eve of the battle of Bosworth, RICHARD sleeps uneasily, and is visited by a cavalcade of ghosts: Prince Edward (son of Henry VI), HENRY VI, CLARENCE, RIVERS, GREY, VAUGHAN, HASTINGS, ANNE, BUCKINGHAM and the Princes from the Tower. After suitably macabre descriptions of how they died and how he caused their deaths, they urge him to 'despair and die'.

Glendower, Owen (*Henry IV Part One*)

Fiery Welsh rebel, with HOTSPUR, against King HENRY. Their quarrel over Glendower's boasting ('I can call spirits from the vasty deep.' 'Why, so can I or any other man./But will they come if you do call for them?') provides a lively dramatic scene and is a symbol of the disunity in the rebels' camp. Some authorities say that he is the same person as the CAPTAIN in *Richard II*, but there is no textual evidence one way or another.

Gloucester *(Henry VI Part Three): see* **Richard**

Gloucester, Duchess of *(Richard II)*
The Duchess (sister-in-law of John of GAUNT, great-aunt of the GLOUCESTER in *Henry IV, Henry V* and *Henry VI*) appears in one short scene only, as a grieving matriarch. Her character echoes Gaunt's: she is passionately loyal to her country (and to the Lancaster line which symbolises it), furious with RICHARD (whom she blames for her husband's murder), and a mistress of moving rhetoric. She is also fiery and implacable, in the manner of Queen MARGARET in *Richard III*, VOLUMNIA in *Coriolanus* or even LADY MACBETH. If she had not disappeared so abruptly from the play in Act II (*Servant*: 'An hour before I came, the Duchess died'), she would have had the makings of one of Shakespeare's grandest female roles, a marvellous stiffener of sinew and summoner-up of blood.

Gloucester, Earl of *(King Lear)*
Gloucester begins the play as a foolish, arrogant old man: save that he lacks dignity, he is LEAR's replica. His decision to bring EDMUND to court after nine years 'out' is as catastrophic as Lear's division of his kingdom; his eager acceptance of Edmund's insinuations against EDGAR suggests that, like Lear, he will listen only to what he wants to hear; he is so intemperate that he has only to read a letter supposedly in Edgar's hand to burst out, 'O villain, villain!... Abhorr'd villain! Unnatural, detested, brutish villain! Worse than brutish!... Abominable villain!...'. He is credulous and despairing, gloomily affected by weather signs and awful omens: 'These late eclipses in the sun and moon portend no good to us... there's son against father, the king falls from bias of nature, there's father against child. We have seen the best of our time...'

All this is interesting, but it remains undeveloped: Lear's moral education, not Gloucester's, is the substance of the play. Gloucester turns into the conventional, suffering old man of Elizabethan tragedy, and his sufferings are not noble and moving, like Lear's, but a crescendo of pathos (he is insulted, arrested, accused of treason, blinded, thrown out in a storm to be looked after by a naked lunatic, and cruelly cheated even of the suicide he craves on the cliffs at Dover): they belong more to melodrama than to tragedy. The 'double plot' of *King Lear* has been regularly criticised by scholars, on the grounds that it makes the play unwieldy if not unstageable. Gloucester's sufferings and his credulous, unsympathetic character are the problem. If he is played too grandly, with too much heroic dignity, he steals light from Lear; if he is played for pathos, his scenes can turn to farce. Balancing between these extremes makes Gloucester an interesting role to play, but it can still underwhelm the audience.

Gloucester, Humphrey, Duke of (*Henry IV Part Two; Henry V; Henry VI Parts One and Two*)
Gloucester is the fourth son of BOLINGBROKE (Henry IV) and the younger brother of Hal (Henry V). He appears very briefly in *Henry IV Part Two*, as one of the retinue of the sick king his father; he is one of the noble lords of *Henry V*, governing and fighting alongside his brother, but speaks only four lines in the whole play. In *Henry VI Parts One and Two*, by contrast, he is a major character. Because HENRY himself is so unassertive a character in these plays, the royal qualities which should by rights be his are shared among other characters. TALBOT is the military leader, unflinchingly heroic and straightforward; YORK is the schemer, the intellectual politician whose every action is designed to make his own position even more impregnable; Gloucester is the statesman, invested with all the dignity of office and with a patriotic concern for his country which should by rights be royal.

Throughout *Henry VI Part One* Gloucester's quasi-regal dignity is a matter of office only. He is Protector of England, and outranks most of the other nobles scrabbling for authority. This should put him above the political battle. But in fact he spends most of the play exchanging insults with WINCHESTER ('peel'd prelate!'; 'unreverent Gloucester!'), and indeed at one point is only stopped from physical assault by the intervention of young King Henry himself. The only difference between his ambition and Winchester's is that he claims the authority of rank and not of religion; the only difference between him and SUFFOLK is that Suffolk's route to power is the queen's bed, whereas Gloucester is happily and loyally married.

In *Henry VI Part Two* Gloucester's statesmanlike qualities have considerably – and unexplainedly – matured. Instead of flaring up at Winchester (now retitled Beaufort, and a cardinal) or at Suffolk, he weathers their insults with calm contempt; even at the moment when his downfall is certain, rather than draw his sword to fight he hurries outside, walks round the garden, then comes back with dignified, conciliatory words. (They fail.) At the start of the play, this growth in dignity, which has consolidated his own position, has also, paradoxically, united all the squabbling nobles in the kingdom – against him. They chip away at his authority, but find him armed with a quality all of them claim but none of them has, concern for England. (How he came by it is never revealed, but it is as powerful, and as moving, as WOLSEY's in *Henry VIII*.)

The weak link in Gloucester's character is his affection for his wife. He lets the Duchess of GLOUCESTER traffic with a gaggle of inept witches, and explains it by saying that she is ambitious for her husband;

his enemies use this to prise his life apart. (He is insulted by the king he has helped to rule, mocked by nobles and commoners alike, and is finally taken behind a hedge and killed.) If he had been as stick-like and undeveloped a character as once he seemed (i.e. in *Part One*), he could have weathered his wife's bizarre behaviour by shedding her for the nation's good; instead, Shakespeare gives him two scenes with her, radiant with affection, and clearly shows these emotions not only as a failing in a statesmanship but as a tragic flaw. This reversal of the usual moral judgement (that love is a 'good' emotion) may seem surprising, but in fact it fits Shakespeare's denunciation, throughout the *Henry VI* trilogy, of all the chivalric values and motives of his 'noble' characters. Not only that, but just as Gloucester's spectacular squabbling with Winchester gives *Henry VI Part One* its moments of greatest dramatic tension, so his fall from moral dignity in *Henry VI Part Two* is tragic and moving, and sets him apart, as a dramatic character, from the marionettes of the other parts.

Gobbo, Launcelot *(The Merchant of Venice)*
SHYLOCK's clownish servant, a lugubrious twin of LAUNCE in *The Two Gentlemen of Verona*. He is so intent on amusing himself that he plays a cruel practical joke on his own blind father (see Old GOBBO); he carries messages for LORENZO and JESSICA with the usual foolish additions of his kind (*Lorenzo*: 'Go in, sirrah, bid them prepare for dinner.' *Gobbo*: 'That's done, sir. They all have stomachs.'); he is described by Shylock as like an unruly pet, 'kind enough, but a huge feeder,/Snail-slow in profit, and he sleeps by day/More than the wild-cat'. His best moment is a scene with Jessica reflecting on the Biblical saw that the 'sins of the father are to be laid on the children': in it, unlike most minor Shakespearean clowns, he achieves genuine, unforced wit.

Gobbo, Old *(The Merchant of Venice)*
Launcelot GOBBO's blind, dim father, who comes up from the country to find out how his son is doing in town, and is cruelly mocked by Launcelot, who at first pretends to be a stranger and tells him his son is dead. Later, Old Gobbo gives BASSANIO 'a dish of doves' to take Launcelot out of SHYLOCK's service, and disappears from the play.

Goneril *(King Lear)*
In the somewhat schematic parcelling-out of villainous character between REGAN, Goneril and EDMUND, Goneril's share is rage, as if she were a humour rather than a character (*see* JAQUES). Thought, 'pleated cunning', underlies both Edmund's schemes and Regan's aloofness; Goneril, by contrast, rages before she speaks. She is determined to provoke a quarrel with LEAR, to give herself a pretext for throwing him out of the castle; she lusts not only for Edmund's help in conspiracy but for his body ('O the difference of man and man! To thee/A woman's services are due...'); when she thinks that Regan has stolen Edmund she poisons her and then furiously rails at her. (*Regan*: 'In my rights/By

me invested, he compeers the best.' *Goneril*: 'That were the most, if he should husband you.' *Regan*: 'Jesters do oft make prophets.' *Goneril*: 'Holla, holla!/The eye that told you so look'd but asquint'.) In the end, when all seems lost, she commits suicide (and the knife, significantly, is 'hot, it smokes'): her death is as intemperate and ill-considered as her life.

Gonzalo *(The Tempest)*
ALONSO's old retainer, he is unimaginative and unquestioning, one of those salt-of-the-earth courtiers whose trust (in Shakespeare's plays, at least) is in the office of Prince rather than in the person who fills it. Although in public he appears to be a colourless bore, and the villains he associates with steal every scene from him, he is the only person in the play – not excepting PROSPERO – to envisage the island as a Utopia for other people's benefit before his own.

Goths *(Titus Andronicus)*
LUCIUS' followers, cutthroat mercenary soldiers. Three of them speak individually; the rest mutter and cheer.

Gough, Matthew *(Henry VI Part Two)*
Leader of the loyal army fighting CADE's 'infinite numbers' at Smithfield; dies without saying a word.

Governor of Harfleur *(Henry V)*
In a single speech of measured dignity, he surrenders his town to HENRY to prevent further loss of blood.

Gower, Captain *(Henry V)*
Gower is the straight-man to FLUELLEN, and the part's chief dramatic function is to give the actor playing Fluellen a calm, unhistrionic partner to play against. Gower is a career soldier, upright, honourable and unimaginative, and the main interest in his character (apart from his restraining influence on Fluellen) is his sharp disdain for cowardly braggarts like PISTOL: 'Why, 'tis a gull, a fool, a rogue, that now and then goes to the wars, to grace himself at his return into London under the form of a soldier. And such fellows are perfect in the great commanders' names; and they will learn you by rote where services were done, at such and such a sconce, at such a breach, at such a convoy...' Regular soldiers have felt, and expressed, identical scorn for irregulars for centuries, but Gower's briskly humorous manner makes him more than a mindless blimp: the part offers character subtlety as well as a stiff upper lip.

Gower, John *(Pericles)*
Fourteenth-century poet (author of *Confessio Amantis*, in which Shakespeare found the story of PERICLES). He speaks a prologue, interludes between the acts and an epilogue, and introduces dumb-shows to demonstrate the action. His verse, by and large, is doggerel, but his explanations (particularly of passing time) are vital aids to

anyone trying to understand the plot.

Gower, Master *(Henry IV Part Two)*
Carries a message from the king to his son; speaks two lines; no
evidence to suggest that he is (or is not) the same man as GOWER in
Henry V.

Grandpré, Lord *(Henry V)*
Fire-eating French lord, 'a valiant and most expert gentleman' whose
impatience for battle leads him to pace out the ground between the
French and English on the eve of Agincourt, and then to stir his fellow-
lords to arms. ('Why do you stay so long, my lords of France?') He is
killed in the fighting.

Gratiano *(The Merchant of Venice)*
ANTONIO's friend, a wit who, as BASSANIO puts it, 'speaks an infinite
deal of nothing, more than any man in all Venice'. When he is with his
Christian friends or his beloved NERISSA, he is light-hearted and
frivolous, but in the trial scene he uses the sharpness of his tongue to
wound, and though many of his insults are justified by SHYLOCK's
savage insistence on his pound of flesh, others have a calculated, gleeful
offensiveness which is Shakespeare's invention, not a gloss by tenderer
twentieth-century sensibilities. His jeering after Portia's trick with the
drop of blood ('O upright judge! Mark, Jew! O learned judge!.../O
Jew, an upright judge, a learned judge!') is particularly unprovoked.
He is tricked by Nerissa in the matter of the ring, and tries to turn it
aside with a joke, as if his tongue is working in overdrive while his
brain catches up with the situation: this gap between speech and
thought marks his character (and makes it rather vile) throughout the
play. (*Nerissa*: Pardon me, my gentle Gratiano./For that same scrubbed
boy, the doctor's clerk,/In lieu of this, last night did lie with me.'
Gratiano: 'Why, this is like the mending of highways/In summer, when
the ways are fair enough./What, are we cuckolds ere we have deserved
it?')

Gratiano *(Othello)*
DESDEMONA's uncle, who goes to Cyprus with LODOVICO. He speaks
less than a dozen lines (of misery at DESDEMONA's death and viperish
rage against IAGO), and shows no character.

Gravediggers *(Hamlet)*
There are two of them. The second is a slack-witted assistant, with few
lines. The first is a joker, able to answer HAMLET's question 'Whose
grave's this, sirrah?' with a perky 'Mine, sir', and to spar with him
verbally like a cross-talk comedian. None the less, the part is tiny, and
(as with the PORTER in *Macbeth*) its fame, and its attraction for actors of
reputation and distinction, seem out of proportion to its scantiness.

Gray, Sir Thomas *(Henry V)*
Third conspirator (with CAMBRIDGE and SCROOP) against HENRY,

arrested at Southampton. He speaks only a few lines, and his character mirrors those of his more distinguished cronies, with whom he invariably agrees.

Green *(Richard II)*
The least vocal of RICHARD's favourites. His handful of lines is purely formal, and he is given no personality to colour them.

Gregory *(Romeo and Juliet)*
Servant of the Capulets, who joins SAMPSON in quarrelling with ABRAHAM at the start of the play. Of the two, he is the more circumspect: 'Say "better" ', he advises the hotter headed Sampson; 'Here comes one of the master's kinsmen.'

Gremio *(The Taming of the Shrew)*
Called a 'pantaloon' in the cast-list (thus prompting all the productions of the play ever seen in *commedia dell'arte* style), Gremio is a foolish dotard, in love with BIANCA and eager to do anything to win her (paying PETRUCHIO's expenses to tame KATHARINA; asking the disguised LUCENTIO to sing her praises to Bianca; trying to outbid TRANIO in an auction for her, and losing – 'Nay, I have offered all. I have no more,/ And she can have no more than all I have'.)

Grey, Lady (later Queen Elizabeth) *(Henry VI Part Three; Richard III)*
From a merry, flirtatious widow courted by EDWARD in *Henry VI Part Three*, Lady Grey is transformed in *Richard III* into a vengeful fury against her brother-in-law RICHARD ('My lord of Gloucester, I have too long borne/Your blunt upbraidings and your bitter scoffs...') then to a very Niobe of wifely sorrow ('O, who shall hinder me to wait and weep,/To chide my fortune and torment myself?'), and finally, after the murder of the Princes in the Tower, back to a Fury, uniting with her old enemy MARGARET in detestation of Richard. The part is comparatively small, but it is written throughout at the peak of young Shakespeare's invention, and its two wooing-scenes (with Edward in *Henry VI Part Three*, with Richard in *Richard III*) dwarf their surroundings.

Grey, Lord (or Sir Richard) *(Richard III)*
Younger son of Queen ELIZABETH, a young man fated to be on the periphery of events and still to die. (He is one of RICHARD's enemies.) He is beheaded at Pomfret, and his ghost is one of the throng haunting Richard at Bosworth. ('Think upon Grey, and let thy soul despair!')

Griffith *(Henry VIII)*
Gentleman-usher in attendance on the sick Queen KATHARINE in Kimbolton, who tells her movingly of the death of her enemy WOLSEY. His account of Wolsey's virtues causes her to say that she would want a chronicler like Griffith.

Grumio *(The Taming of the Shrew)*
PETRUCHIO's servant, belaboured, kicked and absolutely relied on by
his master. His greatest moments are tantalising the starving
KATHARINA by describing the succulent dishes he'd serve if only
Petruchio would let him, and browbeating the TAILOR whose dress
Petruchio dismisses as unworthy of Katharina. He is cheeky, knowing
and not too bright, a counterpart to BIONDELLO rather than to the
sophisticated, witty TRANIO.

Guards *(Antony and Cleopatra)*
Various groups of guards. One stands on watch while the god Hercules
leaves Antony. A second refuses to kill Antony after his botched
suicide. A third carries him to CLEOPATRA after his suicide attempt. Yet
another group guards Cleopatra at the end and later tells OCTAVIUS how
she has killed herself with the asp.

Guiderius *(Cymbeline)*
The elder of CYMBELINE's two long-lost sons who have been brought up
in rural simplicity in Wales. (Guiderius goes under the not-too-Welsh
name of Polydore.) He quarrels with CLOTEN and cuts off his head; he
has the same clean-living, puppyish character as his brother
ARVIRAGUS. But for all their rustic isolation, the brothers are well-
educated, and cultured: when IMOGEN goes to the forest disguised as a
boy, the three of them become soul-mates at once (pure-heartedness
speaking to pure-heartedness), and when the brothers think her/him
dead, they sing the *Dirge for Fidele* ('Fear no more the heat of the sun'),
a composition as sophisticated in construction as it is unaffected in
sentiment.

Guildenstern *(Hamlet): see* **Rosencrantz and Guildenstern**

Guildford, Sir Henry *(Henry VIII)*
Cheerful young man appointed by WOLSEY as master-of-ceremonies at
the banquet before the masked ball at which HENRY first meets Anne
BULLEN. A handful of lines and a smile.

Gurney, Peter *(King John)*
Lady FAULCONBRIDGE's servant. One line.

Haberdasher (*The Taming of the Shrew*)
Brings KATHARINA a cap, only to be told by PETRUCHIO that it was
'moulded on a porringer', that it is 'lewd and filthy' and must be taken
away at once. One line and a deal of cringing is all his part.

Hal, Prince: *see* **Henry**

Hamlet (*Hamlet*)
The challenge and the appeal of Hamlet, both the character and the
play, are that they are open-ended. The text is full of hints and
blueprints of meaning, but leaves almost every option open to the
performers – a fact which also explains the mountain of books, articles
and explanatory essays expounding this or that particular
interpretation. In fact Hamlet's tragedy is precisely that he is *not*
definite: he is unable to interpret himself even to himself.

Throughout the play, Hamlet is convinced of the need for urgent
action. But each time, before he can decide what it is, much less do it,
events ambush his intentions and redirect them. On the few occasions
when he does do something definite, it is either ill-timed and futile (e.g.
stabbing POLONIUS behind the arras) or leads to results far different
from those he had in mind: his feigning madness, for example,
designed to let him spy on CLAUDIUS and GERTRUDE for signs of guilt,
actually sets in train the sequence of disasters which overwhelms almost
everyone of consequence in the play. Because he can never decide how
to purge the rottenness in Denmark in a single, cataclysmic act, he
tinkers with it symptom by symptom, and he never sees that his own
obsessive disgust, and the moral tunnel vision it causes, are major parts
of the sickness he is trying to cure.

Hamlet is no Orestes, with a simple purgative code of death-for-
death. His intention throughout is less to kill Claudius than to make
him admit his guilt: he wants to 'catch the conscience of the king' and
make him writhe. (The ironies are that Claudius is already secretly
racked with guilt, and that none of the forms his remorse might take –
public confession? abdication? suicide? – would do anything at all to
restore Hamlet's peace of mind.)

Hamlet begins the play by straightforward, childish sulking, as if, by
what Claudius calls 'obstinate condolement' and 'peevish opposition',
he can reverse what has happened rather than make it bearable. After

he sees the GHOST, instead of taking urgent action he begins a lengthy, elaborate charade of madness (so much so that some commentators say that he is genuinely deranged). What he seems to want is to affect people as the FIRST PLAYER can, to 'make mad the guilty and appal the free,/Confound the ignorant and amaze, indeed,/The very faculties of eyes and ears'. But instead of producing moral insight in his 'audience' he merely baffles them or confirms their previous opinions: he alarms OPHELIA, distresses Gertrude, insults Polonius, ROSENCRANTZ and GUILDENSTERN and leads Claudius to plot his death. When he has the chance to stab Claudius, alone and at prayer, he draws back, claiming that he has no wish to send him straight to heaven; in fact the unacknowledged reasons are that he needs Claudius alive to feed his own obsessive hatred, and that that hatred has become his reason for existence. Before he leaves for England he persuades his mother to play a charade of watching and waiting, to pretend that everything is as it was – but he never tells her what the pretence is for, what possible good it will do. Until he leaves for England it is still possible for him to control events, if he can ever find the way; but by the time he returns – after being out of the play's action for over half an hour – he has lost the initiative entirely: LAERTES' lust for vengeance after Polonius' death, and Claudius' poisonous plotting, have set up a mechanism which must unwind inexorably to the death of all participants.

The combination in Hamlet's character of an unspecified ache for action and a shrinking back from every specific opportunity has seemed, down the years, to make him emblematic of the human condition, and has made the role endlessly reflect the way we see ourselves and what we are set in the world to do. Hamlet is not an existential coward, the kind who (like the 'poor cat i' the adage' in *Macbeth*) lets 'I dare not' wait upon 'I would'. He believes that he will act resolutely and definitively as soon as the right action presents itself, and his problem is that everything that occurs to him, from mourning to madness, from murder to suicide, offers no cure at all for the sickness of soul he feels. No wonder that he has 'lost all [his] mirth, foregone all custom of exercise', and that 'Man delights [him] not': his father's murder has thrown him out of his element, not merely in the intrigue-busy, poison-in-the-ear Danish court but in his whole moral perception of the world. He has discovered that human existence is not the way 'thinking would have it so', and he has no way either to wish away that knowledge or to cope with it.

Hamlet

On the battlements of Elsinore Castle at night, Prince Hamlet of Denmark listens to his father's Ghost telling him how he (the father) was murdered by his own brother Claudius, now king, and by his own wife Gertrude, now Claudius' queen. This story adds to Hamlet's uneasy manner: Claudius and Gertrude have already criticised him for prolonging his grief for his father well beyond the proper term. Now, to try and trap some sign of guilt in them, he pretends madness, and arranges for a group of visiting Players to perform a play depicting his father's murder. His beloved Ophelia is greatly distressed by his mental state, and is terrified when he reacts to her solicitude – knowing full well that Polonius her father and Claudius are eavesdropping on the conversation – by railing against her for a prostitute. (His cruelty towards her, and grief at her father's death, cause her, later in the play, to go mad and to drown herself.)

Claudius reacts so hysterically to the Players' performance that Hamlet is convinced of his guilt. He comes on Claudius praying, alone, but will not kill him in case his soul goes to heaven, not hell. He is summoned to his mother's bedroom, and they quarrel. Hamlet hears a rustling behind the arras, and stabs dead Polonius (who was eavesdropping behind it). His father's Ghost then appears to remind him of his purpose, and he makes Gertrude agree to go on pretending that he is mad, and to watch Claudius for signs of guilt. In the meantime, Claudius has arranged that Rosencrantz and Guildenstern will take Hamlet to England and see that he never returns alive. But this plot fails, and Hamlet returns to Denmark. Laertes, Polonius' son and Ophelia's brother, who has always distrusted Hamlet, vows vengeance for Polonius' murder, and Claudius arranges for him to fight a duel with Hamlet, poisoning the tip of his rapier and providing a cup of poisoned wine to make sure of success. Ophelia's suicide is announced, and after Hamlet has exchanged gloomy jokes at the graveside with a Gravedigger and reflected on mortality, he quarrels with Laertes and soon afterwards accepts his challenge to the duel. During the duel, Gertrude drinks the poisoned wine by mistake, and in the confusion both Laertes and Hamlet are wounded by the poisoned sword. With his last strength Hamlet stabs Claudius and makes him drink the dregs from the poisoned cup; then, after leaving the Danish throne to Fortinbras prince of Norway, he dies in the arms of his loyal friend Horatio.

Harcourt *(Henry IV Part Two)*
The messenger who brings the king news that his adversaries NORTHUMBERLAND, Lord BARDOLPH and others have been overthrown.

Hastings, Lord *(Henry VI Part Three; Richard III)*
Supporter of EDWARD. He has half a dozen characterless lines in *Henry VI Part Three*, but plays a substantial part in the plotting and counter plotting of *Richard III*. He is made one of the protectors of Queen ELIZABETH and her young sons; he is suspected of treason by RICHARD, framed by CATESBY and treacherously killed. He is dignified and patriotic, but little else.

Hecate *(Macbeth)*
In a single furious scene, Hecate scolds the WITCHES because when they

dared 'to trade and traffic with Macbeth/In riddles and affairs of death'
she was 'never call'd to bear [her] part/Or show the glory of [her] art'.
The monologue is a page long, in short rhymed lines, and scarcely
convincing either as poetry or sinisterness; it and the succeeding scene
(where LENNOX and a Lord voice forebodings about MACBETH) are
often judged the work of lesser minds than Shakespeare's, and are cut
without great loss.

Hector *(Troilus and Cressida)*

PRIAM's son, the chief war-leader of Troy. He is ACHILLES' only rival
for heroic bravery and for prickly, self-conscious pride. When he visits
the Greek camp, full as it is of men who have sworn his death, he
behaves as ceremoniously as a visiting cold-war VIP today, and matches
the Greeks' icy courtesy word for word. (*Agamemnon*: 'From heart of
very heart, great Hector, welcome.' *Hector*: 'I thank thee, most
imperious Agamemnon'.) Only Achilles' hatred goes unsugared – and
with him, too, Hector matches mood for mood. (*Achilles*: 'Tell me, you
heavens, in which part of his body/Shall I destroy him...?' *Hector*: 'It
would discredit the blest gods, proud man,/To answer such a
question.') He is equally imperious with his own family, brushing aside
his father's and wife's forebodings (that fighting Achilles will cause his
death) with an arrogance to match CAESAR's striding out to the Senate-
house on the Ides of March. Lines like 'Aeneas is afield,/And I do stand
engaged to many Greeks,/Even in the field of valour, to appear/This
morning to them' tell us more about his opinion of himself than about
his actual character.

Hector's conceit, and his misreading of pomp for heroism, continue
to the very moment of his death, when he appeals to Achilles' and his
knife-men's adherence to a shared code of honour, with predictable and
fatal results. (*Hector*: 'I am unarm'd. Forego this vantage, Greek.'
Achilles: 'Strike, fellows, strike: this is the man I seek.') In modern
times, when the cynical, despairing tone of the play is emphasised in
production, Hector's pride is often played as foolishness, a self-
defeating, self-destroying arrogance which is the reverse of heroic. In
Shakespeare's time, when pride-in-position was more fashionable and
understood, his behaviour probably seemed more rational and his
progress to death seemed both heroic and noble. Either way, assessing
his tragic stature is a crucial production-decision, since he is the only
major character in the play with any true claims on nobility, whose
faults Shakespeare does not signpost from the start.

Helen(a) *(All's Well that Ends Well)*

Helena is sometimes played as a hardnosed social climber, determined
to marry BERTRAM and keep him whatever he or anyone else thinks or
does. At the start of the play he ousts even her beloved father's memory
from her mind. ('What was he like?/I have forgot him: my imagination/
Carries no favour in't but Bertram's'.) Later, at court, she makes an
unscrupulous bargain with the (equally ruthless) KING OF FRANCE: in

return for her healing him, he will force any lord she chooses to marry her. Finally, in Italy, she bribes her way into Bertram's bed, pretending to be someone else, and so fulfils the silly conditions he has put on plans for their future happiness.

In public, this ruthless image is exactly right for Helena: with other people she is always either briskly forceful or imploring, and there is never any doubt that she will get exactly what she wants. But in private, underneath the brisk façade, she is uncertain and hesitant, desperately hurt by Bertram's indifference and tormented by love for him. ('Poor lord, is't I/That chase thee from thy country, and expose/Those tender limbs of thine to the event/Of the none-sparing war?... O you leaden messengers,/That ride upon the violent speed of fire,/Fly with false aim... do not touch my lord.') If Shakespeare had only given them a final love-scene together, a poetic reconciliation to match the reconciliation in the plot, all would indeed have ended well, and this would have been one of his sunniest, most affecting comedies. As it is, Bertram remains haughty and dour, and all the play's grace, its loveliness, is Helena's. The combination of ruthless behaviour and anxiety is rare in Shakespearean heroines (CLEOPATRA comes nearest, and in her the public and private qualities are reversed), and it makes Helena, whether we like her or loathe her, one of the most 'human' of them all.

Helen (*Cymbeline*)
IMOGEN's maidservant. She says two lines.

Helen (*Troilus and Cressida*)
MENELAUS's wife, living with PARIS in Troy. Whatever other Elizabethan playwrights may have made of her ('the face that launch'd a thousand ships...'), in her one scene in *Troilus and Cressida* she is a minor character, a pleasure-loving girl who dotes on Paris and listens enraptured while PANDARUS sings a love-song.

Helena (*A Midsummer Night's Dream*)
Young woman in love with DEMETRIUS. She is the most fully characterised of all the lovers, and has the longest part. She is tall and blonde (in contrast to short, dark HERMIA), and uses her height to droop about the stage as well as for fury. She follows Demetrius into the wood like a spaniel, only to be first scorned by him and then mocked by what she sees as a pretence of love. When she finds that LYSANDER, too, is in love with her, and that Hermia, her best friend, is apparently joining in the mockery, her patience breaks in a scene of mingled pathos ('If you have any pity, grace or manners,/You would not make me such an argument...') and rage ('O, when she's angry, she is keen and shrewd./She was a vixen when we went to school,/And though she is but little, she is fierce') which is one of the play's high-spots. Her characterisation echoes that of KATHARINA in *The Taming of the Shrew*, written a year or so earlier.

Helenus (*Troilus and Cressida*)
One of PRIAM's sons, a priest. He urges making peace with the Greeks, and his brother TROILUS rounds on him. ('You are for dreams and slumbers, brother priest./You fur your gloves with reasons...'.) His four cautious lines in the play hardly merit such a putting-down: the scene tells us more about Troilus' character than about his.

Helicanus (*Pericles*)
Honest lord left by PERICLES to govern Tyre, and happy to resign his position when Pericles returns. Later, after Pericles loses his wits, Helicanus cares for him and brings him to Mytilene where MARINA cures him. Helicanus is bluff, loyal and one-dimensional, the standard Shakespearean senior courtier.

Henry (*Henry IV Parts One and Two; Henry V*)
Although several other Shakespeare characters appear in more than one play, none shows such a consistent line of development: the three Henry plays contain a 'biography' of a sort common in novels but rare in drama, because the time-span of plays in performance works against the extended exposition of a growing personality. (This growth, in passing, makes *Henry V* less satisfying to see on its own than in relation to the two parts of *Henry IV*. Unless we know what Henry's 'upbringing' has been, some of his behaviour in *Henry V* – his cat-and-mouse game with the conspirators, his wager with WILLIAMS, his trick on FLUELLEN – can seem disconcertingly arbitrary, rather than part of the balance that makes the rest of his personality, the seedbed of his nobility.)

In *Henry IV Part One*, Henry (usually called the Prince, or Hal) is at first shown as a true disciple of FALSTAFF: a merry, unprincipled rogue, spectacularly carefree and able to make the English language turn cartwheels. Almost immediately, however, he tells us in a soliloquy that this is not his true self, that he 'will for a while uphold/ The unyok'd humour of [their] idleness,' and will one day throw off this 'loose behaviour'. This announcement gives the later Gadshill sequences (when he and POINS disguise themselves and trick Falstaff) an edge of irony: we know (as his associates do not) that Henry is playing a role, standing outside the relationship even as he takes part in it, and our pleasure in watching his separateness from his companions, his manipulation of them, makes him a far more interesting and sympathetic character than (say) Poins, who tricks and deceives without giving any reason. Shakespeare brilliantly exploits our expectation of Henry's deviousness in the scenes with his father the king, and in his behaviour with HOTSPUR: we expect not to take his words at face value, and when he turns out to be exactly as patriotic, filial and loyal as he claims he is, we are proved notably and satisfyingly wrong.

In *Henry IV Part Two* the Prince and Falstaff are all but apart throughout the play. Falstaff is in Gloucestershire raising his scarecrow army, Henry is taking the field against his father's enemies, or dealing with matters of state. He takes steps to keep away from his old mentor (*to* BARDOLPH: 'No word to your master that I am yet in town'), and his chief concern is with his father: their reconciliation (in the scene where Henry, thinking his father dead, takes up the crown) is both the climax of Henry's own character-development and the climax of the play. His rejection of Falstaff in the final scene ('I know thee not, old man') at first sight seems blunt and peremptory. But the split between them actually began long before, and was indeed signposted in *Part One*, when Falstaff (playing the part of Henry's father) says 'banish Peto, banish Bardolph, banish Poins, but for sweet Jack Falstaff, kind Jack Falstaff, true Jack Falstaff... banish not him thy Harry's company...', and Henry (playing the part of the king's dutiful son) curtly replies 'I do, I will'.

In *Henry V* (as CANTERBURY and ELY point out at the start of the play), Henry has fully grown into his role as patriot-king, and is truly regal and unhesitatingly brave and patriotic. He shows his regality by his flinty sarcasm to the AMBASSADOR who delivers the DAUPHIN's tennis balls, by his merciless condemnation of the conspirators at Southampton (contrasted with the mercy he shows to the man who insulted him when drunk), and above all by his speeches at the siege of Harfleur ('Once more unto the breach, dear friends') and on the eve of Agincourt (the Crispin's Day speech). But we are consistently shown that this is more than just pomp or pageantry. The heart of the play is not in Henry's battle-speeches, however glorious, but in the scenes with WILLIAMS and the other soldiers before Agincourt, and in his wooing-scene with KATHARINE which ends the play. In the first, he appears disguised to the others, and then (in a fine soliloquy) strips his inner self naked to the audience, showing that the king is just as mortal as other mortals are; in the wooing-scene he affects gaucheness and tongue-tiedness, and we (and Katharine) know perfectly well that this is flirting, a ploy. Throughout his life Henry has delighted in tricks, games, dissembling and disguise, and these two scenes now show how such levity can be used for honest, sincere purposes, a very far cry from the heartless self-indulgence of Falstaff and his band of 'irregular humorists'.

Henry (*Henry VIII*)

Henry is more the play's figurehead than its leading character: his deeds and wishes determine the action, and his presence shadows every scene, but he himself is cardboard. From his courtiers' descriptions he appears autocratic but charming, sly but soft-spoken, capricious but charismatic – and there is never a hint of these qualities in the lines he speaks. It is as if his personality, like the aura of regality which surrounds him, is a conjuring trick, an illusion which works for everyone because no one (not even KATHARINE, not even BUCKINGHAM, not even WOLSEY) ever questions it. We never see Henry in domestic scenes (e.g. wooing Anne BULLEN), but always in full royal formality. The only moments when he shows anything like ordinary human emotion are when he curtly dismisses NORFOLK and SUFFOLK so that he can talk to Wolsey ('We are busy. Go!'), and when he rounds on the council who have been trying to condemn CRANMER for heresy. ('I had thought I had men of some understanding/And wisdom in my council, but I find none./Was it discretion, lords, to let this man,/This good man – few of you deserve that title – /This honest man, wait like a lousy footboy/At chamber door?...') The illusion works in the theatre, too. Gorgeously dressed, grandly spoken, Henry is like a Holbein portrait come to (stiff) life – exactly what the pageantry of his parts of the play requires.

Henry IV: *see* **Bolingbroke**

Henry IV (Parts One and Two)
The historical action of the play follows directly on that of *Richard II*, with England in disarray after the murder of Richard and accession of Bolingbroke (as Henry IV). *Part One* is concerned with the rebellion of Owen Glendower of Wales, Douglas of Scotland and above all Northumberland and his fiery son Hotspur. While King Henry grows ever sadder (and physically sicker), gnawed by remorse for Richard's death and the state of the country, the rebels squabble among themselves and the momentum of their revolt is slow. For all that, Henry is plunged into even deeper sorrow when he compares Hotspur's honour and energy with the apparent heedlessness of state affairs and the gutter tastes of his own son Hal, Prince of Wales. Hal's companions are Falstaff, Bardolph, Poins and the other rogues whose headquarters are the Boar's Head Tavern in Cheapside, and much of the play concerns his relationship with Falstaff (who regards him as a son to be educated in the ways of humanity) and his gradual discovery of the moral balance within himself, the balance between his low-life friends on the one hand and his royal duty on the other. The play's themes are united when Hal is reconciled with his father and kills Hotspur at the battle of Shrewsbury, at which the rebel army is defeated.

In *Part Two* the civil war continues, with the royalists (led by Prince John, Hal's brother) fighting a northern force led by Northumberland (Hotspur's father) and Scroop, Archbishop of York. Mistress Quickly (landlady of the Boar's Head Tavern) tries to have Falstaff arrested for debt, and he goes to Gloucestershire to stay with his old friend Justice Shallow and raise a band of soldiers. While he is collecting the cheapest (and vilest) army in England, and Shallow is revelling in his company and reliving his wild-oats youth, Prince John persuades the rebel leaders that peace will be quicker if both armies are disbanded – and as soon as they do so, arrests them and has them executed for treason. This end of the civil war comes too late, however, for King Henry, whose soul-weariness and physical decline have brought him near to death. Thinking him dead, Hal takes his crown; Henry awakes, and there is a long scene of recrimination and reconciliation, in which Hal finally reveals his change of heart, his abandonment of his low-life companions and his readiness for the role of king. Henry dies, Hal is crowned Henry V, and Falstaff gallops from Gloucestershire to claim high office from his old *protégé*, only to be cruelly rejected with the words, 'I know thee not, old man'. The times have changed; Falstaff and the old order he symbolised have passed away, and a new era of English prosperity (to be seen at its most glittering in the next play in historical sequence, *Henry V*) has begun.

Henry, Prince *(King John)*

John's son and heir-apparent. A holy youth, whose only characteristic is concern for his poisoned father's health.

Henry V

The action is introduced and punctuated by the Chorus, explaining historical intricacies and encouraging the audience to 'piece out our imperfections with your thoughts' by imagining horses, warships and 'the vasty fields of France'. The main part of the play concerns two of Henry's successes in France, the siege of Harfleur and the battle of Agincourt, and is structured to show the king in several different roles (heroic leader, statesman, general with the common touch, vulnerable human being). We are also shown the supercilious, insolent French court, a selection of ordinary British fighting men, and (in two delightful domestic scenes) Henry's future wife, the innocent and charming Katharine, learning English from her maid and responding with shy fascination to Henry's somewhat gauche wooing. The play's 'serious' action is interspersed with scenes involving Bardolph, Pistol and other Falstaffian rogues from Henry's youth, and with the exploits of the Welsh captain Fluellen (especially his quarrels with Macmorris and Pistol). Comic and serious elements are brought together when Henry (disguised) is challenged by the soldier Williams to a fight after the battle, and Henry tricks Fluellen into taking the box on the ear meant for him.

Henry VI *(Henry VI Parts One, Two and Three)*

From the start of the action, nothing goes right for Henry. If this were a soap-opera, he would be one of those big-eyed, honest characters whose main plot-function is to suffer, and whose very colourlessness transfers our sympathy from them to the outrageous villains who harass them. He was, as he plaintively reminds us, dumped on the English throne at nine months old, and no one has ever asked, since then, if he likes the job; he pays for a wife by giving away all the lands his father (HENRY V! What son could live up to that?) won in France; he is cuckolded, abused and plotted against by that same wife; he is persuaded to dismiss the only honest person in the court (GLOUCESTER), and is insulted and mocked (by MARGARET) when he mourns his loss; he is forced to fight for a crown he hardly wants, and finally keeps it only by dispossessing his own son and heir (once again incurring Margaret's fury). He is presented throughout as well-meaning, incompetent and pitiful.

Though such parts seldom steal the notices (people prefer villains to victims) they are juicy to play, and Shakespeare fattens this one with several character-traits which raise it above soap-opera predictability. He consistently links Henry's well-meaningness to a sense of moral, royal duty: Henry may not enjoy being king, but he does his best and is conscious of the dignities of his office as well as its burdens. (His intervention in *Part One* in the quarrel between Gloucester and WINCHESTER shows this, as do, in their different ways, his willingness in *Part Two* to parley with CADE rather than let 'so many simple souls perish by the sword' and his wrangling with YORK at the start of *Part Three* about who is to sit on the royal throne. Although each of these endeavours fails, Henry's moral ambition gives his failure, each time, a dimension which is tragic rather than merely pitiful. And finally, in his scenes of loss and imprisonment in *Part Three*, Shakespeare gives him a loftiness of language, a resignation, which confirms the dignity of his character, makes us wish that he had been given time to prove himself as king after all, and throws the crude power-play of the Yorkists into sharp relief. ('So flies the reckless shepherd from the wolf;/So first the harmless sheep doth yield his fleece,/And next his throat unto the butcher's knife./What scene of death hath Roscius now to act?...')

Henry VI (Parts One, Two and Three)

The action of *Part One* takes place alternately in England and in France. England is reeling from the death of Henry V, when his son is only nine months old. The Duke of Gloucester is Protector of the kingdom, but he and the other nobles spend most of the play squabbling for power. (Gloucester's particular enemy is the Bishop of Winchester: they fight like cat and cat.) Early in the play Richard Plantagenet, Duke of York, sets up two factions, named for a red rose and a white, which give their followers a focus for argument. In France, the French (led by the Dauphin and La Pucelle, Joan of Arc) are progressively winning back the towns captured years before by Henry V; their chief adversary is the brave and noble English Lord Talbot. The period covered by the play is several years, and ends when Henry VI (now a grown prince) marries Margaret of Anjou, and makes peace between France and England. (There is, however, no peace in England: to win her, Henry has surrendered all the French territory his father won, and his ambassador, Suffolk, has seduced Margaret and is having an affair with her, for political as well as personal reasons.)

Part Two is largely concerned with political intrigue. Queen Margaret and Suffolk want to dominate the weak King Henry, and to do this they engineer the downfall of Gloucester (their excuse is his wife's interest in witchcraft). Later, Suffolk is accused of Gloucester's murder and beheaded. York, meanwhile, is vigorously intriguing against the King and all his followers, claiming that the House of York has a better right to the throne than the House of Lancaster. The Yorkists support a people's rebellion led by Jack Cade of Kent, and when it fails York is forced to begin open civil war himself. The play ends with his victory at the battle of St Albans. Its main interest is in the cold-hearted scheming of York, Suffolk and Queen Margaret, and the slapstick antics – albeit dangerous and bloodthirsty – of Cade and his rustic revolutionaries.

Part Three begins in Parliament, with York and Henry squabbling (literally) over the royal throne. Henry agrees to hand power to York's son Edward, if York will only let him (Henry) go on ruling while he lives. This decision infuriates Queen Margaret, whose son (also an Edward) is dispossessed by it. She takes to war in place of her fool of a husband, routs the Yorkists and orders York himself beheaded. In revenge York's sons Edward, Clarence and Richard, helped by Warwick ('the Kingmaker') decimate the royalist forces and seize the throne. The royalists raise a new army and the civil war continues. By now Edward, Clarence and Richard are also squabbling (because Edward has married Elizabeth Grey and not the French princess his brothers and Warwick chose for him). Warwick changes sides and supports Margaret, but even with his help the royalists lose the war, King Henry and Edward Prince of Wales are murdered (by Richard), Queen Margaret is banished, and the play ends as the Yorkists hold all power. (The split between the three brothers remains, however, and Richard's evil plotting, which is to be the main interest in *Richard III*, has already begun.)

Henry VIII

The bones of the plot are the intrigues surrounding Henry's divorce from Queen Katharine and marriage to Anne Bullen, and the power-struggle between the court nobles and the church (as embodied first in Cardinal Wolsey and then in Thomas Cranmer, Archbishop of Canterbury). The play begins with Buckingham leading a discontented group against Wolsey, and being condemned to death himself on an accusation of treason; it ends with Cranmer facing the Council of state to answer a charge of heresy, and evading arrest because of Henry's protection. In between, the action revolves round Henry's love-affair with the innocent, charming Anne Bullen, the dignified and pathetic pleading against divorce of the ageing Queen Katharine, and the machinations of plausible, worldly Wolsey.

In performance, this complex plot is matched by dazzling spectacle. Act One contains a masque (at which Henry, costumed as a shepherd, first meets Anne Bullen); Act Two contains a formal council scene, filled with courtiers, bishops and cardinals in full regalia, at which Katharine's divorce is lengthily discussed; Act Four contains Anne Bullen's coronation and a dream ballet of 'spirits of peace' imagined by the sick Katharine; Act Five contains a second council-scene (the arraignment of Cranmer) and culminates in the pomp and pageantry of the christening of Princess Elizabeth. In all of these, stage directions give detailed instruction for costumes, placing, movement, music and effects; in Shakespeare's time the play was staged with fireworks, cannon shots and other pyrotechnic effects, so uncontrolled at its 1613 première that the Globe Theatre caught fire and burned to the ground.

Herald *(Henry VI Part Two)*
Appears at the scene of ELEANOR's penance to summon GLOUCESTER to answer charges of treason.

Herald *(King Lear)*
Makes the proclamation that 'If any man of quality or degree... will maintain upon Edmund, supposed Earl of Gloucester, that he is a manifold traitor, let him appear...' – a call answered by the disguised EDGAR.

Herald *(The Two Noble Kinsmen)*
Tells THESEUS of the capture of PALAMON and ARCITE before Thebes. Later (as Messenger), announces the arrival of Palamon, Arcite and their KNIGHTS to duel for EMILIA, and then goes to summon the JAILER to supervise the execution of the loser.

Herbert, Sir Walter *(Richard III)*
Follower of RICHMOND. No character.

Hermia *(A Midsummer Night's Dream)*
Young woman in love with LYSANDER. She defends her right to choose him as her husband in defiance of her father EGEUS' desire for her to marry DEMETRIUS. After fleeing to the wood with Lysander, she bears the full brunt of the magic-induced misadventures. Few farce-butts are more delightful or higher-spirited.

Hermione *(The Winter's Tale)*
LEONTES' young queen. Her affability towards her husband's friend (POLIXENES) seems to Leontes like flirting, and provokes his jealous rage against them both. She is bewildered but dignified, both after her arrest ('There's some ill planet reigns:/I must be patient till the heavens look/With an aspect more favourable') and at her trial ('Sir, you speak a language that I understand not./My life stands in the level of your demand, which I'll lay down.'). This dignity, and the charm of the domestic scene before her arrest (when she lets MAMILLIUS whisper a bedtime story in her ear) make her one of the most sympathetic and charming characters in the play. As well as pitying her innocence we warm to her as a person, and this feeling makes particularly moving the moment in the last scene of all when her 'statue' comes to life.

Hero *(Much Ado about Nothing)*
At the start of the play Hero is a lively, bubbly character, with a line in repartee as witty as BEATRICE's and far more charming. (*Don Pedro*: 'Lady, will you walk about with your friend?' *Hero*: 'So you walk softly, and look sweetly, and say nothing, I am yours for the walk...'.) She tricks Beatrice (by letting her overhear how much BENEDICK loves

her) in a high-spirited, guileless way, as if making her cousin fall in love
is nothing more than a game for a summer afternoon, and she discusses
clothes and wedding-preparations with innocent, joyous eagerness.
Then, when she is falsely accused and her world collapses about her,
Shakespeare abandons her as a dramatic character. She has only a
couple of dozen more lines, and they are in the perfunctory, wronged-
innocent style of all his mistreated young heroines. From the audience's
point of view this is perhaps fair enough: the play has moved on and
new characters have taken centre stage. But it hardly helps the actress,
who begins with meat and ends with cartilage.

Hippolyta (*A Midsummer Night's Dream*; *The Two Noble Kinsmen*)
THESEUS' wife, Duchess of Athens. She is a warrior-queen, leader of
the Amazons, and the play-texts refer once or twice to this and to her
martial dignity.

Holland, John (*Henry VI Part Two*)
Follower of CADE who believes that 'it was never merry world in
England since gentlemen came up'. Quiet, mild and insignificant,
swamped by heartier colleagues as soon as the conspiracy takes wing.

Holofernes (*Love's Labour's Lost*)
Pedantic schoolmaster, friend of SIR NATHANIEL who devises the
pageant of the Nine Worthies to entertain the court (and plays at least
three of them himself). He is a linguistic precisian – someone says of
him and Sir Nathaniel, 'They have been at a great feast of languages,
and stolen the scraps' – and polysyllables and Latin tags float in his
speech like twigs in a river: as he puts it himself, facility with language
is 'a gift that I have, simple, simple: a foolish, extravagant spirit, full of
forms, figures, shapes, objects, ideas, apprehensions, motions,
revolutions: these are begot in the ventricle of memory, nourish'd in the
womb of *pia mater*, and delivered on the mellowing of occasion. But the
gift is good in those in whom it is acute, and I am thankful for it.'
    The mockery is affectionate rather than cruel: Holofernes' delight,
unlike that of the courtiers, is in language itself and not in his own
using of it, and when Sir Nathaniel commits a schoolboy howler he
sacrifices pedantry to friendship in a most goodhumoured way: '*Bone?
Bone* for *bene*? Priscian a little scratched? 'Twill serve.'

Horatio (*Hamlet*)
HAMLET's university friend. He is a scholar and a philosopher, the first
person to be brought to see the GHOST and the first person to be shown
OPHELIA's madness, as if his interest in strange phenomena will lead
him to suggest some sort of cure. (It never does: he surrenders moral
initiative to Hamlet throughout the play.) At the end of the duel,
Hamlet dies in his arms, and he promises to tell FORTINBRAS all that
has occurred. The role is quite large, but almost entirely bland: only in
the early scenes with the soldiers does Horatio take any initiative, and
apart from that and his affection for Hamlet he is little more than an

attendant lord.

Horatio *(Romeo and Juliet)*
ROMEO's friend who accompanies him, BENVOLIO and MERCUTIO to the
Capulet's masked ball; he speaks only two lines.

Horner *(Henry VI Part Two)*
Unfortunate man accused of treason by his apprentice PETER because
'when I did correct him for his fault the other day, he did vow upon his
knees that he would be even with me...' He is presented as honest and
bewildered, but accepts trial by combat with Peter and is killed.

Hortensio *(The Taming of the Shrew)*
PETRUCHIO's friend who pays court to BIANCA. Though he says plenty
and is at the heart of the action (disguised as a music-teacher; watching
Petruchio for tips on how to tame a shrew), the dialogue gives him no
character whatever. He is sometimes played as a fool, a *commedia dell'
arte* pantaloon like GREMIO; he could equally well be a serious young
man, LUCENTIO's counterpart. He spends his time either moping,
running farcically about (e.g. with his lute smashed round his ears) or
resolutely behaving in an 'untoward' manner to tame the shrewish
WIDOW he marries instead of Bianca.

Hortensius *(Timon of Athens): see* **Servants**

Host *(The Merry Wives of Windsor)*
Landlord of the Garter Inn in Windsor, whose chief part in the plot is
to set EVANS and CAIUS at each other's throats. (Later, with them, he
makes up a trilogy of comedians who keep turning up, e.g. at FORD's
house, to add an element of linguistic confusion to the general chaos.)
The Host is a forthright, self-educated cynic, and has a robust and vivid
way with words. (To SIMPLE, who has just asked if FALSTAFF is in, he
says: 'There's his chamber, his house, his castle, his standing-bed and
his truckle-bed; 'tis painted about with the story of the Prodigal, fresh
and new. Go knock and call; he'll speak like an Anthropophaginian
unto thee. Knock, I say!')

Host *(The Two Gentlemen of Verona)*
Takes the disguised JULIA where she can overhear PROTEUS serenading
SYLVIA. A jovial man ('Now, my young guest, methinks you're
allicholy. I pray you, what is't?'), but so clay-souled that his response to
Proteus' wooing and singing, and to Sylvia's energetic rejection, is to
fall asleep.

Hostess *(The Taming of the Shrew)*
Indignantly throws SLY out of her tavern, at the start of the Induction,
for refusing to pay for all the glasses he has broken.

Hostilius (*Timon of Athens*): *see* **Strangers**

Hotspur: *see* **Percy, Harry**

Hubert de Burgh (*King John*)
JOHN's chamberlain. He begins as a shifty sycophant, picking up John's nods and nudges about the kind of 'safekeeping' for ARTHUR which 'will not offend your majesty'. But after exposure to Arthur's radiant innocence he turns from bad to good in a conversion as abrupt as the opening of a window – and thereafter finds, to his annoyance, that neither John nor anyone else believes for one moment in his change of heart, and resorts to whining ('If I in act, consent or sin of thought/Be guilty of the stealing that sweet breath/Which was enshrouded in this beauteous clay,/Let Hell want pains enough to torture me'). His change of heart matches that of the BASTARD, and they are superficially similar characters. But for the Bastard villainy was a cloak, and as he throws it off he grows in stature and nobility; for Hubert it was the quality which gave him life, and when he sheds it he becomes the tedious minion others have always thought him. In keeping with the play's general ironical tone, he finds that making the right moral choice not only does his public career no good at all, but destroys his personality.

Hume, John (*Henry VI Part Two*)
Sly priest suborned by BEAUFORT and SUFFOLK (by the promise of a knighthood) to bring ELEANOR fake witches who will show her 'a spirit rais'd from depth of underground/That shall make answers to such questions/As by your Grace shall be propounded him', and so to engineer the downfall of GLOUCESTER.

Huntsman (*Henry VI Part Three*)
Charged with guarding the captive EDWARD, he surrenders him to RICHARD, HASTINGS and others, and then joins them rather 'than tarry and be hang'd'.

Huntsmen (*The Taming of the Shrew*)
In the Induction, the First Huntsman looks after the dogs and the Second Huntsman discovers SLY lying drunk in a ditch.

Hymen (*As You Like It*)
God of marriage. He makes a brief appearance at the end of the play, ushering in ROSALIND in women's clothes and tying all the plot's loose ends. He speaks one speech and sings two songs; his scene lasts only a page, but is vital in clinching the unreal, fairy-tale atmosphere which marks the play.

Hymen (*The Two Noble Kinsmen*)
The play begins with a dumbshow of THESEUS' and HIPPOLYTA's wedding. While it takes place, Hymen sings a beautiful (and notably Shakespearean) wedding song.

Iachimo (*Cymbeline*)

At the heart of *Cymbeline*, all but obscured by the masquerades and misunderstandings of the rest of the plot, is a fascinating confrontation between IACHIMO and IMOGEN: indeed, if this were a Victorian novel, the moral education she gives him might be the burden of the narrative. He begins the play as one of those bored, morally blank young aristocrats Shakespeare seems to associate with Italy, close kin to PORTIA in *The Merchant of Venice* or MERCUTIO and the other young bloods of *Romeo and Juliet*. His days are spent in chatter (about horses, jewels, estates, women), and his way of welcoming a newcomer (in this case, POSTHUMUS) is to test his conversational mettle: his first words to Posthumus, 'You must not so far prefer her fore ours of Italy' are a response to Posthumus' vehement declaration that Imogen is the most virtuous woman in the world, and they are a direct challenge. From there the conversation develops into a verbal duel, involving a wager (that Iachimo can assail and conquer Imogen's virtue) and the promise of a more deadly duel, with swords, if he loses. There is nothing particularly deep or sinister about this, but Iachimo's ensuing behaviour – lying to Imogen, hiding in her bedroom, stealing a bracelet, cold-bloodedly itemising her furniture and the mole under her breast and then hurrying back to Italy to lie to Posthumus – involves a surrender of moral consciousness less Machiavellian than diabolical.

At this point, when he seems one of the blackest-hearted, least admirable rogues in Shakespeare, Iachimo drops out of the action, which concerns itself instead with Posthumus' mistaken fury against Imogen, her own panic-stricken purity, and the true nobility of PISANIO the servant and CYMBELINE's sons GUIDERIUS and ARVIRAGUS who have grown up (we are constantly reminded) untainted by the morals and manners of high society. We next see Iachimo, in a dumbshow, attacked and disarmed by the disguised Posthumus during the Roman invasion of Wales, and when he speaks he immediately announces not the soldierly rage we might expect after such an encounter, but moral contrition: 'The heaviness and guilt within my bosom/Takes off my manhood: I have belied a lady,/The princess of this country, and the air on't/Revengingly enfeebles me...' As soon as he can, he makes a long, public and finely worded confession ('He spake of her, as Dian had hot dreams/And she alone were cold; whereat I, wretch,/Made scruple of her praise, and wager'd with him...'); finally, he kneels to Posthumus and is pardoned by him.

In a play with a less proliferating plot than *Cymbeline*, Shakespeare might have taken time to show us the progress of Iachimo's moral education, the steps along his journey from scheming to penitence. As it is, the attempt on Imogen's virtue is merely there to trigger Posthumus' rage and Imogen's escape to Wales in boy's clothes; Iachimo is an instrument of the plot, and is kept in the background lest his character prove more interesting than the events he causes. Because of this, his change of heart could seem merely silly: each time he pops up in the play, he is wearing new morality like a different suit of clothes. But if his moral growth is taken as a serious strand in the plot rather than as contrivance, it is fascinating, and for the actor, knowledge of the remorse to come in Act Five allows for far greater ambiguity of performance in the apparently carefree callousness of the preceding wager- and bedroom-scenes.

Iago *(Othello)*

As with the parts of RICHARD and BOLINGBROKE in *Richard II*, it has been fashionable in this century for a pair of leading actors to alternate OTHELLO and Iago, as if the balance between them were that of equals, as if the harmonies they make of light and darkness somehow embodied the meaning of the play. This process dignifies Iago, and in so doing weakens the tragic status of Othello, whose personality and actions should bear the main dramatic weight. Iago is a functionary of disaster, and it is his actions and their effects that matter, not their causes: unlike Othello's, his views on life are of neither interest nor importance.

Typical of the weighting of Iago's part is the quest for psychological motivation for what he does: some devil-pact or Machiavellian, not to say Freudian, lust to pollute what is unequivocal and pure. All such 'discoveries' are interpreters' invention. Iago's motives for destroying Othello are, like everything else in his life, manifest and practical. Despite years of loyal and excellent service, he has been passed over for promotion in favour of the 'counter-caster' CASSIO, a man 'That never set a squadron on the field,/Nor the division of a battle knows/More than a spinster' – and for this, Iago vows revenge. He casually introduces elements of class-hatred, race-hatred and sexual suspicion – he 'fears [Cassio] with his nightcap too' – but they are no more than embroidery of his main purpose. If his motives were different, we might see his character evolve in response to the events of the play; as it is, he remains the same person from start to finish, and manipulates people and events as coolly as a chess-player, more for the pleasure of the game than to satisfy some unstated psychological need.

Iago's methods are as direct as his motives. He lies, flatly and deliberately, telling BRABANTIO that Othello has bewitched his daughter, telling RODERIGO that Cassio is a notorious drunk, telling

Othello that DESDEMONA gave Cassio her handkerchief. He is a pure hypocrite, always playing the 'honest ancient' everyone takes him for: lines like 'I had rather have this tongue cut from my mouth/Than it should do offence to Michael Cassio' are typical. It is sometimes said that Iago's methods are so simple, and so transparent to everyone but his victims, because his victims are blinkered by their own noble natures. In fact they are simple because *he* is simple: just as Othello's personality depends on confidence in his own honour, so Iago's involves absolute trust in his manipulative powers, and when things go wrong he collapses, exactly like Othello, into psychological panic and rash, overt and disastrous action.

Throughout the early part of the play (until his insinuations begin to bite, and Othello's jealousy can be left to take its course), Iago is presented in scenes of powerful irony – a method often used in Shakespeare for depicting villainy. With Roderigo in Venice, with Cassio in the drinking scene in Cyprus, with Desdemona, he plays a plausible, ingratiating part with his interlocutors while at the same time clearly showing the audience that he is playing the part for a purpose, and what that purpose is. He speaks dark, direct soliloquies – another characteristic of Shakespeare's villains – and leaves us in as little doubt about his character as does RICHARD in *Richard III*. Shakespeare regularly shows us uncomplex noble characters, and we accept them on their own terms – why need villainy be more complicated? Giving Iago depth is a satisfying game in the seminar-room or rehearsal-hall, but in the theatre it is not the tortuousness of his malevolence but its simplicity which carries the part, and the play, along. If his part truly does counterbalance Othello's, this contrast between undeclared psychological deviousness and declared psychological straight-forwardness is where the balance lies.

Iden, Alexander *(Henry VI Part Two)*
Kentish gentleman who finds CADE in his peaceful garden (a symbol of the England threatened by Cade's rebellion), cuts off his head and is knighted for it.

Imogen *(Cymbeline)*
CYMBELINE's daughter, a woman so pure that virtue shines from her like a light, and who is therefore doomed (in the way of Shakespeare's innocent heroines) to be misunderstood and mistreated by everyone she meets: even her beloved POSTHUMUS suspects her of adultery and sends orders to have her killed. Her beauty of character is shown in lovely lines – for example, her lament at not being allowed to see Posthumus set sail into exile, 'I would have broke mine eye-strings, crack'd them, but/To look upon him, till the diminution/Of space had pointed him fine as my needle,/Nay, follow'd him till he had melted from/The smallness of a gnat to air, and then/Have turn'd mine eye and wept'. But she is not all gush and blush: her unassailable goodness has a core of steel, which she readily reveals, without losing any moral initiative,

when IACHIMO or (in this case) CLOTEN makes insulting advances: 'Profane fellow!/Wert thou the son of Jupiter, and no more/But what thou art besides, thou wert too base/To be his groom...'. This hauteur stops her from being boring-nice: instead of a pallid waif to whom interesting things happen (arrest, death, threats, exile in boy's clothes), she is spirited and unpredictable, a light that can sear as well as shine.

Iras *(Antony and Cleopatra)*
CLEOPATRA's maid, with CHARMIAN. A young girl with no character but cheerfulness, until, presumably heartbroken at having to dress Cleopatra for death in the monument, she drops dead.

Iris *(The Tempest)*
Rainbow-goddess, who takes part in the masque to entertain MIRANDA and FERDINAND. In some productions ARIEL doubles this part.

Isabel, Queen of France *(Henry V)*
In a brief and formal appearance at the end of the play, she assists at the ratification of peace between France and England, and gives her daughter KATHARINE leave to listen to HENRY's courtship.

Isabella *(Measure for Measure)*
Isabella is often played as a far more complex character than the lines suggest. In particular, she is allowed to assent at the end to marriage with the DUKE, and the surrender (or conflict) of principle this suggests, after her apparent vocation for virginity throughout the play, is read back into her earlier speeches and actions, making them seem calculated and hypocritical. In fact she is ANGELO's moral double. She is incapable of changing, and is so petrified to discover her own inflexibility that she walks through the play like an automaton. It is inflexibility, for example, which makes her quite happy for MARIANA to commit fornication in her place, just as it was inflexibility which made her set a higher price on her own virginity even than on her brother's life. She is like the heroine in Sophocles' *Antigone*, a straightforward, simple girl faced with a choice between equally unthinkable disasters – and the only difference between them is that because Antigone is the heroine of a tragedy the choice she makes leads inevitably to her own martyrdom, whereas, because Isabella is the heroine of a comedy, other people (notably the Duke) change the course of events to make her absolute moral choice unnecessary and irrelevant. This leaves Isabella high and dry as a character, and makes her inflexibility in the end seem ludicrous rather than exemplary. But that is no reason to play her as any different from what she is: a girl whose view of right and wrong is so fixed, and so muddle-headed, that she puts principle before people as regularly and as unflinchingly as a robot punches holes in steel.

Jacques *(As You Like It)*
ORLANDO's and OLIVER's brother, not to be confused with JAQUES, the melancholy lord in the same play. He appears once in the play, to announce Duke Frederick's conversion from blackguard to saint; he is a noble, well-spoken youth, with no distinguishing character-traits.

Jailer *(The Two Noble Kinsmen)*
In charge of the prison where PALAMON and ARCITE are lodged. He is not the low-class nonentity of most Shakespearean jailers, but a cultured, amiable man, and although Palamon and Arcite are chained, their imprisonment is more like house-arrest than brute incarceration. When the Jailer's DAUGHTER goes mad for love, the Jailer eagerly agrees to the DOCTOR's scheme of letting the WOOER talk to her in a darkened room, pretending to be Palamon, even kissing and making love to her, to restore her wits.

Jamy *(Henry V)*
Scots captain who appears with GOWER, FLUELLEN and MACMORRIS. He says little, and most of it is in a gibberish dialect which more closely resembles the ranting of a Glaswegian drunk on today's comic stage than it does any kind of comprehensible English. As with the part of Macmorris, this one raises awkward (if academic) questions about racial and comic stereotyping on the Elizabethan stage, and (for modern performers) a rather more urgent question about whether to play the scene for laughs or for real.

Jaquenetta *(Love's Labour's Lost)*
The 'country wench' loved by ARMADO. She says little, and most of it is suitably rustic and deferential ('Good master parson, be so good as to read me this letter...'). Only in her sly, points-scoring dialogue with Armado are there hints that their marriage, like all the others in the play, is likely to be anything but placid. (*Armado*: 'Maid—' *Jaquenetta*: 'Man.' *Armado*: 'I will visit thee at the lodge.' *Jaquenetta*: 'That's hereby.' *Armado*: 'I know where it is situate.' *Jaquenetta*: 'Lord, how wise you are!')

Jaques *(As You Like It)*
Not the same person as JACQUES, ORLANDO's brother in the same play. Shakespeare took the plot and most of the characters of *As You Like It*

from a popular romantic novel called *Rosalynde*, by Thomas Lodge. Lodge's original is full of improbabilities and fancies, as artificial as a madrigal, and though this worked well on the printed page, there was a danger that on the stage the characters' pretty nothings would seem mere silliness. Accordingly, Shakespeare added robuster characters of his own: TOUCHSTONE, AUDREY, WILLIAM and above all Jaques. Shortly before writing the play, he had performed in a production of Jonson's comedy *Every Man in His Humour*, in which each character is governed, to the point of obsession, by a single ruling passion or 'humour', such as anger, pliability or giggliness. Though Shakespeare rarely used this idea in his own work, he did for Jaques, and the humour he chose for him was melancholy.

Jaques, like many of Shakespeare's bored aristocrats, whiles away his time by playing a game with life, choosing and adapting circumstances to suit his mood. (He himself compares human existence to a play, and people to actors: 'All the world's a stage...') He persuades AMIENS to sing to him, claiming that he can 'suck melancholy out of a song, as a weasel sucks eggs'; he eavesdrops on other people (e.g. the fool in the forest) and draws what gloomy lessons he can about life from what he hears; he somewhat self-admiringly sums up his own character thus: 'I have neither the scholar's melancholy, which is emulation; nor the musician's, which is fantastical; nor the courtier's, which is proud; nor the soldier's, which is ambitious; nor the lawyer's, which is politic; nor the lady's, which is nice; nor the lover's, which is all these; but it is a melancholy of mine own compounded of many simples, extracted from many objects and indeed the sundry contemplation of my travels, in which by often rumination, wraps me in a most humorous sadness'.

Although his self-regarding gloominess makes Jaques interesting – and his dark-toned wit, as well as contrasting with the airy nothings of the lovers, makes him a pleasure to listen to – he is in the end as one-dimensional as any of Jonson's 'humorous' characters, far more frivolous than the others he so determinedly mocks. Because he is interested in the human condition only in so far as it relates to himself, and because he regards himself as nature's mirror, he is dependent on other people's dynamism, and as soon as the plot moves away from him (thanks to the gathering impetus of ROSALIND's and ORLANDO's love-affair), he fades from the play. His fascination for us is that he is a well-drawn, colourful personality; his tragedy is that because his character exists in only one dimension, we quickly know everything about him, and he is like a conjuror who runs out of tricks. Moving, in the course of a play, from artificiality to true human emotions is one of Shakespeare's favourite plot-devices, and *As You Like It* is constructed to move from the gloom and uncertainty of the first half (in which Jaques is in his element) to the full radiance of the 'real' love in the second half (in which he is like a fish out of water). The progression helps the play, but it makes Jaques a complicated and somewhat insubstantial part for an actor.

Jessica *(The Merchant of Venice)*
SHYLOCK's daughter. In common with many young girls in Shakespeare
– the range is from BIANCA in *The Taming of the Shrew* to CORDELIA or
JULIET – her apparent demureness is utterly cancelled out by what she
does. She denies her nation and religious heritage, elopes with a
Christian and steals a bag of her father's jewels into the bargain, and
neither maidenly modesty ('Cupid himself would blush/To see me thus
transformed to a boy') nor full-throated love-poetry ('In such a night/
Did Thisbe fearfully o'ertrip the dew...') can glaze over the fact that
she is as ruthless and amoral as any of the Christian aristocrats whose
society she joins.

Jeweller *(Timon of Athens)*
Takes TIMON a rich jewel at the start of the play.

John *(King John)*
If the play *King John* is (as some critics claim) a hollow failure, then
John is no more than the hollow man at its hollow heart, a bombastic,
hypocritical ranter with neither brain nor soul. But if (as seems more
plausible) the play is black farce, a sixteenth-century equivalent to
Jarry's *Ubu Roi* or Heller's *Catch-22*, then John is its key figure, and
far more interesting: a man aware of his own emptiness and trying to
combat it by charades of power, to transmute games into real life. He is
catapulted on to the throne by the departure for the Holy Land and
subsequent death of his charismatic brother Richard; he holds the
throne in trust for his nephew the child ARTHUR, and is uneasily
conscious that his relatives and courtiers all regard him as a stopgap
prince, 'the borrow'd majesty of England'; every time he takes decisive
action to protect himself, it turns to dust in his hands. (When he makes
a marriage-alliance with France, the Pope's legate PANDULPH
excommunicates him; when he orders the murder of Arthur his nobles
turn against him, and when Arthur's life is spared they hold that
against him too; when every knot is tied and he thinks himself secure at
last, he is poisoned and dies.)

As well as hasty and disastrous action, John's attempts to assert his
regality take the form of high-falutin', pompous public utterances: he is
like a boy playing king in a school playground, and his words have a
tone of oddly perfunctory bluster, as if he hardly believes in them
himself. He says, for example, when the kings of Austria, France and
England quarrel, 'Peace be to France, if France in peace permit/Our
just and lineal entrance to our own!/If not, bleed France, and peace
ascend to Heaven!' The jingling repetitions of 'peace', the joggly
rhythm and the spat-out p's make the lines artificial, self-conscious and
precarious, like a dance on stilts. In less public circumstances he still
affects royal dignity, and the way he speaks once again subverts what he
is trying to say – who could take seriously a man who utters sentences
like 'Some reasons of this double coronation/I have possess'd you with,
and think them strong;/And more, more strong than lesser is my fear/I

shall indue you with; meantime but ask/What you would have reform'd that is not well,/And well you shall perceive how willingly/I will both hear and grant you your requests'?

What makes John interesting is not so much this peacock's tail of language as the fact that when it is plucked, when he is left alone to face himself, he becomes credible, pathetic and terrified, a sympathetic and tragic character. His dependency on the BASTARD is total; in his wretchedness at the thought of Arthur's death he speaks sincerely, openly and most unregally to the shifty HUBERT ('O, when the last account 'twixt heaven and earth/Is to be made, then shall this hand and seal/Witness against us to damnation...'); when he is fed poison and realises that he is being consumed as if by fire and must die alone and friendless, the nakedness of his misery is marvellously portrayed ('And none of you will bid the winter come,/To thrust his icy fingers in my maw;/Nor let my kingdom's rivers take their course/Through my burnt bosom...'). We might almost be left grieving for him, so honest and lifelike has he become, except that Shakespeare deliberately subverts this dignified rhetoric by having John die, in true buffoon style, while someone else is giving him urgent news. To the last breath of his life he is a failure, a man who consistently lives down to his own estimate of himself (and everyone else's). He can move us to tears, or be played for laughs, or both; the one option not open is to make bombast the only key to his character, and make his boringness real.

John, Friar *(Romeo and Juliet)*
Friar LAURENCE's fellow-Franciscan. He is sent by him to Mantua to tell ROMEO that JULIET is asleep, not dead, but is delayed by a plague-scare, thus causing the final catastrophe. He speaks few lines and shows little character.

John, Prince, Duke of Lancaster and later of Bedford *(Henry IV Parts One and Two; Henry V; Henry VI Part One)*
Third son of Henry IV (BOLINGBROKE). In *Henry IV Part One* (where the interest is all in his father the king) he speaks five lines; in *Henry V* (where the interest is all in his brother the king) he speaks a dozen; in *Henry IV Part Two*, though he has plenty to say, he is given no character traits except efficiency, and his main claim to fame is tricking the rebels into disbanding their army, and then executing them. In *Henry VI Part One* he is a grizzled and distinguished elder statesman, the Regent of France – a far cry from the owner of the 'maiden sword' in *Henry IV Part One* – but this is about all the characterisation the actor has to bite on.

Jourdain, Margery *(Henry VI Part Two)*
Witch in SUFFOLK's conspiracy against ELEANOR, Duchess of Gloucester.

Julia *(The Two Gentlemen of Verona)*
Julia is the first of the four young people in the play to discover love

and to be transformed by it. At first, her feelings for PROTEUS are intoxicating but uncontrolled, a heady amusement for a summer afternoon. She can't make up her mind whether to accept his love-letter or send it away, to read it or tear it up, and she ends up scrabbling for its torn fragments on the ground and thoroughly enjoying her own discomfort. ('O hateful hands, to tear such loving words!/Injurious wasps, to feed on such sweet honey/And kill the bees, that yield it, with your stings!/I'll kiss each several paper for amends...') This ecstasy of indecision is soon replaced, when Proteus abruptly says he must leave for Milan, first by an anguish of shyness (she gives him a ring, but then runs out without a single parting word) and then by the desperate realisation that she can't live without him – 'his looks are my soul's food' – and by determination to dress as a boy and follow him. We then see her progressively more and more dismayed as she witnesses Proteus' courting of SYLVIA, and trapped (like VIOLA in *Twelfth Night*) by her own self-imposed male disguise from showing what is in her heart. And in a final, most satisfying twist, when the scales fall from Proteus' eyes and he realises that he really loved her all the time, instead of falling into his arms with uncritical rapture, she controls her obvious delight until – as a mature person should – she has told him the moral (about true love and fickleness) which the twists and turns of the plot have been anticipating all the time. ('Behold her that gave aim to all thy oaths,/And entertained 'em deeply in her heart./How oft hast thou with perjury cleft the root!/O Proteus, let this habit make thee blush!/Be thou ashamed that I have took upon me/Such an immodest raiment, if shame live/In a disguise of love:/It is the lesser blot, modesty finds,/Women to change their shapes than men their minds.')

Juliet *(Romeo and Juliet)*

There is a conventional view of Juliet's character, and it makes the part virtually impossible to play, and certainly unrewarding. Since the nineteenth century she has regularly been portrayed as a kind of archetypal ruined virgin, a waif-innocent as depicted by one of the more soulful Pre-Raphaelite painters. She is a beautiful, pure child, and she is ravished before our eyes, first by life and then by death, in a way less spectacular but just as irrevocable as the hapless LAVINIA of *Titus Andronicus*.

To see Juliet in this light is to turn the play from tragedy to melodrama, and to make voyeurs, not spectators, of the audience. And there is no textual justification for it. The only person who describes Juliet at any length is ROMEO, and he quite clearly has in mind an idealised, unique creature, a dream-beloved, and not a real person at all. (He frequently uses images of light – 'O, she doth teach the torches to burn bright'; 'It is the east, and Juliet is the sun'; 'Here lies Juliet, and her beauty makes/This vault a feasting presence full of light.') No one else talks of her with such single-minded rapture. PARIS treats her respectfully but distantly, as befits his future bride in an arranged marriage; even when he visits her in the tomb he is more concerned with his own grief than with her fate ('O woe! Thy canopy is dust and stones,/Which with sweet water nightly I will dew...'). To her parents she is headstrong and disobedient, the very picture of a sullen adolescent daughter; Friar LAURENCE and the NURSE are affectionate but despairing, and spend as much time wringing their hands over her passion for Romeo as they do facilitating it.

One key to Juliet's character, perhaps, is the way she sees, and describes, herself. She is a spirited, lively girl with a will of her own, but for all that is quite happy to go along with her parents' wishes, to marry the man of their choice and presumably to end up as wordly, busy and respectable as her own mother. (In all this, she is an upper-class Italian equivalent of Anne PAGE in *The Merry Wives of Windsor*.) But as soon as she meets Romeo and starts drinking in his love, she utterly moulds her character to his: of all Shakespeare's other plays, only *Antony and Cleopatra* so centres on a relationship rather than on single individuals. She takes up 'quibbling', flirting with words (*Romeo*: 'What shall I swear by?' *Juliet*: 'Do not swear at all;/Or, if thou wilt, swear by thy gracious self,/Which is the god of my idolatry,/And I'll believe thee...'); she emulates his flights of rhetoric, so much so that her poetry outsoars even his ('Gallop apace, you fiery-footed steeds,/ Towards Phoebus' lodging...'); she gulps maturity from their relationship (as he rediscovers childishness), and finds it heady wine.

The change in Juliet's inner self is not, however, matched by outward maturity. To her parents, to Friar Laurence, to the Nurse, she is as impetuous and exasperating as she has always been. Even in the balcony-scene with Romeo, she skips in and out like a girl in a Swiss weather-house; she stamps her foot at her father and flounces at her mother; with the Nurse she is alternately imperious ('Blistered be thy tongue/For such a wish!') and breathlessly dependent ('O God! O nurse, how shall this be prevented?'); she takes Friar Laurence's potion with wide-eyed excitement, like a child playing a party-game, and her discovery of Romeo's body in the tomb, and her subsequent suicide, are given an unreal, artificial feeling as if she were on a stage and watching her own performance. ('What's here? A cup, clos'd in my true love's hand?'... 'O happy dagger! This is thy sheath; there rest, and let me die.') She *is*, in short, a melodramatic heroine, but the melodrama is one she is directing for herself. She makes her life a play, and because she believes (and believes to the end) that it will have a happy ending, we pity not only her circumstances (as we would with a Victorian melodrama-heroine) but also the way her character responds to and affects events.

Juliet(ta) (*Measure for Measure*)
The girl whose pregnancy (by CLAUDIO) causes Claudio's arrest for immorality. She speaks only in one scene, poor waif, agreeing with the disguised DUKE that the 'offenceful act/Was mutually committed', and

expressing her continued love for Claudio and horror at his fate. She reappears in the last act but does not speak.

Julius Caesar

The play's framework is historical: an account of the gathering aristocratic anger against Caesar when he seems likely to assume unconstitutional power in Rome, the growth of Brutus' and Cassius' conspiracy against him, his assassination on the Ides of March and the subsequent war between his followers (led by the triumvirate of Octavius Caesar, Antony and Lepidus) and the conspirators, which culminates in the conspirators' defeat at the battle of Philippi. Shakespeare uses this framework as the basis for a study of different kinds of personality (autocratic Caesar, morally hesitant Brutus, devious Cassius, hidden-depths Antony), and of the politics of personal relationship: the balance of authority between Brutus and Cassius is a major theme. Behind everything are two large groups of people, the cowering, precedent-racked and impotent Senate, and the rowdy, volatile Citizens whose support was Caesar's own power-base and whom Antony, in a single piece of inspired rhetoric ('Friends, Romans, countrymen...') binds to the Caesarian cause even after Caesar himself is dead.

Juno *(The Tempest)*

Queen of heaven, who sings with CERES and IRIS to entertain MIRANDA and FERDINAND. In some productions the part is taken by one of ARIEL's 'airy spirits'.

Jupiter *(Cymbeline)*

Spectacularly descends from the skies in the ghost-scene, sitting on an eagle, hurling thunderbolts, and surrounded by thunder and lightning. In a speech of rolling rhetoric, he bids the ghosts begone from POSTHUMUS, who is under his special protection.

Katharina (also Katherine or Kate) *(The Taming of the Shrew)*

Over the years *The Taming of the Shrew* has consistently been played either as farce or as comedy, and the mode chosen has determined, and depended on, Katharina's character. If the play is farce, and therefore heartless, she is as straightforward as a puppet. She begins as a termagant, tying up and torturing her sister, shrieking insults at her

father, smashing a lute over her music-teacher's head and terrifying
would-be suitors out of the house. As the play proceeds she is tamed by
PETRUCHIO with the same carrot-and-stick technique as one might use
to a stubborn donkey, and she ends up utterly docile, subservient and
even prepared to preach sermons on women's humble role in life. ('I am
asham'd that women are so simple/To offer war where they should
kneel for peace,/Or seek for rule, supremacy and sway/When they are
bound to serve, love and obey...')

In a farce-interpretation, our interest is in action not character, and
the sincerity of Katharina's conversion is of no interest: the fact that she
is tamed is all we need to know. But if *The Taming of the Shrew* is
played as comedy, the emphasis shifts from action to motivation, and
our interest is in Petruchio's and Katharina's characters and in the
developing relationship between them. Now there are interpretative
problems to be solved. Why is Katharina so shrewish? Is she a
disappointed old maid, as some productions make her, a man-hater, a
kind of proto-feminist, or a self-tormentor redeemed by true love in the
way of BEATRICE in *Much Ado About Nothing*? Even less explicable than
her shrewishness is her conversion. How sincere is she? Coming when
Petruchio calls and trampling the cap which, he says, 'becomes her not'
are minor matters, but the vehement speech she makes about a
woman's duty (to 'place your hands below your husband's foot') is quite
another. Is her tongue in her cheek, or is she in some kind of
conspiracy-of-love with Petruchio against the capering zanies of the rest
of the play? It may be that in the climate of Elizabethan opinion about
the respective 'places' of women and men, *The Taming of the Shrew*
never seemed anything but farce, as dazzling and as true to convention
as *The Merry Wives of Windsor*; this view stresses the importance of its
male characters, caricatures rather than people, every one of them.
Playing it as comedy throws attention on Katharina – and while this is
fine for a present-day actress, it creates problems of balance with the
tumbling intrigues of the story. If her 'dilemma' is 'serious', how does
this square, in performance, with the 'silliness' of everything else
onstage?

Katharine *(Henry V)*
Of all Shakespeare's parts for boy-actors, this is one of the cunningest,
written with a true professional's ability to make very little seem very
much indeed. Katharine appears in two scenes, and is innocent, pure
and virginal, a delightful child. This is the kind of part a young boy,
freshly apprenticed, could play with no acting technique at all;
Shakespeare's actor, however, clearly had a pretty ability with French,
and Shakespeare seized on it, wrote most of Katharine's lines in French
(or in charmingly broken English) and so gave the part theatrical
interest and variety without overburdening the performer's slender
skill. Katharine is still best played by a young performer (of either sex):
an adult actress has too little to do, and dissembling adulthood to play a

child-bride is a difficult (and potentially ludicrous) trick.

Katharine (*Love's Labour's Lost*)
The sharpest-tongued of the ladies attendant on the PRINCESS of
France, her role is chiefly to tame DUMAINE, and their sparky sparring
(*Dumaine*: 'But what to me, my love? But what to me?' *Katharine*: 'A
wife? A beard, fair health and honesty.' *Dumaine*: 'Oh. Shall I say I
thank you, gentle wife?' *Katharine*: 'Not so, my lord: a twelvemonth
and a day/I'll mark no words that smooth-fac'd lovers say...') is an
elegant, if somewhat frigid, counterpart to the more stately wooing of
FERDINAND and the Princess, the ecstasies of LONGAVILLE or the good-
humoured raillery of ROSALINE and BEROWNE.

Katharine, Queen (*Henry VIII*)
Henry VIII is full of pageantry and power politics: when its characters
are not processing or banqueting they are lurking behind arrases,
muttering in antechambers, intercepting letters or fulminating against
other people's success. Court life is presented as a series of games, and
the losers toss away their dignity or their lives as cheerfully as
unsuccessful punters discard tickets on a race-course. Up is up and
down is down, and emotion unbalances the equation every time.
   Katharine is dropped into this heartless world like a jewel in a
puddle. She is all humanity. She is no longer young – mature actresses
in search of a superb part need look no further – and has spent most of
her adult life as a queen, equal in respect, if not in power, to HENRY
himself, her husband. Now she is told, not bluntly, but with WOLSEY's
most oblique and oily politeness, that her marriage has all the time been
illegal and that she should agree willingly to a divorce rather than risk
humiliation in the law-courts. The information destroys her, so much
so that she falls ill and has hallucinations. But instead of collapsing into
moping or intrigue, she gathers her dignity and behaves with a
calmness and self-restraint which are not (as they might have been in
this heartless world) a bargaining ploy, but genuine. At the same time,
she is still a queen, and has no hesitation in showing it, even to Wolsey.
(*Katharine*: 'Sir,/I am about to weep, but thinking that/We are a queen
– or long have dreamed so – certain/The daughter of a king, my drops
of tears/I'll turn to sparks of fire.' *Wolsey*: 'Be patient yet.' *Katharine*: 'I
will when you are humble. Nay, before,/Or God will punish me.') The
scene in which Wolsey and CAMPEIUS try to persuade her to accept
divorce, is the only one where she gives way to passion ('Would I had
never trod this English earth,/Or felt the flatteries that grow upon it!),
but she quickly recovers her dignity and ends the scene with polite,
courtly, even ironical apologies ('She now begs,/That little thought,
when she set footing here,/She should have bought her dignities so
dear...').
   The effect on the play of making Katharine the most sympathetic
character is remarkable. Underlying all the pageantry, all the historical
intrigue, is a sustained moral criticism of Henry, his court lords and his

prelates. If Shakespeare had put more of himself into the play (instead of, as is surmised, contributing only half a dozen scenes), he might well have drawn out the contrast and made it the subtext of the whole proceeding (as he did in *Richard II* or *Henry V*, say); as it is, Katharine's and Anne BULLEN's scenes, together with Wolsey's 'long farewell' to worldly ambition, stand apart from the rest of *Henry VIII* and lift it, momentarily, to greatness.

Keeper of the Tower (*Richard III*)

Wakes CLARENCE on the morning of his death, and is told about Clarence's nightmare of drowning. His part is tiny, and chiefly consists of leading questions (e.g. 'What was your dream, my lord?').

Keepers (*Henry VI Part Three*)

Two gamekeepers in 'a chase in the north of England', who are culling a herd of deer when they stumble on HENRY instead, walking alone in the woods with a prayerbook in his hand. He tells them how miserable he is; they answer that they are Yorkists, and arrest him.

Kent (*Richard II*): *see* Surrey

Kent, Earl of (*King Lear*)

With EDGAR, Kent is the bridge between the play's two plots, and like Edgar he spends most of the action in disguise. But Edgar's disguise is always convincing (we soon suspend disbelief in the reality of 'Poor Tom'); Kent's is not. He may be playing the part of Caius the plain-speaking serving-man, but we are always aware of Kent, LEAR's loyal lord, behind the mask. This presence makes 'Caius' shadowy and unconvincing – you feel that no one would be taken in if they were not preoccupied with their own affairs – and it also sets Kent himself at an angle to the action, commentating on it. His purpose is to keep us anchored in the everyday, to remind us that every piece of highflown or extravagant behaviour has implications for ordinary humanity.

This said, Kent remains one of the most mysterious people in the play. What need is there for all his fury against OSWALD at the court of CORNWALL and REGAN – and why does he fall asleep so cheerfully in the stocks soon afterwards ('Fortune, goodnight. Smile once more; turn thy wheel')? Why does he refuse to give his identity to the GENTLEMAN he guides to Lear ('Some dear cause/Will in concealment wrap me up awhile...')? At the end of the play, offered joint rule with Edgar, what – and who – does he mean by 'I have a journey, sir, shortly to go;/My master calls me, I must not say no'? In a play where everyone's thoughts and motives either are declared or become obvious as the action proceeds, he is always an enigma – not sardonic or ironical, merely unexplained – and just as his detachment helps to focus the main action, so his opaqueness of personality makes the part intriguing to perform, closer to the lords in *Measure for Measure* or *The Winter's Tale* (or even to Chekhov's self-blurring characters) than to the more straightforward aristocrats of Shakespearean high tragedy.

King *(Hamlet): see* **Claudius**

King John

King John, the lacklustre brother of Richard the Lionheart, sits
uneasily on the English throne; distrustful of his own courtiers, he
knights his brother's bastard son and makes him his favourite. Philip of
France and the Archduke of Austria demand that John abdicate in
favour of his nephew, a saintly child called Arthur, and though the
quarrel is for a time patched up by a royal marriage (Philip's son
marrying John's niece), it flares up again when the Pope's envoy
Cardinal Pandulph excommunicates John and orders Philip, as a loyal
Catholic, to make holy war on Britain. In the first fighting, the Bastard
kills Austria and John captures the boy Arthur. He gives Arthur into
the 'safe-keeping' of the villainous Hubert de Burgh, on the clear
understanding that safe-keeping means death. Hubert is all set to burn
out Arthur's eyes and kill him when Arthur's waif-like charm persuades
him to relent, but soon afterwards Arthur is killed jumping from the
castle battlements, and news of his death turns John's nobles Salisbury
and Pembroke against him. They join the French, and a huge invasion
force sets sail for England.

John hastily mends his quarrel with the Pope and instructs Cardinal
Pandulph to call off the French, but Philip refuses to withdraw and
defeats John in battle. In the meantime, however, Salisbury and
Pembroke have learned that he (Philip) plans to kill them once England
is his, and they return their loyalty and troops to John. Unfortunately
for John, while this was happening he has been poisoned, and by the
time he hears that the French are retreating to France and begging for
peace he is on his deathbed. The play ends with the announcement that
John's son Henry is to become king, and a speech from the Bastard
proclaiming that no foreigner will ever conquer 'If England to itself do
rest but true' – highly ironical in view of the black farce of deceit,
humbug, treachery and death we have just been watching.

King Lear

Alone of Shakespeare's tragedies (but like many of his comedies), *King
Lear* entwines two stories. Both are about fathers and their children,
both about genuine and pretended love, both about alienation, spiritual
desolation and the search for moral identity. The main plot concerns
King Lear and his daughters Goneril, Regan and Cordelia. At the start
of the play Lear asks which of his daughters loves him most, and says
that he will divide his kingdom according to the answers. Goneril and
Regan reply with unctuous flattery, and are rewarded; Cordelia replies
honestly, and is disinherited and married to the King of France, the
only man willing to take her without a dowry. The Duke of Kent, who
protests against Lear's high-handedness, is exiled. The second plot
concerns Edgar and Edmund, sons of the aged Lord Gloucester. Edgar
is the legitimate heir, an honest and noble youth; Edmund is
illegitimate, a schemer determined to trick his father into dispossessing

Edgar and preferring him.

The plots come together when Lear, who has arranged to live alternate months with Goneril and Regan, is thrown out by Goneril (and her mild husband Albany) because of the arrogance of his hundred knights, is rebuffed by Regan (and her haughty husband Cornwall), and goes to visit his old friend Gloucester. He quarrels with his daughters at Gloucester's castle, and goes into the wilderness in a storm, accompanied only by his fool and by Kent (who has re-entered his service disguised as a blunt, loyal serving-man). In the wilderness they meet Edgar, who has been banished by his father and is disguised as Poor Tom, a lunatic. Lear's sufferings drive him mad, and this part of the play is a counterpoint of insane utterances (real or feigned) between him, Edgar and the Fool.

In the meantime Goneril, Regan and their husbands plot to kill Lear and seize full royal power. Cordelia leads a French army to Britain, and Kent takes the insane Lear to her for safety. Edmund accuses his father Gloucester of complicity in this 'escape' and betrays him to Regan and Cornwall, who blind him and send him into the wilderness to die. (Edgar, still disguised as Poor Tom, rescues him and takes him to safety in Dover.) By now Edmund is conducting love-affairs with both Goneril and Regan. Regan's husband Cornwall is dead, killed by a servant horrified at the blinding of Gloucester; everyone thinks Goneril's husband Albany a spineless nonentity. Goneril sends Edmund a love-letter, but on the way the messenger (Oswald) quarrels with Edgar and is killed, and Edgar takes the letter to Albany and reveals everything.

At Dover, Lear recovers his wits and discovers the truth about Cordelia's love and Kent's loyalty. But Cordelia's army is beaten in battle, and Edmund orders her to be hanged. Albany then forces him to defend himself by armed combat, and he is challenged by the disguised Edgar and fatally wounded; Goneril, who has meantime poisoned Regan, realises that all is lost and kills herself. Albany orders the release of Cordelia, but too late: Lear brings in Cordelia's dead body, grieves over it and dies.

King of France (*All's Well that Ends Well*)
At the start of the play he is suffering from a painful, incurable disease (a fistula), and is physically feeble until HELENA's magic potion restores his health. At once he becomes an arrogant, absolute ruler, ordering his subjects' destinies like a despotic god. (He tells Helena to choose any LORD she likes as husband, and says he will force him to marry her; he threatens ruin and death to BERTRAM at the first hint of disagreement with the future proposed for him.) The part is substantial, allowing the actor to dominate the stage and giving him plenty of lines to speak, but it is one-dimensional.

Knight (*King Lear*)
LEAR's follower, who is sent after the impertinent OSWALD at

GONERIL's castle, and comes back to report, with a mixture of primness and understatement, that '... to my judgement, your highness is not entertained with that ceremonious affection as you were wont...'.

Knights *(Pericles)*
There are five of them, and they appear in dumb-show at the tournament at SIMONIDES' court, while THAISSA describes their armour and the mottoes on their shields. Later, they go to Simonides to ask Thaissa's hand in marriage, and are refused; we last see them politely setting off for home. ('Loth to bid farewell, we take our leaves.')

Knights *(The Two Noble Kinsmen)*
There are six of them, three champions of PALAMON and three of ARCITE. Their quality and appearance are described, before the duel, by PIRITHOUS and the HERALD. Arcite's knights do not speak; Palamon's, doomed to be beheaded with him after he loses the duel, generously and chivalrously give their purses to the JAILER to be his DAUGHTER's dowry. They speak only a couple of flowery lines each, and have no character but nobility.

La Pucelle (Joan of Arc) *(Henry VI Part One)*
Whatever history may say, theatre-goers have known all about the character (or characters) of Joan of Arc for the last six decades. To some, she is the fresh-faced young feminist of Shaw's *St Joan*, a paradox-loving, Fabian debater whose matter-of-factness periodically gives way to bouts of religious mysticism, and whose death is as bloodlessly 'noble' as that of a pre-Raphaelite St Sebastian. For others, she is the stubborn waif of Anouilh's *The Lark*, a saucer-eyed Resistance heroine clutching God's hand for comfort and buffeted by the world's coarseness on every side.

To the young Shakespeare (nearer to St Joan in time, but influenced by generations of English propaganda-history) she showed yet another aspect. He presents La Pucelle ('The Maid') as the very archetype of medieval saintliness, a person impelled by religious certainty to transcend mortal weakness and do great deeds. There is nothing mystical or woolly-minded about her: God's orders are unequivocal, and she carries them out with unquestioning, unflagging efficiency. Her sex is irrelevant: indeed, her way of persuading people to take her seriously is to fight them, wrestling or duelling respect into them. (Only TALBOT refuses this offer, and scornfully rides away to fight 'real men': this tells us about his character, but leaves not a dent in Joan's).

It is refreshing – and historically more plausible, perhaps – to see Joan presented thus, as a crop-headed bully-boy in all but sex. She goes to her death with the same stiff-upper-lipped contempt as any man of action in the play, and WARWICK's concern that she should be spared undue suffering ('because she is a maid,/Spare for no faggots, let there be enow;/Place barrels of pitch upon her fatal stake,/That so her torture may be shortened') seems not so much considerate as impertinent. Even when we 'see' her visions they are satisfyingly, preposterously real, capering fiends from a medieval mystery play with never a psychological or mystical overtone in sight.

One effect of this no-nonsense clarity in La Pucelle's character is to highlight the curious episode at the end of the play, where just before she is dragged away to die she begs mercy on the grounds that she is pregnant, and names the baby's father successively as CHARLES, ALENÇON and REIGNIER. This mightily confuses the English – is she the 'virgin pure' she is supposed to be, God's bride, or a strumpet who has been 'liberal and free', or somehow both at once? – and it can also confuse the audience. Why should her self-confidence falter at this moment and so briefly? Is she really pregnant, or is she desperately inventing excuses to escape the fire? (As soon as the attempt fails, she reverts to her former temper, spitting insults as she is hauled to death.) If this brief scene (less than forty lines) is taken as a guide to her character, it means that human weakness, terrors, must be played into the rest of the part somewhat against the text – and it makes particularly interesting the scene with the SHEPHERD, where the issue of her base or noble parentage is briefly aired. If, on the other hand, she is played consistently as a bluff woman of action, then this momentary collapse is both amazing and moving, a remarkable injection of humanity into the character at the very last moment, and is either a piece of playwriting incompetence or a theatrical surprise as cunning as a conjuring trick.

Ladies *(The Winter's Tale)*
There are three of them, and they play nursery games with MAMILLIUS before he settles down to tell HERMIONE a bedtime story. The First Lady may be the same person as Emilia, who helps Hermione's childbirth in prison and brings PAULINA news of the birth of baby PERDITA.

Lady *(Cymbeline)*
Attendant on the QUEEN and IMOGEN.

Lady Macbeth *(Macbeth)*
Over the years, great actresses have developed a tradition in playing Lady Macbeth which every new performer and director must take heed

of; its origins are certainly in Shakespeare's lines, but interpretations and importations have been added like the accretions on a coral reef. In particular, actresses have developed the ideas of powerful sexuality between Lady Macbeth and her husband, and of its transmutation, before DUNCAN's murder, into a malign, driving ambition which has all the orgasmic irresistibility of sexual passion. This interpretation would have been possible in Shakespeare's theatre, but would have required skill in the boy-actor far beyond the usual demands of Elizabethan female roles.

Everything rests on Lady Macbeth's two soliloquies in the letter-scene. She reads a letter from MACBETH telling her about the WITCHES' prophecy, and proposes, on the grounds that he is 'too full o' th' milk of human kindness/To catch the nearest way', to 'pour her spirits' in his ear and encourage his ambition. ('I may.../Chastise with the valour of my tongue/All that impedes thee from the golden round...') Immediately afterwards a Messenger brings word that Duncan is to visit the castle that night, and she invokes the powers of evil, begging them to 'unsex me here,/And fill me, from the crown to the toe, top-full/Of direst cruelty...'. This speech, the most passionate in the whole play, works up to an enormous climax ('Come to my woman's breasts/And take my milk for gall!... Come, thick night,/And pall thee in the dunnest smoke of hell...'), and at the end of it, virtually interrupting it halfway through a line, Macbeth comes in and she falls on him with an intensity of passion ('Great Glamis! Worthy Cawdor!') which he appears unable to understand or to match: his ambition is not yet stoked to the heat of hers.

If this scene shows the power of Lady Macbeth's ambition for her husband, their next scene shows her transferring that power to him. ('Screw your courage to the sticking-place...'.) She tells him that the deed must be done, explains in detail how to do it, and reassures him about the consequences. Then she leaves him, to greet her guests and (as he puts it) 'mock the time with fairest show', and when we next see her, flushed not with passion but with wine ('That which hath made them drunk hath made me bold'), though she is scornful of Macbeth's psychological panic after the murder and quite happy to go herself and smear the grooms with blood, her mood is a kind of brainless bravado quite unlike her previous calculated energy. When the murder is announced to MACDUFF and MALCOLM, and she faints ('Look to the lady'), her feelings are just as masked. Is her faint genuine, the start of the revulsion which will in the end destroy her, or is it a ploy to distract attention from Macbeth's gory account of how he killed the (supposedly guilty) grooms? The interpretations are mutually exclusive; both are prevalent.

After this scene Lady Macbeth's role declines in importance, and in swagger, as Macbeth's increases: she has surrendered all her psychological power to him, and collapses like a soft balloon. At the banquet, when he starts in horror at BANQUO's ghost (which only he can see), she reassures the guests with empty, hostessy politeness ('Think of this, good peers,/But as a thing of custom...'), and instead of comforting him or buttressing his resolution as she did before, all she can do is lamely suggest that he lacks 'the season of all natures, sleep'. Her own final appearance in the play, one act and the murder of LADY MACDUFF and her children later, is in the sleep-walking scene, and she appears psychologically rudderless, virtually insane and drained with guilt.

Lady Macduff *(Macbeth)*
In a brief scene, she discusses with her SON how they are to live if MACDUFF is killed; their innocent forebodings are interrupted by the MURDERERS, who solve their dilemma by killing them.

Laertes *(Hamlet)*
POLONIUS' son, OPHELIA's brother. He distrusts HAMLET, and thinks his love for Ophelia no more than 'a fashion.../A violet in the youth of primy nature.../The perfume and suppliance of a minute'. He advises her to have nothing to do with Hamlet, and does it in a speech almost as long, sensible and tedious as his father's own speech of advice to him. Later, after his return from France, he is so furious with Hamlet for killing Polonius and causing Ophelia's madness ('I'll not be juggled with!/To hell, allegiance! Vows, to the blackest devil!') that he is easy bait for CLAUDIUS' evil persuasions, and agrees to kill Hamlet in a duel with a poisoned sword – hardly the action one would expect from such a guileless, colourless young man. Only at the very end, fatally wounded, does he see sense at last and beg Hamlet's forgiveness. He is an uncomplicated youth, out of his depth in the murky plots of Elsinore, and doomed by the very heartiness of disposition which is the main attraction of his character. He is often played as older and wiser than his years (late teens), but boyishness, impetuosity, is an important aspect of the role, one of the few qualities he possesses which Hamlet needs, and lacks.

Lafeu *(All's Well that Ends Well)*
Old lord, confidant of the KING OF FRANCE and of the COUNTESS OF ROUSILLON (whose dead husband was his friend). He acts as a father to BERTRAM, in particular trying to warn him against PAROLLES, and when the time comes he acts as a father to HELENA too, writing off the nobles who refuse to marry her with a brusque 'An they were sons of mine, I'd have them whipp'd, or I would send them to the Turk to make eunuchs of'. He is roundly contemptuous of Parolles (who responds by mocking him), impatient with the clown LAVACHE and statesmanlike with his master the king. All through the play, his lines can be taken at face value, as elder-statesman crustiness expressed with a little more vigour than usual, or as determinedly tongue-in-cheek. When, for example, he says after Bertram's two-line recantation in the trial-scene, 'Mine eyes smell onions: I shall weep anon', how serious is he?

Lartius, Titus (*Coriolanus*)
General who with CORIOLANUS and COMINIUS leads the Romans against
the city of Corioli. He is an uncomplicated military man ('So, let the
ports be guarded: keep your duties/As I have set them down'), and
disappears from the play soon after the action moves from Corioli to
Rome, from the battlefield to politics.

Launce (*The Two Gentlemen of Verona*)
PROTEUS' clownish servant, a lugubrious youth whose life is spent
either joking with his jolly fellow-servant SPEED or mournfully
contemplating his mongrel Crab, 'the sourest-natured dog that lives'.
He behaves, indeed, more like Crab's straight man than his master:
when Speed asks, about Proteus and JULIA, 'Tell me true, wil't be a
match?' he answers 'Ask my dog. If he say ay, it will; if he say no, it
will; if he shake his tail and say nothing it will', and his last speech in
the play is a detailed description of Crab's disgraceful behaviour at a
banquet (he had not been under the Duke's table 'a pissing while, but
all the chamber smelt him'), and of how he, Launce, as usual took the
blame and the beating ('Twas I did the thing you wot of'). The only
bright moments in his gloomy, dog-ridden existence come from
imagining his ideal bride, a girl with 'nameless virtues' and a long
catalogue of vices, but who is still a good catch because although she
has 'more hair than wit and more faults than hairs', she also has 'more
wealth than faults'.

Laurence, Friar (*Romeo and Juliet*)
Laurence is an aged bumbler, a collector of herbs and a potterer in
people's lives, as well-meaning and ineffectual as one of the minor
Church of England clergymen in Trollope. He is ROMEO's confessor,
and has chidden him for his love-affair with Rosaline without ever
making him abandon it; as soon as Romeo announces his passion for
JULIET, Laurence falls over himself to facilitate it, on the specious (or
ill-considered) grounds that it might end the feud and bring the families
together. He is drawn further and further into the intrigue, marrying
the lovers in secret, arranging for Juliet's elopement, giving her the
potion – if this were a Greek tragedy, he would be the gods'
clockmaker, winding the machinery of their vengeance and ensuring
catastrophe. And yet, for all his foolishness, and though none of his
words or actions in the play suggest any reason for it, everyone from
Prince ESCALUS to the NURSE treats him throughout with affection and
respect. Some editors have suggested that Shakespeare was too wrapped
up in his play-making to bother giving Laurence depth or consistency
of character. This is a comfortable explanation, for if we were to assume
that Shakespeare *did* consider Laurence at all (and why should he not?),
we would have to admit that few other major characters, in any of his
plays, are depicted with such withering moral scorn.

Lavache (clown) *(All's Well that Ends Well)*
Formerly employed by the old Count of Rousillon, now dead, Lavache
is now a dependant of the COUNTESS. He is an old-fashioned,
melancholy court jester, and his quips and quiddities are so incessant,
and so second-rate, that it seems impossible that Shakespeare can have
meant us to take him seriously. He never stops; he sprays bad jokes
over every conversation he takes part in; the only mystery is why the
Countess, LAFEU, HELENA and the others are so patient with him. His
presence in the play adds nothing, either to plot or atmosphere. Even if
he was played by a famous comedian, and so gave Shakespeare's
audience pleasure we can never share, it is hard to see how he can have
been integrated into any of the scenes we see him in.

Lavinia *(Titus Andronicus)*
TITUS' daughter, beloved by BASSIANUS. In her early scenes she is a
sweet-natured, charming girl, but she is raped and mutilated (hands cut
off, tongue ripped out) about twenty minutes into the action, and
spends the rest of the play gliding gloomily about, giving meaningful
looks, uttering imcomprehensible shrieks and trying to write her
attackers' names with her mouth and stumps of arms. Under the
circumstances there is little scope for characterisation, though the part
must be fun to play.

Lawyer *(Henry VI Part One)*
In the scene of the white and red roses, he chooses white, and tells
SOMERSET his reason in three not-too-fascinating lines.

Le Beau *(As You Like It)*
One of Duke FREDERICK's courtiers, who tells ROSALIND and CELIA of
the impending wrestling-match; possibly the same lord who later takes
Frederick news that the girls and TOUCHSTONE have fled from court.

Le Fer *(Henry V)*
Rich Frenchman captured by PISTOL at Agincourt. He is the only
person in the entire world to be taken in by Pistol's fire-eating manner,
and he cringes and whines most obsequiously. He also does it in
French, which allows the boy playing the PAGE a nice line in ironical
'mugging' as he translates. (This, nowadays, is perhaps more
interesting to the audience than Pistol's abominable puns at the expense
of the Frenchman's language, e.g. when he mistakes the panic-stricken
exclamation 'O Seigneur Dieu' for the man's name and calls him O
Signior Dew.)

Lear *(King Lear)*
However complex and challenging the play *King Lear* may be, Lear's
own character is straightforward and simply drawn. The things he does,
says and is may have wider implications, for the audience, about the
nature and dilemmas of humankind, but he is unaware of them: he is
not a philosopher. Despite a thousand artists' impressions which depict

him as a kind of long-bearded, wild-eyed, Old-Testament patriarch, he is more like one of the no-nonsense heroes of Greek legend, a vessel for higher purposes of which he understands nothing. (Even the FOOL has a clearer view than he does of what things mean.)

For the first half of the play, until he loses his mind, Lear's characteristics are imperiousness and foolishness: of Shakespeare's heroes, only RICHARD (in *Richard II*) combines them to such an extravagant degree. Lear's will, like his rule, is absolute, and his majestic conceit allows no questioning. When he announces his decision to divide his kingdom according to the vehemence of his daughters' love-protestations, for example, his tone short-circuits argument ('Know we have divided/In three our kingdom, and it is our fast intent/To shake all cares and business from our age...') – and when his treatment of CORDELIA *is* questioned, on grounds of common humanity, he reacts with immediate, haughty fury ('Peace, Kent!/Come not between the dragon and his wrath'). The merest hint of insubordination, of absence of flattery, sends his blood-pressure soaring. He dispossesses his beloved daughter in a page of angry rhetoric; OSWALD's impertinence drives him as berserk with fury as if it were something serious; he ends his quarrel with REGAN and GONERIL by rushing out into the storm like a child determined to mortify its parents by doing itself some dreadful hurt. He never wavers from his high opinion of himself (indeed, he has never had to question his own authority before); he shows affection to no one but the Fool; except for Cordelia and KENT, his intimates treat him with formality or awe but not respect.

At first, when Lear's mind begins to topple, it is in the same melodramatic, conceited way. When he sees Kent in the stocks he says, grandly but with a total lack of compassion, 'Oh, how this mother swells up toward my heart!/*Hysterica passio* – down, thou climbing sorrow,/Thy element's below'. When he first faces the storm, he challenges it, tries to dominate it with words ('Blow, winds, and crack your cheeks! Rage! Blow!...'), and is so carried away by his own eloquence that he ignores the Fool's more practical reaction ('O nuncle, court holy-water in a dry house is better than this rain-water out-o'-door. Good nuncle, in, and ask thy daughters' blessing...'). He constantly calls himself aged and impotent ('You see me here, you gods, a poor old man...'), but the description is rhetorical and he rounds on anyone who acts on it.

Lear's madness is the gangway from this histrionic parade to real humanity, regality and moral greatness. If the first stage of his madness is ranting at the weather, the second is a parody of his former powers (the 'trial'-scene: 'Arraign her first: 'tis Goneril. I here take my oath before this honourable assembly, she kick'd the poor king, her father...'), and the last involves total disintegration of personality. ('Ha, Goneril with a white beard! They flattered me like a dog, and told me I had white hairs in my beard ere the black ones were there...'.)

Finally, when he recovers his wits and discovers true humanity, his character becomes serene and gentle, as strong in its 'weakness' as his former blustering 'strength' was weak. Speeches like 'Come, let's away to prison./We two alone will sing like birds i' the cage...' have a radiance, a resonance, absent from all he did or said before. It is no wonder that for two centuries playgoers preferred the play to end happily at this point, with Lear's and Cordelia's restitution: to see him die for grief over Cordelia's corpse, after such a hard-won breakthrough to moral serenity, is catharsis of the grimmest kind.

The symbol of Lear's changed character, and of its place among the wider meanings of the play, comes at the very end. Led by Kent, his courtiers treat him with a deferential affection they never showed in the days of his pomp, and he hardly notices. His sufferings have recreated him, poured humanity into him, and there is nothing left of the hollow, ranting man he was. But the transfiguring love he has found is also, tragically and pointedly, his last emotion on earth, and he dies even as he expresses it. ('Thou'lt come no more,/Never, never, never, never, never./Pray you, undo this button. Thank you, sir./Do you see this? Look on her, look, her lips,/Look there, look there – (*Dies*)'.)

Lennox (*Macbeth*)
Scottish courtier, dismayed by the state of the country after MACBETH becomes king. He joins MACDUFF, MALCOLM and the other rebels. Little character beyond political dismay.

Leonardo (*The Merchant of Venice*)
BASSANIO's servant, who takes Launcelot GOBBO into Bassanio's service.

Leonato (*Much Ado about Nothing*)
HERO's father and BEATRICE's uncle. He is governor of Messina, and part of his character is the stiffness that role demands: he welcomes the victorious DON PEDRO, for example, with formal courtesy, despite Don Pedro's blithe announcement that he and his retinue 'shall stay here at least a month'. But underneath his formality is a youthful, impish glee at the world's solemnity and a willingness, when things are dull, to liven them up with practical jokes and pranks. He organises the masked ball at which Don Pedro courts Hero on CLAUDIO's behalf; he joins wholeheartedly in the trick played on BENEDICK to persuade him that Beatrice is in love with him; even though heartbroken at the breaking-off of Hero's marriage, he goes along with the trick of persuading Claudio that she is dead, and plays the part of the grieving father as if it were really true; he makes Claudio agree to marry his 'niece', and takes the disguised Hero to the altar instead; he ends the play by hosting a second masked ball. He is humorous with Beatrice, businesslike with Dogberry, full of relaxed affection with his friend Don Pedro and his brother ANTONIO. When he is in the pit of despair, believing Hero's guilt (itself an odd thing for a loving father to do so readily), his language has an intensity of suffering worthy – save that this is comedy

– of LEAR himself: 'Wherefore? Why doth not every earthly thing/Cry shame upon her? Could she here deny/The story that is printed in her blood?/Do not live, Hero! Do not ope thine eyes,/For, did I think thou wouldst not quickly die.../Myself would, on the rearward of reproaches,/Strike at thy life.' The hot-blooded, jovial middle-aged are frequent characters in Shakespeare's comedies, and this dark side to Leonato makes him one of the most fascinating of them all.

Leonine *(Pericles)*

Servant of DIONYZA, sent by her to kill MARINA. He takes Marina on a seaside walk, and bids her say her prayers, but before anything else can happen the PIRATES come and kidnap her, and Leonine runs away. He tells Dionyza falsely that he has killed Marina, whereupon she poisons him. He is characterless but his days are full.

Leontes *(The Winter's Tale)*

In the first half of the play Leontes is a monster of jealousy, raging so irrationally and causelessly that he seems insane. ('Is whispering nothing?/Is leaning cheek to cheek? Is meeting noses?/Kissing with inside lip? Stopping the career of laughter/With a sigh?... Horsing foot on foot?/Skulking in corners? Wishing clocks more swift?...') He is abusive to HERMIONE ('O thou thing!), implacable in the trial-scene, and dismissive of the Delphic oracle which proclaims him wrong. Then, when he hears of MAMILLIUS' and Hermione's deaths, he crumples into wretchedness, meekly accepting PAULINA's furious reproaches ('Go on, go on:/Thou canst not speak too much: I have deserv'd/All tongues to talk their bitterest') and brokenly promising what seems, after what he's done, a singularly ineffective penance. ('Once a day I'll visit/The chapel where they lie, and tears shed there/Shall be my recreation... Come, and lead me/To these sorrows.')

In the last part of the play, when the interest has shifted from his generation to that of FLORIZEL and PERDITA, he is hardly characterised at all: his reconciliation with POLIXENES is reported, not shown, and his discovery that Hermione is alive after all is presented less as a piece of drama than as a magic ritual (the coming to life of a statue), and his lines' chief purpose is to show the transfiguration through suffering for which the earlier scenes of the play seemed to be preparing us.

Lepidus, Marcus Aemilius *(Julius Caesar; Antony and Cleopatra)*

Third member, with ANTONY and OCTAVIUS, of the triumvirate which runs Rome after CAESAR's death. In real life he was a banker, a shrewd businessman if no politician. In *Julius Caesar* he appears only in one scene, discussing with the others whose names are to be 'prick'd down for death' in the bloody aftermath of the conspiracy, and his part in the action fits Octavius' scornful opinion of him, 'a slight, unmeritable man,/Meet to be sent on errands...'. In *Antony and Cleopatra* his role is even slighter, chiefly that of a peacemaker between Octavius and Antony. Suspected by Octavius of plotting with POMPEY against him, he is arrested and imprisoned 'till death enlarge his confine'.

Lewis (later King Louis VIII) *(King John)*
Dauphin of France, a young man utterly in the shadow of his father
PHILIP. He is married off to BLANCH, then torn from her into war; he
behaves bravely and nobly, but loses the war and retreats to France.

Lewis (Louis XI) *(Henry VI Part Three)*
King of France. Appears in one scene only, at first refusing to help
Queen MARGARET against the Yorkists because his daughter BONA is to
marry EDWARD, then, when he hears that Edward has married Lady
GREY instead, offering Margaret and WARWICK all the soldiers and
support they need.

Lieutenant *(Coriolanus)*
AUFIDIUS' junior officer, who listens to his complaints that Coriolanus
has changed his loyalty but not his nature and behaves 'more proudlier/
Even to my person, than I thought he would'. The scene is important
for displaying Aufidius' character, but it offers the Lieutenant, a yes-
man, no character-scope at all.

Lieutenant of the Tower *(Henry VI Part Three)*
Guards HENRY until EDWARD's deposition, and is praised by him for
kindness which 'hath made my imprisonment a pleasure,/Ay, such a
pleasure as incaged birds/Conceive, when after many moody
thoughts/At last, by notes of household harmony,/They quite forget
their loss of liberty'.

Ligarius, Caius *(Julius Caesar)*
One of the conspirators, a sick old man whose hatred of CAESAR, in a
brief scene with BRUTUS, jerks him out of feebleness. ('By all the gods
that Romans bow before,/I here discard my sickness!')

Lincoln, Bishop of *(Henry VIII)*
A yes-man, he has one moment of glory, when he claims to have first
suggested to the king the idea of separation from KATHARINE – exactly
what HENRY wants him to say.

Lodovico *(Othello)*
Noble Venetian (a kinsman of BRABANTIO), sent out to Cyprus to recall
OTHELLO. He is bewildered to see Othello humiliate DESDEMONA, and
horrified by the chain of murders and treachery which ensues; he finally
takes command of the situation – too late to mend it – in a handful of
brisk, authoritative lines.

London, Lord Mayor of *(Henry VI Part One)*
A hand-wringing, peace-loving shopkeeper ('I myself fight not once in
forty year') who is caught up in the brawl between GLOUCESTER and
WINCHESTER ('I'll call for clubs if you will not away') and is finally
forced to burst into Parliament and beg the king's help because, as he
puts it with splendid mercantile indignation, 'The Bishop's and the

Duke of Gloucester's men,/Forbidden late to carry any weapons,/Have
fill'd their pockets full of pebble-stones,/And, banding themselves in
contrary parts,/Do pelt so fast at one another's pate/That many have
their giddy brains knock'd out;/Our windows are broke down in every
street,/And we, for fear, compell'd to shut our shops.'

London, Lord Mayor of *(Richard III)*

Self-important local politician, bustling among the nobility. He
welcomes the young Prince EDWARD to London, not realising that he is
doomed to die in the Tower; he is with RICHARD and BUCKINGHAM
when HASTINGS' head is brought in, and they easily convince him that
Hastings deserved to die. (*Richard*: 'Think you we are Turks or
infidels,/Or that we would, against the form of law,/Proceed thus rashly
in the villain's death,/But that the extreme peril of the case,/The peace
of England and our persons' safety/Enforc'd us to his execution?'
Mayor: 'Now fair befall you! He deserved his death...')

Longaville, Lord *(Love's Labour's Lost)*

Attendant lord on FERDINAND, one of the four young gallants at the
heart of the play. Though he is described (by the PRINCESS) as 'a merry
mocking lord' and one of the 'short-liv'd wits' who 'wither as they
grow', his lines seldom bear out this report, and his role is chiefly to be
one voice in an ensemble, either making witty counterpoint with
Ferdinand, BEROWNE and DUMAINE or in duet with his beloved MARIA.
As his name suggests, he is tall – 'Few taller are so young', as Maria
puts it – and the hint this gives of sapling gawkiness is agreeably borne
out by the languishing verse he writes when he finds himself in love.
('Did not the heavenly rhetoric of thine eye,/'Gainst whom the world
cannot hold argument,/Persuade my heart to this false perjury...?')

Lord *(Hamlet)*

Tells HAMLET that it is time to duel with LAERTES.

Lord *(The Taming of the Shrew)*

Finds the drunken SLY at the start of the Induction and sets in motion
the practical joke of persuading him that he is really a nobleman. Jolly,
cheerful and with no human feelings whatever: a typical practical joker
with the added nastiness of being an Elizabethan aristocrat,
unquestioningly obeyed by every underling.

Lord Chamberlain *(Henry VIII)*

A bustling, busy courtier, he introduces HENRY to Anne BULLEN, takes
Anne news that she has been created Marchioness of Pembroke,
conspires with NORFOLK, SUFFOLK and the others against WOLSEY, and
presides over CRANMER's heresy-trial – all without showing the smallest
sign of character.

Lord Chief Justice *(Henry IV Part Two)*

Alerted by Mistress QUICKLY to FALSTAFF's irregular life-style, the
Lord Chief Justice pompously exhorts him to mend his ways, and

complains that he follows the young prince up and down 'like his evil angel'; for his pains, he is roundly abused and mocked, reduced to a quivering 'Fie, fie, fie, Sir John'. At the end of the play, favoured by the new Henry V, he lords it over Falstaff with crowing, old man's malice. He is sometimes played straight, as an outraged official, but he is better as a farce fool, a senile, overweening idiot, a SHALLOW when he speaks prose and a POLONIUS in verse.

Lord Marshal *(Richard II)*
Organises the duel between BOLINGBROKE and MOWBRAY, and contributes (through measured, regularly stressed lines) much of the formality and artificiality the scene requires – a marked contrast with the variety and rhythmic ebb-and-flow of the challenges in the later Parliament scene, an event stage-managed by Bolingbroke. A short and characterless part, but important for dramatic effect.

Lords *(All's Well that Ends Well)*
In the early scenes in the French court, there are four of them, and the KING OF FRANCE asks HELENA to choose a husband from among them. (Despite their courtesy, she picks BERTRAM.) Two of them may also be the same people as the Captains DUMAIN who torment PAROLLES.

Lords *(Cymbeline)*
The two Lords have plenty to say, and most of it is conventional courtiers' stuff, courteous and colourless. But in their scenes with CLOTEN they take on distinct, sharp characters: the First Lord is ironically deferential, and the Second Lord blunt and mocking behind Cloten's back. (*Cloten*: 'Was there ever a man had such luck? When I kiss'd the jack, upon an up-cast to be hit away! I had a hundred pound on't – and then a whoreson jackanapes must take me up for swearing...' *First Lord*: What got he by that? You have broke his pate with your bowl.' *Second Lord, aside*: 'If his wit had been like him that broke it, it would have all run out.') The tone and speed of such dialogue is reminiscent of the TOUCHSTONE scenes in *As You Like It* or (at its best) of the banter of FALSTAFF's followers in *Henry IV Part One*: did Shakespeare's clowns play lords as well as commoners?

Lords *(Timon of Athens)*
Amazed by TIMON's generosity with gold, and lacking all other character. They later attend his second banquet, and are noisily dismayed when he throws hot water over them instead of providing food.

Lorenzo *(The Merchant of Venice)*
ANTONIO's friend, the young nobleman who elopes with JESSICA. For most of the play he is a standard young hero, a nonentity; then suddenly, in the moonlit love-scene in the garden at Belmont, he begins speaking poetry of such radiance that he briefly becomes the play's most watchable character. ('The moon shines bright. In such a night as

this,/When the sweet wind did gently kiss the trees,/And they did make no noise, in such a night/Troilus methinks mounted the Troyan walls/ And sigh'd his soul toward the Grecian tents/Where Cressid lay...'.)

Lovel, Lord *(Richard III)*
Villainous follower of RICHARD, who with RATCLIFF takes HASTINGS to his death, and a few pages later re-enters with his head. No relation to the LOVELL in *Henry VIII*.

Lovell, Sir Thomas *(Henry VIII)*
Lovell has plenty to do, delivering messages (e.g. to GARDINER that Anne BULLEN is in labour), attending the king (e.g. when WOLSEY is disgraced), discussing the latest news (e.g. that foreign fripperies are banished from court). He is discreet, anonymous and elegant: court furniture that moves.

Love's Labour's Lost
Ferdinand, the young king of Navarre, and his nobles Berowne, Longaville and Dumaine vow to give up three years to study, fasting and chastity, and bar all women from the court. Costard the clown is arrested for talking to the country wench Jaquenetta, and is handed into the custody of the fantastical Spaniard Don Armado and his cheeky page-boy Moth. The lords' withdrawal from the world is tested by the arrival of the Princess of France, her ladies Rosaline, Katharine and Maria and a group of lords led by the old *roué* Boyet. The young men and women make frosty, witty conversation, and it becomes apparent that they have fallen in love, Ferdinand with the Princess, Dumaine with Katharine, Longaville with Maria and Berowne with Rosaline. Now begins a chain of cross-purposes. Costard takes a letter from Armado to Jaquenetta, and another from Berowne to Rosaline, and misdelivers them; abandoning their oath, the four lords disguise themselves as Russians and court the ladies, who disguise themselves as one another, with the result that all protestations of love are misdirected. The atmosphere is a mixture of edginess and high-summer frivolity, and in the midst of it all Holofernes, the pedantic schoolmaster, at the lords' behest, plans an entertainment, a pageant of the Nine Worthies, and recruits Armado, Moth, Sir Nathaniel the curate, Dull the constable and Costard to play all the parts he can't manage on his own. After the pageant a messenger brings news of the death of the King of France, the Princess's father. As the ladies prepare to leave, the lords try to convince them of their sincerity, but the ladies order them to wait for a year and a day and then, if their love lasts, come wooing again, and the play ends with music, the Cuckoo-song of spring ('When daisies pied') and the Owl-song of winter ('When icicles hang by the wall').

Luce *(The Comedy of Errors)*
Servant of ANTIPHOLUS II, who encourages DROMIO I not to let her master and his friends into the house, as she thinks that they are there

already.

Lucentio *(The Taming of the Shrew)*
Handsome young hero, in love with BIANCA. He disguises himself as a
Latin teacher, Cambio, and courts her under the pretence of construing
Virgil. (*'Hac ibat* – as I told you before – *Simois* – I am Lucentio – *hic
est* – son of Vincentio of Pisa – *Sigeia tellus* – disguised thus to get your
love').

Lucetta *(The Two Gentlemen of Verona)*
JULIA's servant, who hears her declarations of love for PROTEUS and
helps her disguise herself as a page-boy.

Luciana *(The Comedy of Errors)*
More patient than her sister ADRIANA, she tries to head off her fury
against her absent husband, and later scolds (the wrong) ANTIPHOLUS
for having 'quite forgot/A husband's office', only to be bewildered when
he answers, 'Thee will I love, and with thee lead my life./Thou hast no
husband yet, and I no wife.' The part is small and the lines are few, but
her character, gentle, innocent and unawakened, is as clearly defined as
it is attractive.

Lucilius *(Julius Caesar)*
Friend of BRUTUS: a noble, brave man captured in the fighting, and
proud to hear that Brutus has finally done the right thing and
committed suicide.

Lucilius *(Timon of Athens): see* **Servants**

Lucio *(Measure for Measure)*
Shakespeare calls Lucio a 'fantastic', implying a kind of parrot-brained
fop with no interest in life except the impression he makes on others.
For much of the time this is fair enough: his raillery with the 'two other
like gentlemen', for example, is as shallow and frivolous as his flirting
with women, or, as he puts it, '. . . to seem the lapwing, and to jest/
Tongue far from heart'. There is, however, a much harder edge to his
character. He refuses to go bail for his old joking-companion POMPEY,
however long or hard Pompey's imprisonment will be as a result. ('I
will pray, Pompey, to increase your bondage: if you take it not
patiently, why, your mettle is the more'). He shamelessly slanders the
DUKE to the Friar, not realising that they are one and the same person –
and what reason but foppery has he for claiming acquaintance with the
Duke at all, let alone slandering him to a stranger?; then, when the
'Friar' threatens to reveal everything, he turns on him in a fury which is
anything but frivolous. ('Why, you bald-pated, lying rascal! . . . Show
your knave's visage, with a pox to you! Show your sheep-biting face,
and be hang'd in an hour!') Most unexpectedly of all, he shows himself
a warm, honest and true-hearted friend to CLAUDIO, reaching heights of
eloquence in his urging of ISABELLA to help her brother, and behaving
throughout more like the traditional Shakespearean 'noble friend' than

like a zany. If shallowness triumphs in the end (that is, in his obsequious, ill-timed interruptions in the trial-scene), it is also, ironically, the saving of his life, for when the Duke is unmasked and everything is revealed, he begs the Duke to do anything to him, even whip him or hang him, but not to marry him to a whore – and marriage to a whore is precisely the punishment he gets. He is himself a kind of intellectual whore, constantly prostituting his character to the company he is in, and his comeuppance (or triumph, depending how you look at it) is entirely appropriate, offering a comic equivalent of the catharsis achieved by a hero's downfall in tragedy. With Pompey, Lucio is one of the play's characters most often subordinated in performance, to bring out darker themes and resonances. Because he treads the borderline between tragedy and comedy, the way he is played can determine, more than any other character, the mood and style of a whole production.

Lucius (*Julius Caesar*)
BRUTUS' servant, a mild-mannered boy who sings, and whose presence in the action allows Brutus to reveal both his humanity and his tortured soul. Lucius' main character-traits, both in these scenes and in his scene with PORTIA, are politeness and curiosity.

Lucius (*Timon of Athens*)
False friend of TIMON's whose excuse for not lending him money is that he has unfortunately spent it all the day before. ('What a wicked beast I was to disfurnish myself against such a good time, when I might ha' shown myself honourable.')

Lucius (*Titus Andronicus*)
TITUS' eldest son. His first act in the play is a bloody murder – 'Give me the proudest prisoner of the Goths,/That we may hew his limbs, and on a pile/*Ad manes fratrum* sacrifice his flesh' – and his last, as emperor, is a declaration of terrible justice on AARON (to be buried up to the neck and left to starve) and on TAMORA's body (to be thrown forth 'to beasts and birds of prey'). In between he seems like a noble, honest youth, an avenger banished from Rome for fortitude who returns with an army to cleanse pollution; but if we measure him by deeds and not by glowing words, he is heading, as the play ends, to be as remorseless as his father and as tyrannical as SATURNINUS.

Lucius, Caius (*Cymbeline*)
Roman general who attacks Britain to collect taxes unpaid for many years. A brave soldier.

Lucullus (*Timon of Athens*)
False friend of TIMON's, who refuses to help him on the grounds that 'this is no time to lend money, especially in bare friendship without security'.

Lucy, Sir William (*Henry VI Part One*)
Upright, honourable gentleman who begs first YORK then SOMERSET to

help TALBOT against the French at Bordeaux, and when each of them refuses bewails, in a dignified manner, the way dissension in the English ranks, not French bravery, is losing the day. ('The fraud of England, not the force of France,/Hath now entrapp'd the noble-minded Talbot...')

Lychorida *(Pericles)*
Nurse to whom PERICLES entrusts the infant MARINA.

Lysander *(A Midsummer Night's Dream)*
Young man in love with HERMIA. In contrast with the hot-headed DEMETRIUS, he is unsmiling and serious, but no less fervent for all that. Under the influence of magic, his affections are transferred to HELENA. After many adventures in the wood, the spell is lifted and he once again loves HERMIA.

Lysimachus *(Pericles)*
Governor of Mytilene who visits the brothel looking for 'a dozen of virginities', is appealed to by MARINA, rescues her from the brothel, takes her to PERICLES and later marries her.

Macbeth *(Macbeth)*
At first sight, it is hard to work out precisely what appeal the role of Macbeth has had for star actors down the centuries. The play charts his remorseless moral disintegration, from the 'brave Macbeth' who 'well deserves that name' at the start to the 'hell-hound' of the end. And apart from his (briefly sketched) noble generalship at the beginning, all his qualities are negative: indecision, panic, cunning, superstition, evil-hearted tyranny. Hardly a line solicits sympathy from other people in the play or from the audience. Of all Shakespeare's great tragic roles, Macbeth is the only one which rouses neither our pity nor our admiration. We are fascinated and repelled all at once – a combination common with his villainous secondary roles (IAGO; EDMUND), but unique in his vehicles for stars.

Macbeth's qualities are the stuff of melodrama, and perhaps this is his appeal for barnstorming stars. The play's melodramatic effects are often, nowadays, subordinated to psychological screw-tightening, turned into black farce, or cut, but they permeate the action and it is the fact that Macbeth himself believes in them, with deepest seriousness, that forms his character: his 'tragedy' is that as soon as he surrenders conscience to ambition he becomes, precisely, a two-dimensional, melodramatic personality, a hollow man.

The play moves so quickly that we are left no time to ponder meaning or motivation. No sooner do the WITCHES make their prophecy than Macbeth falls to ambitious musings; no sooner is he back at the castle than LADY MACBETH is stirring him to kill DUNCAN; no sooner is the murder done than he is king, with a throne (if not royal dignity) to protect and only the assassin's knife to help him do it; no sooner does he think the chain of murders ended and his power secure than Birnam Wood moves to Dunsinane and he begins his last, frantic plunge into oblivion. At the beginning of Macbeth's moral descent, when we still have a vestige of sympathy for him, he is given soliloquies, not of self-doubt but of hesitation and foreboding – 'If it were done, when 'tis done, then 'twere well/It were done quickly...'; 'Is this a dagger...?' – and he greedily snatches encouragement from Lady Macbeth, mistaking it for moral authority. But once he orders the MURDERERS to kill BANQUO he is fixed in character and purpose, morally bankrupt and doomed (only a quarter of the way through the play). For the rest of the action, we see him alternately writhing in horror at the ghosts, witches and other manifestations of the power of evil to which he has surrendered, or confidently, swaggeringly, playing the tyrant. At this level, the character is like a soldierly equivalent of Marlowe's bookish Doctor Faustus: Macbeth sells his soul not for knowledge but for power, but just as quickly realises the dreadful implications of his bargain, hurries to gain as much advantage as he can ('No boasting.../This deed I'll do before this purpose cool...') and finally, just before the battle with Macduff that he is sure to lose, throws up his hands and assents cynically, humorously, in his own downfall. ('I 'gin to be aweary of the sun,/And wish th'estate o' th' world were now undone./Ring the alarum-bell! Blow wind, come wrack!/At least we'll die with harness on our back.')

Part of the problem for actors nowadays is that this kind of tough, soldierly fatalism is out of fashion, and has a ring of moral hollowness which would never have occurred to Shakespeare's audiences. For them, Macbeth's courage (regularly signposted throughout the play) would have been a redeeming character-quality, the same kind of leathery integrity as TITUS Andronicus, LEAR or CORIOLANUS possess, for all their vicissitudes, which is present in such utterly different heroes as HENRY V, and whose absence in characters like RICHARD II or HAMLET is such a crippling flaw. We like, nowadays, to see Macbeth played as a kind of moral bladder, pumped full of resolution by his wife at the start of the play and collapsing to flaccidity after her suicide. But in Shakespeare's day – and this is surely what he had in mind as he conceived the roles – Lady Macbeth was entirely subsidiary, and it was the conflict in Macbeth's own character between integrity and villainy and the fluctuation of his moral self-awareness which made the play.

Macbeth

Macbeth, general to King Duncan of Scotland, is promised by three
Witches that he will be Thane of Cawdor and 'king hereafter'; soon
afterwards news is brought that Duncan has made him Thane of
Cawdor. He ponders the rest of the prophecy, and writes of it to his
wife, thus sparking ambition in her. Duncan visits the castle, Macbeth
kills him and Lady Macbeth incriminates the Grooms by smearing their
faces with blood. The King's sons Malcolm and Donalbain flee the
country, and Macbeth is made king. He embarks on a chain of murders
to consolidate his rule, partly inspired by the Witches' prophecies.
Banquo (his fellow-general) was 'to father kings', so he must die. (His
ghost appears soon afterwards in Macbeth's palace at dinner, unseen by
everyone except Macbeth, whose horrified reactions make people
question his sanity.) Macduff is dangerous, so he and all his family
must die. Macduff escapes to join Malcolm in England and when news
is brought that his wife and children have been murdered, he and
Malcolm gather an army to attack Macbeth.

Although Macbeth, buoyed up by the Witches' prophecies that he
cannot fall till Birnam Wood come to Dunsinane, and that 'no man
born of woman' can kill him, grows into a monster of tyrannical
arrogance, guilt crushes his wife. She begins sleepwalking, trying to
wash imaginary blood from her hands and babbling of murder, and
finally commits suicide. Malcolm, Macduff and their army cut branches
from the trees of Birnam Wood and advance under their camouflage on
Dunsinane, where Macbeth has made his lair. So the first prophecy is
fulfilled, and although Macbeth fights bravely, his resolution collapses
when he finds that Macduff was not born normally but was 'ripp'd
untimely from his mother's womb'. He is killed and beheaded, and
Malcolm is proclaimed King of Scotland.

Macbeth, Lady (*Macbeth*): *see* Lady Macbeth

Macduff (*Macbeth*)

One of *Macbeth*'s themes is the contest between light and darkness,
between unregenerate evil and moral purity. In this contest, light
(symbolised by Macduff) eventually and predictably wins, and darkness
(symbolised by MACBETH) has all the best lines. Macduff is as crucial
and about as interesting as the ridge-pole that supports a tent. He is
staunch and noble, so undevious that he fails to see through MALCOLM's
trick of pretending to be wicked to test his loyalty, so devoted that he
reacts with almost comic disbelief to news that his wife and children
have been slaughtered. ('All my pretty ones?/Did you say all? Oh, hell-
kite! All?/What, all my pretty chickens and their dam/At one fell
swoop?') He kills Macbeth in single combat at the end of the play, in
the climactic encounter between light and dark familiar from a
thousand soap-opera epics, ten thousand western films.

Macduff, Lady (*Macbeth*): *see* **Lady Macduff**

Macmorris, Captain (*Henry V*)

Appears in one scene, with the Scots captain JAMY, the Welsh captain
FLUELLEN and the English captain GOWER. There has been vivid
argument about the purpose of the scene (much of which is given over
to Macmorris' and Fluellen's arguing about the respective bravery of
the Irish and Welsh, and to the attempts of the others to keep the
peace). Do they represent how all four nations of Britain achieve
harmony under HENRY? Are they simple comic stereotypes (with
Macmorris the standard stage Irishman)? Are they playing no more
than the kind of Shakespeare 'common-man' scene which nowadays
frequently falls flat? Or is the scene meant to establish Fluellen's bardic
irascibility, which is put to more serious dramatic use later in the play?
Whatever the answer, the scene has to be handled carefully in
performance, or its effect is ruined by Henry's speech before Harfleur
and by KATHARINE's English lesson, which immediately follow it.
Apart from his comic Irish accent, Macmorris is hardly characterised:
his part is better suited to a comic than to a dramatic actor – and this
casting, perhaps, declares the 'meaning' of the scene.

Maecenas, Caius (*Antony and Cleopatra*)

OCTAVIUS' friend, who tries to make peace between him and ANTONY,
and then supports Octavius loyally in his campaigns. Although in real
life he was a fascinating person (a millionaire statesman, who later
became Octavius' – the emperor Augustus' – adviser on culture and a
notable artistic patron), in the play he is unobtrusive and characterless.

Malcolm (*Macbeth*)

DUNCAN's elder son and heir. He is a boy in his teens, and plays no
substantial part in the action until he escapes to England after his
father's murder: the manly, princely lines are given to MACDUFF. In a
powerful scene in England, however, Malcolm pretends to Macduff
that he is ambitious, greedy, lustful, unprincipled and bloodthirsty,
utterly unsuitable to be king – and so tests Macduff's loyalty. The ploy
is an old one, and contrived (though not as hollow-seeming as when
SIMONIDES uses it in *Pericles*), but halfway through the scene news is
brought of the murder of Macduff's wife and children, and we watch
Malcolm simultaneously comforting him and stirring him to 'make
medicines of our great revenge/To cure this deadly grief'. In short, he
demonstrates moral stature, and grows up before our eyes.

Malvolio (*Twelfth Night*)

Everyone is nasty to Malvolio, and no one has any time for him. He is
like POLONIUS in *Hamlet*: every time he speaks people listen, but there
is a distinct feeling that they wish both they and he were somewhere
else; he is a killjoy, a bore and a toady, uncomfortable to be with and
intolerable to work for. (Some scholars say that the character was based
on a real person, and that the part offered Shakespeare's first audiences

the additional pleasure of caricature – it would be very funny so played today – but such an interpretation hardly helps the play.) At another level, Malvolio is a standard comic type, the unbending, unlovable straight-man whom everyone teases and whose downfall (especially if slapstick) is all the funnier for the humourless self-importance which precedes it.

This is farce-characterisation, and people in the play respond to Malvolio in the two-dimensional way of farce, differing only according to their rank in life. OLIVIA, his employer, is either punctilious but distant (e.g. when she sends him to return to 'Cesario' the ring she claims the boy has dropped) or frostily furious (in the 'cross-gartered' scene); Sir Toby BELCH, his social superior but his moral inferior, resorts to schoolboy cheek ('Go, rub thy chain with crumbs!'; 'Sneck up!'); MARIA, his social inferior but moral superior, uses his own self-importance to trip him (in the letter-intrigue), and at the same time makes ironical fun at his expense, by the vulgar references in the letter to Olivia's 'C's, her U's, her T's' and 'the way she makes her great P's', references Malvolio predictably and hilariously fails to understand.

What no one in the play pauses to wonder – and what, in a bad performance, never occurs to the audience either – is what Malvolio's own feelings are about himself. It's easy to play him straightforwardly and farcically, as a bigoted beanpole; some actors add a kind of desperate tragic dignity, investing his 'madness' with LEAR-like intensity and making his final words ('I'll be revenged on the whole pack of you!') a howl of rage to equal anything in *Coriolanus* or *Timon of Athens*. This interpretation, monomania turning to real mania, may fit the character suggested by Malvolio's actual name (Ben Jonson would have been proud to coin it: it means 'I wish ill'), but it is at odds with *Twelfth Night's* autumnal geniality, and in the end isolates Malvolio by making him a different kind of character from any other in the action.

However two-dimensionally he strikes other people in the play, Malvolio is a three-dimensional, real person to himself, a self-tormentor (another stock type in Elizabethan drama) whose bleak attitude to the world arises from neurotic dissatisfaction with himself. From the emotional heights (his elation when he thinks that Olivia wants to marry him) he plunges to the depths (imprisoned as a madman, forced to beg even the despised FESTE to pity him). He says 'I have been most notoriously abused' – and so he has; but the chief agent of his misery is himself, and his final words in the play offer no cure for that, no compromise. This is material for tragedy, not comedy, and as with Feste, the way Malvolio is played can swing the mood of *Twelfth Night* to darkness (if he is played seriously, the only character who ends unhappier than he starts) or to light (if he is played farcically, so that his discomfiture is a cathartic, happy ending for everyone else). The ambiguity in the part mirrors the ambiguity in the play.

Mamillius *(The Winter's Tale)*
Young boy, son of LEONTES and HERMIONE. He is the standard pert, knowing Shakespearean child marked for death, and after a charming if coy domestic scene with Hermione (he whispers a bedtime story in her ear) he is not seen again and we hear that he has died of grief at his mother's false arrest.

Man *(Henry VIII)*
PORTER's assistant who tries with him to keep back the crowd before Princess Elizabeth's christening. Like his master, he is boisterous and good-humoured; bustle is his character.

Marcade *(Love's Labour's Lost)*
Attendant on the PRINCESS of France, he brings his mistress news of the death of the King of France.

Marcellus *(Hamlet)*
The most sensible of the soldiers on guard in Elsinore when the GHOST appears. He encourages HORATIO to ask the Ghost its business, and later brings HAMLET to the battlements to talk to it. Unlike the other soldiers (who are terrified), he seems more curious about the Ghost than afraid of it.

Marcius, Caius: *see* **Coriolanus**

Marcius, Young *(Coriolanus)*
CORIOLANUS' son, a boy of four or five years old. He speaks only one line and a half (in the intercession scene: 'A' shall not tread on me; I'll run away till I am bigger, but then I'll fight'), but his character is well enough sketched for us (by VOLUMNIA and VALERIA in an earlier scene) for us to be grimly certain that he is already, by heredity and environment, his father's unlovely replica.

Marcus Andronicus *(Titus Andronicus)*
TITUS' brother, a stalwart middle-aged lord, hampered by his kindness and honesty from playing a full part in the blood-boltered politics all round him. His bluffness – 'I have dogs, my lord,/Will rouse the proudest panther in the chase,/And climb the highest promontory top' – and his vehement, pure-hearted grief at events – 'Now let hot Etna cool in Sicily,/And be my heart an ever-burning hell!/These miseries are more than may be borne' – make a shining contrast with everyone else's character and behaviour. Titus appropriately calls him 'gentle Marcus'; alas, he is not strong-willed enough, for all his gentleness, to pick up the reins of Rome after the final massacre, but surrenders them to LUCIUS and so ensures the continuation of the storm of blood.

Mardian *(Antony and Cleopatra)*
CLEOPATRA's servant, a eunuch. She mocks him continually, and he stands up manfully if ineffectually for himself. ('... I have fierce affection, and think/What Venus did with Mars'). Cleopatra uses him to

take false news of her death to ANTONY, the event which leads to Antony's suicide. He is, we are told, a singer, but is given no chance to prove it in the play since Cleopatra takes 'no pleasure/In aught a eunuch has'.

Margarelon *(Troilus and Cressida)*
PRIAM's bastard son. He meets THERSITES on the battlefield and orders him to 'turn, slave, and fight'; Thersites refuses on the grounds that he, too, is a bastard. Margarelon speaks three lines altogether, all in the same grim, determined tone.

Margaret *(Henry VI Parts One, Two and Three; Richard III)*
Few Shakespeare characters exhibit such spectacular variety: for the same performer to play Margaret in all four plays, one after another, is a feat of technical virtuosity. In the course of the action she ages thirty years, and passes from the dewy-eyed young girl of *Henry VI Part One* to the embittered, hate-twisted hag of *Richard III*; she flirts with or insults every man she meets; she leads armies with a nobility and regality stolen from her husband HENRY; she passes, as the plays proceed, from self-interest to patriotism and back again; she has some of the liveliest speeches and most flamboyant actions in the plays.

In *Henry VI Part One* Margaret is a cameo role (that is, characterful and fun to play, but short). She is a young woman trapped into a dynastic marriage, and she is by no means as innocent as she appears. (Her dialogue with SUFFOLK, for example, when he courts her on behalf of the absent king, has a sparky, tit-for-tat cheekiness reminiscent of BEATRICE's in *Much Ado About Nothing*.) In *Henry VI Part Two* her love-affair with Suffolk is a mainspring of the action, and the play leaps to life each time she appears because of the sharpness of her tongue: she is particularly vehement, not to say shrewish, with her unfortunate husband Henry, tongue-lashing him one minute for mourning Gloucester and screaming curses at him the next for sentencing Suffolk. (The actress' only puzzle, in this play, is what to do with Margaret's uncharacteristically laconic behaviour when she enters with Suffolk's head in Act Four: being stunned into – comparative – silence is not her usual line.) In *Henry VI Part Three* she once more plays to the hilt her role as termagant (browbeating Henry, insulting loyal followers and enemies alike, jeering at captive YORK, with the paper crown, as zestfully as she slapped Gloucester's Duchess in *Part Two*): she is, as York puts it, a 'tiger's heart wrapp'd in a woman's hide', and in the battle-scenes this fury in her character is given a new, unheralded dimension, patriotism, which channels it and gives it dignity. (Her dignity is also stressed in her motherly scene at the end of the play, when she cradles the blood-stained corpse of her son: it is both filled with forebodings of deaths to come, and a *résumé* of TALBOT's scene with his dead son in *Part One*, save that unlike Talbot Margaret does not go on herself to die.)

In *Richard III* Margaret has another cameo role, appearing in two scenes only as a hate-filled, defeated old woman. In each of them she begins by eavesdropping on the other characters, then sweeps centre-stage and delivers a powerful verse aria: a comprehensive curse, in the first scene, of RICHARD and all his works ('Thou elvish-mark'd, abortive, rooting hog!'), and in the second scene a hymn of savage joy that her son's death has been avenged by the murder of the Princes in the Tower. These outbursts, when *Richard III* is played on its own, steal Richard's own dramatic thunder so convincingly that they are often cut; in the context of Margaret's appearances in *Henry VI*, however, they crown a gloriously imagined, gloriously challenging dramatic character.

Margaret (*Much Ado about Nothing*)
HERO's maid, who dresses in her mistress's clothes and talks at midnight to BORACHIO, thus unwittingly assisting the plot to discredit Hero before her wedding. She is fascinated by clothes ('I like the new tire within excellently, if the hair were a thought browner, and your gown's a most rare fashion, i' faith. I saw the Duchess of Milan's gown that they praise so... By my troth, 's but a nightgown in respect of yours: cloth o' gold, and cuts, and laced with silver, set with pearls...'), and she is pert and witty (*Beatrice*: 'I am stuff'd, cousin: I cannot smell.' *Margaret*: 'A maid, and stuff'd! That's goodly catching of a cold!'). She is determined to better herself, not always to 'keep below stairs', and it is on this ambition that Borachio works to make her help his plot, enticing her with the possibility of marriage.

Maria (*Love's Labour's Lost*)
Attendant on the PRINCESS of France. She is the most genial of the four ladies, and her cheerful bustle effectively contrasts with the fevered languishing of her beloved LONGAVILLE.

Maria (*Twelfth Night*)
OLIVIA's lady-in-waiting, a pert, lively girl, and apparently physically small: Sir Toby BELCH calls her a 'little villain' and 'the youngest wren of nine'. She is sharp-tongued, answering MALVOLIO back, ordering Sir Toby to moderate his row and scolding FESTE like a naughty schoolboy for coming in late. 'Nay, either tell me where thou has been, or I will not open my lips so wide as a bristle may enter in way of thy excuse: my lady will hang me for thy absence.') Her chief part in the play is the plot to fool Malvolio, and she sets about it with a characteristically winsome and self-delighted zest. ('For Mounseer Malvolio, let me alone with him. If I do not gull him into a nayword and make him a common recreation, do not think I have wit enough to lie straight in my bed.') At the end of the play, we are told that she has married Sir Toby.

Mariana (*All's Well that Ends Well*)
Young Florentine solicited by PAROLLES. In a vigorous speech, she warns DIANA against the visiting Frenchmen, telling her to beware of 'their promises, enticements, oaths, tokens and all those engines of

lust...'

Mariana *(Measure for Measure)*

ANGELO's cast-off fiancée who agrees to sleep with him in ISABELLA's place. This is a strange proceeding enough – she cheats him out of affection rather than for revenge – but not half so strange as her behaviour in the last act, when despite all his crimes and his lies to her and to others she pleads for his life and saves him from the gallows. This resolution points to the play being comedy – for if it were serious, what possible chance of happiness could she have, married to such a man?

Marina *(Pericles)*

We first see Marina as a baby in Act Three, then in Act Four as a grown girl of an innocence so single-minded as almost to seem prissy. Her determination to keep her virginity in a brothel is admirable, perhaps, but her methods ('her quirks, her reasons, her master reasons, her knees...') are made to seem more than a little ludicrous. Her disingenuous charm (summed up in the litany 'I never did hurt in all my life:/I never spake bad word, nor did ill turn/To any living creature. Believe me, la,/I never kill'd a mouse, nor hurt a fly;/I trod upon a worm once, 'gainst my will,/But I wept for it...') is too much for both the owners of the brothel and its would-be customers, and results in her being removed to become a seamstress, dancing-teacher and singer.

At this point Marina is brought before her father, the distracted PERICLES, and it would be reasonable to expect that her character would be transfigured, turning her into CORDELIA as he turns into LEAR. But all the delicacy, poetry and subtlety of the scene are his; she has the same hollow niceness as ever, and if her innocence is charming and health-restoring, only he can see it. (He gets lines of the quality of 'Tell thy story./If thine consider'd prove the thousandth part/Of my endurance, thou are a man and I/Have suffer'd like a girl; yet thou dost look/Like Patience gazing on kings' graves, and smiling/Extremity out of act.../Recount, I do beseech thee: come, sit by me'. She gets thumping, expository lines like 'The king my father did in Tarsus leave me,/Till cruel Cleon and his wicked wife/Did seek to murder me...'.) It is tempting, in performance, to read Pericles' view of Marina into her character, and play her as ethereal and radiant throughout the play. But this fights the lines, and changes the character-emphasis not only in the brothel-scene (where it makes her a kind of plaster saint, and the PANDAR, BAWD and BOULT no more than one-dimensional oppressors), but in this scene too. Better, perhaps to play her with all the woodenness the lines suggest, and leave the task of transfiguring the play where it belongs, with Pericles.

Mariner *(The Winter's Tale)*

Delivers ANTIGONUS and PERDITA to the coast of Bohemia. He believes that 'The heavens with that we have in hand are angry' and is drowned with the rest of the ship's company.

Mariners *(The Tempest)*
Swarm over the rigging and decks of the storm-tossed ship, alternately
obeying the BOATSWAIN's orders and crying that all is lost.

Martext, Sir Oliver *(As You Like It)*
The inept priest engaged by TOUCHSTONE for his wedding to AUDREY.
He speaks two lines only, before JAQUES whisks the lovers away to a
'good priest'; the part tells us nothing of his character, and even Jaques'
remarks about him – 'This fellow will but join you together as they join
wainscot, then one of you will prove a shrunk panel and like green
timber warp, warp, warp' – reveal more about Jaques' view of marriage
than about Martext's nature or professional competence. (He *does*
eventually perform the wedding, though we never see him again
onstage.)

Martius *(Titus Andronicus): see* **Quintus and Martius**

Marullus *(Julius Caesar)*
FLAVIUS' fellow-tribune at the start of the play. He says a little more
than Flavius (chiefly a reminder to the CITIZENS of how they once
fawned on Pompey as they now fawn on CAESAR), but has no particular
character.

Master *(Henry VI Part Two)*
Pirate; one bloodthirsty line.

Master *(The Tempest)*
In command of the ship storm-tossed at the start of the play. Two lines
only; he leaves navigation to the BOATSWAIN.

Master-Gunner of Orleans *(Henry VI Part One)*
Eager to uphold the dignity of his position, he aims at and kills a group
of English lords spying on the city.

Master's Mate *(Henry VI Part Two)*
Pirate; one line.

Measure for Measure
Concerned that his rule has been too lax and that certain laws about
morality are being disregarded, the Duke of Vienna pretends to go on a
visit to Poland, but in fact disguises himself as a monk and stays in
Vienna to see what happens. He leaves his puritanical deputy Angelo in
charge of affairs, and Angelo begins enforcing the letter of the law;
apart from minor figures (the bawd Mistress Overdone and her tapster
Pompey, who are arrested by dimwitted Constable Elbow), the chief
sufferer is Claudio, a young aristocrat sentenced to death for making his
fiancée Julietta pregnant. Claudio's sister Isabella, a novice nun, begs
Angelo to spare Claudio's life, and to her horror he agrees to do so only
if she will sleep with him.

The plot now grows more tangled. Isabella goes to the prison and tells Claudio of Angelo's demand, expecting him to surrender his life without hesitation; instead, to her dismay, he begs her to sleep with Angelo. The disguised Duke, overhearing, proposes that instead of Isabella a substitute be sent to Angelo, one Mariana whom he had once promised to marry but abandoned. This is done, but Angelo none the less sends word that Claudio must die. The executioner Abhorson and his new assistant Pompey begin sharpening their axes, and once again the disguised Duke suggests a substitute. First they plan to kill Barnardine, a drunken prisoner, but he refuses to be executed, and instead they send Angelo the head of a pirate who has conveniently died in jail the night before.

The Duke now throws off his disguise and returns to Vienna. Isabella accuses Angelo of fornication, but he brushes her aside. Mariana repeats the charge, and she too is dismissed. Everything hangs on the evidence of the missing 'Friar', and in the end the Duke goes out and returns in friar's robes to confront Angelo, and at the same time to take revenge on Lucio, a frivolous lord who has insulted and mocked the Duke in his absence. Angelo is married to Mariana, and is about to be led away to execution when she, together with Isabella, pleads for his life, and he is pardoned. Claudio and Juliet are free to marry, and Lucio is forced to marry a prostitute who has borne his child. Finally the Duke announces his own intention of marrying Isabella, and in this way justice is dealt to all, measure for measure as each deserves.

Melun (King John)
French lord who staggers in, fatally wounded, and tells SALISBURY and PEMBROKE that PHILIP means treacherously to kill them.

Menas (Antony and Cleopatra)
POMPEY's friend, a pirate captain who, when OCTAVIUS, LEPIDUS and ANTONY, 'the three world-sharers, these competitors' are all drunk on board Pompey's galley, urges him to 'let me cut the cable,/And, when we are put off, fall to their throats:/All then is thine.' Pompey refuses, and Menas mutters 'For this,/I'll never fallow thy pall'd fortunes more'. The part is a cameo, but splendidly, unregenerately bloodthirsty.

Menecrates (Antony and Cleopatra)
Friend of POMPEY.

Menelaus (Troilus and Cressida)
Greek commander, AGAMEMNON's brother and husband of HELEN whose kidnapping by Trojan PARIS provoked the war. He is of similar rank to Agamemnon, nominally his co-commander, but because he is a cuckold he is treated with no respect at all, and remains a cipher throughout the play.

Menenius Agrippa (Coriolanus)
Patrician friend of CORIOLANUS, an old man who describes himself as

his 'father' and 'the book of his good acts'. He spends the play working for reconciliation, between senators and CITIZENS (by telling the fable of the belly), between the Citizens and Coriolanus (in the Act Three brawl) and between Coriolanus and his own nature (when he goes to beg him not to attack Rome). He is sometimes played as a smooth-talking, viperish politician, but the text makes more of his bewilderment. Apart from VIRGILIA, he is the only person in the play who loves Coriolanus – when he hears that he is coming home he breaks into an all-but-embarrassing (to VOLUMNIA and VIRGILIA) verbal jig: 'Ha! Marcius coming home!... Take my cap, Jupiter, and I thank thee. Hoo! Marcius coming home!... I will make my house reel tonight' – and all his pedantic, mother-hen solicitude for Coriolanus ('Do not take/His rougher accents for malicious sounds,/But, as I say, such as become a soldier') springs from this love and is warmed by it. That being so, Coriolanus' rejection of him outside the walls of Rome is cruel and shocking, one of the most savage pieces of behaviour in the play, and has an emotional impact which makes Coriolanus' subsequent explanation to AUFIDIUS sound curtly calculating. ('This last old man,/Whom with a crack'd heart I have sent to Rome,/Lov'd me above the measure of a father,/Nay, godded me indeed. Their latest refuge/Was to send him...'). We are still trembling from it when Volumnia, Virgilia and Young MARCIUS come to intercede in their turn, and Volumnia succeeds where Menenius failed. But although his failure, and the tragic way it is shown, are no more than dramatist's contrivance, they are still unexpected and pitiable, and the reason lies less in Coriolanus' cold character than in Menenius' vigorous warmth.

Menteith *(Macbeth)*
Scottish lord who deserts to MALCOLM and MACDUFF before the final battle.

Merchant *(Timon of Athens)*
Briefly does business with TIMON at the start of the play.

The Merchant of Venice
Portia, an heiress of Belmont, fulfils the conditions of her father's will by setting her suitors a challenge. There are three caskets, gold, silver and lead, and whoever chooses the right one wins her hand; the losers must renounce marriage forever. Bassanio, a Venetian nobleman, wants to try his luck in Belmont, but is penniless. He borrows money from his friend Antonio, who in turn borrows it from the Jewish moneylender Shylock. The arrangement is that if Antonio fails to repay the cash after three months (when his merchant-ships return to Venice), he must pay Shylock a pound of his own flesh. The Christians accept this deal suspiciously, for they hate and fear Shylock as much as he hates them. Shylock's hatred is heated up by his daughter Jessica's love for a young Christian nobleman, Lorenzo, and boils over when he hears that she has eloped with Lorenzo and that Lorenzo's friends (who are

also friends of Antonio) have connived at it.

At this point news comes that Antonio's ships have been lost at sea, and Shylock takes Antonio to court and demands his pound of flesh. Portia (having by now dismissed two suitors, the princes of Morocco and Aragon, who chose the gold and silver caskets respectively, and accepted a third, Bassanio, who chose the lead) disguises herself as a youth, a lawyer, goes to court with her maid Nerissa (disguised as a male secretary), and defeats Shylock on a technicality: he can cut off the pound of flesh providing he sheds not a drop of Antonio's blood. Overjoyed at Antonio's release, Bassanio pays the 'lawyer' with a ring Portia gave him as a keepsake, and his friend Gratiano gives a similar ring to the 'secretary' (Nerissa, to whom he is engaged). Leaving Shylock to hand over half his worldly goods to Jessica and Lorenzo and to convert to Christianity, the young people go back to Belmont, where Portia and Nerissa shed their disguises and demand back their rings, and Bassanio and Gratiano have to beg forgiveness before the trick is revealed and the comedy ends happily.

Merchants (*The Comedy of Errors*)
In a brief scene, the First Merchant advises ANTIPHOLUS I not to admit in Ephesus that he comes from Syracuse, on pain of death. The Second Merchant is owed money by ANGELO the goldsmith, and it is his pressing for payment of the debt which causes Angelo to dun Antipholus II in his turn, and to the arrest of both of them.

Mercutio (*Romeo and Juliet*)
Like his opponent TYBALT, Mercutio plays a small but crucial part in the play's action: it is when Tybalt kills him and ROMEO kills Tybalt in revenge that Romeo is banished from Verona and the tragedy begins its downward course.

Mercutio is named after mercury, and his character is suitably volatile. He takes nothing seriously (not even his own impending death: 'Ask for me tomorrow, and you shall find me a grave man'), and he spends most of his short appearances in the play exchanging meaninglessly witty remarks with Romeo. (*Romeo*: 'Pardon, good Mercutio... in such a case as mine, a man may strain courtesy.' *Mercutio*: 'That's as much as to say, such a case as yours constrains a man to bow in the hams.' *Romeo*: 'Meaning to curtsey.' *Mercutio*: 'Thou hast most kindly hit it.' *Romeo*: 'A most courteous exposition.' *Mercutio*: 'Nay, I am the very pink of courtesy.' *Romeo*: 'Pink for flower...', etc.) He duels with words, and wit-shafts are to him like the *stoccados* or *passados* of a fencer. When he undertakes a real duel (with Tybalt) it is in the same spirit of devil-may-care, ironical affectation, and it is the death of him. He is a victim of the Capulet–Montague feud (as his dying words, 'A plague o' both your houses', famously proclaim); but his insouciant quarrelsomeness is also one of the main causes of its continuing, and a symbol of its pointlessness.

Apart from his witty repartee – he has many of the play's sharpest lines – Mercutio also speaks one of Shakespeare's best-loved anthology-speeches, the description of Mab, Queen of the Fairies, with 'Her waggon-spokes made of long spinners' legs,/The cover, of the wings of grasshoppers,/Her traces of the smallest spider-web,/Her collars of the moonshine's watery beams', and so on. Its dazzling, empty fancy mirrors Mercutio's own character, and also suits the fantastical, artificial atmosphere of the play (so much in contrast with the tragic seriousness of Romeo's and JULIET's love): it is like a cadenza in music, a piece of heartless show whose purpose is not to arouse our emotion but to stun us with admiration. BENVOLIO would never have invented such a speech, because he has heart as well as head; Romeo might have invented it once – but not after he fell in love with Juliet and discovered that the world is real.

The Merry Wives of Windsor

Falstaff and his followers (Bardolph, Pistol and the others) are in Windsor, and broke. Justice Shallow is also there, come from Gloucestershire to help his cloddish nephew Slender court Anne Page, the daughter of a prosperous Windsor citizen. Anne Page is also courted by Fenton, a young nobleman, and by the irascible French Doctor Caius. To raise funds, Falstaff decides to win the hearts of two respectable Windsor ladies, Mistress Page (Anne's mother) and Mistress Ford, and to support himself on the presents they give him. But he bites off more than he can chew. Not only is Mistress Ford's husband pathologically jealous, ready to kill anyone who so much as smiles at his wife (and to disguise himself as 'Master Brook' and fawn on on Falstaff to find out his plans), but the ladies themselves are 'merry wives', well aware of Falstaff's plans and determined to teach him a lesson.

The play's main plot concerns this lesson. Falstaff is invited to assignations with Mistress Ford, and each time Mistress Page bursts in with news that Ford is coming to search the house, Falstaff must hide or disguise himself. He hides in a laundry-basket, and is tipped into the river; he disguises himself as a fat old woman, and Ford, who hates her, thrashes him black and blue. The secondary plot concerns the rivalry for Anne Page's hand, and involves a duel between Dr Caius and the equally peppery Welshman Sir Hugh Evans (who supports Slender). In Act V, all the participants gather in Windsor Forest, where Falstaff is to disguise himself as Herne the Hunter and meet Mistress Ford at midnight. The merry wives have prepared an ambush, a gang of children disguised as fairies who will pinch him and burn him with tapers; during the revels Page plans for his daughter to slip away with Slender, and Mistress Page plans for her to slip away with Caius. In the end she elopes with Fenton, all plots and plans are discovered, everyone is reconciled and the play ends with a genial invitation to a party at Page's house.

Messala (*Julius Caesar*)
Friend of BRUTUS and CASSIUS; no character.

Messenger (*Macbeth*)
Advises LADY MACDUFF to escape while she can. Breathless and panicky; no other character. He may be the same messenger whom MACBETH later scolds for being a 'cream-fac'd loon'.

Messenger (*Much Ado about Nothing*)
Begins the play by telling LEONATO of DON PEDRO's victory and imminent arrival in Messina; discusses BENEDICK with BEATRICE, feeding her scorn. (*Messenger*: 'I see, lady, the gentleman is not in your books.' *Beatrice*: 'No. An he were, I would burn my study'.) Courtesy is his character.

Messenger (*Othello*)
Brings news to the Duke of VENICE and his SENATORS that the Turkish fleet has left Rhodes and is making for Cyprus.

Messenger (*The Two Noble Kinsmen*): *see* **Herald**

Messengers (*Antony and Cleopatra*)
Though fewer appear onstage than the 'twenty several messengers' CLEOPATRA at one point sends after ANTONY, the play nevertheless teems with them. Most bring word of a single incident (e.g. the fact that the pirates are 'strong for Antony', or news of the outcome of battles). But one Messenger has two lively scenes with Cleopatra. In the first he announces that Antony has married OCTAVIA, and Cleopatra boxes his ears, 'hales him up and down' and tries to stab him; in the second he describes Octavia unflatteringly, and Cleopatra fawns on him like a child given a bag of sweets, and pays him with gold.

Messengers (*Richard III*)
There are four of them. The First Messenger wakes HASTINGS in the night to bring news of STANLEY's dream of the boar being 'rasèd off his helm' (a forecast of beheading). The other three messengers bring RICHARD news of uprisings against him in various parts of the country, and he loses his temper ('Out on ye, owls! Nothing but songs of death?'), whereupon they tell him other news, of disaster to his enemies.

Metellus Cimber (*Julius Caesar*)
The conspirator whose request to CAESAR to repeal his brother's exile is the cue for the others to gather round with knives. No individual character.

Michael (*Henry VI Part Two*)
Supporter of CADE; hardly speaks.

Michael, Sir (*Henry IV Part One*)
One of SCROOP's followers; a five-line part, a bearer of messages, not so

much a spear-carrier as a human carrier-pigeon.

A Midsummer Night's Dream

King Theseus of Athens is preparing to celebrate his wedding to
Hippolyta queen of the Amazons, and a group of Athenian rustics,
Quince, Bottom, Flute, Snug, Snout and Starveling, are rehearsing a
play to perform at court. There is, meantime, a love-tangle among four
of Theseus' young courtiers. Lysander loves Hermia, and they decide
to elope because Hermia's father wants her to marry Demetrius.
Demetrius goes after them and he is followed by Helena, who is in love
with him. They all make their way to a wood near Athens, where the
rustics are rehearsing their play. No mortal knows it, but the wood is
enchanted. Oberon and Titania, the fairy king and queen, have
quarrelled over 'a little changeling boy', and Oberon has vowed to
punish Titania. He plans to sprinkle the juice of a magic plant on her
eyelids as she sleeps: when she wakes up, she will dote on the first
person or thing she sees.

Lost in the wood, the four young people wander until they are
exhausted, then sleep. Puck sprinkles some of the love-juice in
Lysander's eyes, and when Lysander wakes up he falls in love with
Helena (who is furious because she still dotes on Demetrius). Oberon
anoints Titania's eyes, and she falls in love with Bottom the weaver,
whom Puck has dressed in an ass's head as he rehearses the play.
Titania dotes on Bottom, who revels in the courtesies offered him by
her fairy servants. The mortal lovers' quarrel grows ever fiercer:
Lysander and Demetrius want to fight a duel over Helena, and Helena
and Hermia, each suspecting the other of tricking their beloveds away
from them, want to scratch each others' eyes out. Once more Puck
leads them through the wood until they fall into an exhausted sleep,
and Oberon changes the love- spell so that the rightful pairs fall in love:
Lysander and Hermia, Demetrius and Helena. He also removes the
ass's head from Bottom and the love-spell from Titania, who surrenders
the 'changeling boy' to him and ends the fairy quarrel. Order once
more restored, the mortals return to court where the two young
couples' betrothals are ratified by Theseus. The rustics, led by Bottom
(who is still marvelling at the 'dream' he had of being an ass), perform
their play, and the enchanted day ends with a fairy-dance, led by Puck,
through the palace to bring joy to all the mortal marriages.

Miranda (*The Tempest*)

PROSPERO's daughter. Brought up on the island with no company but
her father and CALIBAN (she is unable to see ARIEL), she is not
surprisingly somewhat naive. She falls in love with the first visitor she
sees (FERDINAND), and on seeing his father and the wicked lords bursts
out 'O brave new world,/ That hath such creatures in it!', to which we
can only drily answer, with Prospero, 'O,/'Tis new to thee'. Her
innocence is charming, but it's easy to see why Prospero determines to
test her love for Ferdinand, and his for her, before letting their love-

affair develop.

Montague, Lady *(Romeo and Juliet)*
ROMEO's mother. She appears exclusively with her husband, takes little part in the action and says even less.

Montague, Marquess of *(Henry VI Part Three)*
YORK's brother and supporter, he transfers his loyalty to his nephew EDWARD after York's death. He says little, and most of it is tedious, elderly politician's stuff: his disapproval of Edward's marriage with Lady GREY instead of Lady BONA of France, for example, is cautiously wrapped up as 'Yet, to have join'd with France in such alliance/Would more have strengthen'd this our commonwealth/'Gainst foreign storms than any homebred marriage'. After Warwick's defection he joins the Lancastrians (having previously protested vehement loyalty to Edward: 'So God help Montague as he proves true!'), and is killed in the fighting. Edward's epitaph links him with WARWICK – 'two brave bears.../That in their chains fetter'd the kingly lion/And made the forest tremble when they roar'd' – but he does and says little in the play to warrant such hyperbole.

Montague, Old *(Romeo and Juliet)*
ROMEO's father. Though we see a great deal of JULIET's family life, we see nothing at all of Romeo's, and this means that whereas Old CAPULET is a rounded, developed character, Old Montague is a cipher. He has few lines to speak, and they are conventional and unrevealing.

Montano *(Othello)*
OTHELLO's predecessor as governor of Cyprus. Treacherously persuaded by IAGO that CASSIO is a drunkard, he tries to prevent Cassio duelling with RODERIGO and is seriously injured (for which Othello disgraces Cassio). Apart from soldierly honour, and rage at the end of the play when he discovers Iago's treachery, he shows little character.

Montgomery, Sir John *(Henry VI Part Three)*
Proud but laconic supporter of EDWARD; Edward exploits his loyalty at York, manoeuvring him into insisting that Edward claim the throne. ('I came to serve a king, and not a duke'...; 'Ay, now my sovereign speaketh like himself,/And now I will be Edward's champion'.

Mo(u)ntjoy, Lord *(Henry V)*
Chief herald to the French court, a man of dignity and presence, treated by HENRY with personal esteem as well as with the respect due to his office.

Mopsa *(The Winter's Tale)*
Rustic wench in love with the CLOWN, who sings a catch with AUTOLYCUS and DORCAS.

Morocco, Prince of *(The Merchant of Venice)*
PORTIA's suitor, who chooses the golden casket. A Moorish grandee, he

speaks ornate, flowery verse, and betrays only a moment's flash of emotion when he fails the test. ('O hell! What have we here?')

Mortimer, Edmund, Earl of March *(Henry VI Part One)*
Not the same person as the MORTIMER of *Henry IV Part One*. He appears in this play as a sick old man, who on his deathbed tells YORK that he, not HENRY, is the true heir of Henry V.

Mortimer, Lady *(Henry IV Part One)*
This girl, the daughter of GLENDOWER and sister-in-law of HOTSPUR, is chiefly notable because she speaks throughout in Welsh. (Shakespeare seems to have had several Welsh-speaking actors at his disposal: the Welsh figure prominently in *Henry V*, and there is Sir HUGH in *The Merry Wives of Windsor*. *See also* the note on Falstaff's PAGE.)

Mortimer, Sir Edmund *(Henry IV Part One)*
GLENDOWER's son-in-law and HOTSPUR's co-rebel against King HENRY. He speaks no Welsh, a fact which provokes the scene in which Glendower acts as interpreter between him and his wife – a pointless but colourful exchange, perhaps inspired by an unexpected talent in Shakespeare's actors. (It is also a forerunner of the English and French lesson-scenes in *Henry V*.)

Mortimer, Sir Hugh *(Henry VI Part Three)*
Brother of Sir John MORTIMER, killed with him fighting for YORK; he does not speak.

Mortimer, Sir John *(Henry VI Part Three)*
Uncle of YORK, an old man; speaks one line, and is killed in battle one page after he appears in the play.

Morton *(Henry IV Part Two)*
NORTHUMBERLAND's servant who brings news of the rebels' defeat at Shrewsbury and of HOTSPUR's death. His speeches are long, vivid and detailed, patterned after the Messengers' speeches in Greek or Latin tragedy.

Moth *(Love's Labour's Lost)*
ARMADO's page, and with ROBIN (the page in *Henry IV* and *Henry V*) the most satisfying child-character in Shakespeare. He is robustly English, and part of his function is to show up the absurdity of his funny-foreigner master: he does this by correcting his grammar, topping every one of his jokes, and constantly catching him in silky verbal traps. Appropriately, since his name, in Elizabethan pronunciation, is a pun on the French 'mot' meaning 'word', Moth is a master of language, a phrase-maker on the level of BEROWNE himself: he advises Armado, for example, that the best way to win his love is 'to jig off a tune at the tongue's end, canary to it with your feet, hammer it with turning up your eyelids, sigh a note and sing a note... with your hat penthouse-like o'er the shop of your eyes'.

All this would be splendid enough in an adult, but the joke's whole point is that Moth is a child: the contrast is total between the sophistication of what he says and the innocence of his age. He is a mirror not only of Armado's foolish extravagance but of the verbal dalliance of the courtiers, and for this to work at its best he must not be an adolescent, near to them in age, but as small and young a boy as possible. He is cast as the infant Hercules in the play of the Nine Worthies, and this, like his attendance on the beanpole Armado, gains splendid unspoken point if he is diminutive.

Moth (*A Midsummer Night's Dream*): *see* **Fairies**

Mouldy, Ralph (*Henry IV Part Two*)
One of FALSTAFF's unwilling army conscripts, who bribes BARDOLPH to be excused.

Mowbray, Lord (*Henry IV Part Two*)
Son of the NORFOLK of *Richard II*; Lord Marshal of England and chief co-conspirator with SCROOP against HENRY IV. Suspects Prince JOHN's trick over the disbanding of the armies, but none the less trusts his word and is duly arrested and executed. An important man, but a colourless character and a small part.

Mowbray, Thomas, Duke of Norfolk (*Richard II*)
The play opens strongly with BOLINGBROKE's claim that Mowbray is guilty of treason, embezzlement and murder, and his demand that Mowbray prove his innocence by fighting a duel; it continues with RICHARD's arbitrary ending of the duel before it properly begins, and banishing of the participants, after which Mowbray drops out of the play. In his two scenes he is furious, vehement and unbending, and his headstrong rhetoric goes a long way towards establishing the artificial, pageant-like atmosphere so important to the play. Lines like 'Then thus I turn me from my country's light,/To dwell in solemn shades of endless night' can only be delivered ringingly, with a straight face and without a trace of irony. It is small wonder that in many modern productions the part is doubled with the more rewarding one of CARLISLE.

Much Ado about Nothing
After a successful war against his evil brother Don John, Don Pedro of Aragon visits his old friend Leonato, governor of Sicily. He is accompanied by Claudio and by his witty friend Benedick, and also by Don John (whom he has captured and pardoned) and two rascally servants, Borachio and Conrade. Claudio falls in love with Leonato's daughter Hero, and Don Pedro pays court to her on Claudio's behalf and arranges a wedding between them. Leonato's niece Beatrice is a witty, lively young woman, as scornful of Benedick as he is of her; the others agree that it would be fun to make them fall in love with one another, and work the trick by dropping hints to Benedick about how

Beatrice secretly adores him, and vice versa.

Don John, meanwhile, is plotting to break up Claudio's and Hero's engagement. He arranges with Borachio that Borachio will visit Hero's balcony at midnight and make loud, affectionate conversation with 'Hero' (actually her maid Margaret in Hero's clothes), and that Don John will bring Don Pedro and Claudio to witness this from below. The trick is played, but Borachio is arrested by a group of bumbling watchmen led by the self-important Dogberry and the doddering Verges. Dogberry goes to tell Leonato of the arrest, but finds him too busy to listen. The wedding goes ahead, but before it is completed Don John, Claudio and Don Pedro accuse Hero of unfaithfulness and break it off. Hero faints, and they think her dead and leave. Friar Francis (who was conducting the wedding) advises that Leonato should go through a fake burial-service, to see if Claudio will be filled with remorse, and in a spirited scene Leonato and his brother Antonio accuse Claudio of causing Hero's death and challenge him to a duel. So does Benedick, obeying Beatrice's instructions (for he now loves her utterly); for her part, she realises that she may have sent Benedick to his death, and that she loves him, but is still too proud to show it openly. At last the watchmen bring Borachio before Leonato and he confesses. Instead of telling Claudio at once, Leonato makes him promise to marry an unknown masked girl – and it is not until they are before the altar that she reveals herself as Hero. The play ends with Don John in disgrace, the lovers reunited, the watchmen rewarded for a job well done, and Beatrice and Benedick, firmly in love and formally engaged to be married, leading the wedding dance.

Murderers (*Henry VI Part Two*)
Hired by SUFFOLK to kill GLOUCESTER; apart from announcing success 'My good lord, he's dead'), they are all cloak, dagger and silence.

Murderers (*Macbeth*)
Three villains hired by MACBETH to kill BANQUO and the MACDUFF family. They are sometimes portrayed as a crew of cutthroats, sometimes as comic bunglers (who let FLEANCE escape); either way involves pouring character into conventional lines.

Murderers (*Richard III*)
Their task is to kill CLARENCE in the Tower and hide his body in a barrel of wine. The First Murderer is a swaggering, uncomplicated thug ('Take him on the costard with the hilts of thy sword, and then throw him in the malmsey butt in the next room'). The Second Murderer has a pricking conscience ('To be damned for killing him...'), but crushes it in a soliloquy like FALSTAFF's 'honour' speech in *Henry IV* ('I'll not meddle with it: it makes a man a coward... 'Tis a blushing, shame-faced spirit that mutinies in a man's bosom...'), and distracts Clarence's attention ('Look behind you, my lord!') while his colleague stabs him.

Musicians (*Othello*)
In a brief scene, they play for the disgraced CASSIO; the First Musician also acts as straight man in some limp exchanges with the CLOWN.

Mustardseed (*A Midsummer Night's Dream*): *see* **Fairies**

Mutius (*Titus Andronicus*)
TITUS' son, killed by him early in the play for disobedience.

Nathaniel, Sir (*Love's Labour's Lost*)
Elderly curate, bedazzled by the verbal gymnastics of his friend HOLOFERNES. He is the standard foolish old man of farce, but his and Holofernes' mutual affection warmly contrasts with the courtiers' emotionless point-scoring, and their enthusiasm for life (like SHALLOW's and FALSTAFF's in *Henry IV Part Two*) has a mundane zest which lifts the play.

Neighbours (*Henry VI Part Two*)
Support HORNER in his duel with PETER, but to no purpose as he is incontinently killed.

Nerissa (*The Merchant of Venice*)
PORTIA's maid and confidante, who eagerly helps her in the test of the three caskets, and gleefully disguises herself as her male secretary when she goes to court. She is a lively, witty girl, a fit wife for the capering GRATIANO; but the part is too small to let her show much character.

Nestor (*Troilus and Cressida*)
Greek commander, full of years, dignity and experience. He is prone to long, beautifully worded speeches ('...let the ruffian Boreas once enrage/The gentle Thetis, and anon, behold/The strong-ribb'd bark through liquid mountains cut,/Bounding between the two moist elements/Like Perseus' horse...'), but he adds little to the conduct of the war but reminiscence and tedious advice. Everyone treats him with respect, but no one listens to what he says.

Nicanor (*Coriolanus*)
Roman double agent who hurries from Rome with news that Coriolanus' banishment has disheartened the senators, that they are at odds with the common people and that the city is ripe for Volscian

attack. On the road he meets the Volscian ADRIAN and tells him (and us) this news; apart from his friendliness with Adrian, and the fact that he is a spy, he is characterless.

Norfolk, John Mowbray, Duke of *(Henry VI Part Three)*
Minor Yorkist, active on the battlefield.

Norfolk, Thomas Howard, 2nd Duke of *(Henry VIII); see also* **Surrey** *(Richard III)*
The youth of *Richard III*, now grown up and having inherited his father's title. He is a senior statesman, who begins the play by describing the meeting of HENRY and Francis of France at the Field of the Cloth of Gold, and later is the leader of the group of nobles dissatisfied with WOLSEY. Important but colourless.

Norfolk, Thomas Howard, Duke of *(Richard III)*
Military commander in RICHARD's army at Bosworth, who finds a letter pinned to his tent which says, 'Jockey of Norfolk, be not so bold,/For Dickon thy master is bought and sold'. He is killed in the battle.

Northumberland, Henry Percy, Earl of *(Richard II; Henry IV Parts One and Two)*
At first a loyal follower of King RICHARD (he excuses his lord's behaviour on the grounds that he is 'basely led by flatterers'), Northumberland is persuaded by ROSS and WILLOUGHBY to revolt against him. He becomes BOLINGBROKE's trusted lieutenant, his mouthpiece to Richard in the matters of the abdication and the terms of Richard's banishment. He is of the same generation as GAUNT and YORK, but is given none of their individuality of character: his devotion to Bolingbroke is as uninteresting as it is unshakeable. In *Henry IV Part One*, however, he is persuaded by his son HOTSPUR to rebel against Bolingbroke (now Henry IV), because of an insult to their family; in *Part Two*, after Hotspur's death, he at first takes over the rebellion but soon retires to Scotland to watch events from there, and fades from the play. Throughout the plays he is treated by others as a man of rank, dignity and authority, but is otherwise uncharacterised; his finest scene – as often with Shakespeare's secondary historical characters – is domestic, when he hears news of his son's death at the start of *Henry IV Part Two* and tries to steel himself not to mourn.

Northumberland, Henry Percy, Earl of *(Henry VI Part Three)*
Grandson of the NORTHUMBERLAND of *Henry IV*. A fervent Lancastrian (especially loyal to Queen MARGARET and EDWARD Prince of Wales), he arrests YORK before the paper-crown scene, but is subsequently moved to tears by his noble demeanour ('Had he been slaughterman to all my kin,/I could not for my life but weep...'). He plays no further part in the action, and at the end of the play we hear that he is one of the group of 'valiant foemen, like to autumn's corn' which the Yorkists have 'mow'd down in tops of all their pride'.

Nurse (*Romeo and Juliet*)

The Nurse suckled JULIET, she tells us, until the child was two years old, which was 11 years before the play begins: this means that the Nurse is unlikely to be more than 50 years old herself, far short of the foolish old harridan she is made in some productions. She is still Juliet's personal servant (and her *confidante*, helping her for example in the clandestine marriage with ROMEO); but she has by now also graduated to the position of senior servant in the house, as much respected by the Capulet parents as she is desrespectful towards them. (When CAPULET rounds on Juliet over the marriage with PARIS, it is the Nurse and not Juliet's mother who first stands up to him: 'God in heaven bless us! You are to blame, my lord, to rate her so.' Later she tells him to his face that he is a 'cot-quean', that is a busybody male meddling in women's affairs, and he swallows the insult and says nothing.)

The Nurse is full of the dignity of her office (particularly so in the presence of PETER, her own personal servant). She is self-important, and likes to be the centre of events: the scene when she refuses to tell Juliet news of Romeo until she has made the most of her exhaustion after 'jauncing' round Verona is matched only by her extravagant, self-indulgent distress at finding Juliet's apparently dead body: 'O woe! O woeful, woeful, woeful day!/Most lamentable day! Most woeful day,/That ever, ever I did yet behold!/O day! O day! O day! O hateful day!' But for all her personal dignity and her self-admiration, she is a foolish undereducated woman, and her head is filled with old wives' tales, pointless proverbs, pieces of antique superstition and a prodigious vocabulary of innocuous oaths and half-remembered polysyllables. She is in awe of the verbal 'quibbling' of Romeo and MERCUTIO, though she has no time at all for Mercutio himself ('I pray you, sir, what saucy merchant was this, that was so full of his own ropery?'). Some performers, taking their cue from a single line in the play, 'Give me some *aqua vitae*', make her a tippler as well, but there is no need for the line to be taken literally.

For three-quarters of the play, the Nurse provides the warmth, affection and plain human dignity which all the upper-class characters lack. In particular, she is a kind of mother and father to Juliet, and is largely responsible for the feeling that the family environment Juliet abandons for Romeo is loving and close. For the theatre audience she provides comic relief, a welcome earthiness to puncture the high-flown passion of the rest of the plot; but she is essential to the play's main meaning, and not peripheral – and for this reason the part usually works better in the hands of a dramatic rather than of a comic actress.

Nurse (*Titus Andronicus*)

Brings AARON his and TAMORA's newborn child; stabbed dead to stop her telling of its birth.

Nym (*The Merry Wives of Windsor; Henry V*)

One of FALSTAFF's associates in *The Merry Wives of Windsor*, Nym's

main function is to provide contrast with the peppery ranting of
PISTOL. He is a man of little brain, a clod who decides to present
himself to the world as an enigma. He speaks brief, imcomprehensible
sentences, the phrases broken up and dropped in like stones in dough,
and he is prone to short-circuit argument (which might confuse him,
never mind the issue) with a blunt 'That's my humour'. In *Henry V* he
is Pistol's rival (or thinks he is) for Mistress QUICKLY's hand, and after
Pistol marries her he goes into a furious, beetle-browed sulk, so that
BARDOLPH has great difficulty keeping the peace between them. He
goes to fight in France, but turns (like Bardolph) to thieving and is
hanged for it.

Nymphs *(The Two Noble Kinsmen): see* **Wenches**

Oatcake, Hugh *(Much Ado about Nothing): see* **Watchmen**

Oberon *(A Midsummer Night's Dream)*
In his first, angry, scene with TITANIA, Oberon affects a beetle-browed
rage more suited to the demon king in a pantomime than to the king of
the Fairies. He begins, sullenly, 'Ill-met by moonlight, proud Titania',
and ends, all but stamping his foot like a child in a tantrum, 'Well, go
thy way. Thou shalt not from this grove/Till I torment thee for this
injury'. But almost immediately, as if unrelieved malevolence were out
of keeping with the mood of the play, Shakespeare softens and
'humanises' him. The malevolence is handed over to PUCK, and Oberon
becomes a detached director of events, manipulating and guiding what
happens for the good of the participants rather than to feed his own
rage. His deception of the four lovers is benign, not cruel, intended to
show them who they truly love; even his fury against Titania evaporates
as soon as he sees how besotted she is with BOTTOM – 'Welcome, good
Robin. Seest thou this sweet sight?/Her dotage now I do begin to
pity...' – and he is glad, the minute she surrenders the 'changeling
child', to 'undo/This hateful imperfection of her eyes' and restore
harmony to the fairy world. He is often played, on the evidence of the
first scene, with glacial, inhuman glitter; but generous-heartedness,
both to mortals and to his erring queen, is far more the keynote of his
character.

Octavia (*Antony and Cleopatra*)
OCTAVIUS' sister, married to ANTONY in an attempt to heal the breach
between the two men. She is thirty (or so CLEOPATRA'S MESSENGER
guesses), with a round face, a forehead 'as low as she would wish it',
and no intelligence whatever. She understands as little of the political
job she is set to do as if she were a child; she dotes on her brother, and
is determined to make him and Antony friends for no better reason
than that 'Wars 'twixt you twain would be/As if the world should
cleave...'. Ironically, it is Antony's desertion of her which triggers the
fatal war between him and Octavius, and she is the unwitting cause of
all the anguish her marriage was designed to avert. She is left miserable
– 'Ay me, most wretched,/That have my heart parted betwixt two
friends/That do affect each other!' – but the play's action has by then
moved so swiftly away from her that we are given no time to pity her.

Octavius Caesar, Caius (*Julius Caesar; Antony and Cleopatra*)
The future Roman Emperor Augustus is treated by Shakespeare with a
respect which bleaches human interest from his character. His enemies
– CASSIUS, for example – are allowed to call him names ('A peevish
schoolboy... joined with a masker and a reveller'), but his behaviour,
in both plays, is impeccable. He is a fine general, a noble politician, a
loving brother and a trustworthy, capable friend. If this makes him
sound like a prissy head prefect, forever organising games rotas and
healthy hikes, that too is in the texts: he spends most of his time
striding about the stage, either making plans or furious that other
people have let him down. He shows no warmth, no weakness, no
emotion that is not formal: even rage and regret are as rhetorically
expressed as if he were reading from an autocue. This schematic
character, though it shreds the historical record, exactly suits both
plays, making boy-wonder Octavius a marvellously self-possessed foil to
the perplexed BRUTUS and misguided CASSIUS of *Julius Caesar*, and the
inevitable victor (because he never surrenders to, indeed never even
notices, the gross claims of the flesh) in the head-or-heart conflict of
Antony and Cleopatra.

Officer (*The Comedy of Errors*)
Accompanies the second MERCHANT to arrest first ANGELO and then
ANTIPHOLUS II for debt.

Officer (*King Lear*)
Captain in EDMUND's army. Sent by him to supervise CORDELIA's
execution, he makes a joke of his eagerness ('I cannot draw a cart, nor
eat dried oats;/If it be man's work, I'll do't'). Later, he has two half-
lines, one confirming that LEAR 'kill'd the slave' who was hanging
Cordelia, and the other announcing Edmund's death.

Officer of the Court (*The Winter's Tale*)
Reads out LEONTES' accusations of adultery and treason against
HERMIONE.

Officers *(Twelfth Night)*
There are two of them, and they arrest ANTONIO for debt, in the nick of
time for the plot, before he recognises VIOLA despite her boy's disguise.

Old Athenian *(Timon of Athens)*
Asks TIMON to prevent the marriage between his daughter and Timon's
servant LUCILIUS, but quite happily agrees to the match when Timon
offers to pay half the dowry.

Old Lady *(Henry VIII)*
Anne BULLEN's servant and confidante. She appears in two scenes, and
is characterised rather like the NURSE in *Romeo and Juliet*: blunt,
worldly-wise, officious and unceremonious. In her first scene she
robustly advises Anne to accept whatever preferment HENRY gives her.
(*Old Lady*: 'You would not be a queen?' *Anne*: 'No, not for all the
riches under heaven.' *Old Lady*: ''Tis strange: a threepence bow'd
would hire me,/Old as I am, to queen it. But I pray you,/What think
you of a duchess? Have you limbs/To bear that load of title?') In her
second scene she announces the birth of Anne's and Henry's child, is
rewarded with 100 marks and left alone, whereupon she cynically
comments, 'An hundred marks? By this light I'll ha' more.../Said I for
this, the girl was like to him?/I will have more, or else unsay't...'.)

Old Man *(King Lear)*
Leads his blinded master GLOUCESTER to the heath and gives him into
EDGAR's charge, before going home to fetch Edgar a suit of clothes.
Loyalty is his only characteristic.

Old Man *(Macbeth)*
Briefly discusses with ROSS the bad omens following DUNCAN's death,
things which have 'trifled' his 'former knowings' of disaster in the last
seventy years.

Oliver *(As You Like It)*
ORLANDO's black-hearted brother. He has treated him like a savage all
through his childhood, and when Orlando demands his patrimony he
plots for CHARLES the wrestler to break his neck. At the end of the
play, sleeping in a forest, he is on the brink of being killed twice over,
by a 'green and gilden snake' and a 'suck'd and hungry lioness', when
Orlando saves his life; at this, conveniently for the plot but
unconvincingly for character, he turns in an instant from villain to
loving brother, and helps Orlando in his courtship of the disguised
ROSALIND. Whether his melodramatic blackguardry or his sweet-
natured gratitude is harder to play, who can tell? Certainly his character
is always described by others rather than suggested in the lines he has
to say, and the best way to make him convincing is to play him as
straightforwardly, not to say unimaginatively, as the lines suggest.

Olivia *(Twelfth Night)*
There are three female roles in *Twelfth Night*, and over the years a

convention has grown up over how they should be played. VIOLA is the
star part, played by an experienced actress with all the range and
subtlety she possesses, a main vehicle for the 'serious' feelings at the
play's heart; MARIA is a farcical serving-wench, bright as a button and
with no thoughts in her head to deepen her role or distract the
audience; Olivia is equally two-dimensional, a languishing counterpart
to ORSINO, a foil to others (Viola, MALVOLIO) and a clothes-horse for
the costume-designer's loveliest creations.

This interpretation works well in performance (since it never
distracts attention from the main pillars of the action, Viola's distracted
passion and the gulling of Malvolio), but it is markedly unfair both to
the play and to the part of Olivia as Shakespeare wrote it. He gave
Olivia far more lines than a mere foil needs (a great many more than
Orsino, for example), and filled them with a fiery personality which
causes problems to any actress hired to play the part 'straight' and
bland. Like Viola, Olivia straddles the boundary in the play between
farce and comedy; but where Viola is drawn reluctantly into the farce,
Olivia recoils from it, reacting with affronted hostility to Sir Toby
BELCH's drunken familiarities and the cross-gartered caperings of
Malvolio. It was a masterstroke on Shakespeare's part to make these
two characters, Viola and Olivia, opposites, and then to give the 'warm'
character (Viola) cold disgust at the charades she has to play in the plot,
and the 'cold' character (Olivia) the warm emotion of hopeless,
yearning love. (When her yearning is fulfilled by meeting SEBASTIAN,
our pleasure for her is emotional, very like the satisfaction we feel when
Viola finds her heart's desire. This is not so of any of the two-
dimensional characters: who cares, for example, what Orsino feels?)

It is easy enough, reading or studying the text of *Twelfth Night*, to
observe such patterns in the writing. But such observation is of little
help to the actress in the theatre. How is she to give character to Olivia
without stealing scenes from the other characters? In particular, how is
she to play her scenes with Viola (filled with the finest poetry and the
most eloquent emotion in the play) in such a way that the audience feels
for both of them and yet most of all for Viola? Their scenes are like
comic duels, and if one participant plays a passive role there will be no
tension and little dramatic point. Faced with this dilemma, some
actresses generously opt to play Olivia as a stock bootfaced aristocrat,
merely wearing the frocks prettily, standing still and speaking up;
others take their cue from her outrage in the scene with Malvolio cross-
gartered and play her as an unpredictable spitfire throughout the play;
others make her speeches of languishing for 'Cesario' the key to her
character and play her throughout as wistfully distraught, as if her
mind was always on other things. (This last interpretation is the easiest
compromise for a spirited actress, and the one most often used.) It
takes a performer of consummate skill (and a director and fellow-actors
sympathetic to the interpretation) to play the part with its ebb and flow
of feeling left exactly as they are: to make Olivia, in short, as

Shakespeare intended, Viola's emotional mirror-image and (literal) counterpart.

Ophelia *(Hamlet)*

So far as the other people in the play are concerned, Ophelia is a beautiful puppet, not a person. When her brother LAERTES warns her to keep away from HAMLET, he talks to her as if she is an empty vessel just waiting to be filled with his wisdom. ('Fear it, Ophelia, fear it, my dear sister.../Youth to itself rebels, though none else is near.') Her father POLONIUS talks to her with a mixture of sternness and affection, but is quite happy to set her up in the meeting with Hamlet to test Hamlet's 'madness' (the 'Get-thee-to-a-nunnery' scene) – is this because he trusts that her innocence or her vacuity will protect her? CLAUDIUS makes her a pawn in his political intrigues; GERTRUDE realises that she was a real person, with real feelings, only after her suicide. Even Hamlet behaves to her with callous indifference, appearing before her 'with his doublet all unbrac'd' or shouting at her that she is a harlot. Her lines are bland enough to support this interpretation in performance, and the actor/actress is given songs (in the mad scene) into the bargain, of an innocence and poignancy unmatched in any other Shakespeare play.

On the other hand, Ophelia has spent her entire life in, or on the fringes of, one of the most corrupt courts in Europe. Although her father and brother are honest, they are well versed in keeping their own counsel, giving nothing away (exactly as they advise her to do with Hamlet); as for the king, queen, prince and courtiers, they are untrustworthy and murderous. Ophelia is sometimes played as if she, too, is tainted with this deviousness, as if her meek demeanour is a ploy, a behaviour-choice as calculated as Hamlet's charade of madness. If this way is followed, her lapse into (genuine) madness is ironical as well as tragic: the mechanism of self-preservation (isolation from 'normal' society) she once deliberately assumed has become reality, and she is left with no defence at all. Psychological complexity of this kind brings Ophelia to the forefront of the (few) scenes she appears in, and throws yet more light on the duality between truth and deception which is one of the play's main themes. It also gives substance to a role which is otherwise no more than very nearly very interesting, and which gives the performer hardly any character-qualities to match the heart-rending beauty of the lines.

Orlando *(As You Like It)*

Although there are a dozen spirited heroines in Shakespeare, there are very few spirited heroes. The idea seems to have been that a young woman could be as headstrong, pert and coltish as she liked, but a young man had to learn gravity and responsibility early in life, or be written off as frivolous. ROMEO is the pattern of the teenage Shakespearean hero: lively and ardent in his behaviour, but in his thinking already middle-aged and over-serious.

Orlando is a refreshing exception to this rule. At the start of the play he announces his spiritedness in a long complaint to ADAM about his upbringing, and in a fiery adolescent argument with his brother OLIVER ('Now sir, what make you here?' 'Nothing: I am not taught to make anything'); he challenges CHARLES the wrestler, despite Charles' reputation for mangling his opponents; when he finds that Oliver is planning to kill him, he takes Adam's life-savings – and Adam – and sets off into exile without a moment's thought. This is hardly the behaviour Shakespeare's audience might have expected from a noble youth, a gentleman – and the impression Orlando gives of giddiness is increased, not lessened, when he starts carving ROSALIND's name on trees and hanging verses in her honour on every branch in Arden.

Once Orlando meets the disguised Rosalind, and agrees to pay her court even though he thinks her a boy, he seems at first glance to turn into the stock stage lover we expect, a cousin of FENTON in *The Merry Wives of Windsor*, DEMETRIUS and LYSANDER in *A Midsummer Night's Dream* or the young gallant HENRY presents himself as to KATHARINE in *Henry V*. The 'Ganymede'–Orlando relationship is one in which Rosalind (as Ganymede) takes all the initiative, and Orlando's part consists mainly of leading questions ('Did you ever cure any so?') or fervent declarations ('I would not have my right/ Rosalind of this mind, for I protest/Her frown might kill me'). But as the relationship deepens – and it does so, scene by scene, before our eyes – she begins to take on aspects of his lover's character (yearning, fervency, melancholy) and he of hers (wit, self-confidence), until by the end, when flirting has blossomed into love, they are equal partners in a varied, fascinating and ever-changing love-affair.

Orleans, Charles, Duke of *(Henry V)*
Despite his bravado before Agincourt (he jokes with the DAUPHIN and the CONSTABLE), this foppish French lord is killed in the battle.

Orsino *(Twelfth Night)*
Duke of Illyria, who imagines himself in love with OLIVIA. He is passionate and immature, luxuriating in his own romantic melancholy, and the ardent poetry he speaks (not least 'If music be the food of love, play on...') establishes one of the play's main moods. Ecstasies of unrequited longing are his chief character: as soon as his true love (for VIOLA) is discovered (by him) and returned (by her), he reverts to happy but stock ducal formality.

Osric *(Hamlet)*
Foppish young courtier who organises the duel between HAMLET and LAERTES. He is incapable of uttering the simplest sentence without verbal 'flourishes', but he is an empty vessel, and no phrase more tellingly describes his inanity than HORATIO's marvellous description of his swooping about his business: 'The lapwing runs away with the shell upon his head'.

Oswald *(King Lear)*
GONERIL's servant. Instructed by her to 'put on what weary negligence'
he chooses, he is at first off-hand with LEAR, then impertinent ('I'll not
be struck, my lord'), and finally triumphant as Lear is dismissed from
the court and KENT (who tripped Oswald up and threatened to beat
him) is put in the stocks for insolence. Oswald is subsequently used as a
messenger between Goneril and REGAN, and is told that if he kills
GLOUCESTER he will be well rewarded. He comes across him in EDGAR's
company, fights Edgar ('Wherefore, bold peasant, Dost thou support a
publish'd traitor?.../Let go his arm.') and is killed.

Othello *(Othello)*
Pride is the scaffolding of Othello's personality, and he is forever
adding to it, shoring it up and reminding himself of it. He refuses to be
dismayed by BRABANTIO's accusations of enticement and witchcraft, not
because they are false but because 'I fetch my life and being/From men
of royal siege' and 'My parts, my title and my perfect soul/Shall
manifest me rightly'. There is a barefaced nerve about his wooing of
DESDEMONA with talk 'of antres vast and deserts idle,/Rough quarries,
and hills whose heads touch heaven': he knows, and she knows, that his
tales can be as fanciful as he likes, since she loves him for the kind of
man he is and for the general run of 'dangers I had passed', rather than
for any specific adventure.

Love for Desdemona is the only chink in Othello's self-sufficiency,
and its tendency towards obsession is signalled early on, at the moment
of his arrival in Cyprus. ('It gives me wonder great as my content/To
see you here before me. O, my soul's joy!/If after every tempest come
such calms,/May the winds blow till they have waken'd death...')
Taken in conjunction with his next appearance, a torrent of barely-
controlled fury at CASSIO and MONTANO for brawling – 'Now, by
heaven,/My blood begins my safer guides to rule:/And passion, having
my best judgement collied,/Assays to lead the way. If I once stir,/Or do
but lift this arm, the best of you/Shall sink in my reproach' – this makes
the danger in his personality, its potential for self-destruction,
absolutely clear.

The second main plank in Othello's character is honour. Convinced
of his own integrity, he commends the same quality in others as if
handing out school prizes. Cassio is given the lieutenancy because he is
'an honourable man' (a phrase with which Iago later goads Othello);
Iago is given no promotion but is patronisingly praised as 'a man of
honesty and trust'; the Venetian Senators are 'most potent, grave and
reverend signiors'; even Brabantio, despite his hysterical accusations, is
treated with courtesy and dignity. The combination of personal
arrogance, refusal to believe the possibility of evil in others and
obsessive physical love is an explosive one, and Iago sparks off each of
the three qualities in turn. He works most effectively on Othello's love,
and uses it first to give him unaccustomed and psychologically

devastating self- doubts – 'Haply, for I am black,/And have not the soft parts of conversation/That chamberers have, or, for I am declined/Into the vale of years (yet that's not much),/She's gone, I am abused, and my relief/Must be to loathe her' – and then to an outburst of hysteria ending in literal physical collapse (Othello swoons): 'Lie with her! Lie on her! We say lie on her when they belie her. Lie with her! That's fulsome. Handkerchief... confession ... handkerchief...'

Once the fire is lit in Othello's brain, Iago can leave his conflicting personality-traits to work, merely helping the process along by stage-managing confrontations, killing off potential blurters-out of the truth (e.g. RODERIGO) and reiterating his own honesty and discretion whenever occasion offers. It is Othello's own personality, not Iago's urging, that makes him teeter between obsessive love and hatred for Desdemona ('Ay, let her rot and perish, and be damned tonight, for she shall not live ... O, the world hath not a sweeter creature: she might lie by an emperor's side, and command him tasks'), and finally leads him to stifle her, more as a cure for his own soul's turmoil than as punishment for anything she has done.

As soon as she is dead Othello's soul *is* calmed, but he is left with no more than shattered fragments of the emotions which once sustained it. His devotion turns into a pathetic concern for the appearance of the corpse ('O, ill-starr'd wench!/Pale as thy smock!'); his stateliness becomes a kind of exhausted courtesy ('Will you, I pray, demand that demi-devil/Why he hath thus ensnared my soul and body?'); his arrogance is turned to its mirror- image, self-disgust ('O cursed, cursed slave! Whip me, ye devils,/From the possession of this heavenly sight...') Then, in the closing moments of the play, he seems to gather himself before our eyes, and utterly against expectation becomes once more dignified, noble and full of the fascinating unpredictability which marked his earlier character. 'Soft you, a word before you go,' the speech begins, and proceeds to a traveller's tale about a Turk beating a Venetian in Aleppo once, only to end in Othello's own suicide, one of the quietest and most devastating acts of violence in the play. ('I took by the throat the circumcised dog,/And smote him – thus.') This ending is a *coup de théâtre*, a stunning theatrical surprise; it is also a *coup de psychologie*, using to destroy Othello the feline arrogance which underlay his personality until it seemed to have been stripped from him by Iago's machinations. His death, like his life until he met Desdemona, is the product of a prickly code of honour whose moral determinants are his alone to choose. His destruction is caused by the assaults of the outside world, but in his death, as in his life before he admitted love into it, he is an outsider, a man alone.

Othello

Iago, a Venetian soldier, has been passed over for promotion to lieutenant by his general, the Moor Othello, and vows revenge. He begins by telling an old Senator, Brabantio, that Othello has stolen his

(Brabantio's) daughter Desdemona by witchcraft; in open court, however, Othello shows that the only witchcraft he used was love, and Desdemona confirms it. Othello goes to fight the Turks in Cyprus, and Iago begins a different plan of revenge. He takes Roderigo – a fool, and Othello's rival for Desdemona – to Cyprus and tells him to seek occasions to arouse Othello's jealousy. He does the same thing himself, sowing doubt in Othello's mind about Desdemona's faithfulness, hinting that she is sleeping with Cassio (the young man promoted to the lieutenancy which he, Iago, coveted); then he arranges for Othello to find Cassio drunk, and for Desdemona to plead with him not to disgrace Cassio. This fuels Othello's suspicions, and Iago confirms them with circumstantial evidence: he takes a handkerchief which Desdemona has dropped and hides it among Cassio's kit, then tells Othello that he has seen Cassio fondling it in his sleep and babbling Desdemona's name. Othello's mind begins to totter, and he swears revenge, telling Iago to kill Cassio while he kills Desdemona.

Othello humiliates Desdemona before visiting dignitaries from Venice, and later goes to her bedroom, orders her to say her prayers, and despite her terrified protestations of innocence, strangles her. By now Iago's wife, Emilia, has discovered what her husband is doing, and tells Othello the truth about the handkerchief, that Desdemona dropped it by accident and she (Emilia) found it and gave it to Iago. Iago furiously kills Emilia, and Othello attacks him and wounds him before turning his dagger on himself. The Venetian envoys give command of the Cypriot garrison to Cassio, and take Iago back to Venice for punishment.

Outlaws *(The Two Gentlemen of Verona)*
As unterrifying a crew of desperadoes as one could hope to find outside the pages of *Peter Pan*: gentlemen fallen on hard times (they claim), they are so impressed by VALENTINE's gift for languages that they elect him leader on the spot, even accepting his condition that they will do 'no outrages/On silly women or poor travellers'.

Overdone, Mistress *(Measure for Measure)*
Brothel-keeper arrested (twice) by ELBOW. She is POMPEY's employer, but has none of his zest for life: in fact she is less like the raucous, apple-cheeked madam of popular legend than a worried businesswoman, driven almost frantic by the closing of her houses. Her main function in the plot is to tell ESCALUS (and us) of LUCIO's affair with the prostitute Kate Keepdown, a piece of knowledge used against Lucio in the final scene; she contributes little else, either humour or character-interest, to the play.

Oxford, John de, Earl of *(Henry VI Part Three; Richard III)*
Lancastrian; supporter of Queen MARGARET (especially at the French court). After WARWICK's defection from the Yorkists, he is his co-general against them, and is captured at the battle of Tewkesbury

and imprisoned. In *Richard III* he appears briefly in RICHARD's train ('Every man's conscience is a thousand swords/To fight against this guilty homicide'); despite his eminence in both plays, he scarcely speaks.

Page (*Richard III*)
When RICHARD, looking for someone to kill the Princes in the Tower, asks, 'Knows't thou not any whom corrupting hold/Will tempt unto a close exploit of death?', the Page answers 'I know a discontented gentleman.../His name, my lord, is Tyrrel...', and is sent hot-foot to find him.

Page (Robin) (*Henry IV Part Two; Henry V; The Merry Wives of Windsor*)
Somewhat rashly given by Prince HAL to FALSTAFF for education, this young lad becomes an apt, pert pupil, his master's shadow. After Falstaff's death he is taken in by Mistress QUICKLY, and in *Henry V* goes as PISTOL's page to France (where he shows a nimble ability at French, bargaining with the French soldier Pistol captures). He speaks two notable soliloquies, one revealing disgust at the knavish company he is forced to keep, and the other announcing NYM's and BARDOLPH's deaths. He is one of the boys left to guard the English baggage at Agincourt, and is treacherously killed by the French, against all the rules of war.

Page (*The Taming of the Shrew*)
In the Induction, when SLY is being convinced he is a lord, he pertly plays the part of the lord's allegedly sex-starved wife.

Page (*Timon of Athens*)
Serves the same mistress (a money-lender and a brothel-keeper) as the FOOL, and delivers letters to TIMON and ALCIBIADES. Three cheeky speeches only.

Page, Anne (*The Merry Wives of Windsor*)
A grown girl of perhaps 16, Anne Page is the beauty whose courtship (by SLENDER, CAIUS and FENTON) forms the subplot of the play. She is basically a standard farce *ingénue*, pretty and straightforward; but Shakespeare balances her 'serious' love-scenes with Fenton by allowing

her spirit and pertness in her dealings with others (notably Slender). It is a small part, but full of variety and vivacity.

Page, George (*The Merry Wives of Windsor*)
Prosperous Windsor citizen, whose wife is courted by FALSTAFF and whose daughter Anne PAGE is courted by SLENDER (whom Page himself supports), CAIUS (whom his wife supports) and FENTON (who is supported by no one, but wins her in the end). Page is a cheerful counterpart to his friend the brooding FORD: if they were 'humours' in the Ben Jonson sense (*see* JAQUES), he would be all blood and phlegm and his only real preoccupation is with his daughter's happiness. It is a meagre role on paper, but in performance it 'frames' the farcical characters in the other parts, and binds the play.

Page, Mistress (*The Merry Wives of Windsor*)
The more frivolous (and perhaps younger) of the two 'merry wives'. In the tricking of FALSTAFF she is given the task of rushing breathlessly in on the 'lovers' with news that FORD is on his way to search the house. She also devises the last trick of all, a complicated charade involving a wood at midnight, a pack of children dressed as fairies, and Falstaff with deer-horns on his head pretending to be Herne the Hunter. In addition to this feather-light plotting, she is busy with a second intrigue (to bring it about that CAIUS elopes with her daughter Anne), but when the attempt fails she cheerfully confesses everything to her husband. Throughout the action, her bubbliness and his relaxed good humour are magnificently paired: they are happy people, solid citizens, and their warm-hearted humanity contributes much to the atmosphere of this most genial of plays.

Page, William (*The Merry Wives of Windsor*)
George PAGE's son, a boy of about eight (to judge by his rudimentary state of education), has one scene in the play, in which EVANS tests his knowledge (*Evans*: 'What is fair, William?' *William*: 'Pulcher'), and Mistress QUICKLY misunderstands ('Polecats? There are fairer things than polecats, sure.'). The two adults have all the fun of the scene; but part of its success comes from the wide-eyed innocence of William Page (and, quite possibly, from the saucer-eyed self-importance of the little boy playing the part in a real theatre and in a grown-up play).

Painter (*Timon of Athens*)
Always appears with the POET, and apart from the difference in trade, is interchangeable with him.

Palamon (*The Two Noble Kinsmen*)
Of the two young men at the heart of the play, Palamon is by far the more romantic. He is all absolutes, at one moment asking his cousin 'Is there record of any two that loved/Better than we do, Arcite?', and the next snapping his head off for breathing. (*Arcite*: 'Heigh-ho.' *Palamon*: 'For Emily, upon my life! Fool,/Away with this strained mirth! I say

again,/That sigh was breathed for Emily. Base cousin...') When recaptured by THESEUS and told to forswear his love, he breathes implacable defiance (I'll be cut apieces/Before I take this oath'), and when he is beaten in the duel with ARCITE he lays his head on the executioner's block with a bravado which is only just this side of ludicrous. ('Adieu: and let my life be now as short/As my leavetaking.') Having played at life and at love, he is all set to play at death in the same manner – and when he is reprieved, given Emilia and deprived of Arcite all in an instant, his emotions are beggared and he has nothing left but conventional sentiment ('O cousin.../... that nought could buy/Dear love but loss of dear love!'). He is less a shallow character than a shallow person, and, unlike most of Shakespeare's immature young heroes, remains unchanged by his experiences: he ends the play as callow and headstrong as he began it, and his adventures have no moral lesson to teach us, leave no impression at all except what a lucky young man he is.

Pandar *(Pericles)*
Brothel-keeper who buys MARINA from the PIRATES and almost immediately starts losing customers. A heartless, amoral businessman, he is also, endearingly, looking forward to retirement. ('Three or four thousand chequins were as pretty a proportion to live quietly, and so give over...')

Pandarus *(Troilus and Cressida)*
CRESSIDA's uncle. He is a charming man (and a fine singer), flawed by total absence of conscience: he says what the moment requires, never what's truly in his mind, until we begin to wonder if there is actually any real person at all behind the mask. He is a compulsive maker of introductions between one person and another. His method is to praise party A to party B, cheerfully and exaggeratedly, and to try where possible to provoke admiration through jealousy. (He discovers Cressida's true feelings for TROILUS, for example, by telling her a circumstantial tale of HELEN's tickling Troilus' all-but-beardless chin and finding a white hair there.) He brings Troilus and Cressida together for a night of love, and shows them to a chamber with a bed 'which... because it shall not speak of your pretty encounters, press it to death: away!' He is not a professional pandar, since he expects no money for his work, but his hail-fellow-well-met oiliness and his zest for other people's coupling are still to the manner born. At the end of the play, when Cressida has been false to Troilus in Troilus' own sight, he tries in vain to reconcile them and then, insulted and abused by Troilus ('Hence, broker lackey! Ignominy and shame/Pursue thy life!...'), he reflects on the miserable lot in life of go-betweens and points the perverse, bitter moral of the whole play: 'O traders and bawds, how earnestly are you set awork, and how ill requited! Why should our endeavour be so loved, and the performance so loathed?'

Pandulph, Cardinal *(King John)*
Emissary of the Pope who excommunicates JOHN (for failing to accept
the Pope's nominee as Archbishop of Canterbury) and stirs up the
French to attack England, then, when John recants, tries unavailingly
to order the French back home and end the war. He is a silky diplomat
with a touch of steel ('Arm thy constant and thy nobler parts/Against
these giddy, loose suggestions... but if not, then know/The peril of our
curses light on thee,/So heavy as thou shalt not shake them off...'), but
he has only one card (papal authority) in his hand, overplays it at
enormous length – his speeches seem interminable – and is treated by
everyone else with a mixture of politeness and contempt.

Panthino *(The Two Gentlemen of Verona)*
ANTONIO's servant, who urges his master to send PROTEUS away to
Milan 'to practise tilts and tournaments,/Hear sweet discourse, converse
with noblemen,/And be in the eye of every exercise/Worthy his youth
and nobleness of birth'. He is pompous and humourless, and in a later
scene is scurrilously mocked by LAUNCE. (*Panthino*: 'Why should you
stop my mouth?' *Launce*: 'For fear thou shouldst lose thy tongue.'
Panthino: 'Where should I lose my tongue?' *Launce*: 'In thy tale.'
Panthino: 'In my tail?' *Launce*: 'Lose the tide, and the voyage, and the
master, and the service, and the tied...')

Paris *(Troilus and Cressida)*
Prince of Troy, whose kidnapping of HELEN began the war. He is
courteous, handsome and ineffective, always striking poses on the edges
of the action and never at its heart. The part is small, and its chief
characteristic is youthful charm.

Paris, Count *(Romeo and Juliet)*
The husband chosen by the CAPULETS for JULIET, he is a high-born
gentleman, related to Prince ESCALUS himself. He is, on the face of it,
as unlike ROMEO as possible: staid instead of impetuous, boring instead
of lively, predictable instead of mercurial. But for all that, he is no
cipher, and his scene of grieving at Juliet's tomb ('Sweet flower, with
flowers thy bridal bed I strew...') is full of tenderness.

Parolles *(All's Well that Ends Well)*
BERTRAM's confidant and flatterer, a mercenary soldier (a captain) living
by his wits, Parolles – the name means 'words' – is something of a cut-
price FALSTAFF. He has the same verbal gusto, calling two cocky
French lordlings 'worthy fellows, and likely to prove most sinewy
swordsmen', and splendidly urging Bertram to go to Italy with the
words 'To th' wars, my boy, to th' wars!/He wears his honour in a box
unseen/ That hugs his kicky-wicky here at home,/Spending his manly
marrow in her arms,/Which should sustain the bound and high
current/Of Mars' fiery steed'. He is a boaster and a liar, always planning
how to turn events to his advantage. ('I must give myself some hurts,
and say I got them in exploit. Yet slight ones will not carry it – they'll

say "Came you off with so little?" – and great ones I dare not give...')
Beyond saving his own skin, he has no scruples: asked by captors he
thinks are the enemy (but are actually the LORDS in disguise), 'If your
life be saved, will you undertake to betray the Florentine?', he adds,
eagerly tossing his own young master to the dogs of war as well, 'Ay,
and the captain of his horse, Count Rousillon'.

All this would be fine and funny, if Parolles had any of Falstaff's
humanity or moral bulk. But where Falstaff is exuberant, Parolles is
cynical, where Falstaff laughs, he sneers, where Falstaff triumphs, he
trembles. When Falstaff is tricked by disguised friends (HAL and POINS
at Gadshill) and challenged with it afterwards, he masks his cowardice
in a grand bluff: 'By the lord, I knew ye as well as he that made ye...
Was it for me to kill the heir apparent?'; in similar circumstances,
Parolles can only snivel 'Who cannot be crushed with a plot?' When he
is riding high he is arrogant without a trace of Falstaff's generosity of
spirit: there is neither a joke nor a cup of sack in sight. He is summed
up by the First Lord as 'a most notable coward, an infinite and endless
liar, an hourly promise-breaker, the owner of no one good quality
worthy your lordship's entertainment', and by LAFEU as 'a vagabond...
more saucy with lords and honourable personages than the heraldry of
your birth or virtue gives commission'. No one talks of Falstaff with
such flat dislike, and Parolles does nothing in the play to counter such
character-assessments. He is a conventional character, like the pimps or
flatterers in the Roman comedies Shakespeare may have read at school,
and his downfall (when he has to crawl for favour to the clown
LAVACHE and to Lafeu) is grimly satisfying rather than entertaining. If
we pity him, if we feel a shred of sympathy, the triumph is the actor's
over his material.

Patience (*Henry VIII*)
Queen KATHARINE's maid in Kimbolton.

Patroclus (*Troilus and Cressida*)
ACHILLES' catamite, a boy in his mid or late teens. We first hear of him
entertaining his friend by scurrilous impersonations of the Greek
commanders, and we see his frequent, vigorous and wasp-tongued
quarrels with THERSITES, who treats him as a useless fool. He plays no
substantial part in the action until his death: he is killed by HECTOR,
and this rouses Achilles to end his feud with the Greek commanders
and kill Hector in revenge.

Paulina (*The Winter's Tale*)
ANTIGONUS' wife is proud, noble-hearted, forthright and impulsive.
Alone of all LEONTES' courtiers, she tells him exactly what she thinks of
his behaviour. She bursts in on the court with baby PERDITA in her
arms, and repudiates Leontes' claim that it is POLIXENES' bastard by
brandishing the child at the courtiers and crying, 'Behold, my lord,/
Although the print be little, the whole matter/And copy of the father,

eyes, nose, lip,/The trick of's frown...'. After HERMIONE's trial, when she takes Leontes (false) news that Hermione is dead, she dresses it in language of a scalding rage that beggars argument. ('What studied torments, tyrant, hast for me?/What wheels, racks, fires? What flaying, boiling,/In leads or oils?... The queen, the queen,/The sweetest, dear'st creature's dead.') In the last act, however, full of motherly sympathy for Leontes' sixteen-year penance, she is kind and gentle to him: when, for example, he bewails how he 'destroy'd the sweet'st companion that e'er man/Bred his hopes out of,' she sorrowfully answers, 'True, too true, my lord:/If, one by one, you wedded all the world,/Or, from the all that are took something good/To make a perfect woman, she you killed/Would be unparallel'd'. In the last scene, after Perdita has been identified as Leontes' missing child, Paulina reunites Leontes with Hermione, whom she has cared for in secret. With KATHARINE in *Henry VIII*, Paulina is one of the finest and most neglected female roles in Shakespeare, a secondary character who irradiates the play.

Peaseblossom *(A Midsummer Night's Dream)*: *see* **Fairies**

Pedant *(The Taming of the Shrew)*
Old man brought off the street by BIONDELLO to play the part of TRANIO's/LUCENTIO's supposed father. He does it ringingly – 'Soft, son!/Sir, by your leave: having come to Padua/To gather in some debts, my son Lucentio/Made me acquainted with a weighty cause/Of love between your daughter and himself...') – but takes to his heels as soon as the real father arrives, and is not seen again.

Pembroke, William Herbert, Earl of *(Henry VI Part Three)*
Supporter of EDWARD; does not speak.

Pembroke, William Marshall, Earl of *(King John)*
Plotter, with SALISBURY, against John; their forces tip the balance in favour of whichever side they are on, and they are good at showing blustery indignation (e.g. over the body of poor little ARTHUR). But they have no understanding of state affairs, and no concern for anything but their own political position: the BASTARD's scornful phrase, 'They burn in indignation', describes them to a T.

Percy, Harry (Hotspur) *(Richard II; Henry IV Part One)*
The Hotspur of *Richard II* is a thin, unrewarding part: a few score lines, most of them announcements of news ('The grand conspirator, Abbot of Westminster... Hath yielded up his body to the grave') or murmurings of agreement with his father NORTHUMBERLAND. He is a noble stripling, and the part is apt for an apprentice actor: there is no hint of the grandeur to come in *Henry IV Part One*. In that play he is a volatile and dangerous young man, true descendant of John of GAUNT and an apparent candidate for the throne – so much more princely than the Prince of Wales that the king ruefully wonders if they may not have

been exchanged in their cradles. But for all his valorous regality, Hotspur lacks both compassion and humility (two of the qualities Hal is learning and practising, thanks to his low-life activities with FALSTAFF and the others). Hotspur quarrels with GLENDOWER, a major ally, simply because he can't abide the man's boasting; he refuses even to consider handing over the prisoners he has captured, simply because he disapproves of the king's 'ingratitude' – indeed, his anger over this is what gives the rebellion its impetus; his behaviour to his loving, fearful wife is pointlessly callous; his cocky, bully-boy approach to affairs is summed up in his phrase 'Out of this nettle, danger, we pluck this flower, safety'. His uncle Worcester has doubts about his temperament, should he become king, and Worcester is right.

All this works well for the contrast Shakespeare is drawing between the supremacy to be won by political or military prowess in the civil war, and the true qualities required of a king which Hal – and with him, England – is learning as the play proceeds. Hotspur is depicted throughout as untouched by humanity: he therefore has no need, as Hal does, either to understand it in others or to transcend it in himself. The part, though sizeable and full of fiery language, is one-dimensional, and the actor's cue should perhaps be to emphasise Hotspur's headstrong arrogance rather than to portray him as some kind of prototype of the leading character in *Henry V*. He is an anachronism, a yokel lord who clings to a feudal, my-might-is-right view of events in a world which has moved on to subtlety and compromise; he is 'thick of speech', a lover of deeds not words; he is the antithesis not so much to Hal in the play as to that other dinosaur-figure from Britain's idealised, mythical past, Falstaff himself.

Percy, Lady (*Henry IV Parts One and Two*)
Hotspur's wife says little in *Part One*, but in *Part Two* eloquently bewails his death and the waste of war.

Perdita (*The Winter's Tale*)
Beautiful young girl, 'the prettiest... lass that ever/Ran upon the greensward,' 'the most peerless piece of earth.../That e'er the sun shone bright on'. She is the baby daughter LEONTES ordered to be exposed to die, now grown-up and in love with FLORIZEL. We see her as mistress of the rustic jollity of the sheep-shearing festival, and exchanging breathless lovers' vows with Florizel; behind all the pretty-heroine conventionalities, however, her main characteristic is brisk common sense.

Pericles (*Pericles*)
Pericles is less like a play than an episodic fairy-tale: it is closer to *Sinbad the Sailor* than to *King Lear*, and its characters are organised accordingly. Instead of the action arising out of what the people are, it moves with its own independent impetus, and people drop in or out of the plot as they are required, contributing little in the way of individual

personality. The same is true of Pericles, at least for the first four acts.
He is an eager riddle-solver for ANTIOCHUS, then a fugitive; he is a
generous helper of CLEON and DIONYZA; he is a shipwrecked prince in
disguise at Pentapolis, then a knight in unknown armour who jousts for
THAISSA and wins her hand; he is a distraught husband whose wife has
died in childbirth. In Act Four (which is chiefly concerned with
MARINA's adventures in the brothel) he plays no part at all. And then,
utterly without preparation, he turns in Act Five into a LEAR-like
suffering hero, humanity reduced to its essence and learning joy and
humility before our eyes.

The scene in which Marina talks to him and gradually restores his
wits is one of the most luminous pieces of writing in Shakespeare,
paralleled for intensity and for the transcendental simplicity of its
poetry only by the Lear–CORDELIA ending of *King Lear* – and the
theme is identical: the rescue, by dialogue with innocence, of a human
soul all but broken by the world's vicissitudes. ('This is the rarest
dream that e'er dull sleep/Did mock sad fools withal.../I'll hear you
more, to the bottom of your story,/And never interrupt you...'; 'Most
heavenly music!/It nips me into listening, and thick slumber/Hangs
upon mine eyes: let me rest'...) If the earlier acts are fustian, and the
final plot-unravelling before Diana's temple, which follows this scene, is
perfunctory, this section is Shakespeare's art at its most dignified and
most inspired, and Pericles' character is (briefly) transfigured by poetry
just as the scene transfigures the surrounding play.

Pericles, Prince of Tyre
The action of *Pericles* is spread over sixteen years, and each act is
introduced and punctuated by commentary from the poet John Gower
(who wrote the original story in 1390): he recites a prologue, interludes
and an epilogue, and presents dumb-shows of the coming events.

We first see Pericles solving a riddle set by Antiochus of Antioch to
all his daughter's would-be suitors. Unfortunately for Pericles, the
answer involves revealing Antiochus' incest with his daughter, and
Pericles has to flee from Antiochus' hired assassin Thaliard to Tarsus,
where he helps the governor Cleon and his wife Dionyza to end a
famine. Soon afterwards he is shipwrecked at Pentapolis, and after he
and his armour have been rescued by some fishermen he takes part in a
tournament and wins the hand of Princess Thaissa. He stays in
Pentapolis till news comes of Antiochus' death, whereupon he and
Thaissa set sail for home. On the way they are caught in a storm and
Thaissa dies in childbirth. Pericles floats her overboard in a waterproof
chest, and takes his baby daughter Marina to Tarsus, where he asks
Cleon and Dionyza to bring her up.

The chest is washed up near Ephesus, and the healer Cerimon brings
Thaissa back to life. She becomes a priestess of Diana's temple. The
action moves on fifteen years, until Marina is grown up. Dionyza, her
stepmother, angry at the way she outshines Dionyza's own daughter

Philoten, orders her death, but she is captured by pirates in the nick of time and sold to a brothel in Mytilene. Here she scares off all customers by talking of nothing but holy works, and in the end Lysimachus, governor of Mytilene, rescues her. All this time Pericles, thinking her dead, has vowed never to wash, speak or cut his hair, and he now visits Mytilene half out of his mind with grief. Marina is taken before him and tells her story. He recognises her as his long-lost daughter, and when he goes to Diana's temple to celebrate, he finds Thaissa there too, restored to life. Lysimachus marries Marina, Gower announces that the wicked Cleon and Dionyza are dead, and everyone lives happily ever afterwards.

Peter *(Romeo and Juliet)*

Clownish servant of Old CAPULET, who delivers the invitations to the masked ball (and gets ROMEO to read them to him), and subsequently appears with the NURSE and in a knockabout dialogue with the musicians CATLING, REBECK and SOUNDPOST. The part was written for Will Kemp, the comedian who later created the role of FALSTAFF: this throws an unexpected light, perhaps, on Peter's nature, one for which the text gives scanty support. (Perhaps Kemp added to his part in performance, as great comedians will.) Peter is one of those Shakespearean clowns who think themselves far funnier than we, perhaps, do today ('My master is the great rich Capulet, and if you be not of the house of Montagues, I pray, come and crush a cup of wine. Rest you merry!'); but in a play where tragedy is so fast-moving and inexorable, the light relief he provides is essential and effective. The anonymous Serving-man who is told by Capulet 'Sirrah, go hire me twenty cunning cooks' speaks so like Peter ('You shall have none ill, sir, for I'll try if they can lick their fingers... 'tis an ill cook that cannot lick his own fingers; therefore, he that cannot lick his fingers goes not with me') that it could well be the same comedian.

Peter (Thump) *(Henry VI Part Two)*

Apprentice armourer who petitions Queen MARGARET against his master HORNER 'for saying that the Duke of York was rightful heir to the throne', challenges him to a test of combat and kills him, thus proving his accusation if not his honesty. He is presented throughout as a shifty rogue.

Peter of Pomfret *(King John)*

Mad Yorkshire prophet, the 'idle dreamer' who predicts that JOHN will surrender his crown before noon on Ascension Day, and is clapped in jail for it.

Petitioners *(Henry VI Part Two)*

Two of them appear with PETER to ask help of Queen MARGARET. Unfortunately their complaints are against a servant of Cardinal BEAUFORT, whom the queen favours, and against her paramour SUFFOLK, whereas Peter's is against his master HORNER for treason against the king. Horner is preferred and they are sent packing ('Avaunt, base cullions!') with their petitions ripped like confetti about their ears.

Peto (*Henry IV Parts One and Two*)
One of FALSTAFF's crookedest (and slowest-witted) cronies. He speaks all of half a dozen lines, of little liveliness; one's heart goes out to any actor hired to play this part, and this part only, night after night.

Petruchio (*Romeo and Juliet*)
CAPULET's kinsman, who appears in the duel-scene as one of TYBALT's companions, but does not speak.

Petruchio (*The Taming of the Shrew*)
Everything Petruchio does or says belongs to the mode of farce. His motive for coming to Padua is 'to wive it wealthily', and he agrees to court KATHARINA as much because GREMIO and HORTENSIO pay his expenses as because he likes her. He tames her by behaviour even more outrageous and extravagant than her shrewishness (coming to his own wedding dressed in rags; insisting that the moon is the sun and the sun the moon; throwing away the delicious food and beautiful clothes prepared for her). At the end, he treats his triumph, and the hundred-crown wager Katharina's obedience has won him, as casually and cheerfully as if he'd won no more than a hand at cards. There is no hint of moral doubt about him: he knows exactly what he wants and sets about getting it with single-minded, unscrupulous and self-delighting charm.

In productions where the play is taken as comedy, this bare-faced behaviour poses problems of interpretation. Why should such a man pursue such an unlikely marriage in the first place? (There are plenty of other, less violent, heiresses in Padua.) And why should such a girl as Katharina let herself be 'tamed' by him? The usual answer given – though there is no evidence for it in the lines – is that they fall in love with each other in the course of the action, and that what was originally a deadly serious charade on both their parts, a defence against true feeling, turns into a carefree joint conspiracy against the world. If this line is taken (and why should it not be?), it gives the play, and Katharina's and Petruchio's characters within it, a most unexpected extra depth: for just as he tames her, so she, by love, tames him.

Phebe (*As You Like It*)
Shepherdess, loved by SILVIUS but in love with Ganymede (ROSALIND in boy's clothes). She has one meaty scene with Silvius; apart from that most of her part is to stand prettily and dote on her beloved.

Philario (*Cymbeline*)
Italian friend of POSTHUMUS' father, with whom Posthumus lodges when he is exiled in Italy, and at whose house he first meets IACHIMO. He speaks about twenty lines; he is agreeable and hospitable, no more.

Philemon *(Pericles)*
CERIMON's servant.

Philip (Philippe II) *(King John)*
King of France. Urged by everyone to support ARTHUR's claim to the
English throne, he fights a lengthy war against the English, wins so
long as he has the support of the turncoats SALISBURY and PEMBROKE,
but loses when they return to JOHN's side (having heard that Philip
plans treacherously to murder them). He says a good deal, especially in
the quarrel-scenes with John at the start of the play, and later when he
is faced by the furious CONSTANCE, but except for the slightly suspect
courtesy which Shakespeare always attributes to French royalty, he has
little character.

Philo *(Antony and Cleopatra)*
Begins the play by deploring the way in which 'this dotage of our
general's/O'erflows the measure' and how ANTONY, 'the triple pillar of
the world', is 'transform'd/Into a strumpet's fool'.

Philostrate *(A Midsummer Night's Dream)*
THESEUS' master of the revels, a ceremonious court official who
arranges the wedding entertainment, including the rustics' play. ('A
play there is, my lord, some ten words long.../Which, when I saw
rehears'd, I must confess,/Made mine eyes water...')

Philotus *(Timon of Athens): see* **Servants**

Phrynia *(Timon of Athens)*
Whore brought by ALCIBIADES to visit TIMON in exile, and given gold
by him to corrupt the Athenians.

Pinch *(The Comedy of Errors)*
Charlatan brought by ADRIANA to drive out the spirits supposedly
driving ANTIPHOLUS II mad. He has only a dozen lines, but they are in
orotund quack's jargon – 'I charge thee, Satan, hous'd within this
man,/To yield possession to my holy prayers,/And to thy state of
darkness hie thee straight...' – and earn him a well deserved thrashing.

Pindarus *(Julius Caesar)*
Slave persuaded by CASSIUS to hold the sword while he commits
suicide.

Pirates *(Pericles)*
They kidnap MARINA and sell her to the PANDAR. However rollicking
and bloodthirsty they may be made in performance, their lines are as
colourless as water.

Pirithous *(The Two Noble Kinsmen)*
THESEUS' friend. A straightforward lord, with fine words (e.g. his
description of ARCITE's fatal horse-ride in the final scene) but little
character.

Pisanio *(Cymbeline)*
POSTHUMUS' loyal servant. He plays a large part in the action, carrying letters, helping IMOGEN escape to Wales and to disguise herself as a boy, refusing to murder her (and then pretending to CLOTEN that he has), unmasking villainy and protecting innocence. Bustle is the key to his character: like the loyal retainer that he is, he is always more self-effacing than the people he is with, and they (particularly Cloten and Imogen) are the ones whose characters are revealed when they talk with him. When he does speak for himself, e.g. when he reads Posthumus' instructions to kill Imogen, he expresses himself with wooden, conventional vehemence: 'O damn'd paper,/Black as the ink that's on thee! Senseless bauble...' If it's possible to be uncomplicatedly devious, superficially deep, that's what he is.

Pistol *(Henry IV Part Two; Henry V; The Merry Wives of Windsor)*
In FALSTAFF's somewhat dubious military endeavours, Pistol is his 'ancient' (i.e. ensign, or second officer), just as BARDOLPH is his lieutenant and NYM is his corporal. Pistol is a mountebank, a fanatical swashbuckler who wields words as if they were cutlasses. (There is more than a hint of the ham actor: he and the PLAYER KING in *Hamlet* are close kin.) His style is that of a medieval braggart or the Boastful Soldier of Roman comedy (*see* Falstaff): when, for example, he wants to tell Falstaff that Doll TEARSHEET has been arrested, he says, larding his speech to great effect but no purpose with the scraps of a classical education, 'My knight, I will inflame thy noble liver and make thee rage. Thy Doll, and Helen of thy noble thoughts, is in base durance and contagious prison, haled thither by most mechanical and dirty hands. Rouse up Revenge from ebon den, with fell Allecto's snake, for Doll is in. Pistol speaks nought but truth.' This kind of bragadoccio dazzles simple souls like Mistress QUICKLY (whom he marries), and scatters the zanies of *The Merry Wives of Windsor* as a hawk's shadow scatters doves. But in *Henry I* Shakespeare matches Pistol against another word-magician, FLUELLEN, and Fluellen (who is genuinely as brave as he claims) wins the contest and forces Pistol to eat his leek.

Player King *(Hamlet): see* **First Player**

Player Queen *(Hamlet): see* **Second Player**

Poet *(Timon of Athens)*
Opens the play by taking TIMON a flattering ode and being well paid for it. Later, he goes with the PAINTER to Timon in exile, hoping for more patronage, and is cursed and driven away. Oily flattery is all his character.

Poins, Edward (Ned) *(Henry IV Parts One and Two)*
Unlike the other 'irregular humorists' of the comic scenes in these plays, Poins is the confidant not of FALSTAFF but of Prince HAL. (He incites him, for example, to rob the others at Gadshill, and shares in the

later practical joke when he and Hal disguise themselves as Drawers.)
He is a flatterer, a parasite who draws life and colour from his host, and
by the time Hal becomes king he has faded out of the action: we hardly
remember him or care about his fate.

Polixenes (*The Winter's Tale*)
In the first act of the play Polixenes is a young, personable king,
visiting his childhood friend LEONTES and making innocent, polite
conversation with queen HERMIONE, only to be accused of adultery and
forced to flee for his life. In the second half of the play, sixteen years
on, he is a father furious that his son (FLORIZEL) is in love with a
shepherdess, and his language rises to an unconscious and ironical echo
of Leontes' earlier raging against him himself. ('Mark your divorce,
young sir,/Whom son I dare not call. Thou art too base/To be
acknowledg'd; thou art a sceptre's heir,/That thou affect'st a sheep-
hook!') His change of heart, his agreement to Florizel's and PERDITA's
marriage and his reconciliation with Leontes are all reported, not
shown, and this cuts the ground from his character just as it was
beginning to develop.

Polonius (*Hamlet*)
Polonius is a ceremonious windbag, a man who will never say 'Yes' if
'He hath, my lord, wrung from me my slow leave/By laborious petition,
and at last/Upon his will I seal'd my hard consent' will do. Partly for
this reason, and partly because HAMLET keeps treating him as a
dodderer, he is often played as elderly, an old man with a long white
beard and a long black gown. He need actually be no more than forty,
with a son of student age and a daughter only just old enough to be
married (i.e. fifteen or sixteen). What makes him a fool is that he thinks
of himself as an elder and, like many a young actor playing an old
man's role, hams up his performance.

Underneath the foolish veneer, Polonius is one of the shrewdest
people in Elsinore. In a court given over to intrigue, he has risen to
high office by merit, and is treated by everyone (except Hamlet and the
PLAYERS) with respect rather than derision. CLAUDIUS and GERTRUDE
consult him and rely on him because he is honest, not because he is a
crook; his son and daughter listen to his advice (to keep out of mischief
in Paris; to keep away from Hamlet) with respect, not impatience, and
obey him without hesitation. At the end of the Players' play, when
Claudius jumps up in unroyal alarm, it is Polonius, not Gertrude,
Hamlet or anyone else, who takes charge, sending the Players packing
and leading his master out. He may express himself tediously – 'More
matter with less art', Gertrude sharply advises him at one point – but
underneath it all he is decisive, reliable and shrewd.

Polonius' chief weakness, apart from verbosity, is Ophelia. He is a
doting father, strict but kind, determined to shield her from Hamlet's
waywardness even if it means forgoing a princely marriage, and, after
the 'Get-thee-to-a- nunnery' scene, driven almost distracted by the need

to protect her from Hamlet's madness. Until then, his greatest lapse from self-control was losing himself in one of his own sentences (when talking with REYNALDO: 'And then, sir, does he this. He does – what was I about to say? By the mass, I was about to say something...'); now he abandons common sense and begins plotting with Claudius and Gertrude, and it is the death of him, stabbed unceremoniously behind the arras. Unlike the main characters in the play, who suffer as a result of trying to unravel their own identity, Polonius' downfall comes from forgetting his own true nature. He and his children are the most honest people in the Danish court, and their deaths are pitiful – all the more so in Polonius' case, as Shakespeare denies him as much dignity in dying as he did in every one of his earlier appearances in the play.

Pompey *(Antony and Cleopatra)*
Son of the more famous Pompey the Great, he seems likely, at one point in the play, to be as serious a threat to OCTAVIUS as his father was to Julius CAESAR. But his moral sensibilities hamper his ambition – or, as he himself cryptically puts it, ''Tis not my profit that does lead mine honour;/Mine honour it'. Urged by MENAS to kill all three triumvirs during a drunken party on his galley, he indignantly refuses, and is soon afterwards beaten in battle and executed offstage.

Pompey *(Measure for Measure)*
Employed by Mistress OVERDONE, Pompey doubles as tapster and pimp, depending how closely the law is treading on his heels. He is a shameless rogue, happy to confuse the legal process by making a short tale (about what FROTH did to Mistress Elbow in the Bunch of Grapes) preposterously overlong, and to argue the issue of sexual morality with the very judge (ESCALUS) who has the power of life or death over him. ('If you head and hang all that offend that way but for ten year together, you'll be glad to give out a commission for more heads. If this law hold in Vienna ten year, I'll rent the fairest house in it after, three-pence a day. If you live to see this come to pass, say Pompey told you so.') Arrested a second time, and offered the choice of becoming deputy executioner or losing his own head, he revels in his new profession, feeling thoroughly at home in the prison because so many of Mistress Overdone's former customers are there. His cheerful amorality, and above all his funniness, make his appearances a welcome contrast to some of the play's more gloom-ridden examinations of right and wrong: he is not an appendix to the action (as Shakespeare's clowns so often are) but an essential part of both its philosophical meaning and its dramatic pace.

Popilius Lena *(Julius Caesar)*
Unlike his senate-colleague PUBLIUS, he speaks several lines ('I wish your enterprise today may thrive' is the best of them), but adds nothing significant to the play.

Porter *(Henry VIII)*

In a lively comic scene, he and his MAN try to force back a large, vociferous (and unseen) crowd from the gates of the palace yard. The crowd has come to see the baby Princess Elizabeth on her christening-procession; the Porter and his Man are battling to keep the doors shut and the rabble out, and their exuberance and zestful language beautifully help to create a feeling of occasion. *(Man:* 'You, great fellow,/Stand close up or I'll make your head ache!' *Porter:* 'You i' the chambret,/Get up o' the rail; I'll peck you o'er the pales else!')

Porter *(Macbeth)*

One of the most famous cameo roles in Shakespeare, this offers a couple of pages of drunken clowning. The Porter imagines himself as guarding hell's gate, and describes the imaginary visitors; he then tells MACDUFF about the three things which drink provokes ('nose-painting, sleep and urine'). The part is less interesting in itself than for its position, breaking the mood of escalating horror which will culminate in DUNCAN's murder. Its effect on the tension of the play is out of all proportion to its size, and perhaps explains why good actors can be seduced into lending it their talents.

Portia *(Julius Caesar)*

BRUTUS' wife. She is full of loving anxiety for her husband before and during the assassination, and he responds with an affection for her which is most un-Roman. But later, when things go wrong for the conspirators, she remembers the true Stoic virtues (as taught her by her father Cato), and commits suicide rather than face the shame of her husband's dishonour – and news of her death finally disheartens Brutus to the point where he, too, puts death before defeat. Her nature, in short, is a reflection of his, and the tenderness of their relationship (e.g. in the scene where she begs him to tell her who the six or seven men are who 'did hide their faces/Even from darkness') is, like ANTHONY's outburst of affection for dead CAESAR, a moving counterpart to the politics which dominate the play.

Portia *(The Merchant of Venice)*

Like many Shakespearean comedies, *The Merchant of Venice* runs two stories together, the SHYLOCK–ANTONIO plot and the sequence of masquerades, tricks and guessing-games organised by the young aristocrats of Venice and Belmont. Portia plays a central part in both plots, and her presence integrates the play; the challenge of the role is that each plot highlights different character-traits, and the character has to be made consistent without importing comedy to the serious scenes or heartlessness to the comedy.

In the comedy scenes, as Portia's very first line suggests ('By my troth, Nerissa, my little body is aweary of this great world'), her main character-trait is a somewhat self-conscious lassitude with life, and (as many Shakespearean comic aristocrats do) she keeps boredom at bay by

making existence a performance, by devising games. She tests
BASSANIO's love by giving him a keepsake-ring, disguising herself and
beguiling him out of it; she jumps at the chance of impersonating a
lawyer and pleading a case in a real court.

It is during this last game that her character-change begins. To play
the trial-scene as comedy, in the same gay mode as Portia's other
schemes, would involve making Shylock a ludicrous, farcical monster
with no claims on our sympathy; it would involve reducing Portia's
character to that of a heedless gambler (risking her own reputation if
her disguise is discovered and Antonio's life if she loses his case); above
all it would involve ignoring the poetic power and moral affirmation of
the words she speaks – how could anyone seriously play 'The quality of
mercy is not strained' for laughs?

What happens, in effect, is that Shakespeare changes comic course,
as the play develops, from cold-heartedness to romantic warmth, and
uses Portia's character to do it. Until the trial-scene she is interesting
but hardly likeable; after the trial-scene we admire her; in Act Five (the
unravelling of the ring intrigue) we are seduced by poetry into loving
her, and the silliness of her actions (and indeed those of the other
characters) is redeemed by the quality of the words she speaks. If she
and the other aristocrats have been struggling throughout the play to
define themselves and to find reasons for their existence – it is a mirror-
image of the way Shylock loses *his* existential identity – the fact that
self-knowledge comes not from games or dares but from true love (a
genuine and unplanned emotion) and that it is given such heartfelt,
soaring expression, give the play, and Portia's character at the heart of
it, a movement from intellectuality to emotion, from head to heart,
which is complex to describe or to work out in the rehearsal hall, but is
apparent, convincing and satisfying to watch onstage.

Post (*Henry VI Part Two*)
Brings news to court of rebellion in Ireland.

Post (*Henry VI Part Three*)
Busily delivers letters and messages to destinations as far apart as York
and Paris; breathless minor character.

Posthumus Leonatus (*Cymbeline*)
At first, the husband IMOGEN chooses in the teeth of her father's
displeasure seems to have appeal for her alone. He is a passionate but
spineless youth, who takes banishment from his beloved as the cue
more for rhetorical despair ('Write, my queen,/And with mine eyes I'll
drink the words you send,/Though ink be made of gall'...) rather than
for decisive action, and whom the worldly wise IACHIMO readily traps,
in Rome, into foolish protestations of Imogen's faithfulness and an even
more foolish wager to prove it one way or the other. When we next see
him, Iachimo is playing with him like cat with sparrow, describing
Imogen's bedroom, her chimney-piece and the mole under her breast –

and he suddenly loses control, bursts out, 'O that I had her here, to tear
her limb-meal!/I will go there and do't i'the court, before/Her father!
I'll do...something!', and rushes out to write to PISANIO that he must
murder Imogen. Finally, in the last act of the play, he arrives
heartbroken with LUCIUS in Wales, plays a heroic part in the battle
(believing Imogen dead, he has nothing left to live for, and says so at
some length), is visited by dream-visions and given inexplicable
prophecies, and is at last reunited with Imogen and plunged into
ecstasies of mingled remorse and love. A psychiatrist, in short, might
think him a dangerously unstable young man, and advise Imogen to
keep well clear of him; but in the world of Shakespearean lovers his
behaviour is no more inconstant than (say) ROMEO's, and the way his
mind is shown reeling between hope and despair, fury and self-
abasement, is merely a dramatic representation of the sort of calf-love
feelings most people keep privately to themselves. Above all,
Shakespeare stresses his vulnerability (he is Imogen's true mate in that,
at least), and the depth of his love: in the face of soaring lines like
'Hang there like fruit, my soul,/Till the tree die', it is churlish, perhaps
(as well as nothing to do with the play) to wonder what the marriage
will be like in five, ten or twenty-five years' time.

Potpan (*Romeo and Juliet*)
Servant of CAPULET, who appears in the scene of bustle before the
masked ball, and speaks only once.

Priam (*Troilus and Cressida*)
Aged king of Troy, father of HECTOR, TROILUS and PARIS. His part is
tiny, and consists either of handwringing over the Greeks' ultimatums
('Deliver Helen, and all damage else.../Shall be struck off. Hector,
what say you to't?'), or ordering Hector, unsuccessfully, not to go and
fight ACHILLES.

Priest (*Twelfth Night*)
Announces that he has married OLIVIA and SEBASTIAN.

Priest (Sir John) (*Richard III*)
HASTINGS jokes with him, unaware of his own impending arrest. He
speaks only one line, and it is colourless.

Princess of France (*Love's Labour's Lost*)
Like her counterpart FERDINAND, she is chiefly there as leader of an
ensemble, and has little outstanding character of her own. She is
affronted by her cool reception, and for much of the play balances
chilly politeness to Ferdinand with a private nervous exhilaration, as if
she well knows the risks of flirtation; when Ferdinand and his lords
appear dressed as Russians, she organises the ladies' disguises, each
pretending to be the other. At the end of the play, when news of her
father's death and the ladies' imminent departure prompts unfeigned
love declarations from the young gallants, she retreats from their

sentiments into an equally frosty generosity. In short, she begins as a pawn in the diplomatic chess-game and ends up a queen – and the passionless metaphor exactly suits her character.

Proculeius (*Antony and Cleopatra*)
OCTAVIUS' fellow-officer, sent with GALLUS to arrest CLEOPATRA in the monument.

Prologue and Epilogue (*Henry VIII*)
In 32 lines of rhyming doggerel, the Prologue promises the audience a play full of 'such scenes as make the eye to flow', and also a true spectacle which will 'make ye think ye see/The very persons of our noble story/As they were living'. At the end, in a briefer speech, the Epilogue apologises to those of the audience disturbed from sleep by the trumpets, and urges (in a somewhat forced sexual pun) all the 'good women' in the audience to 'bid their men clap'.

Prospero (*The Tempest*)
When ARIEL sings of ALONSO (in 'Ful fadom five') 'Nothing of him that doth fade/But doth suffer a sea-change/Into something rich and strange', he is describing a process of alteration worked on nearly everyone who visits the magic island, and on none so much as Prospero. Before he was cast adrift with the three-year-old MIRANDA, Prospero was one of the least able dukes Milan ever had, virtuous but incompetent: as he himself puts it, 'The government I cast upon my brother,/And to my state grew stranger, being transported/And rapt in secret studies', and '... poor man, my library/Was dukedom large enough.' On the island, for twelve years while Miranda was growing up, he learned worldliness by educating her, and the process was not entirely beneficial. He may have 'done nothing but in care of thee', but his concern for Miranda has also grown into jealousy, both a besotted fatherly obsession with her happiness and a rancorous hatred of his brother ANTONIO and of Alonso, who between them brought about his dismissal from Milan. To everyone on the island but Miranda, he has behaved like a tyrant, wielding his magic as a despot wields his troops. He has enslaved Ariel and CALIBAN, and bends them to his will with threats ('If thou more murmurest, I will rend an oak,/And peg thee in his knotty entrails') or with actual torment ('For this, be sure, tonight thou shalt have cramps,/Side-stitches that shall pen thy breath up...'). The explanations he offers, that Ariel owes him gratitude and that Caliban tried to rape Miranda and 'people the isle with Calibans', are as much reflections of his neurotic self-esteem or over-protectiveness towards Miranda as of his 'justice', objective or otherwise.

Satisfyingly, Prospero's concern for Miranda is the main cause of the 'sea-change' in his character. Although he first reacts to her love with FERDINAND with savage unkindness (designed, he says, to test their love, but no less self-centred and harsh for that), he soon warms to the extent of providing them with fairy entertainment and leaving them in seclusion to play chess together. He is happy in their happiness, and his content gradually loosens his fury against other, less innocent, members of the human race. As he begins to smile on humanity, he finds his 'rough magic' (formerly his solace) more and more unsatisfying and irrelevant, until he abjures it in favour of forgiveness. ('You, brother mine, that.../ Would have killed your king, I do forgive thee,/ Unnatural though thou art...'). He sets Ariel free at last, and even refrains from punishing Caliban for the drunken coup attempt. ('Go, sirrah, to my cell./Take with you your companions. As you look/To have my pardon, trim it handsomely'.) He is accepted by all parties as the true Duke he has become, worldly in the best sense, lordly, wise and just, and he leads them all back home, where, union and amity both restored, 'every third thought shall be my grave'.

As with LEAR, the radiant lines Prospero is given to speak (plus overtones, imagined by critics or real, of Shakespearean autobiography, the old dramatist taking farewell of his created world) have sugared the initial unpleasantness of the character, and can win him our sympathy before it is morally deserved. At the start of the play he is a cold-hearted, obsessive necromancer, and his behaviour in retreat from the world has nothing but strict legal rectitude to commend it. His recognition of fallibility in himself, and thence in all humanity, is a central theme of the play. If it is negated in performance, if he is played throughout as some kind of ethereal puppet-master who renounces his art only when it has served the purpose of humanising everyone else in sight, then *The Tempest*, for all its verbal enchantment, can be little more than a morally vacuous charade.

Proteus (*The Two Gentlemen of Verona*)
Proteus is the kind of young man who has never had to take life seriously, and the play's action shows him growing up: it is a parallel process to ORLANDO's growth in *As You Like It* or BEROWNE's in *Love's Labour's Lost*. At the beginning of the play, he is playing the earnest lover with JULIA, but as soon as he is ordered to leave her and go to Milan, he takes his leave with a pretty speech but no real qualms at all. ('O, how this spring of love resembleth/The uncertain glory of an April day,/Which now shows all the beauty of the sun/And by and by a cloud takes all away.') In Milan, not realising the depths of his friend VALENTINE's love for SYLVIA (for Valentine has always been a broody, passionate youth), he thwarts their elopement by telling Sylvia's father, and then begins courting Sylvia himself, singing her serenades, sending her love-letters, making pretty and unserious speeches. ('Madam, if your heart be so obdurate,/Vouchsafe me yet your picture for my love.../To that I'll speak, so that I'll sigh and weep...'.) He has no idea at all how badly he is behaving, no notion of the distress he is causing Valentine, Sylvia and Julia: even giving Sylvia the ring Julia gave *him* as a keepsake is an act of heedlessness rather than of cruelty. He seems to believe that everyone else's approach to life is as happy-

go-lucky as his own, and takes their vehemence as a joke. (*Sylvia*: 'Had I been seized by a hungry lion,/I would have been a breakfast to the beast/Rather than have false Proteus rescue me...' *Proteus*: 'O, 'tis the curse in love, and still approv'd,/When women cannot love where they're belov'd!') But as soon as Valentine confronts him, and he realises how other people have been affected by his behaviour, he collapses in remorse ('My shame and guilt confounds me...'), and realises, as if hit by a thunderbolt, that he has really been in love with Julia all the time. ('O heaven, were man/But constant, he were perfect!') In a more serious drama, his blindness to other people's feelings would be an alienating defect and his treachery to Julia a dastardly offence; as it is, his whole-heartedness, both when he understands nothing and when the scales fall from his eyes, is mere 'matter for a May morning', and the heartbreak he causes is as insubstantial as froth, needing only to be blown away to reveal radiant, true happiness.

Provost *(Measure for Measure)*
Chief legal officer of Vienna, whose job is to administer justice, admitting people to ANGELO's presence or denying them, supervising trials, ordering or postponing executions. He is a functionary whose chief function is to do what he's told – and this makes his expressed attitude to Angelo's form of justice particularly pointed. He is desperate for ISABELLA to persuade Angelo to spare CLAUDIO's life ('Pray heaven she win him!'), and is later quite happy to delay the execution and to deceive Angelo by sending him a pirate's head instead of Claudio's. If the play is a study of different kinds of morality or immorality, his role is expediency, the morally dubious but admirably practical (indeed, practically admirable) path of compromise in public affairs.

Publius *(Julius Caesar)*
Senator who witnesses CAESAR's assassination and is subsequently 'quite confounded'; he registers dismay without speaking a word.

Publius *(Titus Andronicus): see* **Gentlemen**

Puck *(A Midsummer Night's Dream)*
OBERON's servant. He is a happy-go-lucky practical joker, frightening the 'maidens of the villagery' (as one of the FAIRIES puts it), leading travellers astray and generally making mischief in the mortal world. (He leads LYSANDER and DEMETRIUS a characteristic dance, imitating their voices, issuing challenges and drawing them and the girls deeper and deeper into the wood.) At a more serious level, he is the physical embodiment of Oberon's malevolence, of the amorality of fairyland: his trick on TITANIA has an edge of cruelty quite different from his usual prankishness, and his disdain for QUINCE, BOTTOM and the other 'hempen homespuns' is out of all proportion to their simple (not to say simple-minded) folly. Oberon calls him 'mad spirit' and 'good Robin', and their relationship is like that of Shakespearean kings and their

Fools; but where Fools are wistful or lugubrious commentators on human folly, Puck is a spiteful manipulator, and all his pretty rhymes – he speaks or sings the play's most gossamer verse – are not enough to give warmth to his character. Unlike ARIEL in *The Tempest* (who yearns for freedom, is reluctant to carry out his master's instructions and even admits that pity is – for humans – a powerful and possible emotion), Puck is heartless and heedless, and his presence gives an asperity to the fairy scenes which is welcome in its context – who, outside nursery stories, wants fairies always benevolent and sugarplumsweet? – but which makes us uncomfortable whenever he is onstage. It is hard to give charisma to characters whose effects on others are always more interesting than they are themselves, but that (to say nothing of more mundane skills like singing and dancing) is what the role of Puck demands.

Pursuivant *(Richard III)*
Royal messenger who jokes with HASTINGS just before Hastings is arrested. His appearance adds nothing to the plot, and his three lines allow him no character.

Queen *(Cymbeline)*
An evil-hearted, plausibly spoken witch, as uncomplicatedly villainous as the wicked Queen in *Snow White*. Her trade is deceit, treachery and poison, and it is perhaps fortunate that she says so little, or she might turn the whole play towards melodrama; as things are she goes mad halfway through the action, and dies after a hysterical deathbed confession (reported by CORNELIUS).

Queen *(Hamlet): see* **Gertrude**

Queen *(Richard II)*
There is a recurring female role in Shakespeare, the OPHELIA-character: a young, innocent girl whose plot-function is to suffer. RICHARD'S Queen is a fine example. She has little to say, and stands on the periphery of events. She is ignored or patronised by her husband, and spends her time with courtiers (e.g. BUSHY) or menials (e.g. the GARDENERS) whose tasks are to give her bad news and to comfort her when she grieves at it. In real life, Richard's queen was a child nine years old, and though the queen in the play is adult (and indeed at one

point describes herself as 'pregnant with grief'), she has all of a child-bride's pitiful innocence.

Quickly, Mistress Elizabeth (Nell) *(Henry IV Parts One and Two; Henry V; The Merry Wives of Windsor)*
In both parts of *Henry IV*, and in *The Merry Wives of Windsor*, Mistress Quickly is there to cause mirth in others, and contributes little depth of character to the play's development. In *Henry IV Part One* she appears in two scenes only, and is shown as a woman of wide-eyed simple-mindedness. (She finds FALSTAFF's playing of the Prince's father 'as like one of those harlotry players as ever I see', and is suitably – if unregally – rebuked by him: 'Peace, good pint-pot; peace, good tickle-brain'; she tries to dun Falstaff for the money he owes her, and he mocks and insults her, to her honest but baffled indignation.) In *Part Two* his debt has become pressing, and she calls in the law; this adds anger to her character, and she acquires a splendid liveliness of language, a verbal vividness to equal anything from Doll TEARSHEET or PISTOL. (Indeed, and remarkably for such a minor character, some of her linguistic flights rival those of Falstaff himself.)

In *The Merry Wives of Windsor* she has moved from London to Windsor, and become Doctor CAIUS' house-keeper; she is now full of mother-hen bustle and has filled her head with country maxims and deference to anyone at all of 'quality'. (Her treatment of Falstaff is quite unlike that in the *Henry* plays. In them she understands, and is overcome by, his grandiose roguery; in this play she treats him as one of the gentry whose faults, however glaring, are not for her to comment on. She helps Mistress FORD and Mistress PAGE trick him, but there is no hint of moral condemnation in her actions, as there is in theirs.)

Shakespeare reserves his biggest surprise for Mistress Quickly's brief appearance in *Henry V*. Her main function here is to describe Falstaff's death to her new husband (Pistol), but she does it with a warmth of affection (' 'a babbled of green fields') which transcends everything we know of her character from other plays, and shows that however Falstaff behaved to her or she to him, at heart she loved him.

The part poses a problem to the director of *Henry V*: how is her richness of character to be put across in this one sequence, when she is talking of matters and relationships the audience have never seen? Readers of Shakespeare, and those experienced in his plays, can let knowledge of other plays colour their appreciation of this scene; but an unversed audience – and for directorial purposes, all audiences should be assumed unversed – can be startled at Mistress Quickly's vehement humanity, as if they are eavesdropping on a stranger's grief. In a play-cycle, her character-development would be satisfying and vivid (as is MARGARET's in the three parts of *Henry VI*); over four plays, not meant to be performed in sequence, it is awkward, and what makes it so is Shakespeare's ability to portray vivid and complex personality in a handful of lines, and his profligacy in doing so, apparently at whim, for even the most insignificant of characters.

Quince, Peter (*A Midsummer Night's Dream*)
Athenian carpenter. He is producer, director and probably the author
of the play performed by the rustics ('The most lamentable comedy and
most cruel death of Pyramus and Thisbe'), and has his work cut out
explaining it to them and rehearsing it with them. His chief problem is
not so much the others' denseness or BOTTOM's prima-donna behaviour
as his own literal-mindedness. He considers every suggestion made at
rehearsal (e.g. to have a prologue assuring the ladies in the audience
that the lion, the fighting and the killing are all make-believe), and
answers every question (e.g. 'Doth the moon shine that night we play
our play') with humourless, laborious and delicious pedantry. In the
'play' itself he speaks a long Prologue (in the lumpish metre of 'eight-
and-eight'), and his wooden acting is, as THESEUS says, 'like a tangled
chain, nothing impair'd but all disorder'd'. ('If we offend, it is with our
goodwill./That you should think we come not to offend,/But with
goodwill. To show our simple skill,/That is the true beginning of our
end...')

Quintus and Martius (*Titus Andronicus*)
TITUS' sons, framed and killed for the murder of BASSIANUS.

Rambures, Lord (*Henry V*)
French lord, attendant on the DAUPHIN. Apart from starting the idea of
betting on the number of English prisoners, and scornfully remarking,
'That island of England breeds very valiant creatures: their mastiffs are
of unmatchable courage', he has little else to say. He is killed in the
fighting.

Ratcliff, Sir Richard (*Richard III*)
Apart from CATESBY, Ratcliff is RICHARD's closest confidant. The 'rat'
in his name suggests his character (as the hint of 'caitiff' in Catesby's
does his), and he is a small-scale replica of his master: devious and
dangerous. He tends to lurk in the wings of great events, however; his
chief part in the action is to take RIVERS, GREY and VAUGHAN to death
at Pomfret.

Rebeck, Hugh (*Romeo and Juliet*)
Second of the three musicians who play for the Capulets and discuss
with PETER why music is said to have a silver sound; he thinks it is
'because musicians sound for silver'.

Regan (*King Lear*)
The least fully characterised of LEAR's daughters, Regan is haughty,
distant and taciturn. In the argument-scene between OSWALD and KENT
she takes no part, but stands silently approving her husband
CORNWALL's harsh treatment of Kent until the very end, when it is she
who gives the order for stocking Kent: 'Put in his legs'. In the same
way, she watches impassively as GLOUCESTER is bound, and then
suddenly exhorts the soldiers to fasten him 'Hard, hard!' She joins in
his interrogation ('To whose hands have you sent the lunatic king?/
Speak.'), stabs the SERVANT who tries to stop Cornwall blinding him,
and sends Gloucester into the storm ('Go, thrust him out at gates, and
let him smell/His way to Dover...') with as little compunction as she
earlier let her father go to possible death from exposure ('O sir, to
wilful men/The injuries that they themselves procure/Must be their
schoolmaster. Shut up your doors...'). In her plotting with Oswald (to
kill Gloucester) and with Edmund (to supplant GONERIL) she is ruthless
and unlikeable; even when she is poisoned by Goneril she continues to
spit at her to the very end, like a dying cat. Her ice is a foil to Goneril's
fire and Edmund's banked-embers scheming, and like them she is one-
dimensional on her own: the full picture of malevolence demands all
three.

Reignier, Duke of Anjou (*Henry VI Part One*)
Loyal French lord, MARGARET's father. He is lightly characterised as a
brave old courtier who stoically accepts her capture by SUFFOLK.

Reynaldo (*Hamlet*)
POLONIUS' servant, sent with LAERTES to France to look after him and
to keep him, 'by lecture and advice', out of mischief.

Richard (*Henry VI Part Three*; *Richard III*)
If ever there was a one-role play, *Richard III* is it. So long as Richard is
onstage, the entertainment zips along; when he goes, it sags. His
characterisation is so persuasive that people even mistake it for real:
earnest Plantagenet-rehabilitators have spent years and spilled gallons of
ink proving that Richard was really a twinkly-eyed knight in shining
armour, and that Shakespeare was some kind of Tudor Goebbels.

But Shakespeare was writing plays, not history-books, and all his
character-decisions about Richard are dramatic. Something about the
circumstances of this play – Shakespeare's growing theatrical
experience? a prestigious commission? the personality of Richard
himself? – inspired him to work of dazzling genius, as far surpassing
the 'promising newcomer' excellence of *Henry VI* and *Titus Andronicus*
as eagles outsoar jays. The effect of inspiration was to liberate Richard's

character from the constraints of historical accuracy. In *Henry VI Part Three* (which is still hobbled by facts) Shakespeare could do no more than sketch the blacker character-traits in Richard (there called Gloucester) which were to become the main interest in *Richard III*. He gives him self-delighted soliloquies announcing villainy to come (e.g. that EDWARD must be 'wasted, marrow, bones and all'), panache in action (e.g. the repeated stabbing of HENRY's corpse, 'Down, down to hell, and say I sent thee thither', or the 'Judas kiss' – his own description – he gives Edward's baby son) and a lip-licking, saturnine sexuality (in the scene where he and CLARENCE banter about Edward's courtship of Lady GREY) which was to reappear, dramatically transformed, in the scene in *Richard III* where he woos Lady ANNE across her father-in-law's bier.

The problem, in *Henry VI Part Three*, is that these qualities are merely single strands in a matted dramatic texture: the play has other schemers, other villains just as satisfying as Richard. In *Richard III*, therefore, Shakespeare decided – or perhaps was persuaded by a leading actor hot for a juicy role – to isolate Richard from the main action, to subordinate every other character and to make his personality, not his deeds (as in *Henry VI*), the main interest of the play.

In technical terms, the isolation of Richard's part is simply done. He is the only character in the play to speak directly to the audience, and his soliloquies take us into his confidence, reveal what wickedness he is going to do, how he is going to do it and what his long-term purpose is, with the result that we watch the play more like conspirators than spectators, taking grim pleasure in seeing each of Richard's schemes work out exactly as he said it would.

Shakespeare reveals Richard's character in three of the play's most highly charged dramatic scenes. In the first, the magnificent declarative scene which begins the play, Richard's sardonic, narcissistic and sadistic nature is first presented in a soliloquy ('Since I cannot prove a lover... I am determined to prove a villain'), and is then demonstrated in action, in the seduction of Lady Anne. Richard's method in this seduction is the same as he uses with everyone else: patiently, inexorably, he hypnotises her with words till she agrees with him – whereupon he cuts the encounter short and leaves the stage. There is no excess dialogue: each word is as precisely placed, and as essential, as a brick in a wall.

The second major scene, the apex of the action, is the one in which Richard pretends to be 'at holy work' with two prelates, and has BUCKINGHAM plead with him to accept the crown. This scene is a piece of ironical playacting, pretence for political ends, and it is 'staged' by Richard from start to finish. The combination of relaxation in the 'performance' he gives and nervous tension in the dialogue is identical to the quality of 'danger', of precisely calculated risk, which great actors import into theatrical performances.

At first sight the third scene, the ghost-scene and its aftermath at the end of the play, appears to destroy Richard's character instead of demonstrating it, to strip off his actor's mask and show the wretch he really is. The last thing we want to see in such a consummate performer is genuine contrition, and if the scene is played that way the play collapses into bathos. An alternative, subtler, reading is to use the ghost-scene to peel yet one more layer from the onion, to show yet one more facet of Richard's character. Until now, he has successfully used words to control every situation; now events (over which, as a cripple, he has no control) take over, and he momentarily loses himself. His soliloquy in the ghost-scene shows him psychologically rudderless; his battlefield fury ('A horse! A horse!') shows him winding himself up physically to command events; before he has time to succeed or fail, he is abruptly killed ('*Enter Richard and* RICHMOND; *they fight; Richard is slain*'). His collapse is in one sense disappointing for the audience, since he has long ago won our sympathy; but it also shows us a magician trapped by his own magic, a high-wire artist falling without a safety-net, and the pleasure it gives is grim, cathartic and one-hundred-per-cent theatrical.

Richard *(Richard II)*

No other Shakespearean character apart from LEAR and MACBETH so closely conforms to the conventions of classical drama, as outlined by Aristotle and practised by the great Greek tragedians. Richard has both a tragic flaw (unshakeable faith in his own quasi-divinity) and the self-destructive arrogance which the Greeks called *hubris*; his utter lack of humour is matched by a pigheadedness in the face of fate which everyone else can see will be a main cause of his downfall. He commits a motiveless crime (sequestration of GAUNT's property) which begins the crisis and from which there is no going back. He recognises the inevitability of his doom (in Act Three, in the pivotal scene of the play, he says 'Down, down I come, like glistering Phaethon...'), and seems from that moment onwards to conspire in it. His collapse is unremitting, fatal for him personally, and a clear moral lesson for the audience.

Although the play's plot is like a clockwork engine (once wound up, unstoppable), and although the presentation of Richard's character is schematic (unpicking him and displaying him for us piecemeal from scene to scene), Shakespeare avoids any effect of alienating didacticism by bejewelling the lines with poetry. Few of his works are so peacock-rich, so fantastical, and although every speaker has a share of lovely lines, the most exquisite verbal music is Richard's. At first, in the early scenes of the play, his glamour is physical: he is like the king in a gorgeous tapestry, dazzling everyone he looks on (even BOLINGBROKE), and confining himself to elegant, ornately formal utterances. But once Bolingbroke begins to threaten his physical security, once his state (literally) begins to reel, he turns increasingly from real to imagined glory, and the pomp is in the poetry. He is giving a theatre-show – even his despair is artfully displayed – and his most appreciative audience is himself. When his supporters are trying desperately to rally their cause, all he can offer is the invitation 'Let's talk of graves, of worms and epitaphs.../Let's choose executors and talk of wills.../For God's sake, let us sit upon the ground/ And tell sad stories of the death of kings...' – fine words but useless generalship. When he abdicates it is like an archbishop dispensing the Host at some glittering State Eucharist: 'With mine own tears I wash away my balm;/With mine own hands I give away my crown;/With mine own tongue deny my sacred state...' He may be stripped of power, but he never once resigns the dramatic initiative; even to himself, penned in Pomfret Castle, he plays the star: 'I have been studying how I may compare/This prison where I live unto the world' – and so on for fifty or so lines. The only stage characters so to revel in their own dejection are the broken-hearted clowns and dying courtesans of Italian Grand Opera – and as with opera, Shakespeare evades cardboard melodrama only by dressing it in sounds of genius.

The result of all this is to make *Richard II* more a glittering pageant than a play, and then to trump that by making its central character a confidence-trickster who believes his own patter, a popinjay who deserves none of our sympathy but wins it every time he opens his mouth. Shakespeare's technique is sleight-of-hand, illusion – and the way the poetry elevates Richard from buffoon to tragic hero is the essence of what theatre is, and does.

Richard II

At the start of the play Richard is an absolute monarch, sure of his own divine right to rule, presiding over a country which is gradually slipping into bankruptcy, corruption and civil war. His cousin Bolingbroke accuses him of complicity in the murder of their uncle Gloucester, and is challenged to a duel (by Mowbray) and then banished (by Richard). But when Bolingbroke's father John of Gaunt dies, and Richard usurps the money and lands that should be his (to finance a war in Ireland), Bolingbroke returns from exile and civil war is declared (not by Bolingbroke himself, but by Northumberland and others acting in his name). One by one, Richard's supporters desert him, and finally he himself is captured; he abdicates and is imprisoned in Pomfret Castle. The legality of his abdication (and of Bolingbroke's assumption of royal power, if not of the name of king) is hotly debated by the nobles, and a revolt is planned against Bolingbroke by two churchmen and the turncoat Lord Aumerle. (It is discovered and the churchmen are banished; Bolingbroke however spares Aumerle at the request of his mother, the Duchess of York.) Misunderstanding a chance remark of Bolingbroke's, Sir Piers Exton goes to Pomfret Castle (where Richard is gloomily – and exquisitely – pondering his own imprisonment) and murders him. At the end of the play Bolingbroke is named king (Henry IV), but is tormented by guilt at the responsibility of regicide, and plans a journey of expiation to the Holy Land.

Richard III
Presented with the chance of becoming king of England, Richard seizes it eagerly, even though winning or securing his throne means a chain of murders, chiefly of close relatives. His victims include his brother Clarence and his two nephews (the Princes in the Tower), as well as several opposing lords and knights (Hastings, Buckingham, Rivers, Grey, Vaughan). In addition to murder, Richard puts dynastic marriage to powerful use with Anne (widow of the Prince of Wales he killed before the play began).

Throughout the play, our delight is less in these dark doings than in the mocking, self-admiring soliloquies with which Richard announces each step in his gory plan. He is surrounded by flatterers and villains (Catesby and Ratcliffe, evil toadies; Buckingham, a high-born dolt), and is opposed, in scenes of fishwifely fury, by the royal women Queen Margaret (widow of Henry VI), Queen Elizabeth (widow of Edward IV), Elizabeth of York (his mother) and Queen Anne (his wife). As his evil becomes ever more apparent, his nobles desert him for the Earl of Richmond (the future Henry VII), and when he refuses to give Buckingham a promised preferment, Buckingham too deserts and raises an army. The play culminates in the battle of Bosworth, on the eve of which Richard is visited by the ghosts of all his victims, and in the course of which he is killed by Richmond, who closes the play by proclaiming that civil wars are ended and peace reigns in England once again.

Richmond, Henry, Earl of *(Henry VI Part Three; Richard III)*
The future Henry VII appears as a child in *Henry VI Part Three*, but does not speak; in *Richard III*, grown up, he comes in like an avenging fury at the beginning of Act Five, leads the rebellion against RICHARD and finally kills him at the battle of Bosworth and pridefully proclaims that 'Now civil wounds are stopp'd, peace lives again;/That she may long live here, God say Amen!'

Rivers, Lord *(Henry VI Part Three; Richard III)*
Brother and confidant of Lady GREY. He says little of note in *Henry VI Part Three*, while his sister's star is rising; in *Richard III* he is one of a queue of people whom RICHARD regards as dynastic obstacles, and is beheaded.

Roderigo *(Othello)*
Roderigo is a one-dimensional character, a fool. He is sometimes played as a yokel, burly and blockish, but is more usually given the slightly camp fussiness which the lines suggest. He opens the play by expostulating 'Tush, never tell me. I take it most unkindly/That thou, Iago, who hast had my purse/As if the strings were thine, shouldst know of this', and never stops whining until he is stabbed in the back and dies. The 'humour' (see JAQUES) of his folly is melancholy: he is prone to self-pitying remarks like 'I do follow here in the chase, not like

a hound that hunts, but one that fills up the cry' or 'I will incontinently drown myself'. Because the play is so tightly organised and moves so swiftly, there is little time for comic relief, and for this reason Roderigo's part is regularly cut down, stripped of its funniness or played for pathos. This is a pity: he may be a pricked balloon of a human being, an 'empty mask' (in the Greek theatre's evocative slang phrase for a minor actor), but his presence beautifully highlights the saturnine, zestful malevolence that is a main ingredient of IAGO's character. (*Iago*: 'Didst thou not see her paddle with the palm of his hand? Didst thou not mark that?' *Roderigo*: 'Yes, that I did, but that was but courtesy.' *Iago*: 'Lechery, by this hand: an index and obscure prologue to the history of lust and foul thoughts.')

Romeo (*Romeo and Juliet*)

How old is Romeo? He has been played by 16-year-old boys and by grandfathers, by actors of every age and kind from film-matinée idols to the 12-year-old William Betty ('the young Roscius'), whose treble lispings must have delivered the play's passionate sexual poetry in a way Shakespeare can hardly have envisaged. Whatever Romeo's age, the decision made about it affects the play's whole 'flavour'. If he is a teenage innocent, a mirror-image of JULIET, the passion is entirely different than if he is a mature 35, her mother's contemporary. He is certainly several years older than Juliet: he has finished his education (perhaps even his university education), and he, MERCUTIO and BENVOLIO speak to each other as mature, if irresponsible, grown men. Shakespeare may have had the early 20s in mind for him – and if that makes casting difficult, so be it.

In fact, whatever his actual age, Romeo seems to grow younger, not older, as the play proceeds. At the start he is a true companion to Benvolio: an underoccupied, over-serious young aristocrat, not old enough for family or state responsibility, but old enough to feel the weight and dignity of the social position which will one day be his. He spends his time making conversation with Mercutio and Benvolio in a self-consciously witty manner which is all cleverness and no substance: even his miserable love-affair with Rosaline is made a subject not for real sighs but for repartee. (*Romeo*: 'In sadness, cousin, I do love a woman.' *Benvolio*: 'I aimed so near, when I supposed you loved.' *Romeo*: 'A right good marksman! And she's fair I love.' *Benvolio*: 'A right fair mark, fair coz, is soonest hit. *Romeo*: 'Well, in that hit you miss. She'll not be hit/With Cupid's arrow...'). His duels with the Capulets are undertaken in the same frivolous manner, more as a way of passing the time than out of real feeling, and so is his decision to go to the Capulets' masked ball: it is an escapade, a game whose deadly outcome (if he is discovered) is perhaps a main part of its attraction.

So far, Romeo is no different from a thousand bored young Italians, ten thousand over-bred, over-educated university graduates from any country. But then he meets Juliet, and his sophistication vanishes. ('It is my lady, O!, it is my love!/O that she knew she were!/She speaks, yet she says nothing. What of that?/Her eye discourses: I will answer it...' This is very like his earlier manner, full of peacocking wordplay, but it is underlain by genuine feeling, as that is not, and its tone is bewildered and insecure as well as heady and frivolous.) The more he centres his being on Juliet, the more he sheds his former character: as cancer-victims in the terminal stages seem to become their illness, so he becomes his love. He kills TYBALT almost in a fit of abstraction; his mind is on Juliet, and his every thought is of how to be with her. This is a tragic fixation, and he stumbles to his fate as blindly and inexorably as any Antigone or Oedipus.

The combination of tragic dignity and adolescent impetuosity makes Romeo a complex, fascinating role to play. And once again, his supposed age affects the balance of these qualities. A young Romeo will tend to seem a helpless, unknowing victim of fate, his life consumed by the very love which gives it meaning, and he and Juliet will have to work hard not to look like prototypes of the Babes in the Wood. An older Romeo, by contrast, more experienced in the world's affairs, can be played as aware of what is happening, a tragic victim assenting in his own delirious downward destiny – and this makes the play a tragedy on the level of *Richard II*, and the leading part as challenging.

Romeo and Juliet

Two of the noblest families in Verona, the Capulets and the Montagues, are engaged in a deadly feud. No one knows how it started, but it involves everyone from the servants to the most distant cousins, aunts and acquaintances. One day Romeo Montague, hearing that his ex-girl-friend Rosaline is to be at a masked ball that evening at the Capulets', decides to go there too. He dances with Juliet, the Capulets' 13-year-old daughter, and the two young people fall in love. They meet secretly that night in the Capulets' orchard, and Romeo arranges for his confessor, Friar Laurence, to marry them the next day. (The wedding-plans are assisted by Juliet's garrulous old Nurse.) In the meantime, however, Juliet's parents have arranged another wedding for her, to Count Paris, a relative of Prince Escalus of Verona.

The lovers are married, and that same morning Romeo's friend Mercutio quarrels with Tybalt and is killed by him. For this Romeo kills Tybalt, and he is banished from Verona on pain of death. Juliet's parents order her to prepare for her wedding to Paris in three days' time, and in despair she asks Friar Laurence for help. He gives her a potion which will make her lie for 42 hours as if dead, and says that once she is laid in the tomb he, Laurence, will send word to Romeo to come and fetch her away to Mantua. Juliet takes the potion, and is duly laid in the tomb for dead. But Friar Laurence's message is delayed, and the news Romeo gets is that Juliet is dead. He buys poison, gallops back to Verona, finds her lying in the tomb as if dead and drinks the poison. When she wakes up and finds his dead body, she stabs herself.

Rosalind (*As You Like It*)
In a play whose chief mode is artificiality, Rosalind begins as one of the most artificial characters of all. She decides to 'forget the condition of her estate' (she is the daughter of a banished Duke) by 'devising sports', and the sport she chooses is falling in love; she watches ORLANDO wrestling, and somewhat abruptly chooses him as the object of her affection; when she is banished in her turn, she decides to disguise herself as a boy, and to steal the court jester as a travelling companion. It is a high-spirited romantic adventure, and unless you enter into its mood both it and Rosalind, who leads the dance, can seem no more than silly.

Once Rosalind is in the forest of Arden, however, and begins finding Orlando's love-poems hung on every tree, her mood and her character both change. What was an artificial and arbitrary choice of emotion (love) becomes real and deep, and her boy's disguise (as so often with Shakespeare's heroines) becomes a prison, forcing her to hide her true nature. In short, tension enters the character and gives backbone to the play. When she meets Orlando in the forest, and proposes that he ease his love-pangs by courting her (i.e. the boy Ganymede) under the pretence that she is Rosalind, the irony is not frivolous but affecting, and her flirting with Orlando has power to break the heart. Until now, JAQUES' melancholy has seemed more 'real' than hers; when she meets him now, he is put out of countenance by her and Orlando's genuine emotion, and abruptly leaves the stage ('Nay then God buy you, an you talk in blank verse').

Nonetheless, and although the play now has 'true' emotion at its heart instead of sawdust, the surroundings are still artificial, and our anxiety is to see how Rosalind's love can be fulfilled against flimsy but overwhelming odds. She is in the same dilemma as VIOLA in *Twelfth Night*, and Shakespeare resolves it in the same way, by a dramatist's trick: in *Twelfth Night* SEBASTIAN arrives unexpectedly from a shipwreck, and the fact that he is Viola's identical twin untangles every knot; in *As You Like It* Orlando saves OLIVER's life, and Oliver's immediate change of character from all-bad to all-good opens the way to happiness. The whirl of disguise continues until HYMEN, god of weddings, ushers in Rosalind in girl's clothes, the scales fall from everyone's eyes, and the play moves to a romantic ending free from the irony and verbal conceits which have marked its development up till now.

Only one other Shakespeare heroine, CLEOPATRA, uses irony as consistently as Rosalind, and in Cleopatra's case her true feelings are left unstated, so that *Antony and Cleopatra* centres on a mystery. Rosalind leaves us in no doubt about what is in her heart, and our knowledge that every word she says is play-acting for Orlando's benefit gives *As You Like It* an exhilarating double-edge: we want her to continue the charade, and at the same time we ache for Orlando to find her out. This walking-on-eggshells feeling, coupled with its marvellous verbal duelling (*Phebe*: 'Good shepherd, tell this youth what 'tis to love.' *Silvius*: 'It is to be all made of sighs and tears,/And so am I for Phebe.' *Phebe*: 'And I for Ganymede.' *Orlando*: 'And I for Rosalind.' *Rosalind*: 'And I for no woman...') make it one of the subtlest of all Shakespeare's comedies, and Rosalind one of his most imaginative and attractive heroines.

Rosaline (*Love's Labour's Lost*)

Although the number of her lines and the fact that she is courted by BEROWNE make Rosaline a leading role, in fact she is less individually characterised than either KATHARINE or MARIA. She is nearest in seniority and stateliness to the PRINCESS herself, and indeed exchanges roles with her, in a marvellously hoity-toity scene with the four lords disguised as Russians. One reason for her prominence, perhaps, is that what she says sums up and sets the changing moods of the play, from the insouciant gaiety of flirtation to the autumnal seriousness of the ending. ('A jest's prosperity lies in the ear/Of him that hears it, never in the tongue/Of him that makes it...') The part looks simple on the page, but in performance takes colour from the actress' own personality, and thus, more than all the others, depends on casting to make its effect.

Rosencrantz and Guildenstern (*Hamlet*)

Lords sent by CLAUDIUS to take HAMLET to England, with sealed orders that he is to be killed. They are absolutely interchangeable characters, a Danish Tweedledum and Tweedledee – *King*: 'Thanks, Rosencrantz and gentle Guildenstern.' *Queen*: 'Thanks, Guildenstern and gentle Rosencrantz.' – and they never appear or speak separately. Hamlet pretends to them that he is mad, and they fail to pick up all his hints (e.g. 'I can tell a hawk from a handsaw') that he is saner than he seems. They vanish from the play, unmourned, as soon as they leave for England, and their death is announced, for anyone who still cares, in the very last scene of the play. Tom Stoppard, in his play *Rosencrantz and Guildenstern are Dead*, dazzlingly imagines their life 'backstage' as it were, waiting in the wings of life while the main action unfolds somewhere else; none the less, the fact remains that in Shakespeare they have nothing of note to say or do, and all character in performance (e.g. making them fops or fools) must be supplied by the actors and not inferred from the lines they speak.

Ross (*Macbeth*)

Scottish lord, a soldier whose loyalty is turned by events from MACBETH. He has a good, caring scene with LADY MACDUFF, and later appears with the army which fights Macbeth; honesty is his character.

Ross, Lord (*Richard II*)

A supporter of BOLINGBROKE, with WILLOUGHBY. He has few lines and little character.

Rousillon, Countess of (*All's Well that Ends Well*)
BERTRAM's mother, a domineering matriarch. She is businesslike with
LAFEU, her son's elderly mentor, brisk to the point of impatience with
the clown LAVACHE, and alternately tells Helena to call her 'mother'
and addresses her like a junior executive in some family firm.

Rugby, John (*The Merry Wives of Windsor*)
CAIUS' servant. The part is small, and consists mainly of breathless
bustle: Rugby is that standard comic character, the person inexplicably
bullied by everyone else onstage.

Rumour (*Henry IV Part Two*)
Henry IV Part Two is preceded by an Induction, a kind of 'the story so
far' in high-falutin' verse and spoken by the allegorical figure of
Rumour, a crawling beast with many legs and a body covered in
wagging tongues. (The play then begins, suitably enough, with a
mistaken report to NORTHUMBERLAND of victory at Shrewsbury.) It
ends with an Epilogue – spoken by 'a dancer' – promising more plays
about FALSTAFF and specifically stating that he is not based on the real-
life Sir John Oldcastle – one of the first examples of an author's (or
publisher's) disclaimer, which fools no one. These live-action
programme-notes are nowadays one of the most bizarre parts of a
Shakespeare production; the ones here, wooden and over-elaborate,
make one long for the superb CHORUS who introduces *Henry V*.

Rutland, Edmund, Earl of (*Henry VI Part Three*)
YORK's youngest son, a child, murdered by Young CLIFFORD in
revenge for Lord CLIFFORD's death.

Sailor (*Othello*)
Brings news to the Duke of VENICE and his SENATORS that the Turks
have attacked Rhodes.

Sailors (*Pericles*)
There are two of them, and they superstitiously beg PERICLES to throw
THAISSA's dead body overboard before the ship sinks in the storm.

Salarino and Solanio (*The Merchant of Venice*)
Venetian friends of ANTONIO, BASSANIO and GRATIANO. Their main
function is to carry news from one person to another, for example that

SHYLOCK's daughter has eloped or that Antonio's ships are lost at sea. They also bring the disguised PORTIA and NERISSA to court to plead Antonio's case. They are a Venetian ROSENCRANTZ and GUILDENSTERN, equally indistinguishable and equally in need of Tom Stoppard's redeeming skill.

Salisbury, Earl of *(Henry V; Henry VI Part One)*
Son of the SALISBURY of *Richard II*, this lord appears briefly in *Henry V*, as one of the commanders at Agincourt, and even more fleetingly in *Henry VI Part One*, where he is one of the lords shot by the MASTER-GUNNER at Orleans. His character, such as it is, is that of an honourable military man, a professional soldier bright for battle.

Salisbury, Earl of *(Richard II)*
One of RICHARD's courtiers, Salisbury hears of the defection of the Welsh and brings the heavy news to his master. Although characterless, he is given gorgeous lines to speak: Shakespeare's minor characters often do better out of misery than joy. 'Ah Richard, with the eyes of heavy mind/I see thy glory like a shooting star/Fall to the bare earth from the firmament./The sun sets weeping in the lowly west...' are typical.

Salisbury, Richard Neville, Earl of *(Henry VI Part Two)*
No relation of the SALISBURY killed at Orleans in *Henry VI Part One*, this old man is a featureless courtier, whose loyalty is at first for HENRY but who is then convinced (by historical arguments) that YORK is the rightful king of England. Even so, his conviction never leads to decisiveness: even when he tells Henry of his change of loyalty, his words are measured, ponderous and as boring as the minutes of a government committee: 'My lord, I have consider'd with myself/The title of this most renowned Duke,/And in my conscience do repute his Grace/The rightful heir to England's royal seat.' York calls him 'a winter lion', but his toothless roaring hardly bears out the description or explains why anyone should hold him in such high regard.

Salisbury, William Longsword, Earl of *(King John)*
Turncoat noble who deserts JOHN after the death of ARTHUR, only to return when he discovers that his new master, PHILIP of France, is planning to kill him. He and PEMBROKE are a sinister double-act, always hovering and plotting on the fringes of the action; malevolence is their stock-in-trade.

Sampson *(Romeo and Juliet)*
Quarrelsome servant of the Capulets, who, with GREGORY, opens the play by picking a fight with ABRAHAM. He is hot-headed and bullying. ('I do not bite my thumb at you, sir, but I bite my thumb, sir...') Later, in the preparation for the Capulets' masked ball, he speaks with some authority to the other servants ('Away with the joint-stools, remove the court-cupboard, look to the plates; good thou, save me a

piece of marchpane'), in a lively (and often unjustly cut) scene of domestic light relief.

Sands, Lord *(Henry VIII)*
Merry gentleman who makes puppyish, lascivious small talk with the ladies at WOLSEY's supper-party before the masked ball where HENRY first meets Anne BULLEN. He calls himself 'an honest country lord', and says that if he were a ladies' confessor they would find penance 'as easy as a down-bed would afford it': this undergraduate heartiness is his only character.

Saturninus *(Titus Andronicus)*
Villainous emperor of Rome, cuckold-husband of TAMORA. In public he likes to appear the beetle-browed tyrant, ordering a death here, a mutilation there, a political *coup* somewhere else; but nature has given him utterly inadequate equipment to play the role. He is weak-willed and timorous, and every time he blusters, he collapses into immediate recantations and qualifications. Saturninus is putty in TAMORA's hands and is oblivious of both her political scheming and her love-affair with AARON. Towards the end, when the Andronican conspiracy seems to be getting out of hand, all he can do is wring his hands at the affront it offers his own dignity. ('Was ever seen/An emperor in Rome thus overborne,/ Troubled, confronted thus, and for the extent/Of egal justice, used in such contempt?...') The one determined act of his life is stabbing TITUS at the end of the play, and he only stirs himself to this after he has been served the heads of Tamora's sons in a pie and seen Titus stab Tamora before his eyes: provocation enough, one would imagine, for even the most lily-livered of men.

Say, Lord *(Henry VI Part Two)*
Lord Treasurer of England, captured by CADE and his followers. He pleads for his life, but unfortunately does so at great length and with a profuse use of Latin tags; he dies.

Scales, Lord *(Henry VI Part Two)*
Keeper of the Tower of London who sends GOUGH to defend Smithfield against CADE and his followers.

Scarus *(Antony and Cleopatra)*
ANTONY's officer. He is vehemently brave in battle – 'We'll beat 'em into benchholes' – and, though seriously wounded, is made Antony's second-in-command after the defection of ENOBARBUS.

Schoolmaster *(The Two Noble Kinsmen)*
Because the morris-dancing COUNTRYMEN are too busy dancing to be full-heartedly funny, the Schoolmaster who trains them is given all the clownish lines. He is a fussy, fretful pedant, and his speech to THESEUS introducing the dancers is as ridiculously pompous as anything Peter QUINCE manages in *A Midsummer Night's Dream*. ('Dainty Duke, whose doughty dismal fame/From Dis to Daedalus, from post to pillar,/Is

blown abroad, help me, thy poor well-willer,/And with thy twinkling
eyes look right and straight/Upon this mighty "Morr" of mickle
weight;/"Is" now comes in, which being glued together/Makes
"Morris", and the cause that we come hither...')

Scrivener *(Richard III)*
Scribe who brings in a proclamation he has just spent eleven hours
writing out 'in a set hand'. It is the indictment of HASTINGS, to be read
in St Paul's, and its contents appal him. ('Bad is the world, and all will
come to naught/When such ill-dealing must be seen in thought'.)

Scroop, Lord *(Henry V)*
Co-conspirator against HENRY with CAMBRIDGE and GRAY, notable for
his fierce advocation that the drunk who railed at HENRY's person
should be punished 'lest example breed, by his sufferance, more of such
a kind' – advice which is subsequently and satisfyingly turned against
the conspirators themselves.

Scroop, Richard, Archbishop of York *(Henry IV Parts One and Two)*
A Yorkist, brother of the (Sir Stephen) SCROOP who supported
RICHARD II against the then BOLINGBROKE (later Henry IV). He aids
HOTSPUR and the other rebels in *Part One*; after Hotspur's death he
transfers his loyalty to NORTHUMBERLAND, and is one of those tricked
(in *Part Two*) by Prince JOHN into disbanding his army, and executed.
Uncle of the SCROOP in *Henry V*. In history Scroop was apparently a
saintly, other-worldly man; in the plays he is hardly characterised at all,
and for all his importance as a rebel leader, his part is small.

Scroop, Sir Stephen *(Richard II)*
Supporter of RICHARD, who brings him the devastating news that
(among other disasters) 'Whitebeards have arm'd their thin and hairless
scalps/Against thy majesty; boys with women's voices strive/To speak
big and clap their female joints/In stiff unwieldy arms against thy
crown...' This leads to Richard's speech, 'Let's talk of graves, of
worms and epitaphs...', after which Scroop (perhaps feeling himself
outclassed) says no more for the duration of the play.

Seacole, Francis *(Much Ado about Nothing): see* Watchmen

Seacole, George *(Much Ado about Nothing): see* Watchmen

Sebastian *(The Tempest)*
ALONSO's villainous younger brother. Jealous of his power, he is urged
by ANTONIO to murder him. He is vituperative with underlings (e.g. to
the BOATSWAIN: 'A pox o' your throat, you bawling, blasphemous,
incharitable dog!'); he is mercilessly witty about his equals (e.g. of the
tedious GONZALO, 'Look, he's winding up the watch of his wit. By and
by it will strike'); he has no pleasant or human qualities, and is the one
visitor to the magic island apart from Antonio whose character remains
unchanged.

Sebastian (*Twelfth Night*)
VIOLA's twin brother. At first a somewhat stuffy hero, a mixture of gush and abruptness ('My kind Antonio,/I can no other answer make but thanks,/And thanks, and ever thanks... What's to do?/Shall we go see the relics of this town?'), he is transported by love into ecstasies of poetry whose ardour surpasses even ORSINO's.

Second Player (Player Queen) (*Hamlet*)
In one short scene, this actor plays a melodramatic accessory to murder, and the speeches ('Nor earth to me give food, nor heaven light!/Sport and repose lock from me day and night!') are aptly characterised in GERTRUDE's dry comment, 'The lady doth protest too much, methinks'.

Seleucus (*Antony and Cleopatra*)
CLEOPATRA's treasurer. Tells OCTAVIUS that she has misled him about her assets.

Sempronius (*Timon of Athens*)
Of all TIMON's false friends, he has the most ingenious way of avoiding lending him money. He pretends to be offended at being asked third instead of first. ('Has Ventidius and Lucullus denied him,/And does he send to me...?/Must I be his last refuge?.../Who bates mine honour shall not know my coin').

Sempronius (*Titus Andronicus*): *see* **Gentlemen**

Senators (*Cymbeline*)
In a brief scene, the First and Second Senators tell the TRIBUNES that LUCIUS has been appointed General against the British. Like the GENTLEMEN who begin the play, they are walking notice-boards and need no character.

Senators (*Othello*)
Anxiously debate with the Duke of VENICE what to do about the Turkish invasion of Cyprus, and then react with dignified horror to BRABANTIO's accusations against OTHELLO.

Senators (*Timon of Athens*)
At first they hold to the strict letter of the law, refusing to pardon ALCIBIADES' drunken friend who killed a man, and banishing Alcibiades for challenging their authority. Later, when Alcibiades attacks Athens, they beg TIMON (in vain) to return to the city, and then stand on the battlements and ask Alcibiades to spare the citizens on the grounds that 'we were not all unkind, nor all deserve/The common stroke of war'. They are elderly, reverend and foolish, functionaries rather than individuals.

Sergeant (*Macbeth*)
The 'bloody man' who tells DUNCAN, at the start of the play, that MACBETH has won a victory against the rebels, in particular facing 'the

merciless Macdonwald' and with a single sword-blow 'unseaming' him 'from the nave to th' chops'. Twenty lines, revealing no character but crammed with poetry.

Sergeant-at-Arms *(Henry VIII)*
Goes with BRANDON to arrest BUCKINGHAM for treason.

Servant *(Troilus and Cressida)*
In a scene with PANDARUS, while never actually being rude to him, he makes it perfectly clear that he despises both him and the 'sodden business' he engages in. It is not precisely clowning, though its starting-point is a typically clownish misunderstanding of Pandarus' question 'What music is this' ('I do but partly know, sir: it is music in parts'): his lines are more full of scorn than mirth; no character.

Servant *(The Two Noble Kinsmen): see* **Gentleman**

Servant *(The Winter's Tale)*
At the sheep-shearing festival, he announces to his master the SHEPHERD a string of visitors including 'three carters, three shepherds, three neat-herds' who 'have a dance which the wenches call a gallimaufry of gambols'. Nice phrases.

Servants *(King Lear)*
Ordered by CORNWALL to blind GLOUCESTER, the First Servant is so appalled that he draws a sword and wounds his master, whereupon REGAN comes up behind him and stabs him dead. The three other servants, horrified, plan to desert Cornwall and help Gloucester, but none the less disappear from the play after this scene, leaving Gloucester in EDGAR's care.

Servants (Lord's) *(The Taming of the Shrew)*
There are three of them, and in the Induction they ply the bemused SLY with fine clothes, rich food and assurances that he is really of noble birth.

Servants (Petruchio's) *(The Taming of the Shrew)*
They bring food, clothes and welcome to their master and their new mistress KATHARINA, only to be kicked and insulted for their pains. Their names are Nathaniel, Joseph, Nicholas, Philip, Peter, Walter and Sugarsop. Walter and Sugarsop are silent; the others each speak a line or two.

Servants (Pompey's) *(Antony and Cleopatra)*
On board POMPEY's galley, they serve the banquet and pass caustic comments on their betters' drunkenness.

Servants *(Timon of Athens)*
There are over a dozen servants in the play, bustling about TIMON's house, begging loans on behalf of their masters or demanding payment of Timon's debts. Those named are Timon's servants Flaminius,

Lucilius and Servilius and his creditors' servants Caphis, Philotus,
Titus and Hortensius. They speak a handful of lines each, and have no
character, apart from Timon's (unnamed) Servant who rails at the
senator SEMPRONIUS for refusing to help his master. ('Of such a nature
is his politic love./This was my lord's last hope; now all are fled.')

Servilius (*Timon of Athens*)*: see* **Servants**

Serving-Men (*Coriolanus*)
Three clownish servants of AUFIDIUS at Antium. When CORIOLANUS
comes to the house in disguise, they treat him scornfully. After
Aufidius reveals his true identity and takes him in, they discuss him
excitedly, and grow particularly hot at the prospect of war with Rome.

Serving-men (*Henry VI Part One*)
The quarrel between GLOUCESTER and WINCHESTER is reflected in the
brawling between their servants, which culminates in a riot on the steps
of Parliament itself: stones are thrown, pates are bloodied, and, as the
First Serving-man puts it, 'if we are forbidden stones, we'll fall to't
with our teeth'.

Sexton (*Much Ado about Nothing*)
Briefly appears in the scene where DOGBERRY interrogates CONRADE
and BORACHIO. The part is tiny (14 lines), but full of delightful
pedantry as he tries to keep the voluble, bombastic Dogberry to the
point.

Seyton (*Macbeth*)
MACBETH's personal servant, who helps him arm.

Shadow, Simon (*Henry IV Part Two*)
One of FALSTAFF's scarecrow army; he speaks only twice, and his name
occasions a bout of lame hilarity.

Shallow, Robert (*Henry IV Part Two; The Merry Wives of Windsor*)
Like many other characters from *Henry IV* carried over into *The Merry
Wives of Windsor*, Shallow loses most of his character on the way. In
The Merry Wives of Windsor he is a doddery old fool, pursuing
FALSTAFF with impotent fury because 'you have beaten my men, killed
my deer and broke open my lodge' (*Falstaff*: 'But not kiss'd your
keeper's daughter'). He is one of a group of zanies, and is as shallow a
creation as his name implies. In *Henry IV Part Two* he is altogether a
more robust character: a lively old gentleman, delighted to welcome
Falstaff to Gloucestershire and to reminisce about the good old days,
sixty years before, when he was a young lawyer at Clement's Inn in
London, called 'mad Shallow', 'lusty Shallow' or 'By the Mass... call'd
anything'. 'Jesu, Jesu,' he cries, 'the mad days I have spent!' – and his
self-delight is as infectious, as heart-warming, as his railings in *The
Merry Wives of Windsor* are tedious and pitiful. *Henry IV* is often
claimed as a panegyric to the old 'Merrie England' of blessed memory:

the Gloucestershire scenes in *Part Two*, and Shallow's contribution to them, are the chief creators of that happy mood.

Shepherd *(Henry VI Part One)*
Bewildered but dignified peasant, brought in by the English to prove that LA PUCELLE is his daughter and not, as she claims, 'descended of gentler blood'. Her rage ('Peasant, avaunt!') breaks his heart, and he curses her ('I would the milk/Thy mother gave thee when thou suck'st her breast/Had been a little ratsbane...') and stumbles out.

Shepherd *(The Winter's Tale)*
Good old man who rescues the infant PERDITA, brings her up and eventually restores her to her real father and sees her married to a prince. He seldom takes centre-stage, but is always busy on the fringes of the action, discussing business with his son (the CLOWN), supervising rustic jollity, travelling anxiously to Sicilia to sort out the tangle the plot is in, and regularly, gloriously, taking AUTOLYCUS at his word and regretting it.

Sheriff *(Henry IV Part One)*
Comes to arrest FALSTAFF for the robbery at Gadshill, and is persuaded by Prince HAL – who wants to use the robbery for his own ends – to delay the arrest for twenty-four hours.

Sheriff *(Henry VI Part Two)*
Leads ELEANOR on her penance through the streets.

Sheriff of Wiltshire *(Richard III)*
Leads BUCKINGHAM to execution. Says only two half-lines.

Shylock *(The Merchant of Venice)*
Because of Shylock's religion, more controversy has surrounded *The Merchant of Venice* than any other Shakespeare play – and people's views of his Jewishness often affect production-styles, not always to the play's advantage. In Shakespeare's own time, and for many years afterwards, it was acceptable to play Shylock as little more than a bloodthirsty monster, and to make the trial-scene a triumph of justice over malignity. In recent times, partly as a result of this century's appalling treatment of the Jewish people, interpretations have veered to the opposite pole, presenting Shylock as the only whole person in a sick society, and the trick played on him in the trial scene as a typical piece of bloody-minded persecution; in neither interpretation is the play's moral weighting once in doubt.

In fact Shylock's religion is merely the peg on which Shakespeare hangs his character. He is a man divided against himself (one of Shakespeare's favourite character-types: MACBETH, LEAR, HAMLET, BRUTUS and OTHELLO also, in their different ways, conform to it); his private and public personalities are at odds; he selects a moral attitude for each situation, and it is this schizophrenic approach to life (of which Jewish orthodoxy symbolises only part) which destroys him. In his public life he has the same ruthless, heartless approach to business as everyone else in Venice. He and ANTONIO are moral twins: neither lets compassion affect his commercial judgement, and if the situation were reversed Antonio's bond against Shylock, and enforcement of it, would be no less implacable. Shakespeare gives dramatic flesh to their mutual callousness by making them religious antagonists – Antonio, in Shylock's words, 'hates our ancient nation' and shows it by cold contempt; Shylock for his part goes out to dinner 'in hate, to feed upon the prodigal Christian' – but the specific details of Jewishness have as little to do with this as would specific Christianity.

In private, Shylock is a different man. He lives his life by a strict moral code, a set of predetermined laws and observances which are the binding forces of his personality: he is what he believes. (Again, the details are Jewish, but the approach to life is common.) In particular, he centres his emotional life on his daughter JESSICA, and her acceptance of his moral code is essential to his peace of mind. Thus, when she abandons him – and for someone he regards as wholly immoral, a child of the devil – Shylock's inner resources are ripped to shreds. He rails against Jessica for stealing his ducats, and claims that he would gladly see her dead at his feet if only his jewels were safe: but this is the raving less of a monster (as it is sometimes played) than of a man in emotional shock, clutching at inessentials because the real agony is too huge to contemplate. Significantly, Shakespeare combines the announcement of Jessica's elopement with news that Antonio's argosies are lost at sea and the bond is forfeit, and Shylock's impotence over Jessica turns into a neurotic lust for vengeance on Antonio. Throughout the trial-scene he behaves like someone mentally unbalanced, suffering a nervous breakdown, and when the trial is over he stumbles out of Venetian business life, and out of the play, for good.

There has been enthusiastic debate about Shakespeare's own feelings about Jewishness, and the feelings of the society for which he wrote the play. Certainly the anti-Jewish jibes in the trial-scene (notably those uttered by GRATIANO) have an uncomfortable, real-life racist edge, and though Shakespeare's depiction of Shylock never falls entirely into the rabid anti-semitism of Marlowe's *The Jew of Malta* (performed half a dozen years before *The Merchant of Venice*, and hugely popular), it none the less keeps losing track of itself and turning into a caricature of miserly malignity (in a way which his portrayal of other villains, e.g. IAGO or EDMUND, never does). His own ambivalence is debatable, but the ambivalence in the play is not. Save that it would involve tampering with the dialogue, it might be instructive to play Shylock not as a Jew at all, but as Arab, Chinese, Eskimo or protestant Scot.

Sicinius Velutus (*Coriolanus*)
The hotter-headed of the two tribunes who stir up the Roman people against CORIOLANUS. He is an elderly demagogue, characterised by Coriolanus as an 'old goat' and a 'tongue o' the common mouth'; during

the brawl scene in Act Three he is so vehement, shouting that
Coriolanus is a traitor and should be thrown from the Tarpeian Rock,
that Coriolanus has to be held back from physically assaulting him. But
although his demagoguery is fuelled by class-hatred and by personal
loathing for Coriolanus, it arises from genuine concern for the common
people he represents, as his words after Coriolanus' self-banishment
make clear. ('We do make his friends/Blush that the world goes well;
who rather had . . . behold/Dissentious numbers pest'ring streets, than
see/Our tradesmen singing in their shops . . .')

Silence *(Henry IV Part Two)*
Gloucestershire Justice of the Peace. The part is small, and he is little
more than SHALLOW's *confidant*; like all Shakespeare's Gloucestershire
characters, he is aptly named.

Silius *(Antony and Cleopatra)*
VENTIDIUS' junior officer in Syria.

Silvius *(As You Like It)*
Young shepherd in love with PHEBE. His love prompts him to blank
verse ('O dear Phebe,/If ever, as that ever may be near,/You meet in
some fresh cheek the power of fancy,/Then shall you know the wounds
invisible/That love's keen arrows make . . .'), but he is abashed by the
fact that (as he thinks) she loves one of his betters, the boy Ganymede
(really ROSALIND in disguise), and manfully keeps out of the way rather
than mar her happiness. He marries Phebe at the end of the play. There
is little character in the lines, but there are enough lines to give him a
certain amount of colour (making him, for example, one of the 'noble
shepherds' of classical literature or Elizabethan madrigal verse, a simple
soul ennobled by emotion).

Simonides *(Pericles)*
King of Pentapolis who organises the tournament at which PERICLES
wins marriage with THAISSA. Despite one brief, somewhat contrived
dramatic scene (he pretends to think Pericles a traitor, to test his
mettle), he is a cardboard king: the fact of rule defines his character.

Simpcox, Mistress *(Henry VI Part Two)*
Wife and accomplice of the fake beggar of St Albans; her sad
explanation, 'Alas, sir, we did it for the money', is not enough to
prevent a beating.

Simpcox, Saunder *(Henry VI Part Two)*
Tries to persuade the king, GLOUCESTER and others that thanks to a
miracle he has recovered both his sight and the use of his legs
(paralysed when he fell out of a plum tree). The nobles prove (by
questioning) that he is still blind and (by ordering a beating) that he can
run like a hare.

Simple, Peter (*The Merry Wives of Windsor*)
SLENDER's servant, a yokel from Gloucestershire. He says little, and
what he does say shows that he is aptly named.

Sir Andrew Aguecheek (*Twelfth Night*): *see* **Aguecheek**

Sir Toby Belch (*Twelfth Night*): *see* **Belch**

Siward, Old (*Macbeth*)
Earl of Northumberland who supports MACDUFF and MALCOLM against
MACBETH. He has less than a dozen lines, when he is told of his son's
death, but they are of a dignity and nobility all the more striking for the
blood-boltered context in which they come. ('Then he is dead?'...
'Had he his hurts before?'... 'Why then, God's soldier be he!/Had I as
many sons as hairs,/I would not wish them a fairer death.')

Siward, Young (*Macbeth*)
Adolescent son of Old SIWARD, the English leader against MACBETH.
He faces Macbeth in single combat ('Thou liest, abhorred tyrant! With
my sword/I'll prove the lie thou speak'st'), and is killed.

Slender, Abraham (*The Merry Wives of Windsor*)
SHALLOW's nephew, come with his uncle from Gloucestershire to
Windsor to court Anne PAGE. He is a country squire, a beanpole (kin to
that other slack-witted zany, AGUECHEEK in *Twelfth Night*), and the
loam of Gloucestershire seems to have clogged his brain as well as his
boots: he spends his time vacantly sighing for love ('O sweet Anne
Page!'), making embarrassed and ineffective conversation with his
beloved ('I bruised my shins the other day with playing at sword and
dagger with a master of fence... and by my troth, I cannot abide the
smell of hot meat since...'), and being pushed around by Shallow,
PAGE and everyone else in sight.

Sly, Christopher (*The Taming of the Shrew*)
Drunken tinker tricked, in the Induction to the play, into believing that
he is really a lord. He spends his time either bewildered at the attention
shown him or drunkenly enjoying it, and disappears from the action at
the end of Act One, Scene One.

Smith (*Henry VI Part Two*)
Weaver who supports CADE. He is particularly vehement against the
CLERK OF CHATHAM.

Snare (*Henry IV Part Two*)
One of the law-officers brought by Mistress QUICKLY to arrest
FALSTAFF. He is fiercer than his sidekick FANG, but no more
successful.

Snout, Tom (*A Midsummer Night's Dream*)
Athenian tinker, who plays the Wall in QUINCE's production. He is the
archetype of the utterly untalented amateur actor, who plants himself

foursquare onstage, recites his lines like a string of sausages ('In this same interlude it doth befall/That I, one Snout by name, present a wall...'), and then stumps off with almost audible relief. ('Thus have I, Wall, my part discharged so;/And, being done, thus Wall away doth go'.) As THESEUS comments, 'Would you desire lime and hair to speak better?'

Snug (*A Midsummer Night's Dream*)
A plain man, who introduces himself as 'Snug the joiner' without Christian name, he takes the part of Lion in QUINCE's play, and despite initial anxiety ('Have you the lion's part written? Pray you, if it be, give it me, for I am slow of study') turns into one of the most eager members of Quince's troop, making rehearsal suggestions, asking what he thinks are helpful questions, and finally gaining courtly approval ('Well roared, lion!'), if not a round of applause, for his performance.

Solanio (*The Merchant of Venice*): *see* **Salarino and Solanio**

Soldier (First Soldier) (*All's Well that Ends Well*)
Assists the LORDS to trick PAROLLES. Like them, he is chiefly characterised by the zest of his masquerade as a cutthroat foreign mercenary, and by the absurd made-up words he speaks.

Soldier (*Henry VI Part Two*)
He speaks only four words, but unfortunately they are 'Jack Cade! Jack Cade!' and come just after CADE has declared himself Lord Mortimer. SMITH kills him, and then grimly remarks, 'If this fellow be wise, he'll never call ye Jack Cade more: I think he hath a very fair warning.'

Soldier (*Timon of Athens*)
Sent to fetch TIMON from the seashore, he finds his tomb and (since he is illiterate) takes a wax impression of the inscription back for ALCIBIADES to read.

Soldiers (*Antony and Cleopatra*)
A dozen individual soldiers speak in the course of the play. ANTONY's are confused and angry at the lack of direction in the fighting; OCTAVIUS's witness ENOBARBUS' death.

Somerset, Edmund Beaufort, Duke of (*Henry VI Part Two*)
Younger brother of the SOMERSET of *Henry VI Part One*, older brother of the SOMERSET of *Henry VI Part Three*, he takes over the family feud against the House of York. He joins the nobles' conspiracy against GLOUCESTER, and tries to broaden it to attack BEAUFORT, his own illegitimate relative ('Yet let us watch the haughty Cardinal:/His insolence is more intolerable/Than all the princes in the land beside...'). After this he draws back from the main action until the rebellion of YORK, when he is killed (by RICHARD) at the battle of St Albans. He plays a small and somewhat futile part in great events, but his language is vigorous and his hatred for the Yorkists is as lively as it

is unreasoning.

Somerset, Edmund, Duke of *(Henry VI Part Three)*
Minor lord who defects from EDWARD after his marriage to Lady GREY, helps WARWICK to snatch him from his tent and depose him, takes part in the battle of Tewkesbury, is captured and is executed – all without saying more than half a dozen lines.

Somerset, John Beaufort, Duke of *(Henry VI Part One)*
Grandson of John of GAUNT Duke of Lancaster, and therefore leader of the Lancastrian faction in opposition to his uncle YORK. At the scene of the choosing of the roses, he chooses red, and shows a splendid line in dynastic abuse of York: 'We grace the yeoman in conversing with him'. In the rest of the play, their quarrel is somewhat overshadowed by the wrangle between GLOUCESTER and WINCHESTER, but it surfaces at the coronation of HENRY (*York*: 'Will not this malice, Somerset, be left?' *Somerset*: 'Your private grudge, my lord of York, will out/Though ne'er so cunningly you smother it'), and they are so preoccupied with it that they later refuse to help TALBOT on the battlefield in France. After this, Somerset disappears from the play, and indeed from the Dukedom: the SOMERSET of *Henry VI Part Three* is his younger brother.

Somerville, Sir John *(Henry VI Part Three)*
Brings WARWICK news that reinforcements are on their way to Coventry.

Son of Clarence (Edward) *(Richard III)*
Pathetic child who with his sister first bewails the murder of their father and then refuses to weep with Queen ELIZABETH for the death of his uncle EDWARD.

Son of Macduff *(Macbeth)*
A bright, pert child ('Was my father a traitor, Mother?'), he is cut down by the MURDERERS before his mother's eyes.

Son of the Master-Gunner of Orleans *(Henry VI Part One)*
Small boy, sent by his father to keep lookout.

Son that hath kill'd his father *(Henry VI Part Three)*
While HENRY is mooning about a battlefield, the Son comes in with a corpse to loot, and is horrified to find that it is his own father's. Shortly afterwards, a FATHER THAT HATH KILL'D HIS SON comes in on the same grisly business. Neither of them sees Henry, but their lamentations prompt him to gloomy reflections on the plight of England, torn by civil war.

Soothsayer *(Antony and Cleopatra)*
In a lively scene, he tells the fortunes of CLEOPATRA's maids. Later, to ANTONY, he acutely assesses the fatal difference between him and OCTAVIUS. ('Thy demon, that's thy spirit which keeps thee, is/Noble, courageous, high, unmatchable,/Where Caesar's is not; but near him,

thy angel/Becomes a fear, as being o'erpower'd: therefore,/Make space enough between you.') As with all soothsayers' advice in Shakespeare, this is ignored and the results are fatal.

Soothsayer *(Julius Caesar)*
Wild-eyed seer whose advice ('Beware the Ides of March!') is as unheeded as it is spectacular. He has one brief additional scene with PORTIA, but it is designed more to build tension (because of her unreasoning alarm) than to display his character.

Soothsayer (Philharmonus) *(Cymbeline)*
Roman follower of LUCIUS, who expounds and explains a lengthy prophecy at the end of the play: 'When as a lion's whelp shall, to himself unknown, without seeking, find and be embraced by a piece of tender air, and when...'. He shows ingenious learning but not much personality.

Soundpost, James *(Romeo and Juliet)*
Third musician (despite his name, a singer) who performs for the Capulets. He is asked by PETER his view of why music is said to have 'a silver sound', and (prudently conserving his voice, perhaps) answers nothing more than 'Faith, I know not what to say'.

Southwell, John *(Henry VI Part Two)*
Sorcerer involved in SUFFOLK's plot against ELEANOR Duchess of Gloucester; he does not speak.

Speed *(The Two Gentlemen of Verona)*
VALENTINE's clownish servant, a cheeky, carefree youth with a relish for language like DROMIO I's in *The Comedy of Errors* (a part perhaps written for the same actor): asked, for example, how he knows his master is in love, he says, 'You have learned... to wreathe your arms like a malcontent, to relish a lovesong like a robin-redbreast, to walk alone like one that hath the pestilence, to sigh like a schoolboy that hath lost his ABC, to weep like a young wench that hath buried her grandam...' and so on for half a page. He spends much of his time in this kind of harmless fooling, or acting as straight man to his gloomy friend LAUNCE (e.g. in the discussion of the virtues – few – and faults – 'more than hairs' – of Launce's ideal wife); he disappears from the play when he and Valentine are captured by the OUTLAWS.

Spirit *(Henry VI Part Two)*
Conjured up by BOLINGBROKE, JOURDAIN and the other false witches, it predicts (to a script prepared in advance, and later found by YORK) the fates of HENRY, SUFFOLK and SOMERSET, but fails to predict the arrest of the people who called it into being.

St Albans, Mayor of *(Henry VI Part Two)*
Sends for the BEADLE to thrash the impostor SIMPCOX.

Stafford, Lord *(Henry VI Part Three)*
Supporter of EDWARD; does not speak.

Stafford, Sir Humphrey *(Henry VI Part Two)*
Sent to persuade CADE and his followers not to revolt, he adopts entirely the wrong tone ('Rebellious hinds, the filth and scum of Kent,/ Mark'd for the gallows, lay your weapons down'), and is sent packing.

Stafford, William *(Henry VI Part Two)*
Brother of Sir Humphrey STAFFORD, who accompanies him on his abortive attempt to crush CADE's rebellion.

Stanley, Sir John *(Henry VI Part Two)*
Takes ELEANOR to exile on the Isle of Man.

Stanley, Sir William *(Henry VI Part Three)*
Helps HASTINGS and RICHARD free EDWARD from house-arrest in Yorkshire, but does not speak. Brother of the STANLEY (Lord Derby) in Richard III.

Stanley, Thomas, Lord (later Earl of Derby) *(Richard III)*
At first an uneasy follower of RICHARD, he is turned by such events as HASTINGS' murder into the king's enemy, and joins forces with RICHMOND. His daughter marries Richmond, and Richmond creates him Earl of Derby. He is a nonentity for most of the play, but springs to life (and to virile poetry) in his scene with Richmond before the battle of Bosworth. ('The night hours steal on,/And flaky darkness breaks within the east./In brief, for so the season bids us be,/Prepare thy battle early in the morning/And put thy fortune to th'arbitrament/Of bloody strokes and mortal-staring war ...')

Starveling, Robin *(A Midsummer Night's Dream)*
Athenian tailor, who plays Moonshine in QUINCE's production. He has only one speech as Moonshine ('This lantern doth the horned moon present;/Myself the man in the moon do seem to be'), but he is so rattled by questions and comments from the courtly audience that he steps out of character and makes matters absolutely clear. ('All that I have to say is, to tell you that the lantern is the moon, I the man in the moon, this thornbush my thornbush, and this dog my dog.')

Stephano *(The Merchant of Venice)*
PORTIA's servant, who brings LORENZO and JESSICA news of her imminent return to Belmont.

Stephano *(The Tempest)*
Drunken butler, whose tattered dignity persuades CALIBAN and TRINCULO that he is the right man to be king of the island in PROSPERO's place. His secret hoard of wine – 'My cellar is in a rock by th' seaside, where my wine is hid' – takes the place, for his companions, of Prospero's magic, and in the same way, instead of true dignity and authority of speech he favours a drunkard's pomposity. ('My man-

monster hath drowned his tongue in sack. For my part, the sea cannot drown me. I swam, ere I could recover the shore, five and thirty leagues off and on. By this light, thou shalt be my lieutenant, monster, or my standard.')

Steward (*All's Well that Ends Well*)
Manages the house and estate of the COUNTESS OF ROUSILLON. Dignified and middle-aged.

Strangers (*Timon of Athens*)
Three Strangers (of whom the third only speaks half a line) are walking with LUCILIUS when SERVILIUS asks him for a loan to help TIMON, and he refuses. They reflect on Timon's generosity of character and on human ingratitude. The second Stranger is addressed as Hostilius; the others are unnamed.

Strato (*Julius Caesar*)
BRUTUS' slave, the only one willing to hold the sword while his master runs on it.

Suffolk, Charles Brandon, Duke of (*Henry VIII*)
With NORFOLK, the senior courtier opposed to WOLSEY. After Wolsey's fall we see Suffolk briefly as the king's confidant, a man allowed to play him at cards and beat him; but his lines are sparse and his character elusive. (If anything, he is heartier and bluffer than Norfolk, an older version of SANDS. But that is like saying that chalk is more fascinating than china-clay.)

Suffolk, William de le Pole, Duke of (*Henry VI Parts One and Two*)
Of all the lords bickering for power, Suffolk is the most deceitful and devious, spitting hatred at the Yorkists and setting up the fake witches to discredit GLOUCESTER ('Say but the word, and I will be his priest'). Unlike the others, however, he lets passion outweigh diplomacy, and it is the death of him. He falls in love with MARGARET, cunningly arranges to woo her on HENRY's behalf, then conducts an open affair with her in which political power and sexuality go hand in hand ('Madam, be patient: as I was cause/Your Highness came to England, so will I/In England work your Grace's full content'). Peeping from Margaret's protection like a cheeky schoolboy, he insults Gloucester ('Why, as you say, my lord,/An't like your lordly lord-Protectorship'); eventually he arrests him and organises his murder. Like his adultery with the queen, this is ill-judged politics: the nobles round on him to put him in his place (*Warwick*: 'Madam, be still (with reverence may I say):/For every word you speak in his behalf/Is slander to your royal dignity') and he responds like a striking snake ('Blunt-witted lord!... Thy mother took into her blameful bed/Some stern untutor'd churl, and noble stock/Was graft with crab-tree slip, whose fruit thou art...'); he is finally banished, captured by pirates, and killed.
　　To the end he is imperious and insufferable ('O, that I were a god, to

shoot forth thunder/Upon these paltry, servile, abject drudges!.../It is impossible that I should die/By such a lowly vassal as thyself...'); the miracles are that such a creature should have risen so far, and that he should have been so beloved by Margaret, whose sorrow now, when she is presented with his head, is as heartfelt and sexually charged as was her love for his body when he was alive. ('Ah, barbarous villains! Hath his lovely face/Rul'd, like a wandering planet, over me,/And could it not enforce them to relent/That were unworthy to behold the same?')

Surrey, Earl of *(Henry VIII)*

NORFOLK's son and BUCKINGHAM's son-in-law, he rages at WOLSEY both behind his back (*Norfolk*: 'He's vex'd at something.' *Surrey*: 'I would 'twere something that would fret the string/The master-cord on's heart!') and face-to-face ('I'll startle you/Worse than the sacring bell, when the brown wench/Lay kissing in your arms, lord Cardinal.' *Wolsey*: 'How much, methinks, I could despise this man,/But that I am bound in charity against it.'). He itemises the charges against Wolsey, and is implacable against him even after his fall, responding to the LORD CHANCELLOR's plea 'O my lord,/Press not a falling man too far... My heart weeps to see him/So little of his great self' with a curt, sarcastic 'I forgive him'.

Surrey, Thomas Fitzalan, Earl of *(Henry IV Part Two)*

Appears in one scene, as a fellow-retainer of the king with WARWICK, but does not speak.

Surrey, Thomas Holland, Duke of (also Earl of Kent) *(Richard II)*

Surrey speaks twice in the Act IV Parliament scene, spitting accusations and insults at FITZWATER ('Dishonourable boy!/That lie shall lie so heavy on my sword/That it shall render vengeance and revenge/ Till you the lie-giver and that lie do lie/In earth as quiet as thy father's skull...'). The part is so short, and so like the others round about, that it is often cut.

Surrey, Thomas Howard, Earl of *(Richard III); see also* Norfolk *(Henry VIII)*

A youth, a minor courtier who fights at Bosworth on RICHARD's side.

Surveyor *(Henry VIII)*

Former employee of BUCKINGHAM who gives a detailed account of his master's treasonable utterances and brings about his death-sentence. He is a shifty rogue, and each time the truth of what he is saying is questioned, he produces even more circumstantial, explicit and damning evidence. ('... he stretch'd him, and with one hand on his dagger,/Another spread on's breast, mounting his eyes,/He did discharge a horrible oath, whose tenour/Was...')

Sylvia *(The Two Gentlemen of Verona)*

Each of the four lovers in the play is given a different kind of ardour, and Sylvia's is the sort that literally takes her own breath away. When she first realises that she loves VALENTINE, she can hardly finish a sentence for excitement – 'A pretty period! Well, I guess the sequel;/ And yet I will not name it; and yet I care not;/And yet take this again; and yet I thank you,/Pleasing henceforth to trouble you no more' – and when she gives back Valentine the very letter he has written for her to give to a 'known beloved', it is a piece of bravado, a declaration of love for him so sudden and so impulsive that he fails utterly to understand. Later, she flirts with him in the presence of THURIO, with infectious daring and self-delight, and when he is exiled and she decides to follow him she pours out her heart to EGLAMOUR in a headlong rush of words, sentences six, seven, eight lines long. She is one of those people who live as if in the pages of a romantic novelette, and her life appropriately passes from flirting to planned elopement, from fighting off unwelcome suitors (to PROTEUS: 'My will is even this,/That presently you hie you home to bed,/Thou subtle, perjured, false, disloyal man!') to running away from home to find her beloved and being captured immediately by outlaws ('O Valentine, this I endure for thee!'). There is no depth to her character – but when the shallows are so disarming and so enchanting, who cares?

Taborer *(The Two Noble Kinsmen)*
Drummer for the morris-dance. He does not speak.

Tailor *(The Taming of the Shrew)*
Brings a beautiful gown for KATHARINE, and robustly defends himself when PETRUCHIO and GRUMIO tell him it is unsuitable.

Talbot, John *(Henry VI Part One)*
Brave young son of TALBOT, who refuses to escape from Bordeaux without his father. He fights fiercely (among other things, striking sparks from the helmet of CHARLES himself), but is finally killed. Soldiers carry his body before his father, who speaks a memorable epitaph ('Thou antic death, which laugh'st us here to scorn...') before he, too, dies.

Talbot, Lord (later Earl of Shrewsbury) *(Henry VI Part One)*
There are several dozen lords in *Henry VI Part One*. All are named after counties or cathedral cities, all are as like one another as the figures on the Bayeux Tapestry, all bicker and brawl in the same relentless, five-

beat verse. Some of them, to be sure, acquire character in the later parts of the trilogy, but in this play they are one another's clones, and sorting out who is who is about as easy as distinguishing individual bees in a busy hive.

Only one lord, Talbot, stands apart from the insensate, endless wrangling, and Shakespeare symbolises his separateness by keeping him in France, not England, throughout the play. Unlike the home-staying lords, Talbot is a man of action, not words, a member of no faction but his own. He is the first example of a standard Shakespeare character: the no-nonsense soldier, patriotic, honourable and professional. Talbot shares character-traits with such men as ENOBARBUS in *Antony and Cleopatra*, CASSIO in *Othello*, BOLINGBROKE in *Richard II*, and above all HENRY V himself, the very model of patriotic heroism; similar qualities underlie two of Shakespeare's most complex 'noble' characters, EDGAR in *King Lear* and CORIOLANUS in *Coriolanus*.

These are high claims for Talbot, and it must be said that at this early stage in his career Shakespeare's powers of characterisation hardly matched his ambition. He gives Talbot depth by showing him in two 'private' scenes (contrasting with the public ones of war): his visit to the Countess of AUVERGNE early in the play and the moving dialogue with his son just before his death. The Countess scene shows Talbot's bluff soldierly humour: when she complains that he is no Hercules, no second Hector, but a 'child, a silly dwarf... a weak and writhled shrimp', he counters by calling in his soldiers and saying 'these are [his] substance, sinews, arms and strength' – a grim joke which wins her instantly. The scene with his son, a precursor of many similar father-and-son scenes in Shakespeare, gives him a gruff humanity which is intended to bring tears to our eyes, and very nearly does: his elegiac speech as he cradles the young man's body ('Thou antic death, which laugh'st us here to scorn...') contains some of the finest verse in the whole play, poetic flights quite outside the range of the aristrocrats bickering over roses back in England. As with AARON in *Titus Andronicus*, Talbot in this play might make us wonder what Shakespeare would have done with the character in a later, maturer play – except that *Henry V* exists to show us.

The Taming of the Shrew

In the In(tro)duction to the play, a practical joker of a Lord picks up a drunken tinker, Christopher Sly, and he and his household make him believe that he is really a nobleman woken up from a fifteen-year sleep. They dress him in finery, feed him a banquet and settle him down to watch strolling Players perform a play.

In the play, Baptista has two daughters, shrewish Katharina and beautiful Bianca. He says that no one will marry Bianca until Katharina is off his hands, and so two of Bianca's suitors, the old fool Gremio and the young fool Hortensio, persuade Petruchio, a visiting fortune-hunter, to tame Katharina and marry her. Petruchio does this by alternately praising her beauty and disagreeing with everything she says, until she is so confused that she submits rather than annoy him. While all this is going on, Lucentio, a handsome young man, is paying court to Bianca. He disguises himself as Cambio, a Latin teacher, and under the guise of teaching Bianca, flirts with her. Also in Baptista's house are Hortensio, disguised as the music-master Licio, and Lucentio's servant Tranio, disguised as Lucentio and distracting Baptista's attention by pretending to be Gremio's rival for Bianca's hand. The Bianca plot reaches its climax when Vincentio, Lucentio's father, arrives, the deceptions are revealed, and Lucentio and Bianca announce that they have secretly gone to a priest and been married. The Katharina plot reaches its climax at the banquet held to celebrate Baptista's daughters' weddings, when Katharina shows that she has learned her lesson, and is a more obedient wife than Bianca or than the shrewish Widow Hortensio has found for himself.

Tamora *(Titus Andronicus)*
Queen of the Goths, mother of DEMETRIUS and CHIRON. She is a two-faced, smooth-tongued villain, out to wheedle what power she can and happy, when wheedling fails, to unsheathe the knife. Married to the weak emperor SATURNINUS, she has a love-affair with AARON ('My lovely Aaron.../My sweet Moor, sweeter to me than life') and bears him a half-caste child in secret. She presides over the murder of BASSIANUS and the mutilation of LAVINIA, and when she thinks TITUS is mad with grief, feeds his insanity by appearing to him disguised as Revenge, urging him on to what will be a fatal rebellion. She is later forced to eat her own sons baked in a pie, and is then stabbed to death – a fittingly melodramatic end for a character who never quite leaves the realm of pantomime.

Taurus *(Antony and Cleopatra)*
OCTAVIUS' officer.

Tearsheet, Dorothy (Doll) *(Henry IV Part Two)*
A prostitute, FALSTAFF's bedfellow, with a spectacular line in vulgar abuse: 'Away, you cut-purse rascal, you filthy bung, away! By this wine, I'll thrust my knife in your mouldy chaps if you play the saucy cuttle with me. Away, you bottle-ale rascal, you basket-hilt stale juggler, you' – and this is to someone who merely wished her the time of day.

The Tempest
Prospero, banished Duke of Milan, lives with his daughter Miranda on an enchanted island, and uses his magic powers to dominate its natural inhabitants, especially the ethereal spirit Ariel and the deformed monster Caliban. He broods on revenge against the three men (his brother Antonio, King Alonso of Naples and Alonso's brother Sebastian) who dethroned him from his dukedom, and when they sail near the island he raises a supernatural tempest which shipwrecks them

(though it leaves their boat and sailors intact).

For most of the play the three villains (together with Alonso's honest courtiers and the loyal old lord Gonzalo) are led about the island by Ariel, and Alonso is made to believe that his wickedness is being punished by the drowning of his son Ferdinand. (In fact Ferdinand is not drowned, but has met Miranda and fallen in love with her.) Antonio and Sebastian plot to murder Alonso where he sleeps, but Ariel wakens Gonzalo just in time for him to shout a warning of some unknown impending disaster. At the same time, Caliban has met Alonso's butler Stephano and his jester Trinculo, and they stumble drunkenly about the island plotting to overthrow Prospero and make Stephano king of the island in his place, and being led through bogs and middens by Ariel. Finally, his revengeful heart thawed by seeing Miranda's and Ferdinand's love, Prospero abandons his magic, gathers the bemused visitors and shows them mercy and humanity. He frees Ariel and Caliban, accepts back his ducal power, and leaves with the others, purified and 'sea-changed', to return to the mortal world.

Thaissa *(Pericles)*
SIMONIDES' daughter, the princess of Pentapolis whom PERICLES woos and wins. Later, thought to be dead in a storm, she is rescued and brought back to life by CERIMON; fifteen years after that, as a dignified priestess of Diana's temple at Ephesus, she is reunited with Pericles. Her lines are few, and her character is non-existent.

Thaliard *(Pericles)*
Villainous servant of ANTIOCHUS, sent by him to poison or shoot PERICLES. He chases him from town to town, always arriving a few moments after Pericles has left for somewhere else. His master Antiochus dies before the murder can be carried out, and Thaliard disappears, unlamented, from the play.

Thersites *(Troilus and Cressida)*
'Deform'd and scurrilous Grecian' (according to the cast-list) favoured by ACHILLES because he insults and mocks the Greek commanders. Except that his wit is bitter rather than smiling, he is a standard Shakespeare clown, firing words like grapeshot at everyone he meets. (AJAX, he says, is a 'mongrel, beef-witted lord' who 'wears his wit in his belly and his guts in his head'; NESTOR's wit, he tells the Greek lords, 'was mouldy ere your grandsires had nails on their toes'; PATROCLUS is so paltry that 'if I could have remembered a gilt counterfeit, thou wouldst not have slipped out of my contemplation: but it is no matter'.) Entertaining though his lines are (and a welcome contrast to the bombast of the whippersnapper lords he mocks), he would be as peripheral to the action as most other Shakespearean comedians, were it not that he views the whole Greek enterprise at Troy with the same rancorous cynicism, and so provides a moral framework to the play. (The war, he says, is 'too much blood and too little brain', and 'all the

argument is a cuckold and a whore – a good quarrel to draw emulous factions and bleed to death upon...'.) Though his own behaviour is despicable (battering people with words but cringing from physical confrontation – 'I am a rascal, a scurvy railing knave, a very filthy rogue'), his unique moral perception makes him a pivotal character, as important for dramatic meaning as HECTOR or CRESSIDA themselves.

Theseus *(A Midsummer Night's Dream; The Two Noble Kinsmen)*
Duke of Athens, a standard Shakespearean ruler, imperious and authoritative. In both plays, he is full of good humour because of his wedding to HIPPOLYTA, and encourages rustic entertainers (QUINCE and his 'rude mechanicals' in *A Midsummer Night's Dream*, the SCHOOLMASTER and morris-dancers in *The Two Noble Kinsmen*). In *The Two Noble Kinsmen* we also see glimpses of him as a warrior-prince, razing Thebes to the ground to punish evil done by its king Creon; that and a certain arrogant implacability (as when he decrees that whichever of PALAMON and ARCITE loses the duel for EMILIA's hand shall be beheaded) is all his character.

Third Player *(Hamlet)*
Melodramatic poisoner. He has only one speech, but it is an effective one. ('Thoughts black, hands apt, drugs fit and time agreeing...'.)

Three Queens *(The Two Noble Kinsmen)*
Widows of three enemies of Creon king of Thebes. They beg THESEUS to destroy Creon because 'He will not suffer us to burn their bones,/To urn their ashes, nor to take th'offence/Of mortal loathsomeness from the blest eye/Of holy Phoebus...' Later, after Theseus' war against Thebes (in which PALAMON and ARCITE are captured), the Queens appear with their husbands' bodies in a solemn funeral procession, complete with dirge.

Thurio *(The Two Gentlemen of Verona)*
The standard silly-ass lover of farce, he is VALENTINE's rival for SYLVIA. He huffs and puffs at him (*'Thurio*: 'How!' *Sylvia*: 'What, angry, sir Thurio? Do you change colour?' *Valentine*: 'Give him leave, madam: he is a kind of chameleon.' *Thurio*: 'That hath more mind to feed on your blood than live in your air.' *Valentine*: 'You have said, sir?' *Thurio*: 'Ay, sir, and done too, for this time'), and he presses Proteus eagerly – and disingenuously – to urge his virtues on Sylvia ('What says she to my valour?'). In the end, when Valentine offers to fight him for Sylvia, he backs off very fast indeed. ('Sir Valentine, I care not for her, I./I hold him but a fool that will endanger/His body for a girl that loves him not...'.)

Thyreus *(Antony and Cleopatra)*
Messenger who carries OCTAVIUS' ultimatum to CLEOPATRA, that she must hand ANTONY over or lose her kingdom. Antony bursts in on them and has him whipped.

Timandra (*Timon of Athens*)
PHRYNIA's fellow-whore.

Time (*The Winter's Tale*)
In a single speech, he announces the passing of sixteen years, and firmly refuses to tell us anything the characters have said or done in all that time, except that they have grown older.

Timon (*Timon of Athens*)
Scholars think that *Timon of Athens* is not a finished play, but a first draft left unrevised and unperformed in Shakespeare's lifetime. The main evidence for this in the play itself is Timon's own character. Superficially he is like LEAR, a man who gives away all he has, for love, and regrets it; but there are none of the resonances in the part which make Lear great, no use of the character to symbolise the moral and philosophical plight of humanity at large. And from the actor's point of view, there is an even more serious lack, of motivation. Halfway through the play, Timon's personality turns inside-out, from happy to tormented, from philanthropic to misanthropic, and although the events of the plot explain the change, there is nothing in his earlier speeches or actions to prepare us for the unremitting bleakness and savagery he shows. Some modern, psychological interpretations give him a nervous breakdown, and though this is a neat and convincing solution to the problem, it is imposed from outside and not inherent in the play.

There are, to be sure, forebodings of disaster in the early scenes, at least for those who know how the plot will turn out. There is, for example, bitter irony when Timon says, as he sends money to bail VENTIDIUS, 'I am not of that feather to shake off/My friend when he most need me', or remarks expansively at the first, happy banquet, 'My good friends... the gods have provided that I shall have much help from you: how had you been my friends else?' and 'O, what a comfort 'tis to have so many, like brothers, commanding one another's fortune!' In the same way, APEMANTUS' refusal to believe in the sincerity of Timon's flatterers, and FLAVIUS' complaints about the ebbing of Timon's finances, are perfectly clear signposts of what is to come. Even Timon's outburst in the second banquet scene – 'May you a better feast never behold,/You knot of mouth-friends' – and his hurling of the water-dishes at his flatterers, are extreme but understandable behaviour. What is not explicable is the savagery of his curse on Athens as he leaves it – 'O thou wall,/That girdlest in those wolves, dive in the earth/And fence not Athens! Matrons, turn incontinent!/Obedience fail in children! Slaves and fools/Pluck the grave, wrinkled senate from the bench/And minister in their steads!...' – or his back-to-front behaviour when he finds the buried gold, giving it to BANDITS (providing that they 'love not themselves'), to whores (providing that they infect the whole state with pox) and to Flavius (providing that he 'hate all, curse all, show charity to none'). He has turned from a human being into an allegorical monster – hatred – and nothing persuades him out of it: not Apemantus' churlish kindness, not the tears of Flavius, not the entreaties of the SENATORS.

In the end, as if consumed by what he has become, Timon crawls into his cave and dies – a far cry from the moving and pointful deaths of Lear, HAMLET or OTHELLO. If Shakespeare had reworked this ending, giving Timon's suffering (not to mention his character) some kind of moral dignity, the play might have been on the level of his greatest tragedies; as it is, it is intellectually vacuous, a mere tract against ingratitude, and because Timon's sufferings demonstrate a point which was never in doubt from the start, they leave us neither wiser nor sadder, not so much purged by what we have seen as quite indifferent.

Timon of Athens
Timon, a rich Athenian, lavishes gifts on everyone: his friends, the senate, poets, merchants, painters and petitioners of every kind. At a banquet, the cynical philosopher Apemantus suggests that people's love of him is skin-deep, and his faithful steward Flavius wrings his hands at the low state of Timon's coffers. Soon Timon's creditors begin demanding payment, and his debts are so huge that he has to ask his former friends for loans. On one pretext or another, all refuse. Timon's only loyal friend, Alcibiades, pleads in the senate-house for mercy on a soldier who killed another in a drunken fight, and is exiled for his pains.

Timon gives a last banquet for his 'friends', but instead of food serves bowls of hot water, which he hurls at them. Then he, too, goes into exile. He lives in a seaside cave, and digs for roots to eat. One day he finds a hoard of gold, which he gives away to passers-by, including a trio of Bandits and two whores whom Alcibiades brings to visit him on his way with an army to attack Athens. Timon comprehensively curses humankind, and finds only one honourable man, Flavius, to whom he gives the rest of the gold on condition that he hate the human race. He drives away the Poet, Painter and Apemantus, and throws stones at the Senators who try to persuade him to return to Athens and make Alcibiades spare the city. At last, out of his mind with despair, he dies. The play ends with the Athenian senators surrendering their city to Alcibiades and a soldier describing Timon's tomb on the seashore; there is no true conclusion, happy or otherwise, and no moral is drawn.

Titania (*A Midsummer Night's Dream*)
Fairy queen. At the beginning, when she quarrels with OBERON over the 'little changeling boy', she is as haughty as he is ('Set your heart at rest./The fairyland buys not the child of me'), and he punishes her by making her dote like a pony-mad child on BOTTOM in his ass's head. ('Thou art as wise as thou art beautiful'; 'I have a venturous fairy that shall seek/The squirrel's hoard, and fetch thee hence new nuts'). These two scenes are (apart from brief contributions to the fairy songs and dances) all the opportunity she has to show character, as opposed to

beauty of appearances or costume; once the enchantment is lifted and she is reconciled with Oberon, she scarcely speaks.

Titinius (*Julius Caesar*)
Friend of CASSIUS who commits suicide on hearing of his death; nobility is his chief character-trait.

Titus (*Timon of Athens*): *see* **Servants**

Titus (*Titus Andronicus*)
At the beginning of the play, Titus has one daughter and many sons. One by one, they are killed or mutilated, and his reaction is to wield his own knife with gusto on anyone who crosses him. Where a modern vigilante film would give the deaths verisimilitude by hideous camera-virtuosity, Shakespeare uses the power of his verse, and the result is just as horribly irresistible: we are made gourmets of violent death.

Titus' personal predicament holds the seeds of tragedy. If he were presented as a noble soul driven distracted by his children's death, if his lust for vengeance were a facet of character, of a 'great mind o'erthrown' (as OTHELLO's grisly strangling of DESDEMONA is), we might be edified as well as entertained. But Shakespeare evades that interpretation from the start. The first murder in the play (we must discount the deaths of a score of Titus' sons before curtain-up, in battle) is done at Titus' command, and is particularly brutal: the hacking to pieces of a noble prisoner-of-war to 'appease the shadows' of his dead soldier-offspring. This event triggers all the subsequent violence – and Titus is not the innocent party, as in a vigilante film, but is tainted with implacable guilt. He could have shown mercy; he could have expressed reluctance or remorse at having to carry out a barbaric, arcane law; he does neither. The decision for the execution is brief and blunt ('die he must'), and sets a tone of inhuman heedlessness which marks every subsequent murder throughout the play (not to mention the rape of Titus' daughter LAVINIA, the lopping off of her hands and the tearing out of her tongue to prevent her revealing her attackers' names). Towards the end of the play (after Titus has discovered his daughter's attackers, killed them, baked them in a pie and served them to their own mother), he suddenly says of his own daughter, 'Die, die, Lavinia, and thy shame with thee', and stabs her, apparently with as little premeditation and concern as one swats a fly.

The effect of this lack of any context of humanity is to throw attention not on the people but on the events – and it must be said that, stomach-churning or not, *Titus Andronicus* is a fast-moving, engrossing and beautifully constructed play. It used to be thought that the only way to 'save' it for today's audiences was to deepen Titus' character, to make him either some grim-faced moralist of the 'antic Roman stamp' (cousin, as it were, to CORIOLANUS), or – better for the actor – to turn him into a kind of suffering colossus, a hero unhinged by the wrongs done to him. This is false to the text. It is better to play *Titus*

Andronicus absolutely deadpan, as a chain of bloody revenges set in a state where ethics and conscience are words unknown, and leave the audience to love it or hate it as they please. To do this makes AARON, not Titus, the most complex character in the play, and though this may be hard on the actors, it exactly follows Shakespeare's text.

Titus Andronicus

The victorious Roman general Titus brings home Tamora, Queen of the Goths, and her three sons, as prisoners-of-war. He cruelly executes Tamora's eldest son, and Tamora vows revenge. The Roman emperor Saturninus, who was due to marry Titus' daughter Lavinia, unexpectedly marries Tamora instead, and so opens the way to her vengeance and Titus' downfall. The rest of the play is a seesaw of bloody murders and even bloodier revenge. Tamora's sons (helped by her lover, the scheming Moor Aaron) murder Bassianus, brother of the emperor, and rape Lavinia (cutting out her tongue and chopping off her hands to prevent her naming her attackers), then frame two of Titus' sons for Bassianus' murder. Titus' sons are executed; their brother Lucius finds out from Aaron what has happened, and goes to raise an avenging army among the Goths. Meanwhile, in Rome, Titus avenges his sons by killing Tamora's and stabs his own daughter Lavinia dead to blot out her shame. He bakes Tamora's sons in a pie, serves them to their mother and then kills her. Tamora's husband the emperor now kills Titus, and he himself is murdered by Lucius (now returned with a Gothic army to become the new emperor). Aaron, the play's chief schemer, is the only main character not to come to a bloody end: instead, he is buried up to the neck and left to starve.

Touchstone (clown) *(As You Like It)*

There is nothing particularly clownish about Touchstone: he is one of those Shakespearean fools who say silly things with a serious face, a deadpan comedian. His jokes, therefore, depend less than usual on obscure (and nowadays virtually incomprehensible) puns, and his part remains genuinely funny. His scene with the shepherd CORIN ('[It is a] simple sin in you, to bring the ewes and the rams together, and to offer to get your living by the copulation of cattle...') and his love-affair with his gawky mistress ('Bear your body more seemingly, Audrey') are gifts to a comic character-actor rather than a comedian. His name suggests that he is there to show up others' true natures (touchstone was a dust used to test the amount of gold in a metal alloy), but there is no suggestion of this in the text, and if that part of his work is done at all it is done by JAQUES.

Townsman of St Albans *(Henry VI Part Two)*

Announces to HENRY, GLOUCESTER and others the imminent arrival of SIMPCOX, fresh from recovering his sight. ('A miracle! A miracle!')

Tranio *(The Taming of the Shrew)*

LUCENTIO's servant. Though humbly born ('son of a sailmaker in

Bergamo'), he is well educated, able to quote Italian and Latin and to play the nobleman (when he disguises himself as his master) as if he had been nothing else all his life. He is the standard cheeky servant of farce, and nothing baffles him, not even the arrival of his real master, Lucentio's father, just after he has persuaded a stranger from the street (the PEDANT) to play the part.

Travers (*Henry IV Part Two*)
NORTHUMBERLAND's servant who brings him first news of his son's (HOTSPUR'S) death.

Trebonius, Caius (*Julius Caesar*)
One of the minor conspirators. His task is to spirit ANTONY out of the way during the assassination; he does so without speaking, and indeed says no more than half a dozen sentences in the whole play.

Tressel (*Richard III*)
Lady ANNE's attendant.

Tribunes (*Cymbeline*)
Receive the news from the SENATORS that LUCIUS is about to invade Wales; they are no more than a plot-contrivance, ears on legs.

Tribunes (*Titus Andronicus*)
Organise the choice of emperor at the start of the play, and declare that the people will support any decision TITUS makes.

Trinculo (*The Tempest*)
ALONSO's jester, made lugubrious by drink. He spends his time with CALIBAN and STEPHANO, plotting to instal Stephano in PROSPERO's place. For most of the time his wits are soused in sack, but he has occasional flashes of insightful asperity, to remind us of his true calling. ('The folly of this island! They say there's but five upon this isle. We are three of them. If th'other two be brained like us, the state totters.')

Troilus (*Troilus and Cressida*)
PRIAM's son, prince of Troy. He is young (early twenties), and his entire adult life has been shadowed by the war. He begins the play by announcing his soul-weariness to PANDARUS ('Why should I war without the walls of Troy/That find such cruel battle here within?'), and Pandarus shrewdly deduces that the cause is not only despair at the impotency of the fighting but also love for CRESSIDA. For a time thereafter, Troilus' discovery of that love fulfils his character: it satisfies his ambition as well as his lust, it becomes the thing he lives for. His wooing of Cressida, doomed though we know their love must be (because we see, as they do not, the Greeks bargaining for her exchange with ANTENOR even as she sleeps in Troilus' arms), is the heart of the play, and the ardour of the verse wings their passion in a way equalled only in *Romeo and Juliet*. (*Cressida*: 'Are you aweary of me?' *Troilus*: 'O Cressida! But that the busy day,/Wak'd by the lark, hath rous'd the

ribald crows,/And dreaming night would hide our joys no longer,/I
would not from thee.')

In the last act of the play, Troilus' discovery of Cressida's
unfaithfulness turns his love inside-out: he is as full of uncomplicated
ardour as ever, but now it is hate not love, agony not ecstasy. He rails
at the absent Cressida ('O Cressid! O false Cressid! False, false, false!')
and pursues DIOMEDES across the battlefield with a demented energy
which is, in terms of the greater human purposes outside his love-affair,
absolutely pointless. The whole Trojan War has been undertaken with
equal intensity and equal pointlessness on an equally insignificant
pretext (the kidnapping of HELEN), and Troilus' part in it typifies the
energetic nullity, the orgasmic sterility, of the entire undertaking. He is
like one of the ardent, doomed youths in A.E. Housman's First-World-
War poetry, and our feeling for him is less pity than the bleak
fascination with which we might watch a rat trapped in a laboratory
maze.

Troilus and Cressida
Seven years after the start of the Trojan War, there is stalemate. The
Greeks (led by Agamemnon, Nestor and Ulysses) in their camp outside
the city, and the Trojans (led by Priam and his sons Hector and
Aeneas) cooped up behind their city walls, are prickling with boredom,
spending their time in banquets, jousts and high-flown, empty chivalry
(epitomised by Hector's beginning a duel with Ajax, and breaking it off
as soon as he realises that Ajax, as well as one of his most hated
enemies, is also his cousin), or in bitter squabbles among themselves.
Whenever there is fighting it is bitter, bloody and inconclusive, and the
only way to reach some conclusion would be if Achilles, noblest of
Greeks, and the only man able to match Hector in battle, would rouse
himself to fight. But despite the machinations of Ulysses and the scorn
of the other Greek leaders, Achilles stays in his tent, nursing injured
pride while his catamite Patroclus and the surly, bitter-tongued
Thersites amuse him by cruelly impersonating or insulting their fellow-
Greeks.

Troilus, a young Trojan prince, tells Pandarus that he is sick of
fighting and also love-sick for Pandarus' niece Cressida. Pandarus
arranges for the two of them to meet, and after initially pretending
indifference Cressida joins Troilus for a night of love. But now her
father Calchas, a renegade Trojan priest, says that he will only stay to
help the Greeks if they bring him his daughter, and an exchange is
organised, Cressida for the captured Trojan prince Antenor. Diomedes,
the Greek lord sent to fetch Cressida, lusts after her, and she flirts with
him and finally – spied on by Troilus – gives him a love-token which
Troilus has given her earlier and agrees to sleep with him. Troilus rages
against all Greeks, but his fury is forestalled by news that Achilles,
enraged by Hector's killing of Patroclus, has accepted Hector's
challenge to single combat. Instead of meeting Hector in fair fight,

TUBAL

Achilles treacherously surrounds him with armed men who stab him
dead, and then drags his body, tied behind a warhorse, round the walls
of Troy. Troilus is left futilely raging, and Pandarus closes the play
with a cynical epilogue about the state of the world where go-betweens
and Pandars are given none of the honour they deserve.

Tubal (*The Merchant of Venice*)
Jewish friend of SHYLOCK, who takes him news of ANTONIO's lost
treasure-ships, and hears him lamenting the elopement of his daughter.

Tutor (*Henry VI Part Three*)
Tries to protect his charge RUTLAND from CLIFFORD's fury, but is
'forc'd off' by Clifford's soldiers.

Twelfth Night
Duke Orsino of Illyria loves Countess Olivia, but she is in mourning
and rejects his advances. Viola, a young girl from nearby Messaline, is
shipwrecked on the Illyrian coast and enters Orsino's service disguised
as Cesario, a page-boy. Orsino sends her/him with love-messages to
Olivia, and Olivia falls headlong in love with him/her, just as much as
Viola has meanwhile fallen in love with Orsino. Olivia's other suitor is
the brainless country squire Sir Andrew Aguecheek, and he is egged on
by Sir Toby Belch (Olivia's uncle), Feste the Clown, Maria the
chambermaid and Fabian the upper servant. Aguecheek and Viola/
Cesario are spurred on to fight a duel, something neither of them wants.
   While this intrigue develops, Sir Toby and the others are conducting
a feud with Olivia's puritanical steward Malvolio. He threatens to turn
them out of the house; they retaliate by making him believe that Olivia
is in love with him, and encouraging him to appear in yellow stockings,
cross-gartered, before her. She indignantly has him arrested as a
madman. Meanwhile, Viola's twin brother Sebastian is wandering
about Illyria (not drowned in the shipwreck, as everyone imagined),
and confusion mounts as he is mistaken for Cesario/Viola, and vice
versa. In the end Olivia marries him, and Orsino discovers that Viola is
really a girl and declares his love for her. The trick played on Malvolio
is revealed and he is freed from jail. We hear that Sir Toby has married
Maria, but we are never told how Sir Andrew and the others come out
of it, and the play ends autumnally with Feste singing the song 'When
that I was and a little tiny boy'.

The Two Gentlemen of Verona
Valentine leaves Verona to seek his fortune in Milan, and soon
afterwards his friend Proteus is ordered by his father to leave Julia, the
girl he loves, and go to join his friend. Proteus and Julia exchange rings
as keepsakes. After Proteus has left, Julia disguises herself as a boy
('Sebastian') and follows him. The young men's clownish servants
Speed and Launce go with their masters; Launce takes his surly, ugly
dog Crab with him. In Milan, Valentine falls in love with Sylvia, the
Duke's daughter, and plans to elope with her before she can marry

Thurio, the rich fool her father has chosen as her husband. When
Proteus arrives, Valentine tells him the plan, and Proteus tells the
Duke, who banishes Valentine from Milan. On their way out of the
city, Valentine and Speed are captured by outlaws, who are so struck
with Valentine's qualities of leadership that they make him their chief.

Meanwhile, in Milan, Proteus is paying secret court to Sylvia, much
to her annoyance; he even serenades her (singing 'Who is Sylvia?'),
pretending to the Duke that he is doing it on Thurio's behalf. Julia,
disguised as Sebastian the page-boy, watches aghast, and is even more
horrified when Proteus engages her/him as messenger to take Sylvia a
love-letter and a keepsake-ring (the very one Julia once gave to him). As
Sylvia's forced wedding with Thurio comes ever nearer, she escapes
from Milan in the care of the bluff old knight Sir Eglamour, only to be
captured by the outlaws. Thurio and Proteus rescue her, and Proteus
declares his love – at which Valentine, who has overheard, angrily
accuses him of treachery. Proteus repents; 'Sebastian' faints and is
discovered to have been Julia all the time; the Duke arrives, and after
Thurio has given up all claim to Sylvia (rather than fight a duel with
Valentine), the lovers are united and the play ends happily.

The Two Noble Kinsmen

Palamon and Arcite are cousins and close friends. They are Thebans,
and are captured defending their city against Theseus Duke of Athens.
They are imprisoned, and the Jailer's Daughter falls in love with
Palamon. From their cell the cousins see Emilia, Theseus' sister-in-law,
and they both fall in love with her. They agree to remain friends in
every matter except love, in which they are to be deadly rivals. At this
point Arcite is freed from jail and banished from Athens; he disguises
himself as a wrestler and goes to Theseus' court, where he wins
Theseus' favour and is promised Emilia's hand in marriage.

In the prison, the Jailer's Daughter sets Palamon free, and he goes
into a trackless forest to escape pursuit. Here Arcite meets him, and
gives him food, clothes and weapons. The two friends agree that next
time they meet it will be to duel for Emilia's hand. They make their
way to court, unrecognisable in knightly armour. Meanwhile the
Jailer's Daughter, trying to find Palamon in the woods, goes mad with
unrequited love, joins a band of morris-dancers who appear before
Duke Theseus, and is returned, babbling, to her father and the loyal
Wooer who still loves her. Palamon and Arcite reveal their identities to
Theseus, and when Emilia refuses to choose between them he decrees
that they must fight for her, and that the loser will be executed. Arcite
wins the duel and takes Emilia; but just as Palamon lays his head on the
block for execution, news comes that Arcite's horse has thrown him and
fatally injured him, and just before he dies he surrenders Emilia to
Palamon and the friends are reconciled. The story of the Jailer's
Daughter ends happily, too: by talking to her in a darkened room,
disguised as Palamon, the Wooer gradually restores her wits, and she

marries him.

Tybalt (*Romeo and Juliet*)

Lady CAPULET's nephew, a bristling, easily provoked and dangerous young man. (He is constantly compared by others to a cat, for the unguessability of his temper and the sharpness of his claws.) He first appears in the play as a duellist; as BENVOLIO says, 'He breathed defiance to mine ears,/He swung about his head and cut the winds,/ Who, nothing hurt withal, hissed him in scorn'. As with a gunslinger in a Western film, his stock-in-trade is an impression of uncoordinated fury. He recognises ROMEO at the Capulets' masked ball, and old CAPULET has to shout him down to prevent his challenging him to a duel on the spot./('Go to! Go to!/You are a saucy boy! Is't so indeed?.../You must contrary me? Marry, 'tis time!.../You are a princox, go!...') Later, he picks a quarrel with Romeo ('Boy, this shall not excuse the injuries/That thou hast done me; therefore turn and draw'); MERCUTIO challenges him ('Tybalt, you ratcatcher, will you walk?'), and Tybalt treacherously kills him, slipping past Romeo who is trying to part them. At once Romeo kills Tybalt, and for this is banished from Verona. Tybalt's part is small, but crucial to the plot, and although he has little to say, his lines are full of the same unpredictable peremptoriness which people find in his character: Mercutio sums him up as 'prince of cats', and his feline regality sets him apart from the other young men of the play, and (together with the swordfighting) enlivens every scene he appears in.

Tyrrel, Sir James (*Richard III*)

The 'discontented gentleman' bribed by RICHARD to kill the Princes in the Tower. He is a man of feeling, but crushes his conscience in the interests of self-advancement: both qualities are shown in his soliloquy describing the murder, a splendid piece of double-think which gives grounds for remorse without once showing it. ('Dighton and Forrest, whom I did suborn/To do this ruthless piece of butchery,/Albeit they were flesh'd villains, bloody dogs,/Melting with tenderness and mild compassion,/Wept like two children in their death's sad story./"Lo, thus," quoth Dighton, "lay the gentle babes" –/"Thus, thus," quoth Forrest, "girdling one another/Within their innocent alabaster arms:/ Their lips were four red roses on a stalk..."...')

Ulysses (*Troilus and Cressida*)
Ulysses and THERSITES are the only people in the play who realise that
the lords around them are behaving less like heroes than like spoiled
children. Thersites reacts by pointing it out, and is kicked and insulted
for his pains; Ulysses reacts more subtly, by playing on their
childishness to make them do exactly what he wants. His aim is to
topple Troy as soon as possible, and he thinks that the way to do it is to
break the stalemate (in which 'everything includes itself in power,/
Power into will, will into appetite...') by shaming or shocking
ACHILLES, the only Greek able to beat HECTOR, out of his sulk and into
battle. His strategy is first to make Achilles feel that he is disregarded
by the commanders (which he does by the childish ploy of getting them
to walk past his tent without acknowledging his existence) and then to
insult him by getting the doltish AJAX to answer Hector's challenge to
the bravest of the Greeks to meet him in single combat (which he brings
about by flattering Ajax as grossly as one might soft-soap a backstreet
bully-boy). With Achilles himself he is all commiseration, but the sugar
of his sympathy coats a calculated lesson about human ingratitude.
('Time hath, my lord, a wallet at his back/Wherein he puts alms for
oblivion,/A great-siz'd monster of ingratitudes...'.) Next, leaving this
strategy simmering, he takes Troilus where he can overhear DIOMEDES
flirting with CRESSIDA, and so stirs him to bloodlust. And after that he
disappears from the play. The reason is perhaps the original myth:
Troy fell in the end not because of Achilles' quarrel with Hector or
Troilus' fury with Diomedes, but thanks to the trick of the Wooden
Horse. This fact means that all the enterprise and action in this play is
futile, and that Ulysses, who stage-manages much of it, is as ineffectual
as anyone else. Though he is not childish like the others, maturity is
systematically replaced in his character by cunning, and his conceit in
his own wiliness is in the end as unjustified and as pointless as his
companions' conceit in their force of arms.

Ursula (*Much Ado about Nothing*)
HERO's maidservant. We see her flirting at the masked ball with Hero's
uncle, the elderly ANTONIO, and she plays a lively part in the scene
where Hero lets BEATRICE overhear how much BENEDICK adores her.
Apart from that she says little, and is mainly characterised by giggly

cheerfulness.

Urswick, Sir Christopher (*Richard III*)
STANLEY's chaplain, to whom he announces his intention of joining
RICHMOND. Urswick's contribution to the scene is a list of all the other
nobles who also 'resort to him'.

Valentine (*Twelfth Night*)
ORSINO's courtier.

Valentine (*Titus Andronicus*): *see* **Gentlemen**

Valentine (*The Two Gentlemen of Verona*)
Valentine's whole existence is spent in a whirlwind of emotion. He
begins the play in a passion for travel which brooks no argument
('Cease to persuade, my loving Proteus'), and as soon as he gets to
Milan converts it first to a passion for flirting and then to the
extravagant transports of unrequited love. When PROTEUS offers to
introduce his own beloved, when he has one, to Valentine's lady,
Valentine pours out a reply worthy of ROMEO himself: 'She shall be
dignified with this high honour,/To bear my lady's train, lest the base
earth/Should from her vesture chance to steal a kiss,/And, of so great a
favour growing proud,/Disdain to root the summer-swelling flower/And
make rough winter everlastingly'. When he is forbidden to see SYLVIA
and banished from Milan, his despair is expressed in language of equal
self-absorption: 'And why not death,' he broods, 'Rather than living
torment?/To die is to be banished from myself,/And Sylvia is myself:
banished from her/Is self from self – a pretty banishment!' Later, he
tells us how much he enjoys living in the woods because 'Here I can sit,
unseen of any,/And to the nightingale's complaining notes/Tune my
distress and record my woes'. It is because he enjoys the slings and
arrows of fortune so much, one feels, that he does absolutely nothing to
change his condition, and it is only at the very end, when THURIO
threatens to snatch his beloved from under his nose, that he springs
into action at last and puts his ardour to some practical use. ('Thurio,
give back, or else embrace thy death.') He remains the same moody,
excitable person throughout the play, and no other character in
Shakespeare so exactly epitomises the agonies and ecstasies of
adolescence.

Valeria *(Coriolanus)*
Roman matron, friend of VIRGILIA. She is aptly characterised, in
Shakespeare's own phrase, as one of Virgilia's 'gossips': a garrulous,
empty-headed friend with more concern for a pregnant neighbour who
needs visiting than for Virgilia's agony of soul.

Valerius *(The Two Noble Kinsmen)*
Lord who announces to PALAMON and ARCITE that war is coming
between Athens and Thebes, that 'Theseus, who where he threats
appals, hath sent/Deadly defiance' to Creon of Thebes, and 'is at hand
to seal/The promise of his wrath'.

Varrius *(Antony and Cleopatra)*
POMPEY's friend and lieutenant.

Vaughan, Sir Thomas *(Richard III)*
Noble supporter of RIVERS and GREY, imprisoned and executed with
them at Pomfret.

Vaux, Sir Nicholas *(Henry VIII)*
Takes BUCKINGHAM to execution.

Vaux, Sir William *(Henry VI Part Two)*
One of BEAUFORT's entourage, who brings news to MARGARET that his
master is on the point of death.

Venice, Duke of *(The Merchant of Venice)*
Hears SHYLOCK's case against ANTONIO, reluctantly admitting his right
to the pound of flesh and then eagerly rounding on him when PORTIA
plays the trick of the drop of blood.

Venice, Duke of *(Othello)*
Presides over the council of war after news of the Turkish attack on
Cyprus, and hears BRABANTIO's case against OTHELLO. He is a formal
head of state, no more, and speaks a couple of dozen dignified, weighty
lines.

Ventidius *(Antony and Cleopatra)*
Loyal friend and general of ANTONY, who defeats the Syrians for him:
one of the eastern victories which most alarms OCTAVIUS. In real life he
was a soldier of fortune, something of a scoundrel, but in his brief
appearance in the play he shows no character but loyalty.

Ventidius *(Timon of Athens)*
Lord freed from debtor's prison when TIMON pays his debt. At the
banquet Timon gives to celebrate his release, he is fawning and
grateful, but later in the play, when he has inherited a fortune and
Timon is bankrupt, he refuses to send help in turn. He speaks only in
the first banquet scene; his later appearance (in the second banquet
scene, where he is one of the lords showered with water) is silent.

Verges *(Much Ado about Nothing)*
Headborough, or parish officer, second in command to DOGBERRY.
Dogberry describes him as 'an old man, sir, and his wits are not so
blunt as, God help, I would desire they were, but i' faith, honest as the
skin between his brows' – and this is all the character he needs, for he is
one of a group of interacting comedians, there chiefly as straight man
for Dogberry to play against.

Vernon *(Henry VI Part One)*
Quarrelsome follower of YORK, whose fight with BASSET over red or
white roses leads HENRY to try to unite the warring factions of York and
Lancaster.

Vernon, Sir Richard *(Henry IV Part One)*
One of HOTSPUR's less vocal supporters, chiefly used to give news of
political and military developments. Executed with WORCESTER after
the battle of Shrewsbury.

Vincentio *(The Taming of the Shrew)*
LUCENTIO's father, a 'sober ancient gentleman' (in the words of his
servant TRANIO), who is greatly taken aback when he arrives in Padua
to find Tranio pretending to be Lucentio, Lucentio pretending to be a
servant and the PEDANT pretending to be him (Vincentio).
Bewilderment and a (hardly surprising) tendency to pepperiness are his
character.

Viola *(Twelfth Night)*
Throughout *Twelfth Night* Shakespeare achieves a balance between two
distinct dramatic genres, comedy and farce. The 'high' characters
(OLIVIA, ORSINO, SEBASTIAN) play comedy, and our pleasure is in
watching their personalities change and develop in response to each new
situation. (They are like real human beings: mysteriousness of character
is what makes them interesting.) The 'low' characters (Sir Toby BELCH,
Sir Andrew AGUECHEEK, MARIA), by contrast, are playing farce: their
personalities are established from the start, and our pleasure is in
watching how each new situation confirms rather than changes what we
know of them, in what they do rather than what they are.

Apart from FESTE (a farce-character given depth by music) and
Malvolio, the main bridge between the two worlds, and between the
two dramatic genres, is Viola. She is a dramatic character caught in a
comic role, and the development of her personality (as she realises, and
struggles to control, her love for Orsino) is the ingredient which propels
the plot. But she is trapped in farce. Everyone else in the play thinks
her nothing more than a pretty boy, and expects one-dimensional
responses from her while she aches to express humanity; she spends a
large part of her time carrying vain love-messages from Orsino to
OLIVIA (which she adapts to express her own longings), or in arid
repartee with characters with whom she has nothing in common and
wants nothing more to do. Her trap is that of everyone who is

emotionally tongue-tied, and it is a source of relief as well as pleasure to the audience when events take over (the arrival of Sebastian) and resolve Viola's dilemma in a happy ending (marrying Orsino) she was quite incapable of engineering for herself. (That we should feel relief and pleasure on behalf of a person in a play, as if for a real human being, is a measure of the powerful characterisation Shakespeare gives the part.)

Emotional ambivalence of another kind is crucial both to the play and to Viola's role in it. The constant conflict between what she wants and what she gets sets up a feeling of irony: that is, the audience shares her feelings about what is happening, feelings of which the other characters are unaware. Viola's state of mind and her entrapment in an artificial role-playing she detests are symbolised by her boy's disguise; it forces her into literal combat – the ludicrous duel she fights with Sir Andrew, slapstick in intention and utterly at odds with her true character.

One thing Viola shares with all Shakespeare's major comic characters (and, as it happens, with none of the other characters in *Twelfth Night*) is that we know at every stage what she is thinking, the turmoil in her heart. Shakespeare gives the performer every assistance (e.g. by making 'real' Viola speak verse and 'trapped' Viola speak prose throughout the play); but even so, the challenges of expressing wildly shifting emotions while at the same time performing ludicrous, marionette farce-actions, are both the problem and the reward of playing this part.

Violenta (*All's Well that Ends Well*)
Companion of the WIDOW of Florence, DIANA and MARIANA. Silent part.

Virgilia (*Coriolanus*)
CORIOLANUS' wife. She is timid and retiring – Coriolanus calls her 'my gracious silence' – and is utterly overshadowed by her mother-in-law VOLUMNIA. None the less, and although she scarcely speaks (she says only seven lines in the whole intercession scene, for example), her silence is an effective foil to Volumnia's furious rhetoric, and Coriolanus speaks no more melting lines in the whole play than when he says to her, 'Best of my flesh,/Forgive my tyranny; but do not say,/ For that, "Forgive our Romans". O, a kiss/Long as my exile, sweet as my revenge!/Now, by the jealous queen of heaven, that kiss/I carried from thee, dear; and my true lip/Hath virgin'd it ever since'.

Volscian (Adrian) (*Coriolanus*)
Messenger who meets the ROMAN spy Nicanor on the road and hears his news. His chief characteristic is the pleasure he gets from meeting a fellow-professional: the freemasonry of espionage, it seems, transcends even patriotism.

Voltimand and Cornelius (*Hamlet*)
Courtiers sent to Norway at the start of the play. They return to announce FORTINBRAS' friendship for Denmark.

Volumnia (*Coriolanus*)
CORIOLANUS' mother, who has fostered his arrogant genius from
infancy and finds, in the intercession scene, that it is galloping out of
control, that instead of persuading or trusting him she must break him
like a headstrong horse. Her ruling passion, like his, is fury – she says
of herself, 'Anger's my meat; I sup upon myself' – and she is as
vehement as he is against the common herd: 'Rats, that can judge as
fitly of his worth/As I can of those mysteries which heaven/Will not
have earth to know'. She claims for herself a more controlled spirit, 'a
brain that leads my use of anger/To better vantage', but when she,
Coriolanus or Rome are under threat she resorts to furious, unyielding
rhetoric. Altogether, she is less a rounded character than one of Ben
Jonson's 'humours', the sanguinary, and her undeviating nature,
answering adversity with more of the steeliness which provoked it, is at
once the source of Coriolanus' haughtiness and a notable contrast with
it. His rage is like a disease which bewilders even as it exhilarates; hers,
by contrast, is not external but springs from her very self, and if the
result of 'supping upon herself' is 'to starve with feeding', there is
magnificent consistency in that.

Volumnius (*Julius Caesar*)
Soldier, friend of CASSIUS and BRUTUS; he refuses to help Brutus
commit suicide. ('That's no office for a friend, my lord').

Wart, Thomas (*Henry IV Part Two*)
A potential recruit for FALSTAFF's army, he is rejected on account of his
name. (Warts are catching.)

Warwick, Richard Beauchamp, Earl of (*Henry IV Part Two; Henry V*)
Retainer of Henry IV, chiefly used by him as his go-between with
Prince HAL, whose behaviour at one point he vigorously defends. He
appears in *Henry V*, but speaks only a single line (to FLUELLEN: 'How
now, how now, what's the matter?').

Warwick, Richard Neville, Earl of (*Henry VI Parts One, Two and
Three*)
Throughout the trilogy, Warwick is presented as one of the ablest lords
in England, a consummate warrior and a subtle politician – and yet he
remains the lieutenant and never the commander, the kingmaker and

never the king. As a youth, in the scene of the choosing of the roses, he picks a white rose for YORK, and thereafter spends most of his meagre lines in *Henry VI Part One* flattering York ('sweet prince') or working zealously for his cause ('Accept this scroll, most gracious sovereign,/ Which in the right of Richard Plantagenet/We do exhibit to your majesty'); the only time we see him really moved is at the trial of LA PUCELLE, when he tempers York's vehemence ('Away with her to execution') with a kind of regretful, hard man's mercy ('spare for no faggots... /Place barrels of pitch upon the fatal stake,/That so her torture may be shortened').

In *Part Two*, older and more central in state affairs, Warwick baldly announces his intentions ('I'll plant Plantagenet, root him up who dares'), and spends the play plotting vigorously against SOMERSET and supporting GLOUCESTER against the conspirators. He fades out of the action during CADE's rebellion, only to return at the battle of St Albans, when he challenges Clifford to single combat and is called off by his master York like an over-eager terrier ('Hold, Warwick! Seek thou out some other chase,/For I myself must hunt this deer to death'). In *Part Three* he is presented as an elder statesman, York's mouthpiece ('Plantagenet shall speak first; hear him lords,/And be you silent and attentive too,/For he that interrupts him shall not live); then, after York's murder, he becomes the adviser and protector of his sons EDWARD and RICHARD, who respond with what is either affection or – since we know their treacherous natures – flattering contempt (*Richard*: 'Ay, now methinks I hear great Warwick speak:/Ne'er may he live to see a sunshine day/That cries 'Retire' if Warwick bid him stay.' *Edward*: 'Lord Warwick, on thy shoulder will I lean;/And when thou faintest – as God forbid the hour! – /Must Edward fall, which peril Heaven forfend!'). He is, with them, leader of the Yorkist army, first against HENRY then against MARGARET and her forces, and his career seems to have achieved its goal when Edward is finally crowned king and Warwick goes to France to arrange a dynastic marriage which will unite the countries.

At this point, after thirty years of unwavering, stockish service to the cause of York, Warwick's loyalty receives a death-blow. While he is in France, Edward marries Lady GREY and peremptorily dismisses the political union planned for him. Warwick at once becomes a fanatical Lancastrian, and is tinged with the same heroic futility as besets the royal house itself: one by one his followers desert or are killed, and finally he himself is wounded, dragged to the battle's edge by his former protégé Edward, and dies after a death-scene in which, for the first time in the trilogy, his thoughts are not about England but entirely about himself. ('I must yield my body to the earth... /Thus yields the cedar to the axe's edge,/Whose arms gave shelter to the princely eagle,/ Under whose shade the ramping lion slept... /These eyes, that now are dimm'd with death's black veil,/Have been as piercing as the mid-day sun/To seek the secret treasons of the world... ')

Whatever Warwick's historical importance – and without him, some authorities claim, no aspirant to the English throne was ever taken seriously – in Shakespeare's trilogy he is presented as an honourable, unbending and utterly trustworthy second-in-command, whose loyalty is unshakeable to the very last moment and whose change of heart, at the end of *Part Three*, leads to as much confusion and collapse in his own personality as it does in the soldiers he commands. If the trilogy is performed complete, this crack in the boring solidity of his character can be prefigured and prepared, and the part can develop; when each play is separately performed the line of the part is harder to see, the lack of imagination that is Warwick's hurdle to greatness is difficult to demonstrate, and he becomes – alas, for his speeches are full of vigorous imagery – little more than one more noble cipher, given voice in discussion and sinew in battle but never for one moment flesh-and-blood reality.

Watchmen *(Henry VI Part Three)*
Guarding EDWARD in his tent, they run for help when WARWICK, OXFORD and others come to arrest him, leaving the king in his nightgown and to his fate.

Watchmen *(Much Ado about Nothing)*
There are three of them: Hugh Oatcake, George Seacole and Francis Seacole. We first see George Seacole being recruited by DOGBERRY, who reminds him and the others of how discreetly a true watchman should behave ('The most peaceable way for you, if you do take a thief, is to let him show himself for what he is, and steal out of your company...'); then we see Hugh Oatcake and George Seacole arresting BORACHIO and CONRADE, mightily perplexed at the absence of a third conspirator, the 'vile thief' known as Deform'd; finally we see (but don't hear) them at the interrogation of Borachio and Conrade, where Francis Seacole comes into his own because he can read and write.

Wenches *(The Two Noble Kinsmen)*
Countrywomen: Friz, Maudlin, 'little Luce with the white legs', 'bouncing Barbary' and 'freckled Nell that never failed her master'. Invited by the SCHOOLMASTER to dance – or, as he puts it, to 'Swim with your bodies,/And carry it sweetly and deliverly' – they discover that one of their number is missing (Cicely the Sempster's daughter), and the Schoolmaster recruits the Jailer's DAUGHTER in her place. The Wenches dance, giggle and flirt, but do not speak. (Their parts were probably taken by the same dancers as played Nymphs in HYMEN's wedding-dumbshow which began the play.)

Westminster, Abbot of *(Richard II)*
After RICHARD's abdication, the Abbot invites AUMERLE and CARLISLE to supper, with the promise to 'lay a plot shall show us all a merry day'. Is this a reference to Aumerle's plot against BOLINGBROKE? We have no way of knowing, since the Abbot does not appear again.

Westmoreland, Earl of *(Henry VI Part Three)*
Grandson of the WESTMORELAND of *Henry IV* and *Henry V*. In the
opening scene of the play, hot for the Lancastrians, he curses YORK
('Plantagenet, of thee and these thy sons,/Thy kinsmen and thy friends,
I'll have more lives/Than drops of blood were in my father's veins'),
and then rounds on HENRY for abdicating in York's favour ('Farewell,
faint-hearted and degenerate king,/In whose cold blood no spark of
honour bides'). He is not seen again.

Westmoreland, Ralph Neville, Earl of *(Henry IV Parts One and Two;
Henry V)*
In *Henry IV Part One*, Westmoreland appears briefly as a brisk military
commander undeviatingly loyal to the king. In *Part Two*, while
maintaining the same bluff character, he is one of Prince JOHN's main
agents in persuading HASTINGS, SCROOP and MOWBRAY to disband their
army, and then arrests them for treason. In *Henry V* he is one of the
main courtiers of the young king, and adds to the clipped military
presence we have seen before a mellifluous turn of phrase ('For once the
eagle England being in prey,/To her unguarded nest the weasel Scot/
Comes sneaking, and so sucks her princely eggs...'). Before Agincourt,
it is he who says, 'O that we now had here/But one ten thousand of
those men in England/That do no work today', and so inspires HENRY's
St Crispin's Day speech. His part, in short, scarcely rises above that of
attendant lord, but it offers the actor more character-hints than usual,
as well as a handful of rewarding speeches.

Whitmore, Walter *(Henry VI Part Two)*
Pirate who captures SUFFOLK and is given the pleasure of killing him.
('Come, Suffolk, I must waft thee to thy death...')

Widow *(All's Well that Ends Well)*
Old woman of Florence with whom HELENA lodges. She accepts a large
sum of money to let Helena take DIANA's place in BERTRAM's bed, but
such is the dignity of her lines that we never once think of her as
unprincipled.

Widow *(The Taming of the Shrew)*
Loud-mouthed wife found in the end by HORTENSIO. At the banquet in
the play's last act, she quarrels with KATHARINA about women's duty to
men, and later refuses to come to Hortensio when he sends for her. The
lines give her no character, but she is clearly meant to be not the sort of
woman any sane Paduan would marry if he had the choice.

William *(As You Like It)*
TOUCHSTONE's rival for the love of AUDREY: a yokel, outfaced by little
more than the power of Touchstone's vocabulary ('You clown, abandon
– which is in the vulgar, leave – the society – which is in the boorish,
company – of this female – which in the common, is woman – which
together is, abandon the society of this female, or clown thou

perishest...'). If the put-upon RUGBY of *The Merry Wives of Windsor* has a Forest of Arden cousin, this is he.

Williams, Michael (*Henry V*)

A common soldier who quarrels with the disguised king HENRY before Agincourt, gives him a glove to wear on his hat and says he will reclaim it with a box on the ear if they both survive the battle. (Henry later gives the glove to FLUELLEN.) Williams is forthright (particularly about the king's lack of understanding of ordinary people), and expresses himself with fire and eloquence. 'If the cause be not good, the king himself hath a heavy reckoning to make, when all those legs and arms and heads, chopped off in a battle, shall join together at the latter day and cry all "We died at such a place"...' His dramatic purpose is to teach Henry a lesson in humility, and to lead up to the great soliloquy before the battle ('What have kings that privates have not too, Save ceremony, save general ceremony...?' – a heightened equivalent of FALSTAFF's soliloquy on honour in *Henry IV Part Two*); his chirpiness of character makes him interesting as well as useful to the plot, and he is like one of the cheerfully cynical cockneys who man the lower decks in those stiff-upper-lip British films of the Second World War. (He is often played as Welsh, though there is no hint of it in the dialogue.)

Willoughby, Lord (*Richard II*)

In a kind of minor-character double-act with ROSS, he persuades NORTHUMBERLAND to revolt against RICHARD. The part demands more standing-around than speaking, and more of both than of character-acting.

Winchester, Bishop of; later Cardinal Beaufort(*Henry VI Parts One and Two*)

Ambitious, worldly priest, the bastard son of John of GAUNT. We see him in Parliament, on the battlefield, hunting and hawking in the company of kings and lords, but never once in church – as his rival GLOUCESTER tartly puts it, 'Name not religion, for thou lov'st the flesh,/And ne'er throughout the year to church thou go'st/Except to pray against thy foes'. His quarrel with Gloucester is one of the main dramatic glories of *Part One*, the two of them trading insults like present-day parliamentarians. (*Gloucester*: 'Thou bastard of my grandfather!' *Winchester*: 'Ay, lordly sir, for what are you, I pray,/But one imperious in another's throne?' *Gloucester*: 'Am I not Lord Protector, saucy priest?' *Winchester*: 'And am I not a prelate of the church?')

In *Part Two* Winchester (by now created Cardinal) plays a leading part in the conspiracy to trap Gloucester through his wife's addiction to witchcraft; but he is blamed, with SUFFOLK, for Gloucester's fall, his own fortunes wane, and we last see him on his deathbed, raving with remorse: 'Died he not in his bed? Where should he die?/Can I make men live, whe'r they will or no?/O, torture me no more! I will confess!/

Alive again? Then show me where he is:/I'll give a thousand pound to look on him'.

Although the interest of the part is spread over two plays (and is therefore dissipated when either is performed separately), Beaufort's characterisation is strong: a devious, arrogant, superficially courteous and utterly untrustworthy gentleman, whose bastardy is a moral taint and whose whole life is a search for the legitimacy of power his birth has denied him.

The Winter's Tale
Leontes, King of Sicilia, is driven so insane with jealousy by the friendship between his wife Hermione and his boyhood friend Polixenes, king of Bohemia, that he orders Polixenes to be poisoned, Hermione to be tried as an adultress and their new-born infant daughter to be exposed in a lonely place to die. Polixenes escapes (thanks to the warning of the loyal lord Camillo), but Leontes is told that Hermione is dead, that his son Mamillius has died of grief and that the Delphic Oracle has declared Hermione's innocence and his own deep guilt. He vows a lifetime of penance.

Meanwhile, the old courtier Antigonus has taken baby Perdita to the coast of Bohemia, and leaves her there; soon afterwards he is pursued by a bear and eaten. Perdita is discovered by a Shepherd and his clownish son, and brought up as the Shepherd's daughter. Sixteen years pass, and we next see Perdita as Queen of the sheep-shearing festival, surrounded by rustics (including the con-man Autolycus) and by dancers, and deeply in love with young Florizel, who is Polixenes' son and prince of Bohemia. Polixenes and Camillo visit the sheep-shearing festival in disguise, and Polixenes forbids his son to marry a commoner. But Camillo helps the young couple to elope to Sicilia, where Perdita is revealed to be Leontes' long-lost daughter. So the young people's marriage can go ahead, and there is a further joy in store for Leontes: he is taken by Paulina (his wife's old friend, the lady who told him she was dead) to see a 'statue' of Hermione, which 'comes to life'. Leontes and Hermione are reunited.

Witches (Macbeth)
Although the lines the three Witches speak are (a) redolent of pantomime ('Fair is foul and foul is fair ...'), and (b) so well-known that audiences tend to mouth them as they listen, the Witches still remain terrifying rather than preposterous. The reason is the unsoftened malignity of everything they say, and the scene which prints that on our minds is the one where they vow vengeance on the sailor whose wife refused to share her chestnuts. ('I will drain him dry as hay;/Sleep shall neither night nor day/Hang upon his penthouse lid;/He shall die a man forbid ...'.) Not even their fawning on HECATE or their stage-managing of the dumb-show of the eight kings, fustian and Jacobean-conventional as they are, can shake our feeling – at least in a good performance – that we are in the presence less of a creaking stage-

show than of genuine dark powers.

Wolsey, Thomas, Cardinal (*Henry VIII*)

Shakespeare is thought to have written *Henry VIII* in collaboration with John Fletcher, and though no one knows which playwright wrote which scenes, the character of Wolsey changes so radically and so abruptly in the middle of the play that it seems, more than anything else, to show the effects of two men's work.

Wolsey begins the play urbane, confident and as trustworthy as a rattlesnake. When he is challenged by HENRY to explain why illegal taxes have been raised in the king's name, he replies, with affable humbug but no attention to the issue, 'These exactions/Whereof my sovereign would have note, they are/Most pestilent to the hearing, and to bear 'em/The back is sacrifice to the load', and continues humbly, 'If I am/traduc'd by ignorant tongues... let me say/'Tis but the fate of place, and the rough brake/That virtue must go through'; as soon as the taxes are revoked, he tells his secretary to put it about that this is thanks to his personal influence with the king. He is equally relaxed with CAMPEIUS the Pope's legate, who tells him that he is being traduced in Rome; his method of persuading KATHARINE to agree to the annulment Henry wants is to smother her with silky speeches; greatly daring, he even challenges Henry before his own court. ('Most gracious sir,/In humblest manner I require your highness/That it shall please you to declare, in hearing/Of all these ears... whether ever I/Did broach this business to your highness...') It is small wonder that he provokes such violent hostility in NORFOLK, SUFFOLK, SURREY and the other nobles. Norfolk's thoughts on him are a scarcely exaggerated description of the man we have seen so far: 'The king-cardinal!/That blind priest, like the eldest son of Fortune,/Turns what he list...'

Once the conspiracy against him gathers momentum – it involves intercepting treasonable, ambitious letters and passing them to the king – the great change in Wolsey's character begins. Instead of collapsing like a card-house, he becomes dignified, resigned, gentle and genuinely humble (it is an exact parallel to what happens to Katharine when her sufferings begin); he abandons human concerns and turns to God. He has already implied, in a brief soliloquy about Anne BULLEN, that his motivation has always been religious, not political: 'A knight's daughter/To be her mistress' mistress!... What though I know her virtuous/And well deserving? Yet I know her for/A spleeny Lutheran, and not wholesome to/Our cause... Again, here is sprung up/An heretic, an arch one, Cranmer: one/Hath crawl'd into the favour of the king/And is his oracle'. Now, having made 'a long farewell' to all his greatness, comparing himself to Lucifer (who 'falls never to hope again'), he retires from Court life to an abbey at Leicester, falls sick and dies. He spends his last hours, we are told, in 'repentance,/Continual meditations, tears and sorrows' – and this is exactly true to the Wolsey we have just seen deliver a moving and striking rejection of the force which has governed his whole court life: 'Cromwell, I charge thee, fling away ambition./By that sin fell the angels – how can Man, then,/The image of his Maker, hope to win by it?/O Cromwell, Cromwell.../Had I but serv'd my God with half the zeal/I serv'd my king, he would not in mine age/Have left me naked to mine enemies'. There may be nothing to evoke tears in this – Wolsey in defeat is no more sympathetic than Wolsey in triumph – but there is plenty to admire: his renunciation of his former self is as thoroughgoing and genuine as it is unheralded, strongly reminiscent of the stories of saints' conversions from uplifting Catholic literature.

Woman *(The Two Noble Kinsmen)*
EMILIA's servant, who walks with her in the garden of the jail and discusses flowers.

Woodville, Richard *(Henry VI Part One)*
Lieutenant of the Tower of London, ordered by WINCHESTER not to admit GLOUCESTER or his men – the first inkling we have of the quarrel between the lords. He speaks five lines.

Wooer *(The Two Noble Kinsmen)*
The JAILER's friend and would-be son-in-law, who comes into his own after the Jailer's DAUGHTER goes mad, when he agrees to disguise himself as PALAMON and make love to her. He is earnest and humourless rather than ridiculous, either middle-aged or a youth old beyond his years.

Worcester, Thomas Percy, Earl of *(Henry IV Part One)*
HOTSPUR's uncle and fellow-rebel against King HENRY. He is older and wiser than Hotspur, and this and his former loyalty and personal friendship for the king make his a voice for moderation (e.g. he supports Henry's offer of an amnesty if the rebels surrender). He is captured at the battle of Shrewsbury and executed. A less colourfully drawn character than his historical importance might suggest, and a minor part.

York, Cicely Neville, Duchess of *(Richard III)*
Widow of the YORK of *Henry VI Parts One and Two*, and mother of
RICHARD and his brothers EDWARD and CLARENCE. She is with her
grandchildren, bewailing the death of their father Clarence, when
Queen ELIZABETH comes in grieving for the death of her husband (the
Duchess' son Edward). In a powerful antiphonal scene (reminiscent of
the grief choruses in Greek tragedy), they mourn. Later, after hearing
of the murder of the Princes in the Tower, the Duchess and Queen
Elizabeth are once again mourning when Queen MARGARET (widow of
HENRY VI) gloats over their distress, in another powerful scene. Like
Elizabeth, the Duchess veers between two hysterical emotions, grief
and rage; the part is too compact, and too powerfully written, to need
more developed character.

York, Duchess of *(Richard II)*
Wife of YORK, mother of AUMERLE, the Duchess is trapped by her
loyalty to both of them in the conspiracy-scene. Shakespeare finely
shows her inner struggle, as she lets mother-love outweigh her distaste
for Aumerle's treason, and he gives her a powerful scene of intercession
with BOLINGBROKE, in which the dignity of her age and rank are set
against the deferential, pitiful role she takes it upon herself to play.
(The scene is sometimes claimed to be spurious, and some of its lines –
e.g. 'Speak it in French, king; say *Pardonne-moy*' – hardly sound like
Shakespeare; but the way the three characters, devious son, implacable
father and anguished mother, are deployed, and the way the Duchess'
motherly passion gradually sweeps the action to a climax, are
wonderfully Shakespearean.) Some producers, faced with the
dichotomy between dramatic power and linguistic ineptitude, play the
scene for comedy, a solution which works in the theatre but diminishes
the Duchess' character.

York, Edmund Langley, Duke of *(Richard II)*
York is a bluff, loyal servant of his country. He shares his brother
GAUNT's horror at the way RICHARD is buying and selling it, but argues
that the king should be excused because he is young and 'young hot
colts do rage the more'. He believes in the 'divinity that doth hedge a
king', and this leads him first to accept the regency (while Richard is
away in Ireland) and to round on BOLINGBROKE when he returns

unbidden from exile, and then, after Richard abdicates and
Bolingbroke takes the crown, to transfer his loyalty absolutely to him.
His doggedness (he is loyal to country and king, whoever it is who
wears the crown) is contrasted with his son AUMERLE's shiftiness
(Aumerle is loyal only where his own advantage lies), and leads to his
denouncing Aumerle to Bolingbroke as a traitor, subordinating his
fatherly feelings to his patriotism. It is a somewhat tract-like role,
demonstrating one argument in a thesis rather than personal character;
but in the hands of a powerful actor, York's burly presence can
splendidly contrast with the self-admiring intellectual aesthetes of
Richard's court. Indeed, Shakespeare allows York a neat line in
exasperation, his loyalty constantly fighting his dislike of the men to
whom he owes it.

York, Lord Mayor of (Henry VI Part Three)
At first he bars the gates against EDWARD, claiming that the city is loyal
to HENRY; Edward protests that he is only coming as Duke of York,
and the Mayor hands over the keys.

York, Richard Duke of (Richard III)
Younger son of EDWARD IV, a child. (He and his brother EDWARD are
the Princes in the Tower.) He is young enough to play prettily with
RICHARD's dagger and sword, and then to ask, 'because I am little, like
an ape', to ride piggy-back on Richard's shoulder. When he is taken
with his brother to the Tower, we have a touching scene full of all-too-
accurate foreboding (he says, 'I shall not sleep in quiet at the Tower');
later, he is one of the GHOSTS who haunt Richard at Bosworth. ('Let us
be lead within thy bosom, Richard!')

York, Richard Plantagenet, Duke of (Henry VI Parts One, Two and Three)
In the welter of fine dialogue, promising plot-lines and colourful
characters struggling to get out of Henry VI, one of the greatest
casualties is the character of Richard, Duke of York. At first sight, he
seems to be the hub of the action. In Part One he establishes the
factions of the red rose and the white, and so focusses the quarrel
between the nobles; he spends Part Two intriguing melodramatically at
court (announcing his dark intentions, from time to time, in soliloquies
to the audience); he begins Part Three by usurping the throne and
refusing to give it up till HENRY agrees to grant succession to York's son
EDWARD; he is arraigned as a traitor, defeated in battle and beheaded;
Part Three ends with his sons squabbling among themselves for royal
power, but with the Plantagenet dynasty riding high.

For all that, there is something unsatisfactory about York's character
throughout the trilogy. Perhaps the constraints of history were against
Shakespeare, and other plotters (e.g. SUFFOLK in Part Two) steal
limelight that in a perfectly made drama would be York's alone.
Perhaps he dies too soon in Part Three, and the focus of interest shifts

too spectacularly to his sons. Perhaps the characterisation itself wavers, and the high-flown, black-hearted rhetoric of *Part Two* and the bluntness of the quarrels (*Henry*: 'I am thy sovereign.' *York*: 'Thou'rt deceiv'd. I'm thine.') give way too easily to blandness in the battle-scenes, to a sameness of heroics with everyone else which cuts off dramatic stature at the knees.

A good actor could find ways round this, taking his cue perhaps from York's malevolence in *Part Two* and playing him as a twisted villain throughout the trilogy, a true father to his 'foul stigmatic' son RICHARD (in *Richard III*). This would give an ironical edge to his wooden nobility in the battle-scenes (as if he were merely playing the noble part), and a superb, scowling magnificence when he is cornered, in the scene in *Part Three* where MARGARET taunts him with the paper crown. The only problem with such an interpretation is that it weights the whole trilogy in his favour, and makes his death three-quarters of the way through a dramatic hurdle of a different but no less awkward kind. Not only that, but giving him such prominence cuts the other main parts – TALBOT, Suffolk, WARWICK, Margaret, even Henry – down to a size not warranted by their importance either in the historical events or in Shakespeare's dialogue. The trilogy is often trimmed and reshaped to fit such an interpretation, but it is closer to Shakespeare's intentions (and perhaps to history) to play York as he appears in the play, one of a number of equals, who struts his hour upon the stage then disappears abruptly to make way for someone else. No one objects when this happens to Talbot, Suffolk or even CADE; that we mind in York's case is a sign of the strength of character latent in his lines.

York, Thomas Rotherham, Archbishop of (*Richard III*)
Gives Queen ELIZABETH sanctuary.

Young Lucius (*Titus Andronicus*)
TITUS' grandson, a child. He spends his time in the gruesome company of his mutilated aunt LAVINIA, and it is his copy of Ovid's *Metamorphoses* (the story of Procne and Tereus in particular) which gives her the clue to how to reveal her attackers' names although she is tongueless and handless. He is proud and defiant in his childish way ('I say, my lord, that if I were a man/Their mother's bedchamber should not be safe/For these bad bondsmen...'), but the part is too small to have much character.